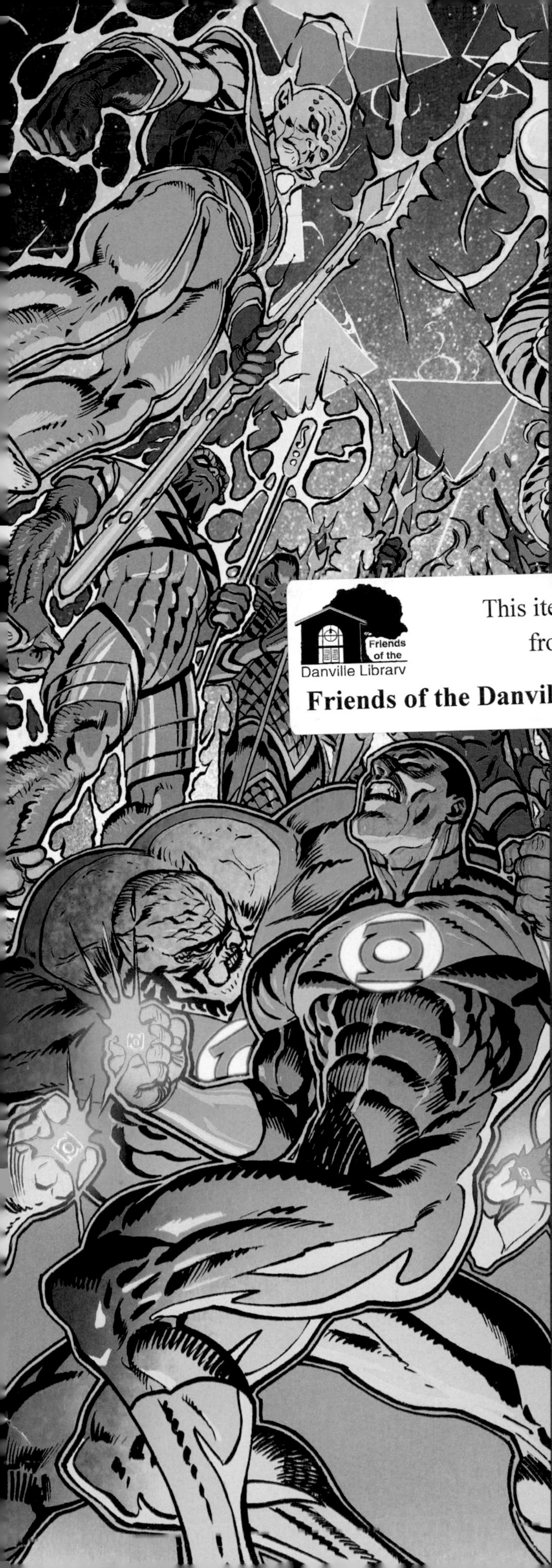

THE LOST ARMY

GREEN LANTERN CORPS

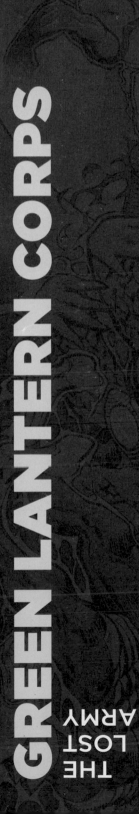

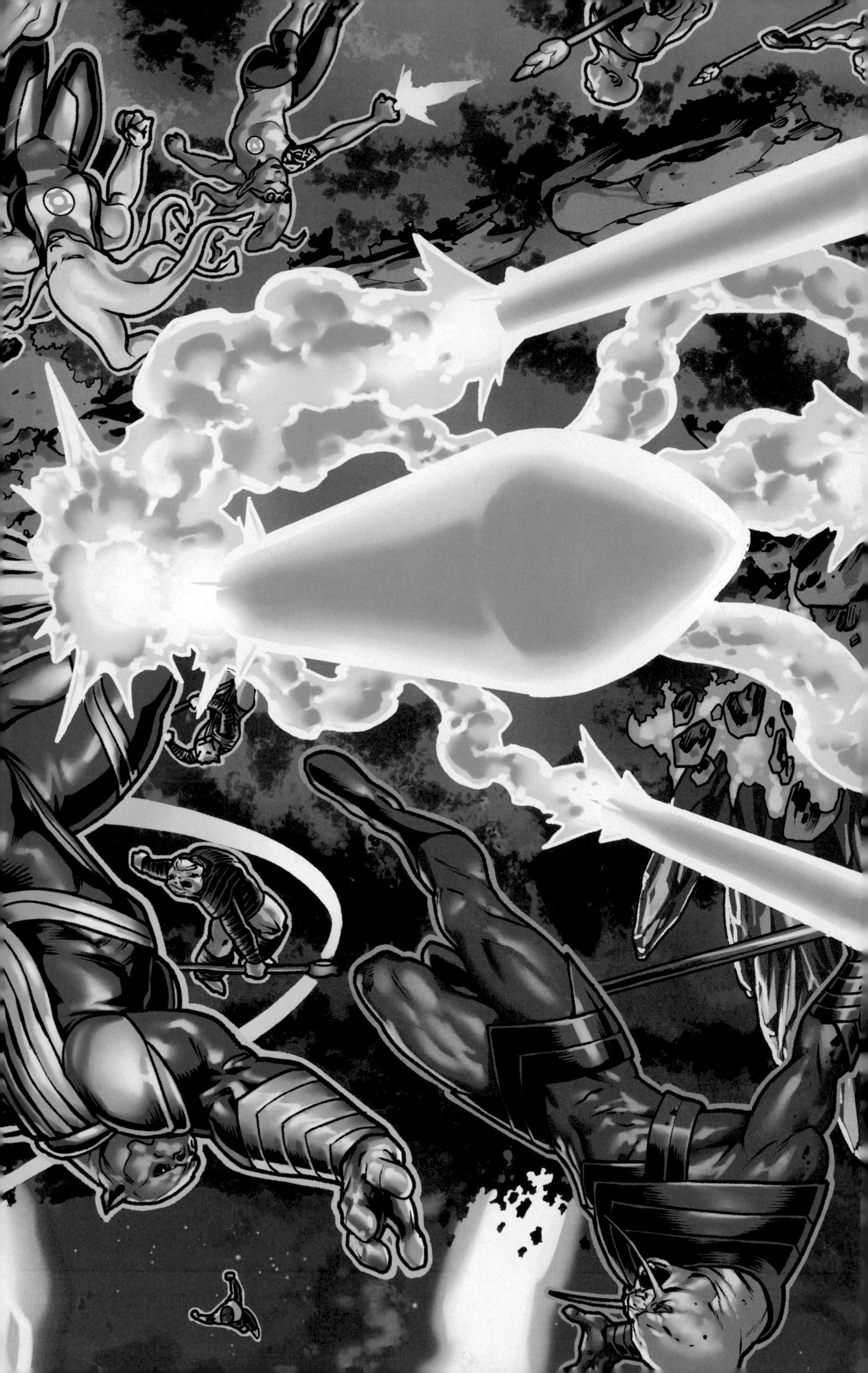

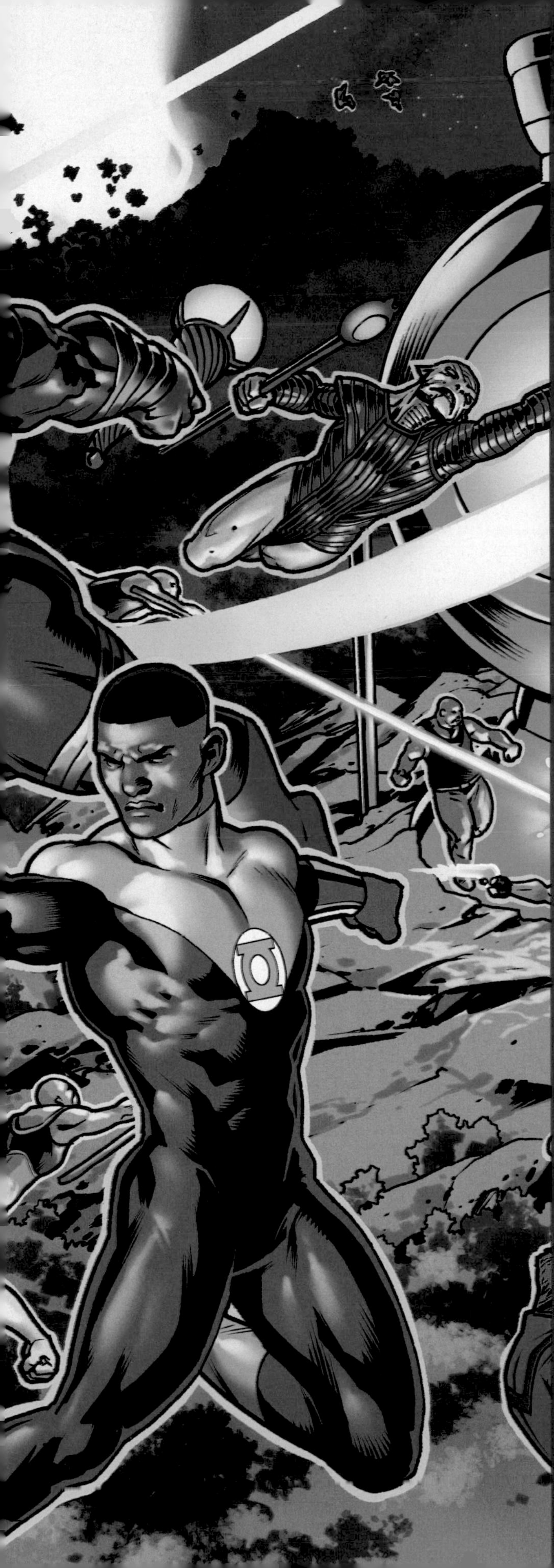

GREEN LANTERN CORPS

THE LOST ARMY

WRITTEN BY
CULLEN BUNN

ART BY
JESUS SAIZ
CLIFF RICHARDS
JAVIER PIÑA

COLOR BY
JESUS SAIZ
MICHAEL ATIYEH
CHRIS SOTOMAYOR

LETTERS BY
DAVE SHARPE

COLLECTION COVER ARTIST
JESUS SAIZ

GREEN LANTERN CORPS: THE LOST ARMY

Published by DC Comics. Compilation and all new material Copyright © 2016 DC Comics. All Rights Reserved.
Originally published online as GREEN LANTERN: LOST ARMY SNEAK PEEK and in single magazine form as GREEN LANTERN: LOST
ARMY 1-6 Copyright © 2015 DC Comics. All Rights Reserved. All characters, their distinctive likenesses and related elements featured in
this publication are trademarks of DC Comics. The stories, characters and incidents featured in this publication are entirely fictional.
DC Comics does not read or accept unsolicited ideas, stories or artwork.

DC Comics, 2900 West Alameda Ave., Burbank, CA 91505
Printed by RR Donnelley, Owensville, MO, USA. 3/4/16. First Printing.
ISBN: 978-1-4012-6126-9

Library of Congress Cataloging-in-Publication Data

Names: Bunn, Cullen, author. | Saiz, Jesus, illustrator. | Richards, Cliff,
illustrator. | Piña, Javier, illustrator. | Atiyeh, Michael, illustrator.
| Sotomayor, Chris, illustrator. | Sharpe, Dave, illustrator.
Title: Green Lantern Corps : lost army / Cullen Bunn, writer ; Jesus Saiz,
Cliff Richards, Javier Piña, artists ; Jesus Saiz, Michael Atiyeh, Chris
Sotomayor, colorists ; Dave Sharpe, letterer.
Description: Burbank, CA : DC Comics, [2016]
Identifiers: LCCN 2015044873 | ISBN 9781401261269 (paperback)
Subjects: LCSH: Graphic novels. | BISAC: COMICS & GRAPHIC NOVELS /
Superheroes. | GSAFD: Superhero comic books, strips, etc.
Classification: LCC PN6728.G742 B86 2016 | DDC 741.5/973–dc23
LC record available at http://lccn.loc.gov/2015044873

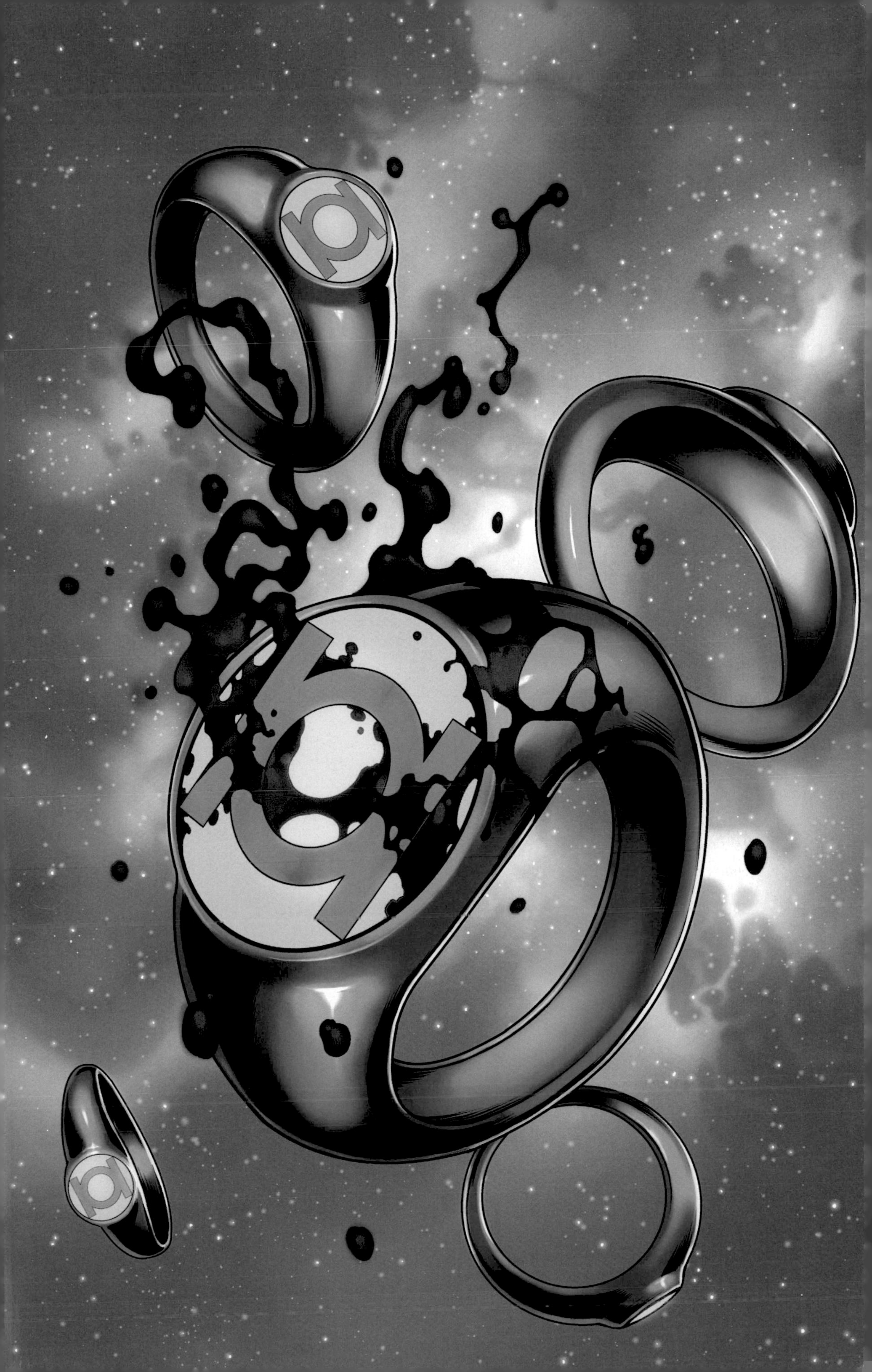

CULLEN BUNN writer **JESUS SAIZ** artist, colorist & cover **DAVE SHARPE** letterer

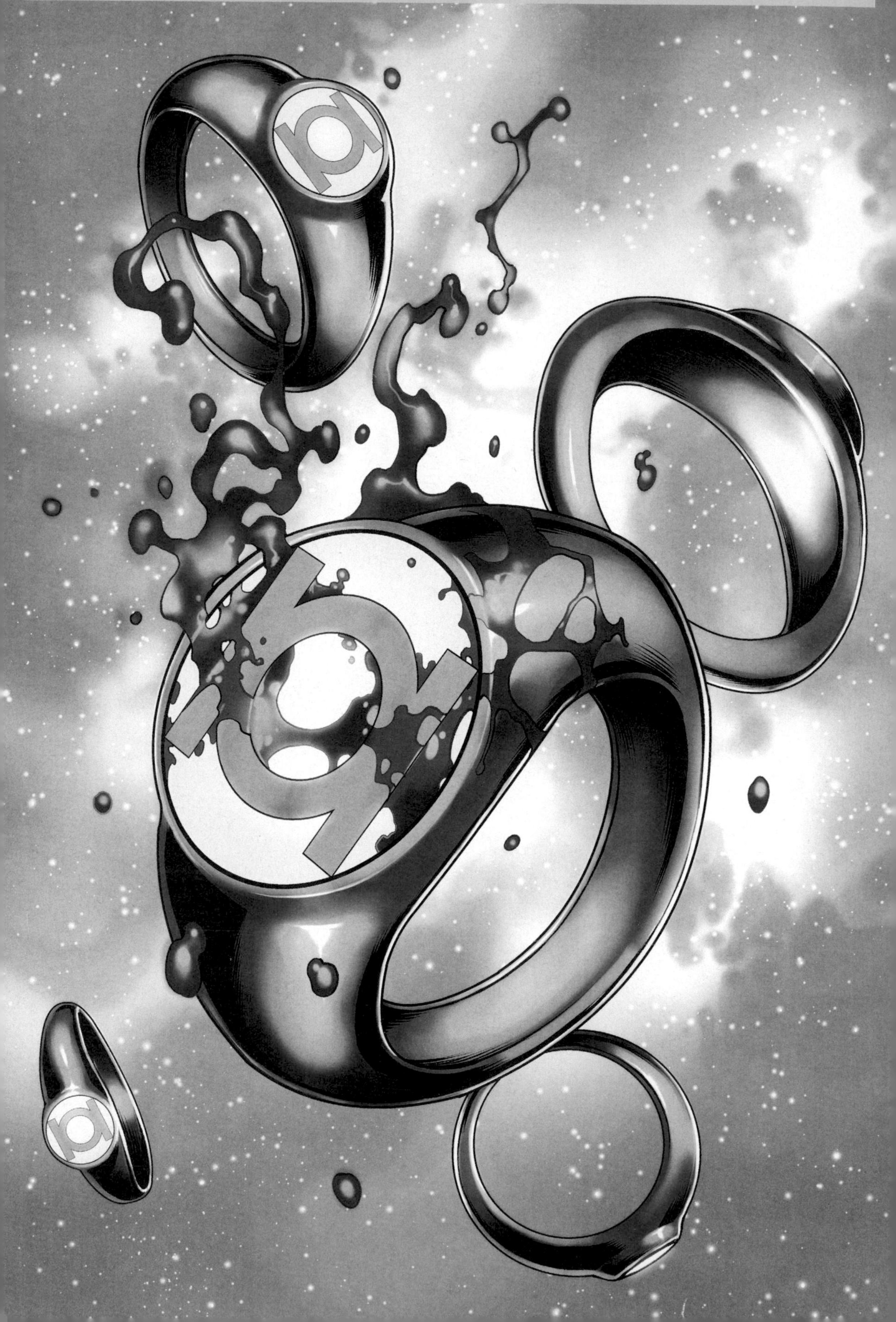

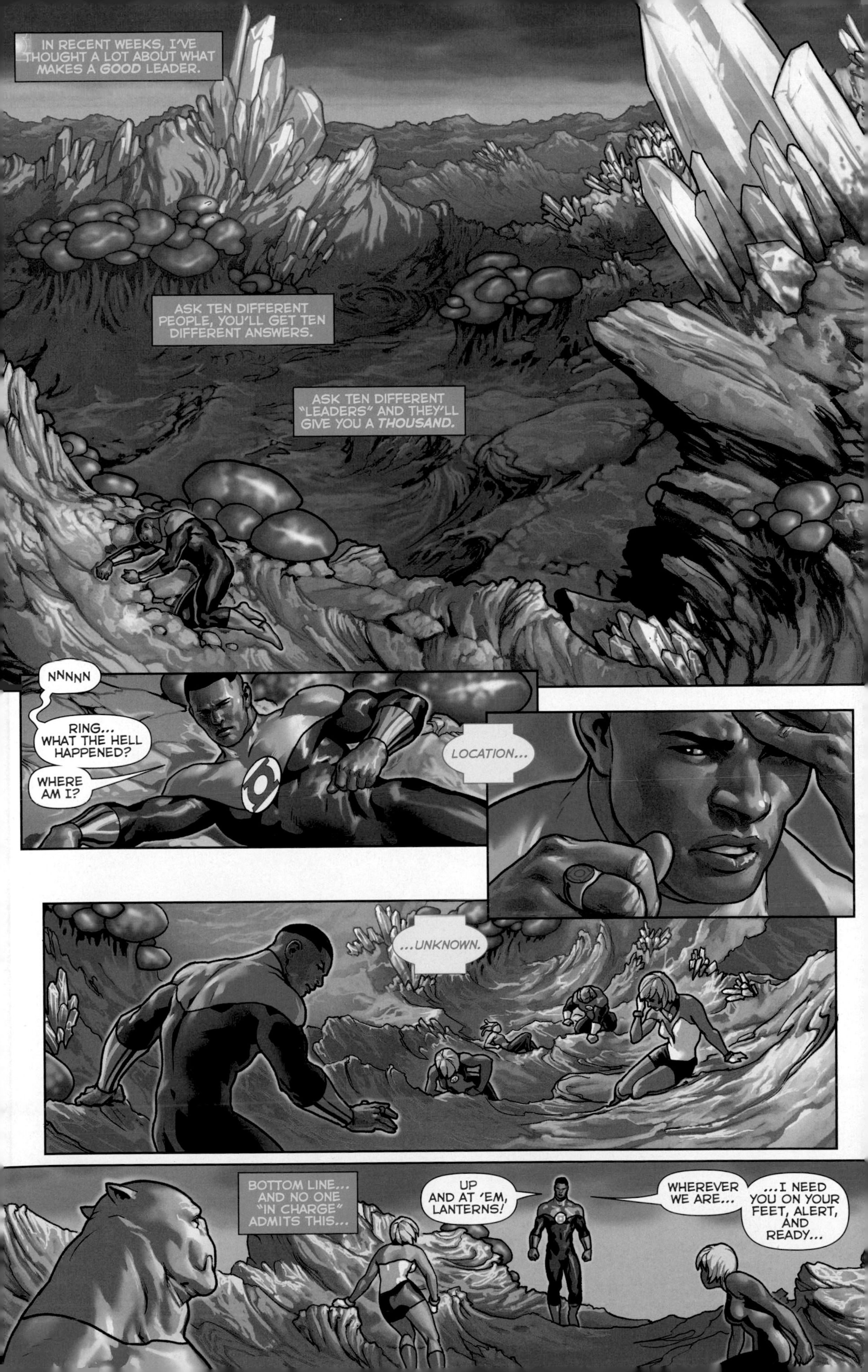

IN RECENT WEEKS, I'VE THOUGHT A LOT ABOUT WHAT MAKES A *GOOD* LEADER.
ASK TEN DIFFERENT PEOPLE, YOU'LL GET TEN DIFFERENT ANSWERS.
ASK TEN DIFFERENT "LEADERS" AND THEY'LL GIVE YOU A *THOUSAND.*
NNNNN
RING... WHAT THE HELL HAPPENED?
WHERE AM I?
LOCATION...
...UNKNOWN.
BOTTOM LINE... AND NO ONE "IN CHARGE" ADMITS THIS...
UP AND AT 'EM, LANTERNS!
WHEREVER WE ARE...
...I NEED YOU ON YOUR FEET, ALERT, AND READY...

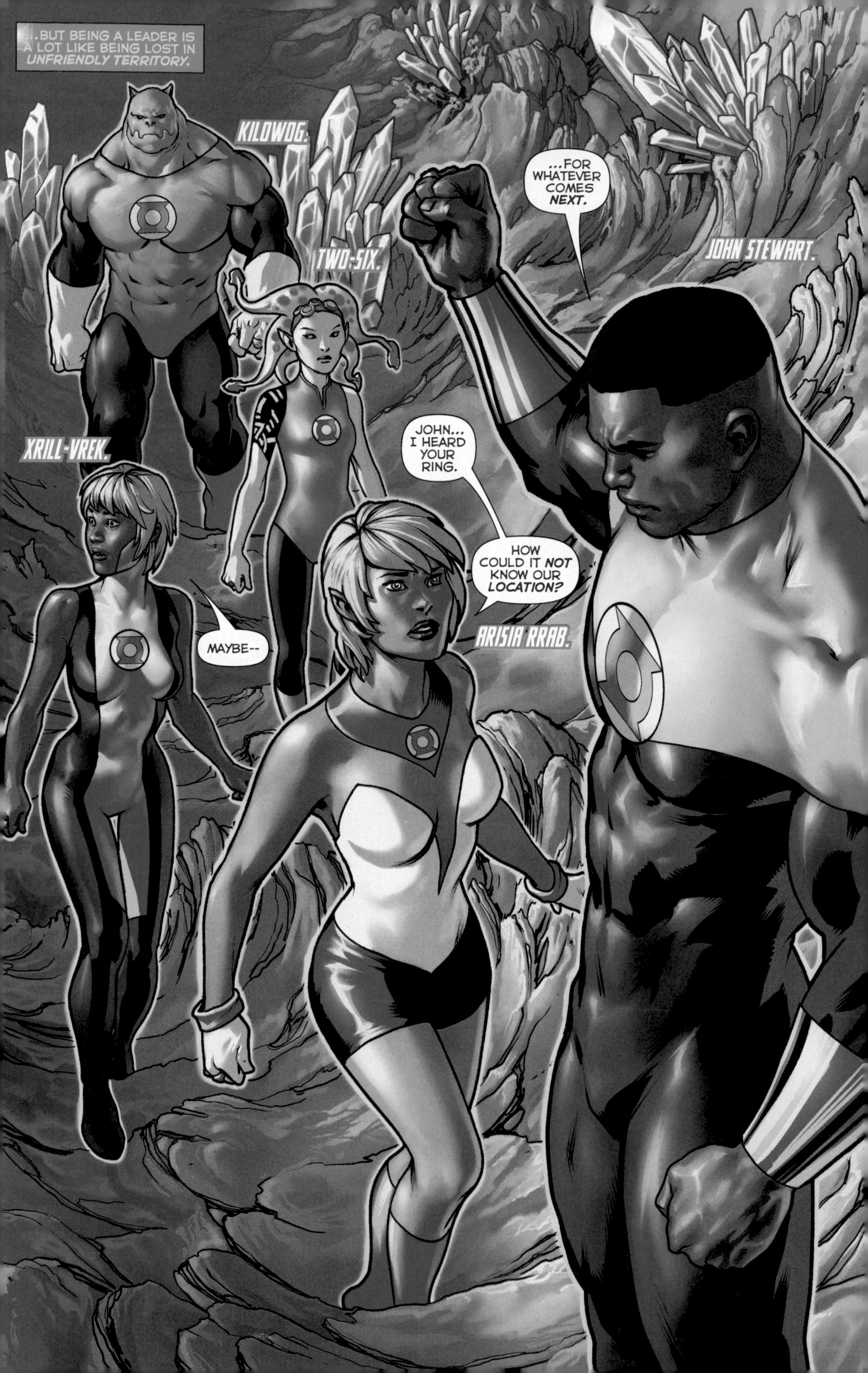
...BUT BEING A LEADER IS A LOT LIKE BEING LOST IN UNFRIENDLY TERRITORY.
KILOWOG.
TWO-SIX.
...FOR WHATEVER COMES NEXT.
JOHN STEWART.
XRILL-VREK.
JOHN... I HEARD YOUR RING.
HOW COULD IT NOT KNOW OUR LOCATION?
MAYBE--
ARISIA RRAB.

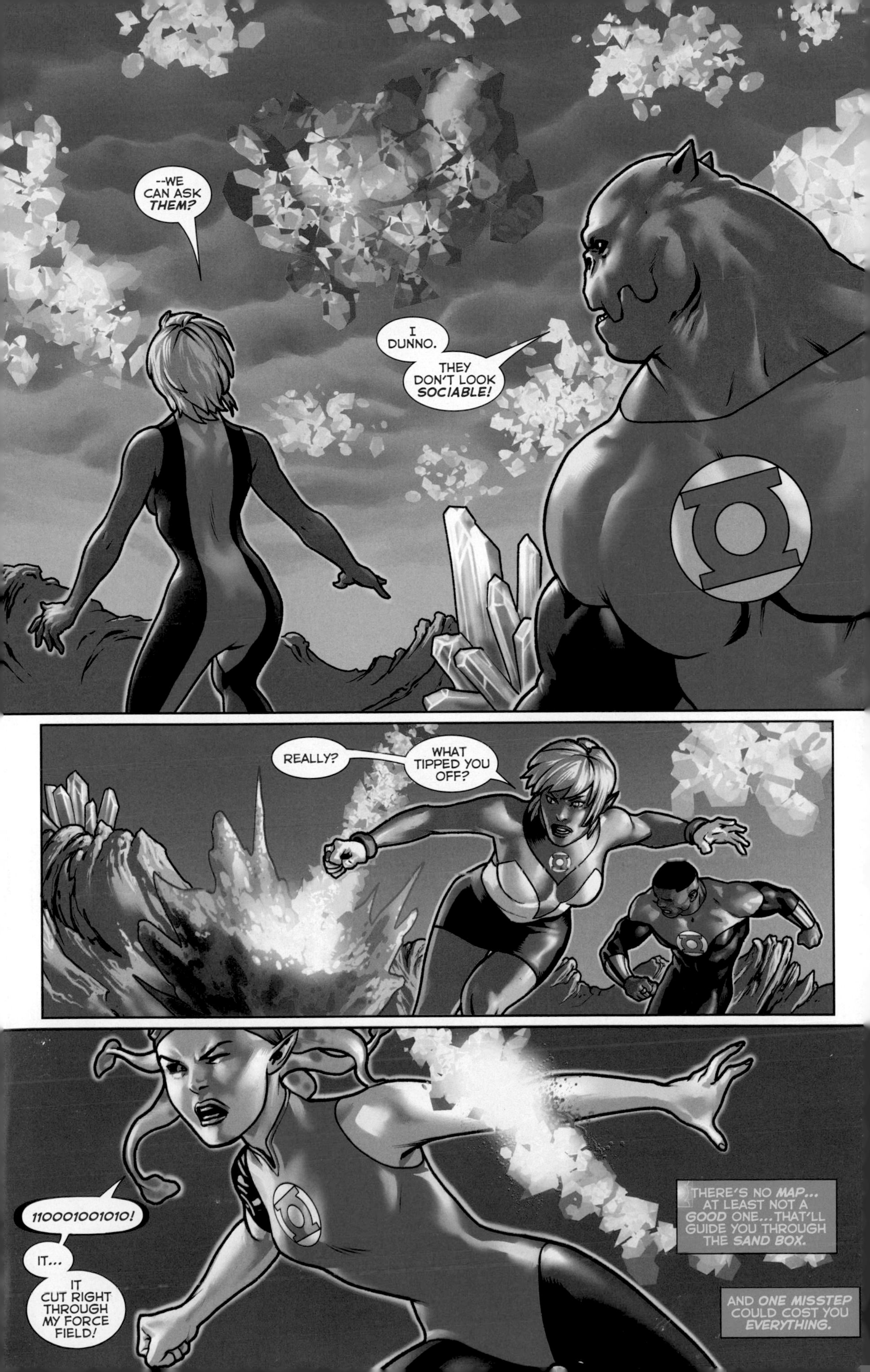
--WE CAN ASK *THEM?*
I DUNNO.
THEY DON'T LOOK *SOCIABLE!*
REALLY?
WHAT TIPPED YOU OFF?
110001001010!
IT...
IT CUT RIGHT THROUGH MY FORCE FIELD!
THERE'S NO *MAP*... AT LEAST NOT A *GOOD* ONE... THAT'LL GUIDE YOU THROUGH THE *SAND BOX.*
AND *ONE MISSTEP* COULD COST YOU *EVERYTHING.*

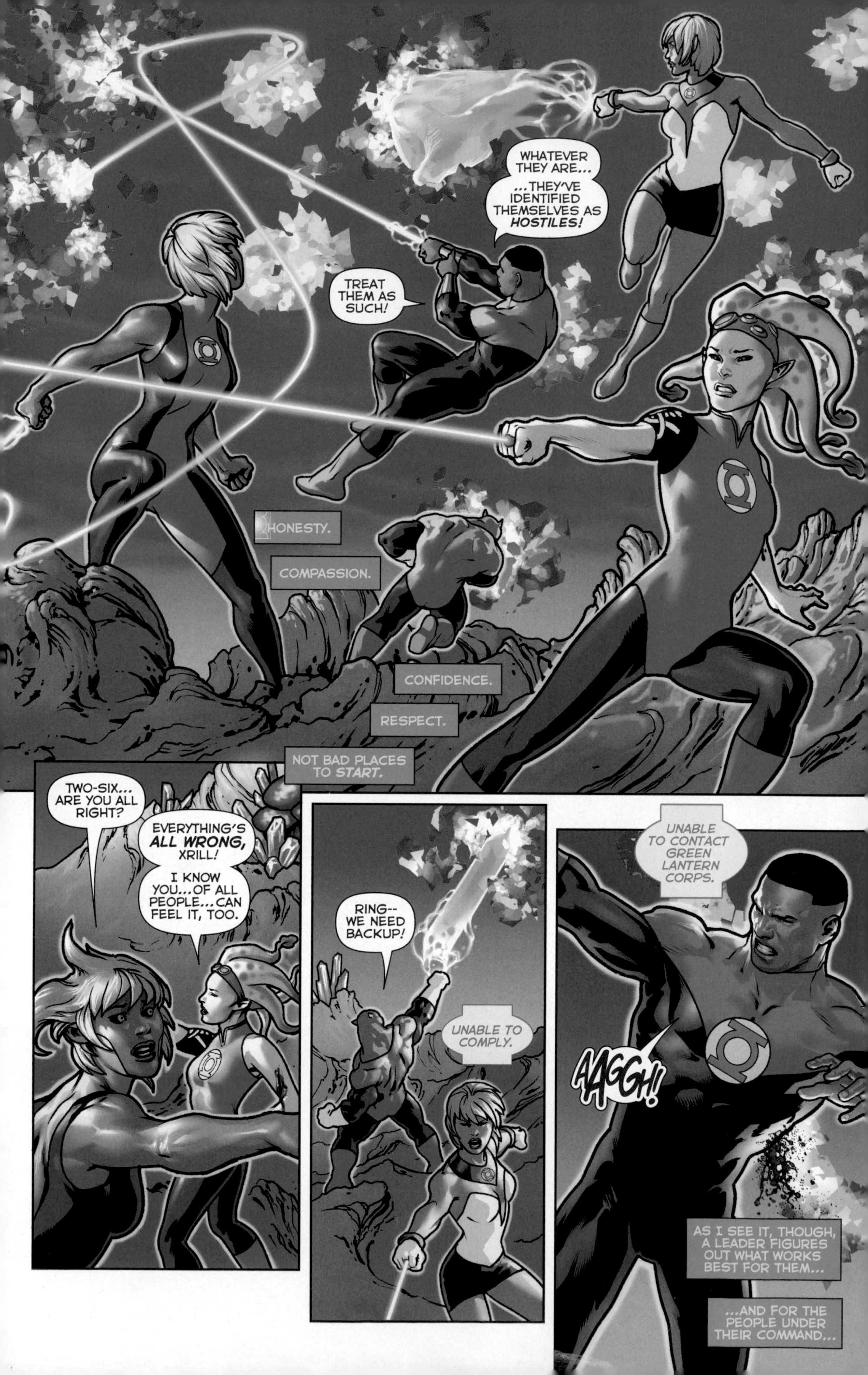

WHATEVER THEY ARE... ...THEY'VE IDENTIFIED THEMSELVES AS HOSTILES!
TREAT THEM AS SUCH!
HONESTY.
COMPASSION.
CONFIDENCE.
RESPECT.
NOT BAD PLACES TO START.
TWO-SIX... ARE YOU ALL RIGHT?
EVERYTHING'S ALL WRONG, XRILL!
I KNOW YOU...OF ALL PEOPLE...CAN FEEL IT, TOO.
RING-- WE NEED BACKUP!
UNABLE TO COMPLY.
UNABLE TO CONTACT GREEN LANTERN CORPS.
AAGGH!
AS I SEE IT, THOUGH, A LEADER FIGURES OUT WHAT WORKS BEST FOR THEM...
...AND FOR THE PEOPLE UNDER THEIR COMMAND...

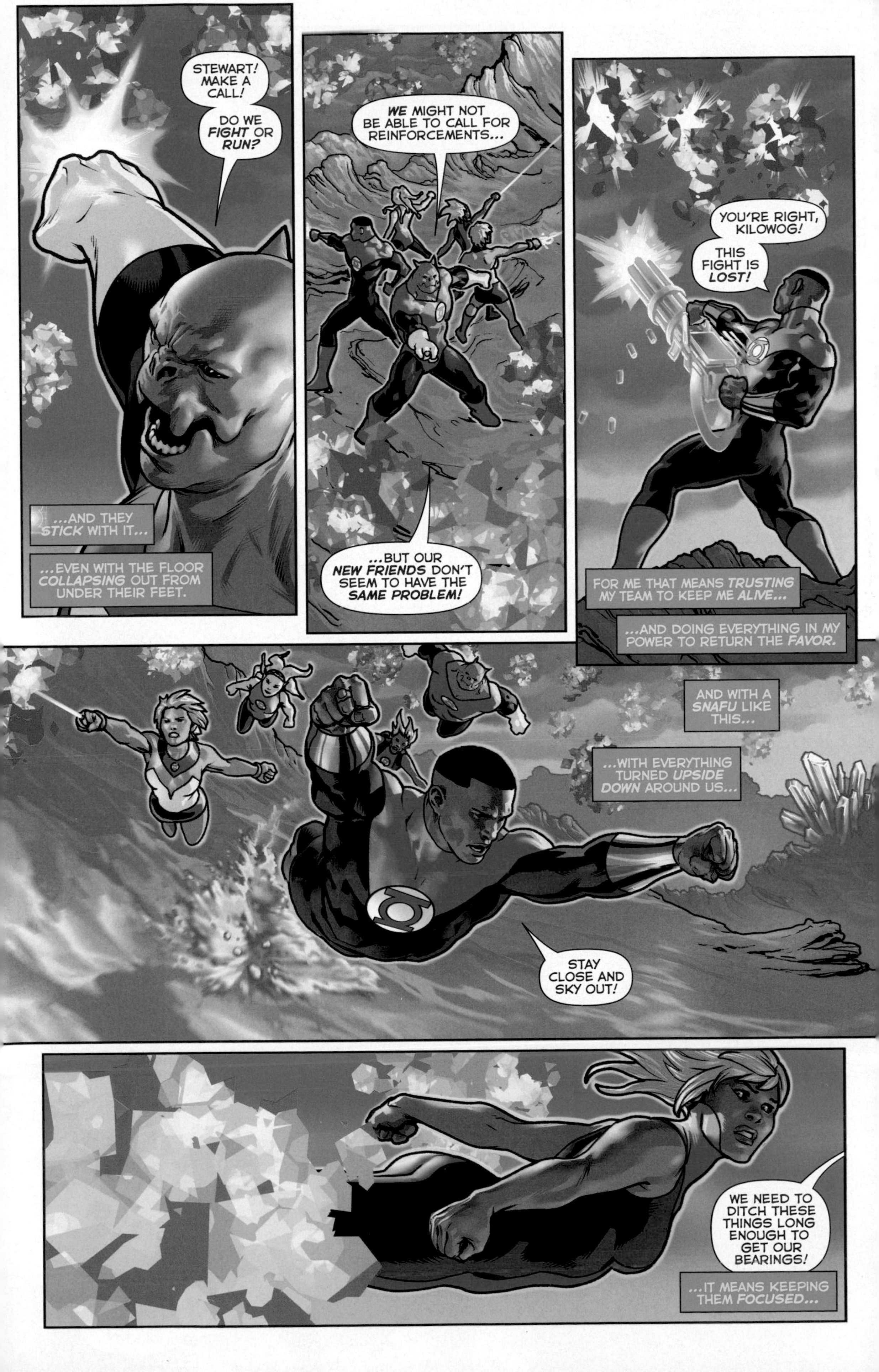
STEWART! MAKE A CALL!
DO WE FIGHT OR RUN?
...AND THEY STICK WITH IT...
...EVEN WITH THE FLOOR COLLAPSING OUT FROM UNDER THEIR FEET.
WE MIGHT NOT BE ABLE TO CALL FOR REINFORCEMENTS...
...BUT OUR NEW FRIENDS DON'T SEEM TO HAVE THE SAME PROBLEM!
YOU'RE RIGHT, KILOWOG!
THIS FIGHT IS LOST!
FOR ME THAT MEANS TRUSTING MY TEAM TO KEEP ME ALIVE...
...AND DOING EVERYTHING IN MY POWER TO RETURN THE FAVOR.
AND WITH A SNAFU LIKE THIS...
...WITH EVERYTHING TURNED UPSIDE DOWN AROUND US...
STAY CLOSE AND SKY OUT!
WE NEED TO DITCH THESE THINGS LONG ENOUGH TO GET OUR BEARINGS!
...IT MEANS KEEPING THEM FOCUSED...

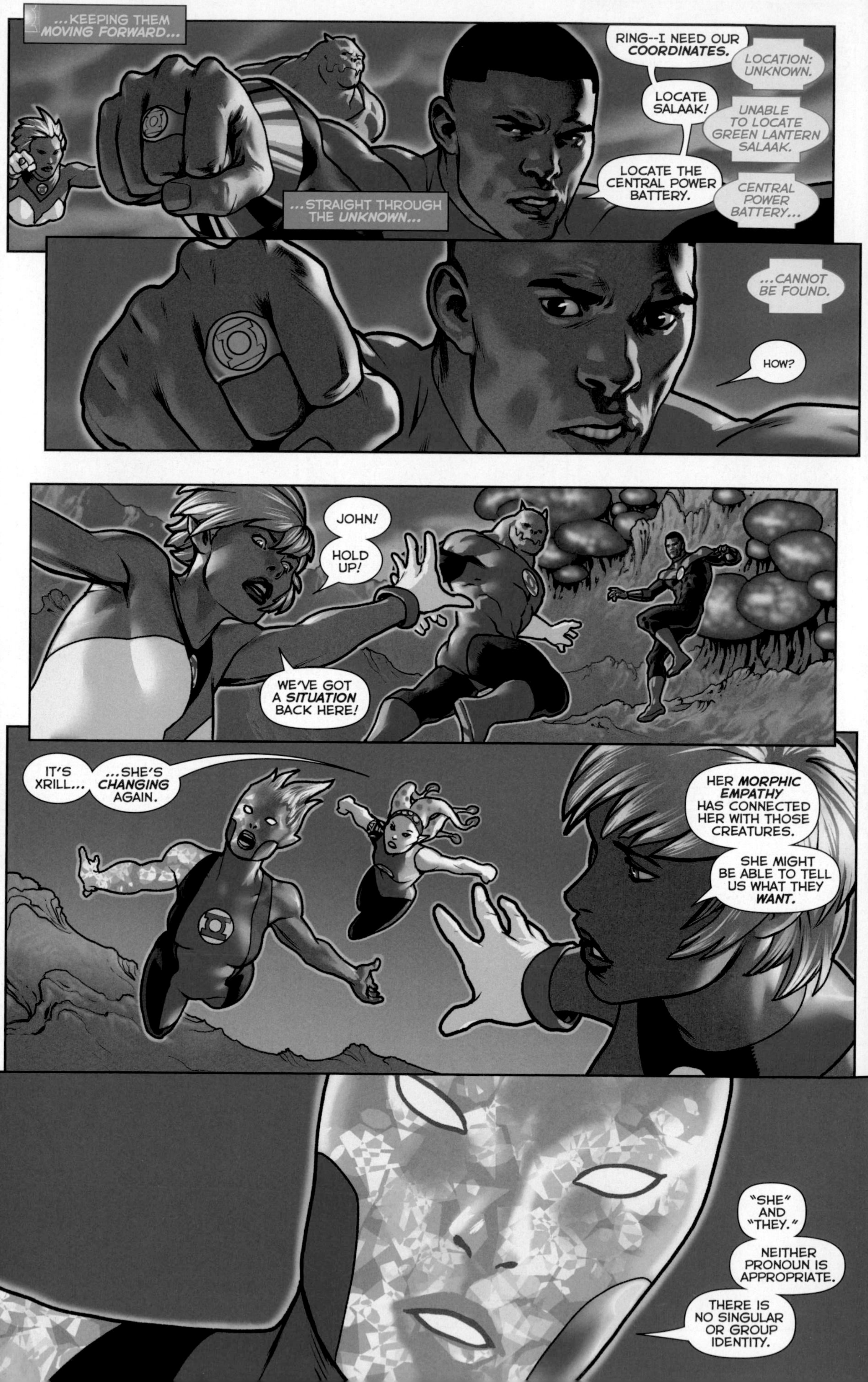
...KEEPING THEM MOVING FORWARD...
RING--I NEED OUR COORDINATES.
LOCATION: UNKNOWN.
LOCATE SALAAK!
UNABLE TO LOCATE GREEN LANTERN SALAAK.
LOCATE THE CENTRAL POWER BATTERY.
...STRAIGHT THROUGH THE UNKNOWN...
CENTRAL POWER BATTERY...
...CANNOT BE FOUND.
HOW?
JOHN!
HOLD UP!
WE'VE GOT A SITUATION BACK HERE!
IT'S XRILL...
...SHE'S CHANGING AGAIN.
HER MORPHIC EMPATHY HAS CONNECTED HER WITH THOSE CREATURES.
SHE MIGHT BE ABLE TO TELL US WHAT THEY WANT.
"SHE" AND "THEY."
NEITHER PRONOUN IS APPROPRIATE.
THERE IS NO SINGULAR OR GROUP IDENTITY.

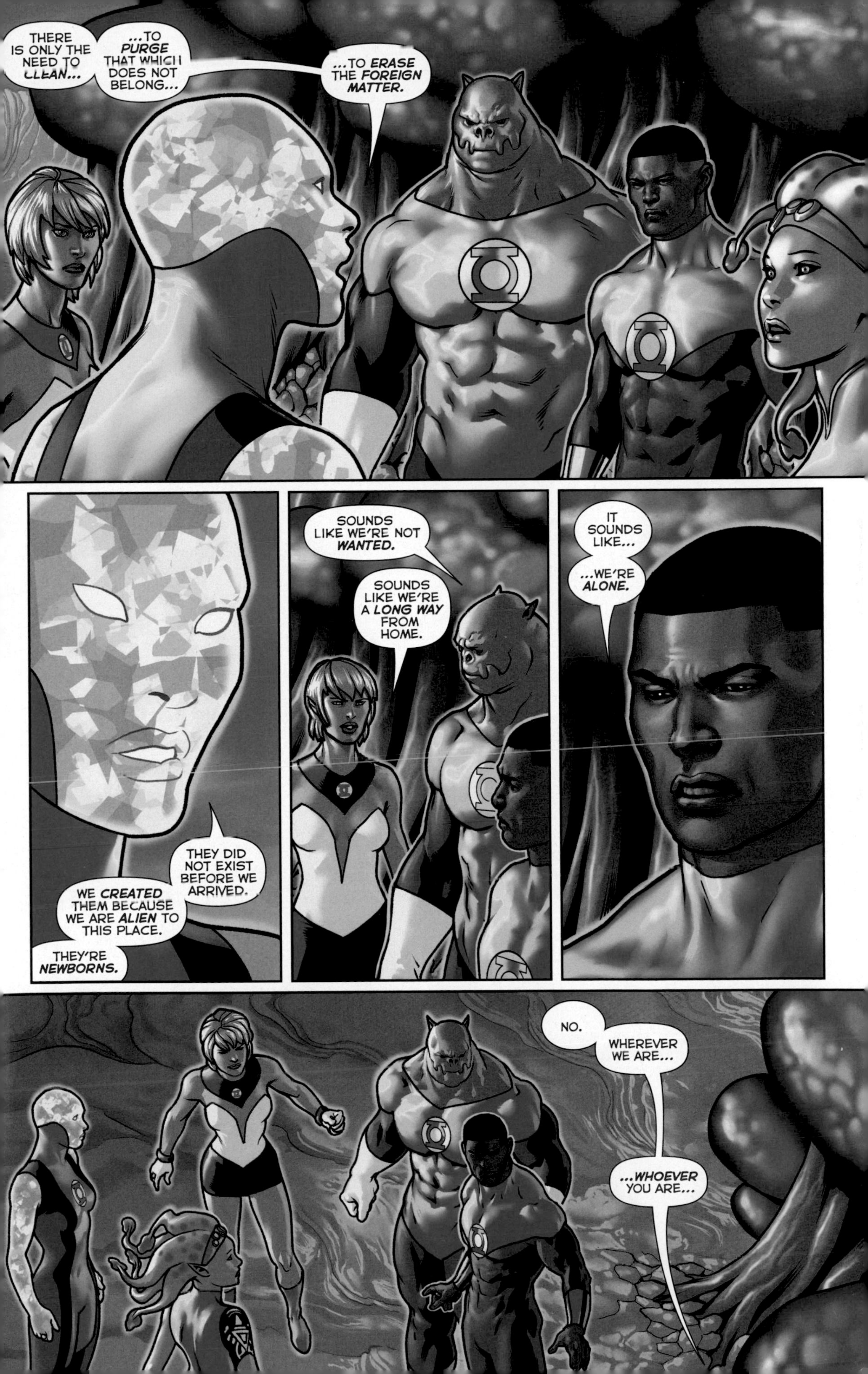

THERE IS ONLY THE NEED TO CLEAN...
...TO PURGE THAT WHICH DOES NOT BELONG...
...TO ERASE THE FOREIGN MATTER.
THEY DID NOT EXIST BEFORE WE ARRIVED.
WE CREATED THEM BECAUSE WE ARE ALIEN TO THIS PLACE.
THEY'RE NEWBORNS.
SOUNDS LIKE WE'RE NOT WANTED.
SOUNDS LIKE WE'RE A LONG WAY FROM HOME.
IT SOUNDS LIKE...
...WE'RE ALONE.
NO.
WHEREVER WE ARE...
...WHOEVER YOU ARE...

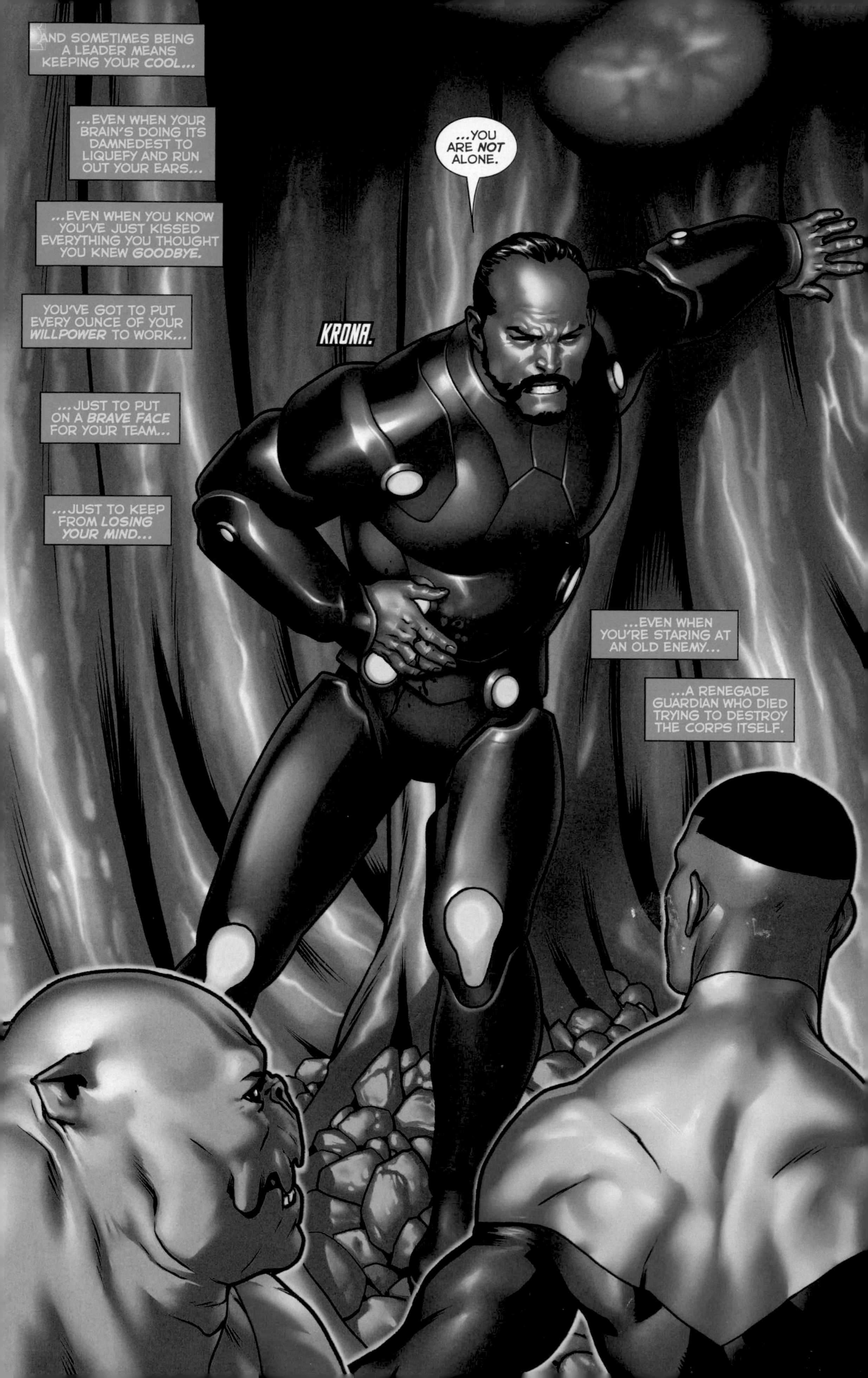
AND SOMETIMES BEING A LEADER MEANS KEEPING YOUR COOL...
...EVEN WHEN YOUR BRAIN'S DOING ITS DAMNEDEST TO LIQUEFY AND RUN OUT YOUR EARS...
...EVEN WHEN YOU KNOW YOU'VE JUST KISSED EVERYTHING YOU THOUGHT YOU KNEW GOODBYE.
YOU'VE GOT TO PUT EVERY OUNCE OF YOUR WILLPOWER TO WORK...
...JUST TO PUT ON A BRAVE FACE FOR YOUR TEAM...
...JUST TO KEEP FROM LOSING YOUR MIND...
...YOU ARE NOT ALONE.
KRONA.
...EVEN WHEN YOU'RE STARING AT AN OLD ENEMY...
...A RENEGADE GUARDIAN WHO DIED TRYING TO DESTROY THE CORPS ITSELF.

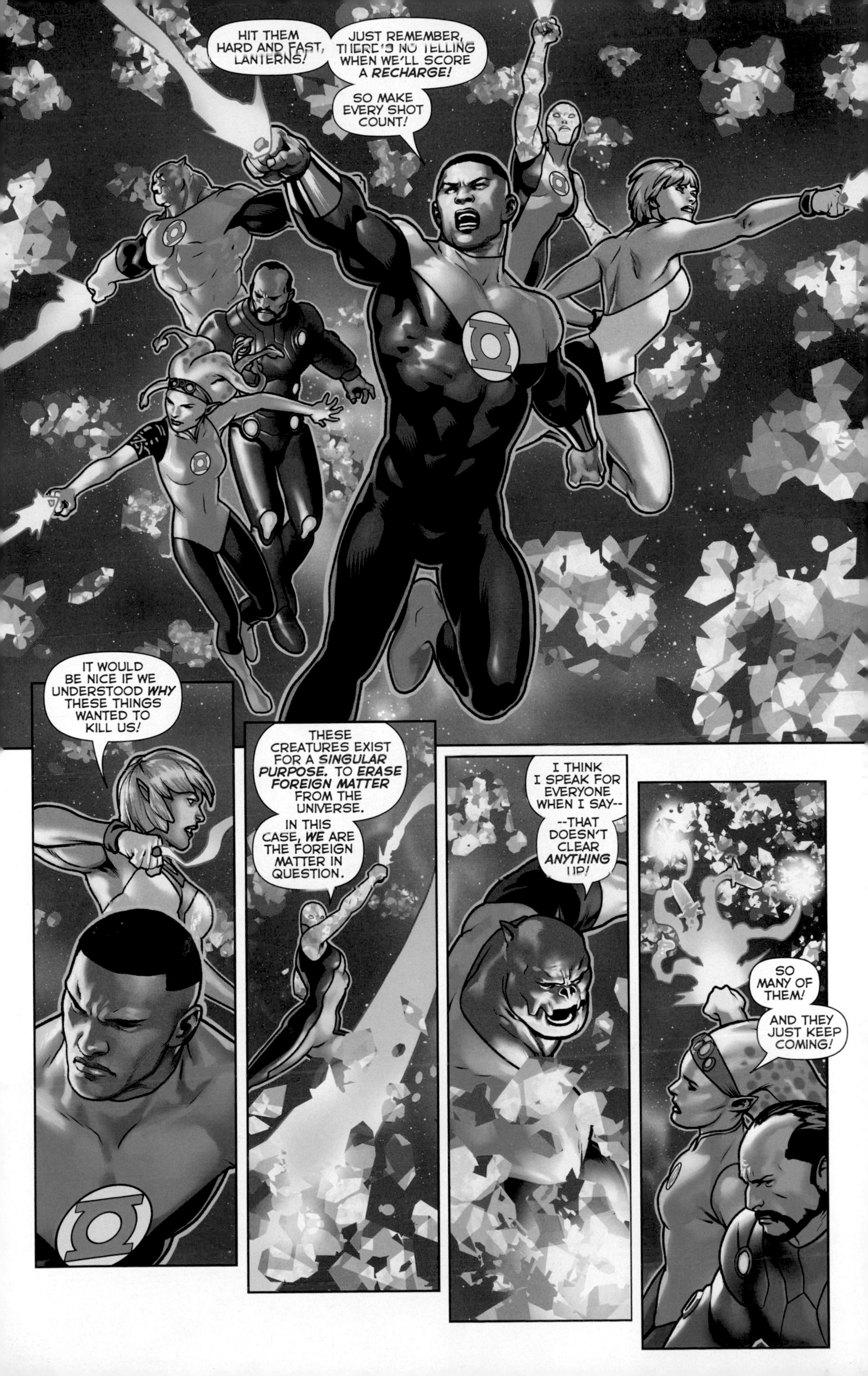
HIT THEM HARD AND FAST, LANTERNS!
JUST REMEMBER, THERE'S NO TELLING WHEN WE'LL SCORE A **RECHARGE!**
SO MAKE EVERY SHOT COUNT!
IT WOULD BE NICE IF WE UNDERSTOOD **WHY** THESE THINGS WANTED TO KILL US!
THESE CREATURES EXIST FOR A **SINGULAR PURPOSE.** TO **ERASE FOREIGN MATTER** FROM THE UNIVERSE.
IN THIS CASE, **WE** ARE THE FOREIGN MATTER IN QUESTION.
I THINK I SPEAK FOR EVERYONE WHEN I SAY--
--THAT DOESN'T CLEAR **ANYTHING** UP!
SO MANY OF THEM!
AND THEY JUST KEEP COMING!

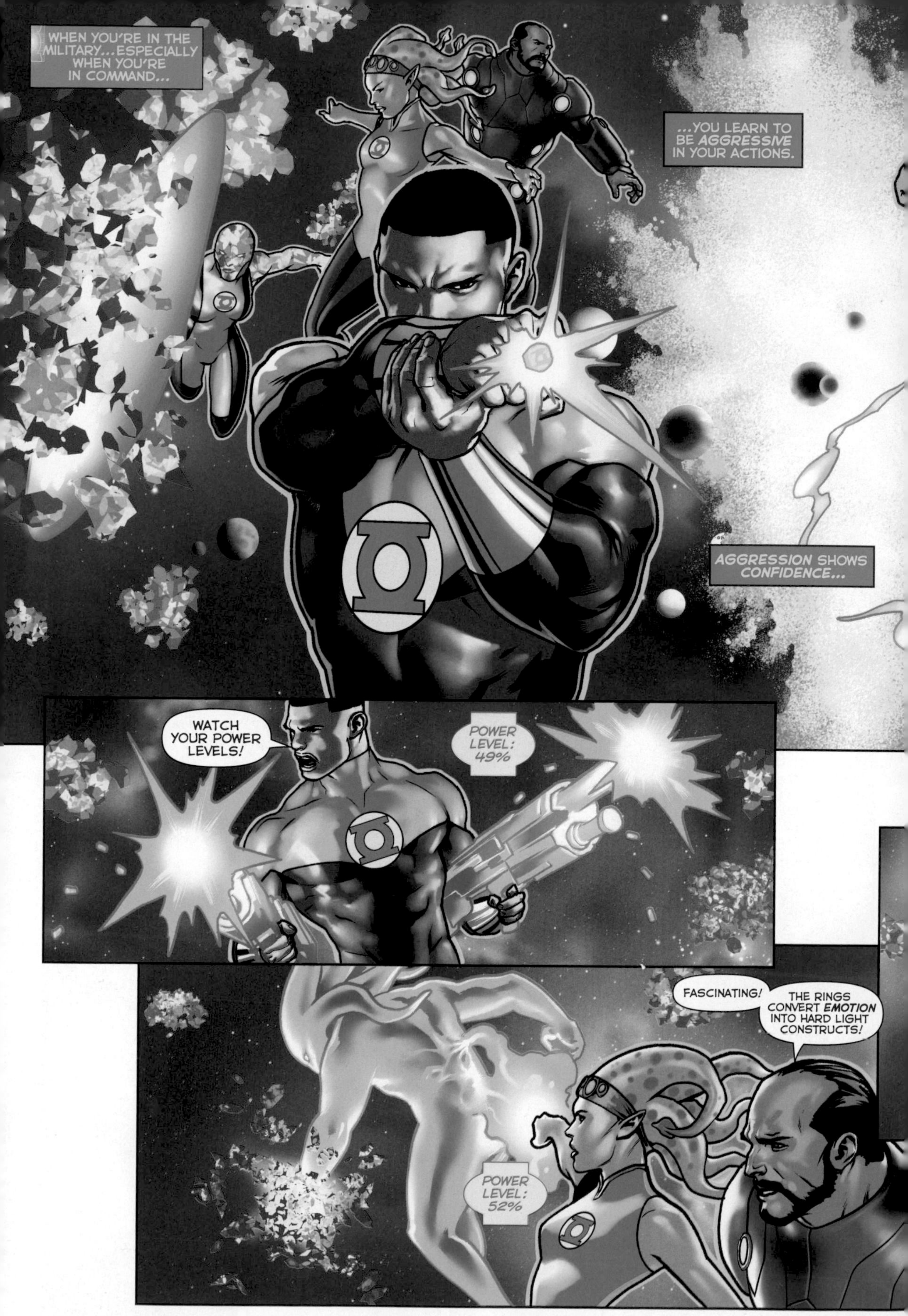

WHEN YOU'RE IN THE MILITARY... ESPECIALLY WHEN YOU'RE IN COMMAND...
...YOU LEARN TO BE AGGRESSIVE IN YOUR ACTIONS.
AGGRESSION SHOWS CONFIDENCE...
WATCH YOUR POWER LEVELS!
POWER LEVEL: 49%
FASCINATING!
THE RINGS CONVERT EMOTION INTO HARD LIGHT CONSTRUCTS!
POWER LEVEL: 52%

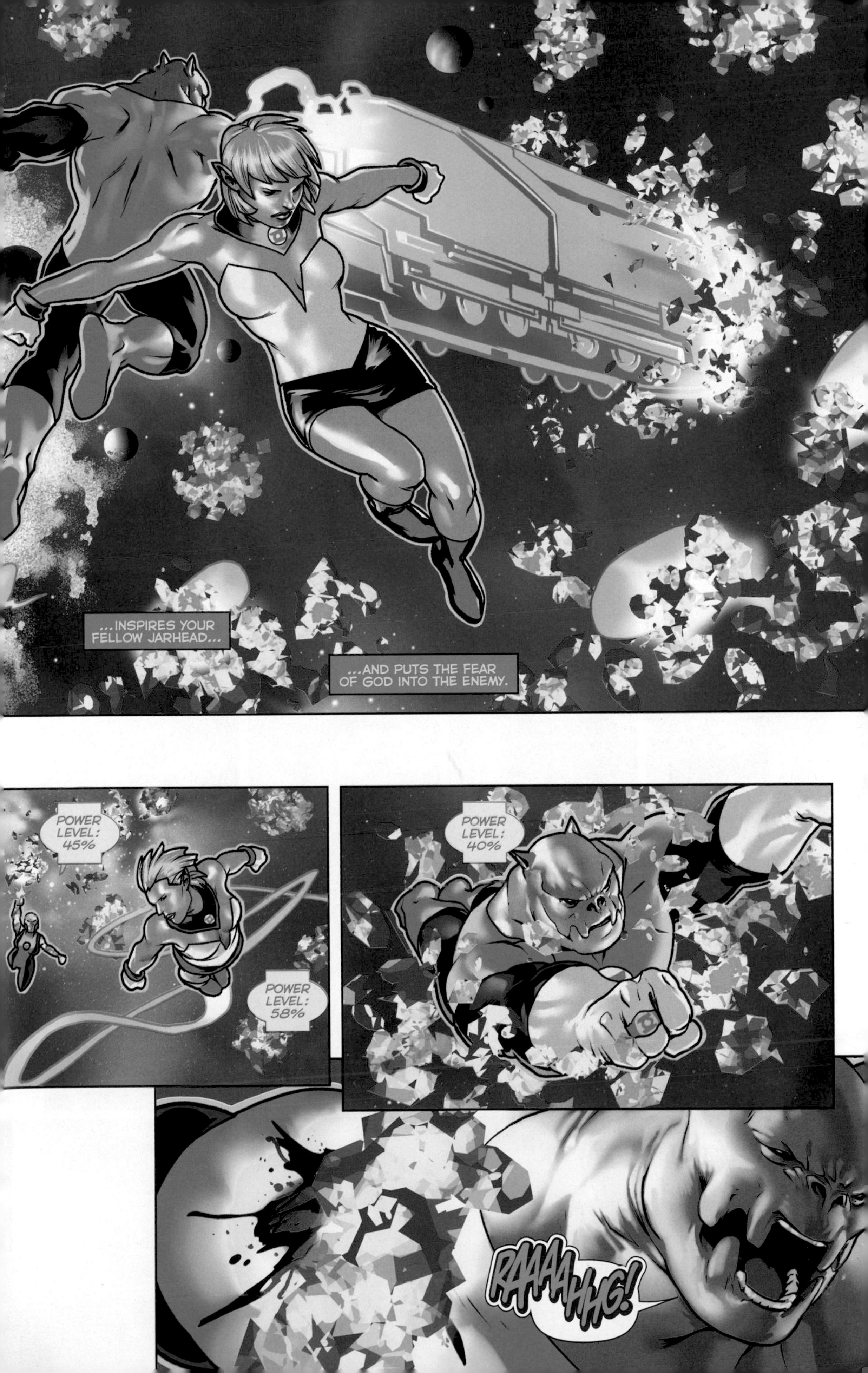
...INSPIRES YOUR FELLOW JARHEAD...
...AND PUTS THE FEAR OF GOD INTO THE ENEMY.
POWER LEVEL: 45%
POWER LEVEL: 58%
POWER LEVEL: 40%
RAAAAHHG!

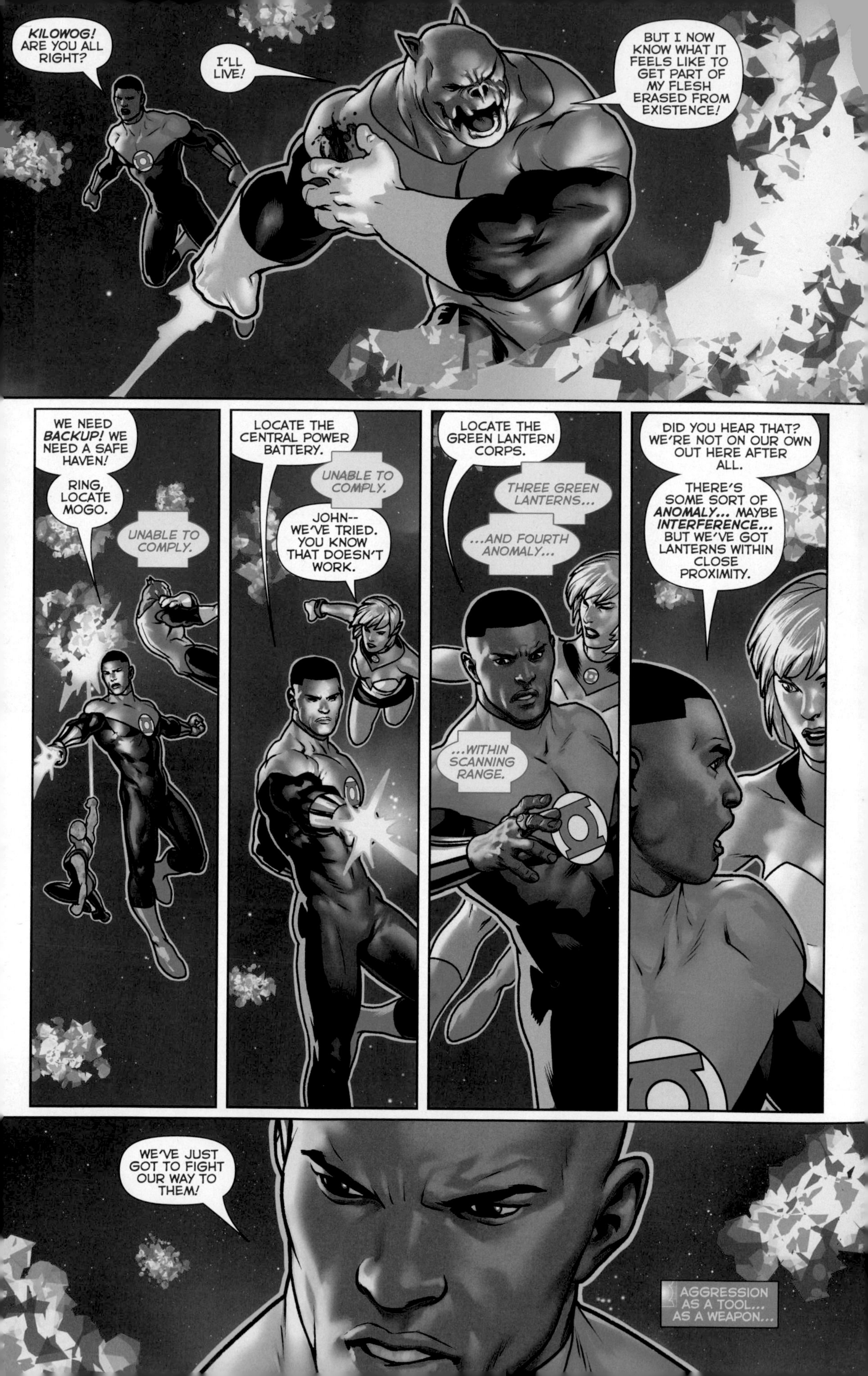
KILOWOG! ARE YOU ALL RIGHT?
I'LL LIVE!
BUT I NOW KNOW WHAT IT FEELS LIKE TO GET PART OF MY FLESH ERASED FROM EXISTENCE!
WE NEED BACKUP! WE NEED A SAFE HAVEN!
RING, LOCATE MOGO.
UNABLE TO COMPLY.
LOCATE THE CENTRAL POWER BATTERY.
UNABLE TO COMPLY.
JOHN-- WE'VE TRIED. YOU KNOW THAT DOESN'T WORK.
LOCATE THE GREEN LANTERN CORPS.
THREE GREEN LANTERNS...
...AND FOURTH ANOMALY...
...WITHIN SCANNING RANGE.
DID YOU HEAR THAT? WE'RE NOT ON OUR OWN OUT HERE AFTER ALL.
THERE'S SOME SORT OF ANOMALY... MAYBE INTERFERENCE... BUT WE'VE GOT LANTERNS WITHIN CLOSE PROXIMITY.
WE'VE JUST GOT TO FIGHT OUR WAY TO THEM!
AGGRESSION AS A TOOL... AS A WEAPON...

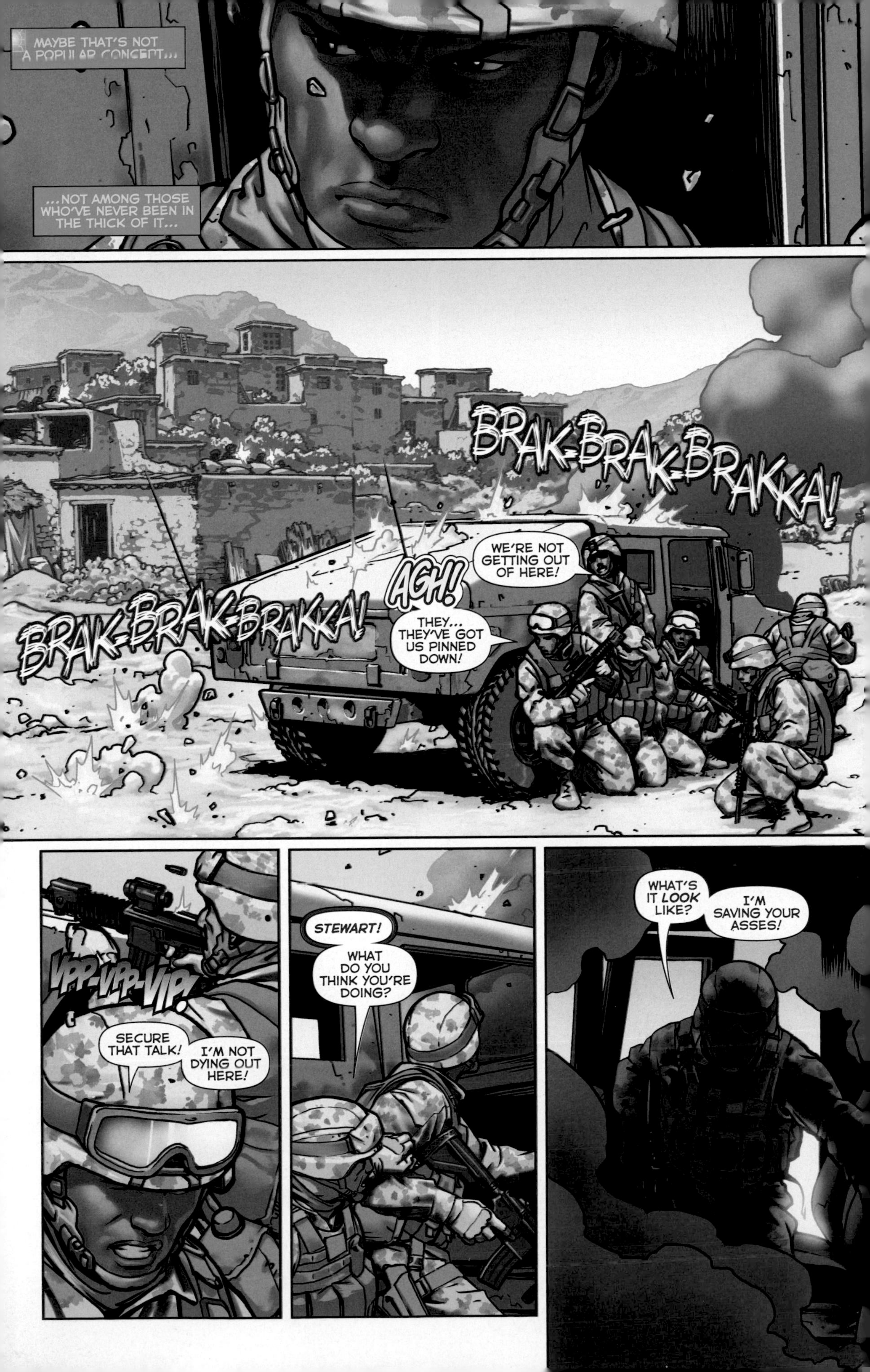
MAYBE THAT'S NOT A POPULAR CONCEPT...
...NOT AMONG THOSE WHO'VE NEVER BEEN IN THE THICK OF IT...
BRAK-BRAK-BRAKKA!
WE'RE NOT GETTING OUT OF HERE!
AGH!
BRAK-BRAK-BRAKKA!
THEY... THEY'VE GOT US PINNED DOWN!
VPP-VPP-VIP!
SECURE THAT TALK!
I'M NOT DYING OUT HERE!
STEWART!
WHAT DO YOU THINK YOU'RE DOING?
WHAT'S IT LOOK LIKE?
I'M SAVING YOUR ASSES!

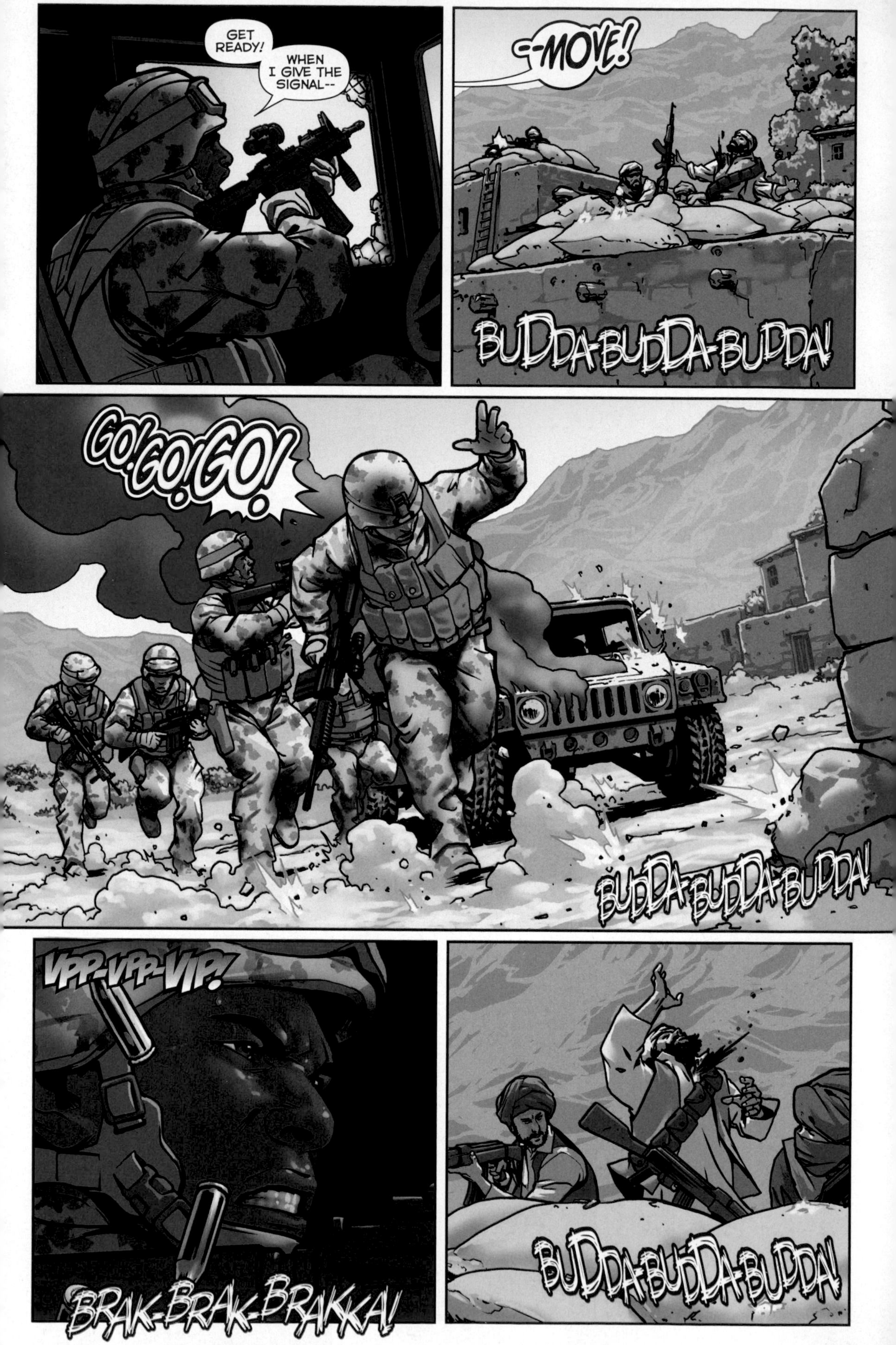
GET READY!
WHEN I GIVE THE SIGNAL--
--MOVE!
BUDDA-BUDDA-BUDDA!
GO! GO! GO!
BUDDA-BUDDA-BUDDA!
VPP-VPP-VIP!
BRAK-BRAK-BRAKKA!
BUDDA-BUDDA-BUDDA!

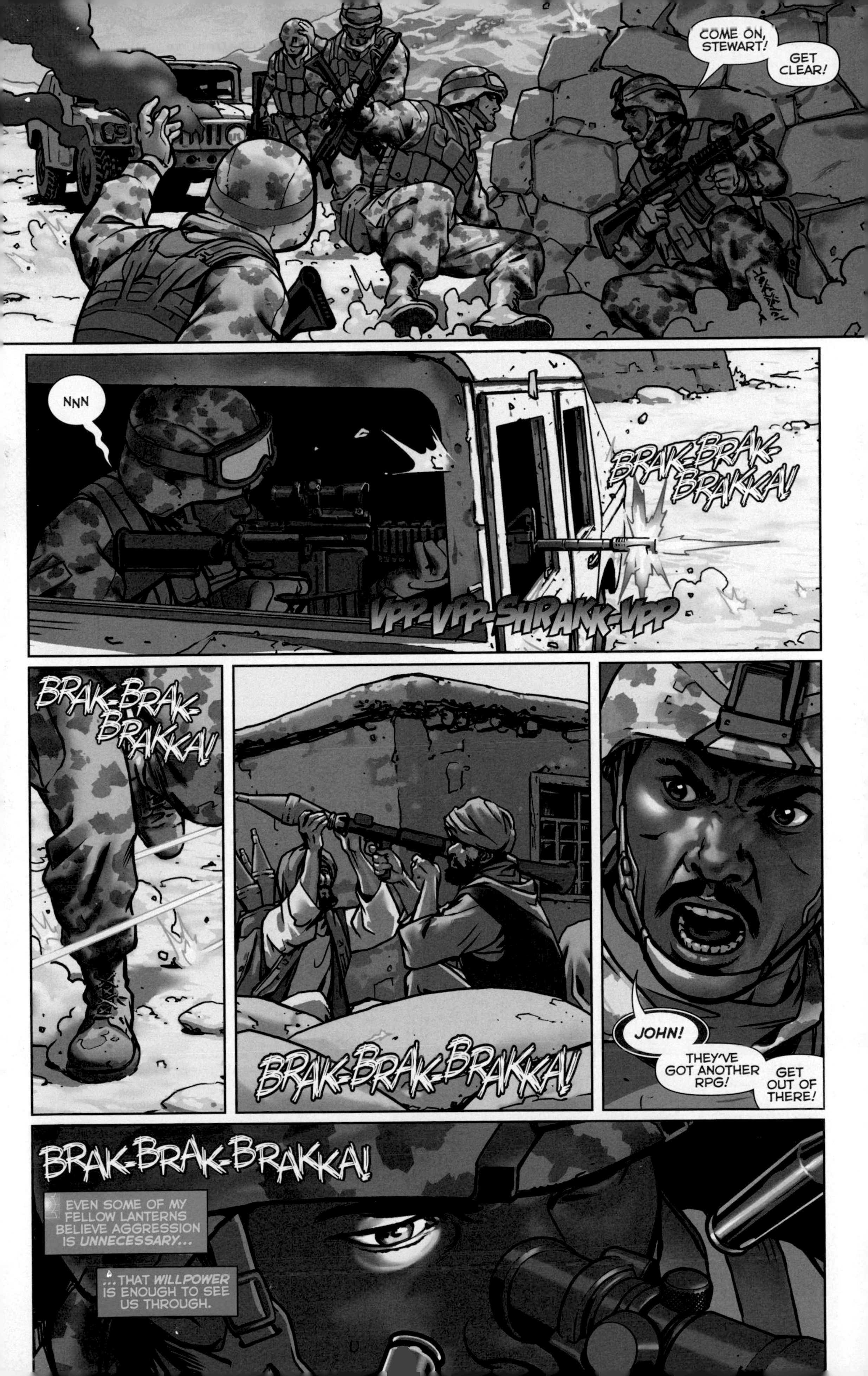
COME ON, STEWART!
GET CLEAR!
NNN
BRAK-BRAK-BRAKKA!
VPP-VPP-SHRAKK-VPP
BRAK-BRAK-BRAKKA!
BRAK-BRAK-BRAKKA!
JOHN!
THEY'VE GOT ANOTHER RPG!
GET OUT OF THERE!
BRAK-BRAK-BRAKKA!
EVEN SOME OF MY FELLOW LANTERNS BELIEVE AGGRESSION IS UNNECESSARY...
...THAT WILLPOWER IS ENOUGH TO SEE US THROUGH.

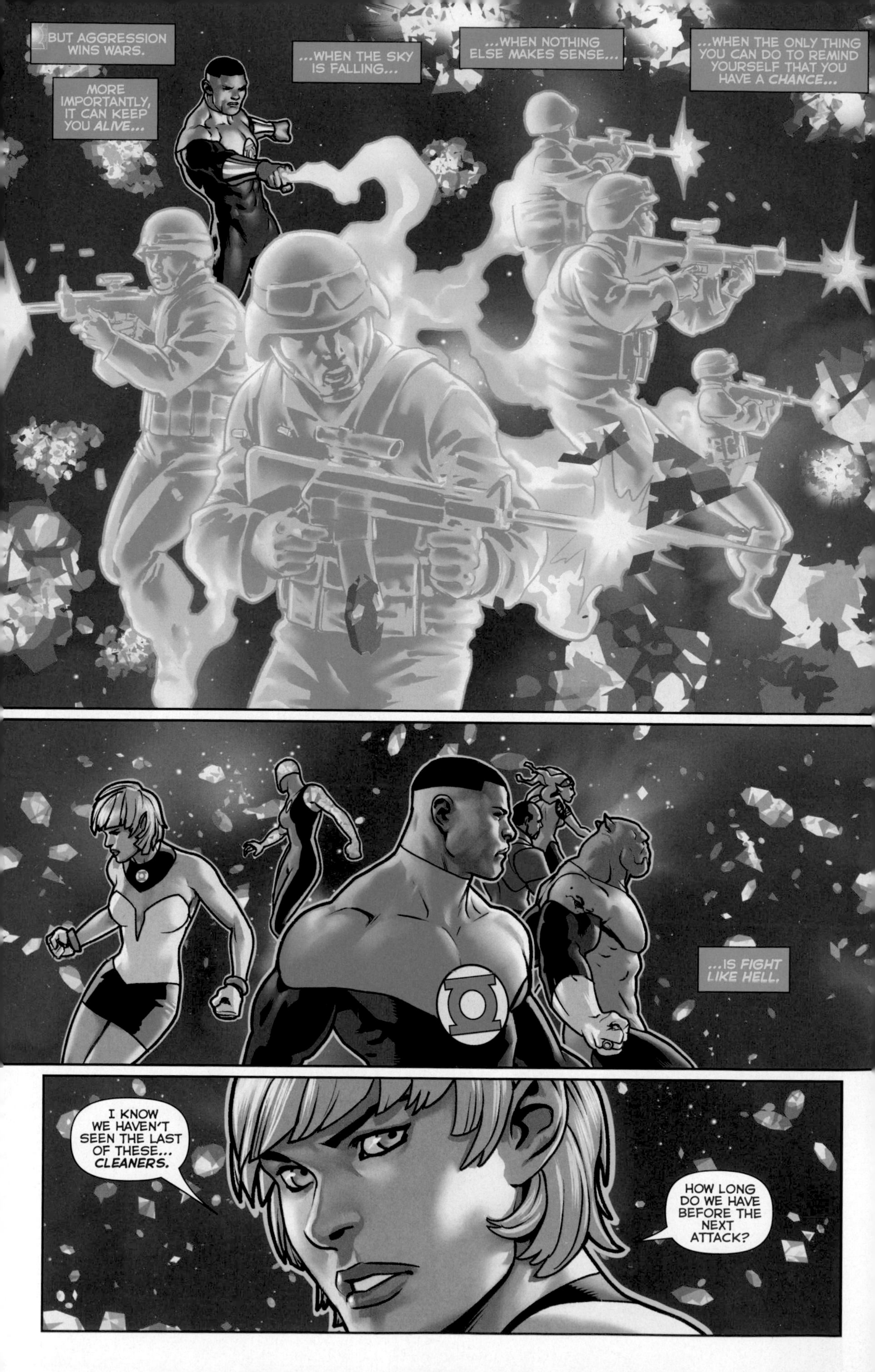
BUT AGGRESSION WINS WARS.
MORE IMPORTANTLY, IT CAN KEEP YOU ALIVE...
...WHEN THE SKY IS FALLING...
...WHEN NOTHING ELSE MAKES SENSE...
...WHEN THE ONLY THING YOU CAN DO TO REMIND YOURSELF THAT YOU HAVE A CHANCE...
...IS FIGHT LIKE HELL.
I KNOW WE HAVEN'T SEEN THE LAST OF THESE... CLEANERS.
HOW LONG DO WE HAVE BEFORE THE NEXT ATTACK?

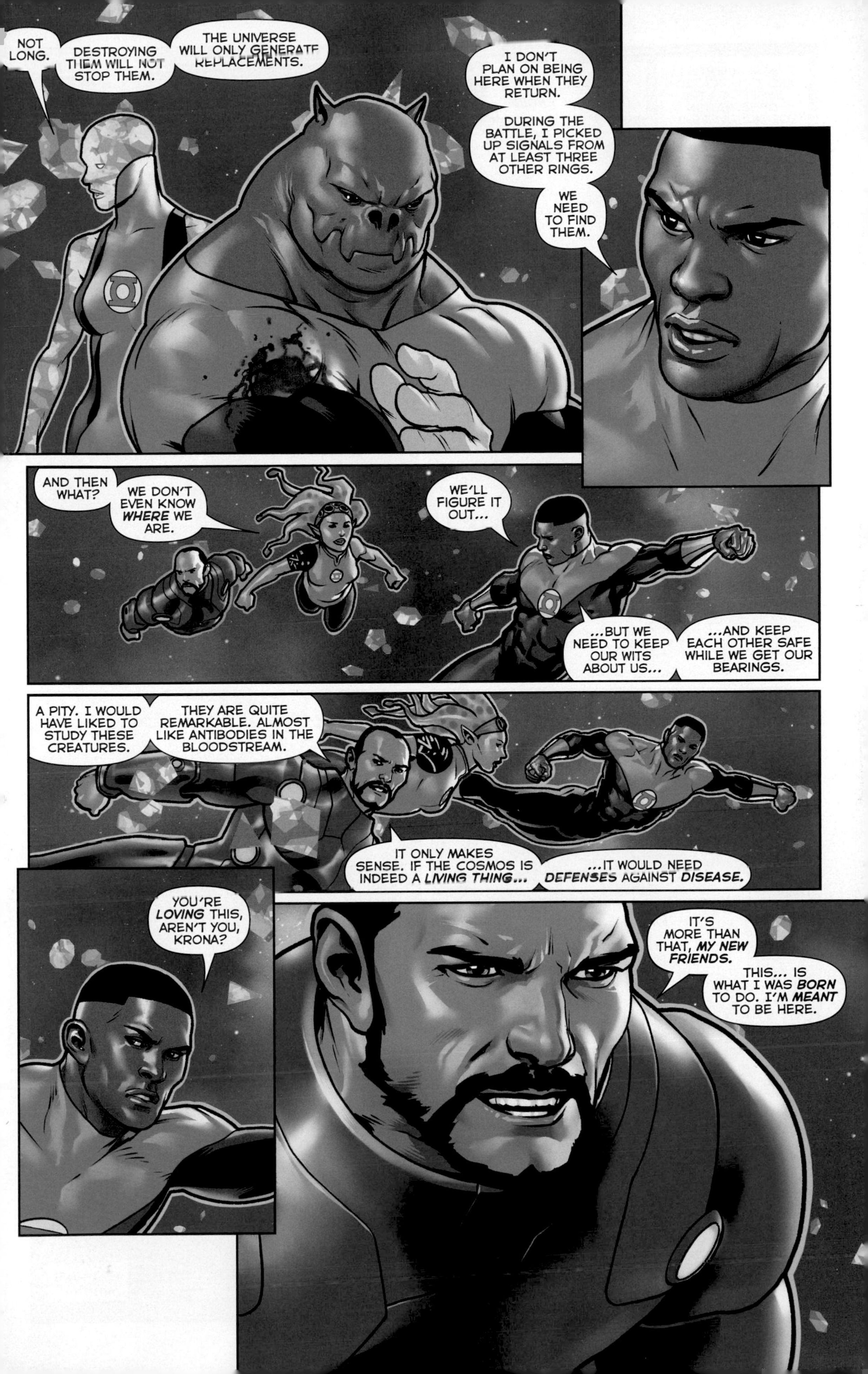
NOT LONG.
DESTROYING THEM WILL NOT STOP THEM.
THE UNIVERSE WILL ONLY GENERATE REPLACEMENTS.
I DON'T PLAN ON BEING HERE WHEN THEY RETURN.
DURING THE BATTLE, I PICKED UP SIGNALS FROM AT LEAST THREE OTHER RINGS.
WE NEED TO FIND THEM.
AND THEN WHAT?
WE DON'T EVEN KNOW *WHERE* WE ARE.
WE'LL FIGURE IT OUT...
...BUT WE NEED TO KEEP OUR WITS ABOUT US...
...AND KEEP EACH OTHER SAFE WHILE WE GET OUR BEARINGS.
A PITY. I WOULD HAVE LIKED TO STUDY THESE CREATURES.
THEY ARE QUITE REMARKABLE. ALMOST LIKE ANTIBODIES IN THE BLOODSTREAM.
IT ONLY MAKES SENSE. IF THE COSMOS IS INDEED A *LIVING THING...*
...IT WOULD NEED *DEFENSES* AGAINST *DISEASE.*
YOU'RE *LOVING* THIS, AREN'T YOU, KRONA?
IT'S MORE THAN THAT, *MY NEW FRIENDS.*
THIS... IS WHAT I WAS *BORN* TO DO. I'M *MEANT* TO BE HERE.

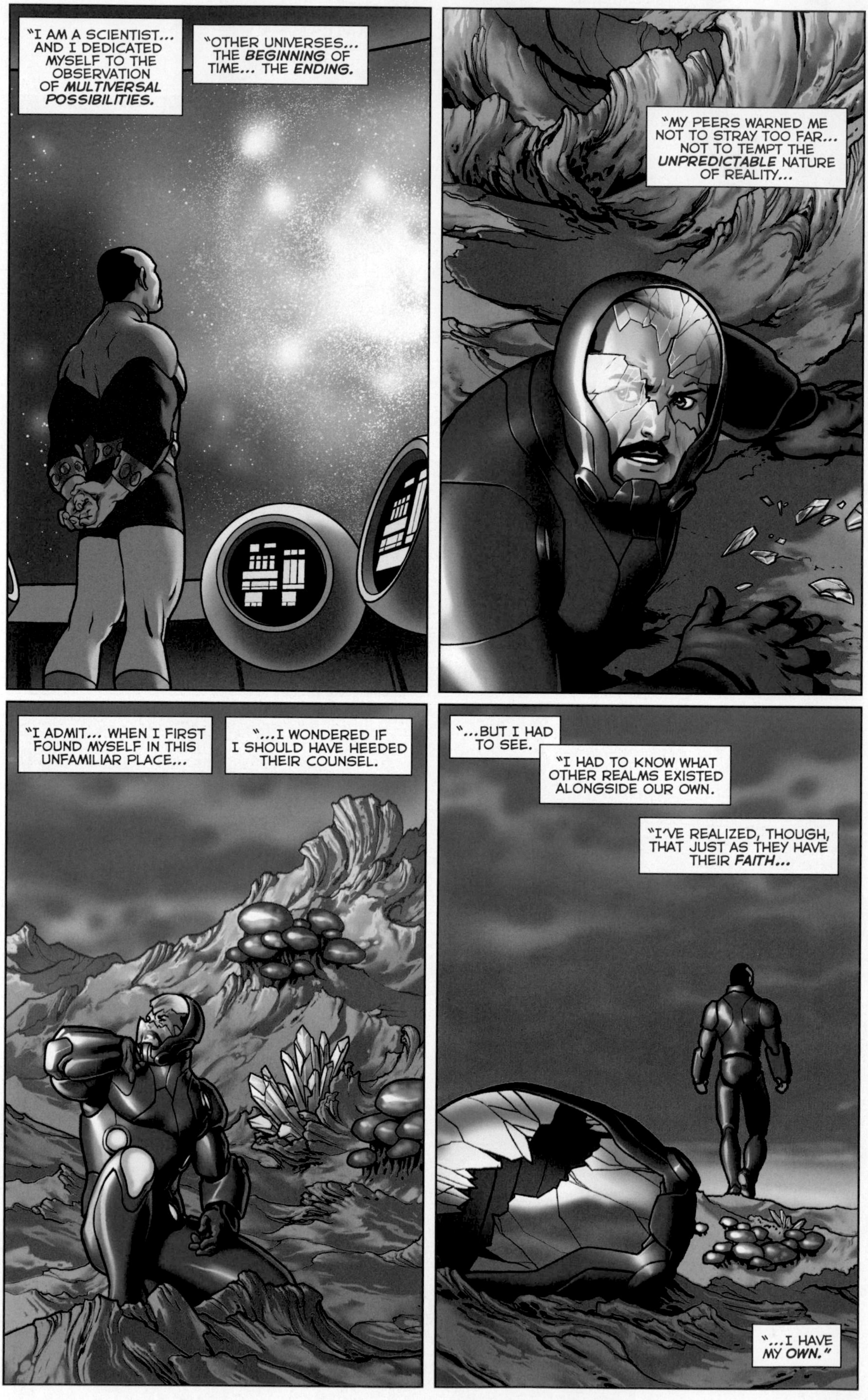
"I AM A SCIENTIST... AND I DEDICATED MYSELF TO THE OBSERVATION OF MULTIVERSAL POSSIBILITIES.
"OTHER UNIVERSES... THE BEGINNING OF TIME... THE ENDING.
"MY PEERS WARNED ME NOT TO STRAY TOO FAR... NOT TO TEMPT THE UNPREDICTABLE NATURE OF REALITY...
"I ADMIT... WHEN I FIRST FOUND MYSELF IN THIS UNFAMILIAR PLACE...
"...I WONDERED IF I SHOULD HAVE HEEDED THEIR COUNSEL.
"...BUT I HAD TO SEE.
"I HAD TO KNOW WHAT OTHER REALMS EXISTED ALONGSIDE OUR OWN.
"I'VE REALIZED, THOUGH, THAT JUST AS THEY HAVE THEIR FAITH...
"...I HAVE MY OWN."

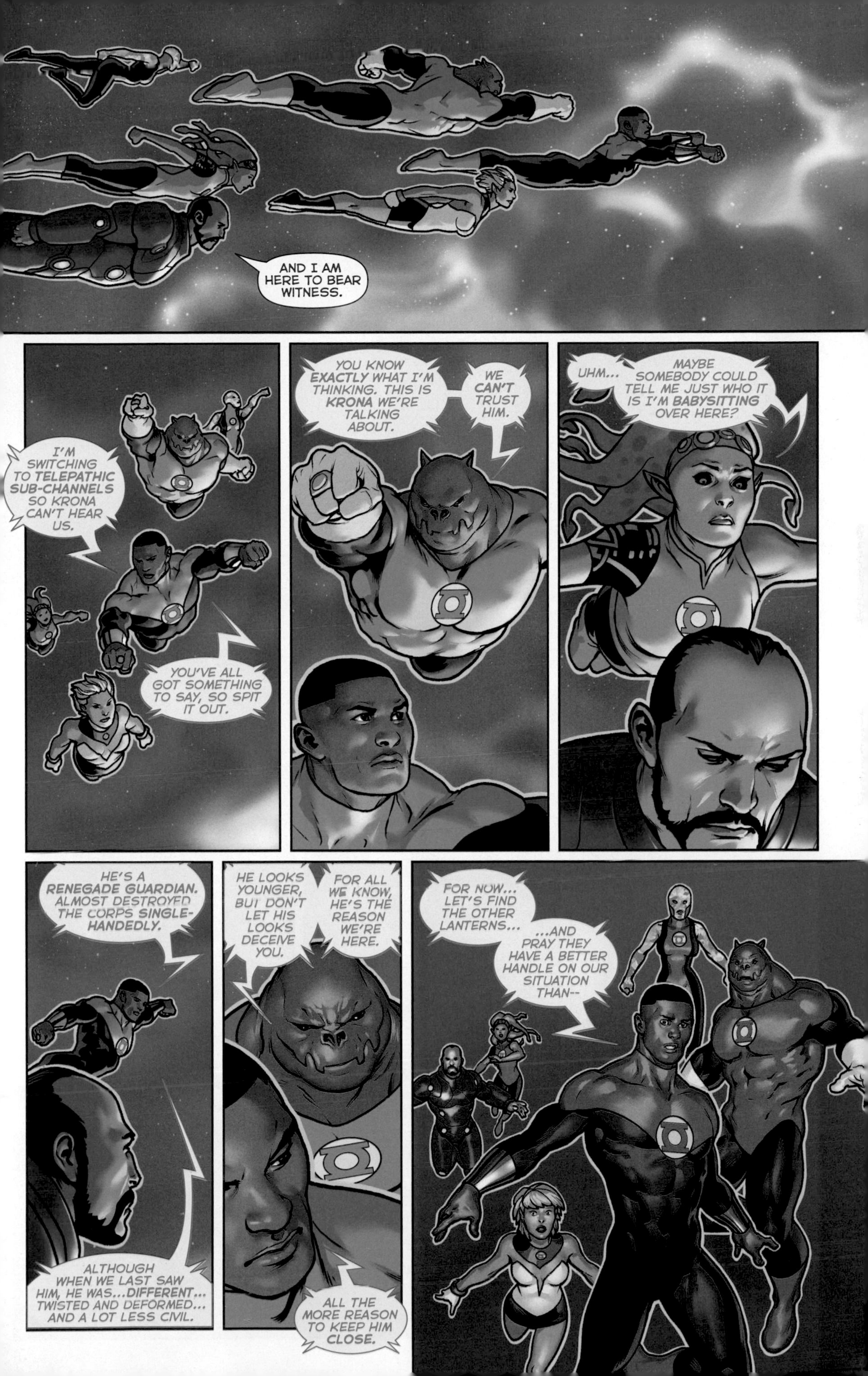
AND I AM HERE TO BEAR WITNESS.
I'M SWITCHING TO TELEPATHIC SUB-CHANNELS SO KRONA CAN'T HEAR US.
YOU'VE ALL GOT SOMETHING TO SAY, SO SPIT IT OUT.
YOU KNOW EXACTLY WHAT I'M THINKING. THIS IS KRONA WE'RE TALKING ABOUT.
WE CAN'T TRUST HIM.
UHM...
MAYBE SOMEBODY COULD TELL ME JUST WHO IT IS I'M BABYSITTING OVER HERE?
HE'S A RENEGADE GUARDIAN. ALMOST DESTROYED THE CORPS SINGLE-HANDEDLY.
ALTHOUGH WHEN WE LAST SAW HIM, HE WAS...DIFFERENT... TWISTED AND DEFORMED... AND A LOT LESS CIVIL.
HE LOOKS YOUNGER, BUT DON'T LET HIS LOOKS DECEIVE YOU.
FOR ALL WE KNOW, HE'S THE REASON WE'RE HERE.
ALL THE MORE REASON TO KEEP HIM CLOSE.
FOR NOW... LET'S FIND THE OTHER LANTERNS...
...AND PRAY THEY HAVE A BETTER HANDLE ON OUR SITUATION THAN--

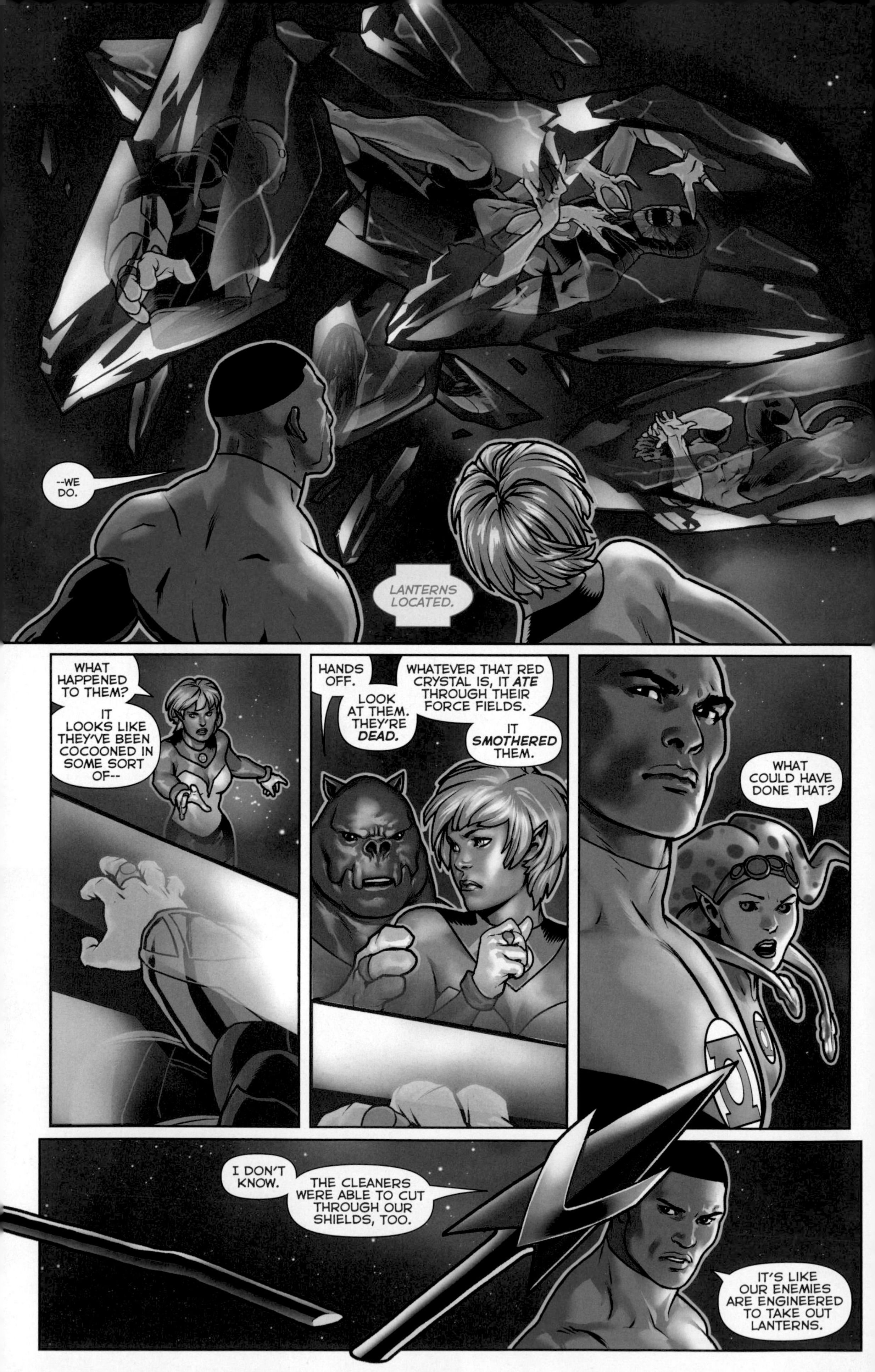
--WE DO.
LANTERNS LOCATED.
WHAT HAPPENED TO THEM?
IT LOOKS LIKE THEY'VE BEEN COCOONED IN SOME SORT OF--
HANDS OFF.
LOOK AT THEM. THEY'RE DEAD.
WHATEVER THAT RED CRYSTAL IS, IT ATE THROUGH THEIR FORCE FIELDS.
IT SMOTHERED THEM.
WHAT COULD HAVE DONE THAT?
I DON'T KNOW.
THE CLEANERS WERE ABLE TO CUT THROUGH OUR SHIELDS, TOO.
IT'S LIKE OUR ENEMIES ARE ENGINEERED TO TAKE OUT LANTERNS.

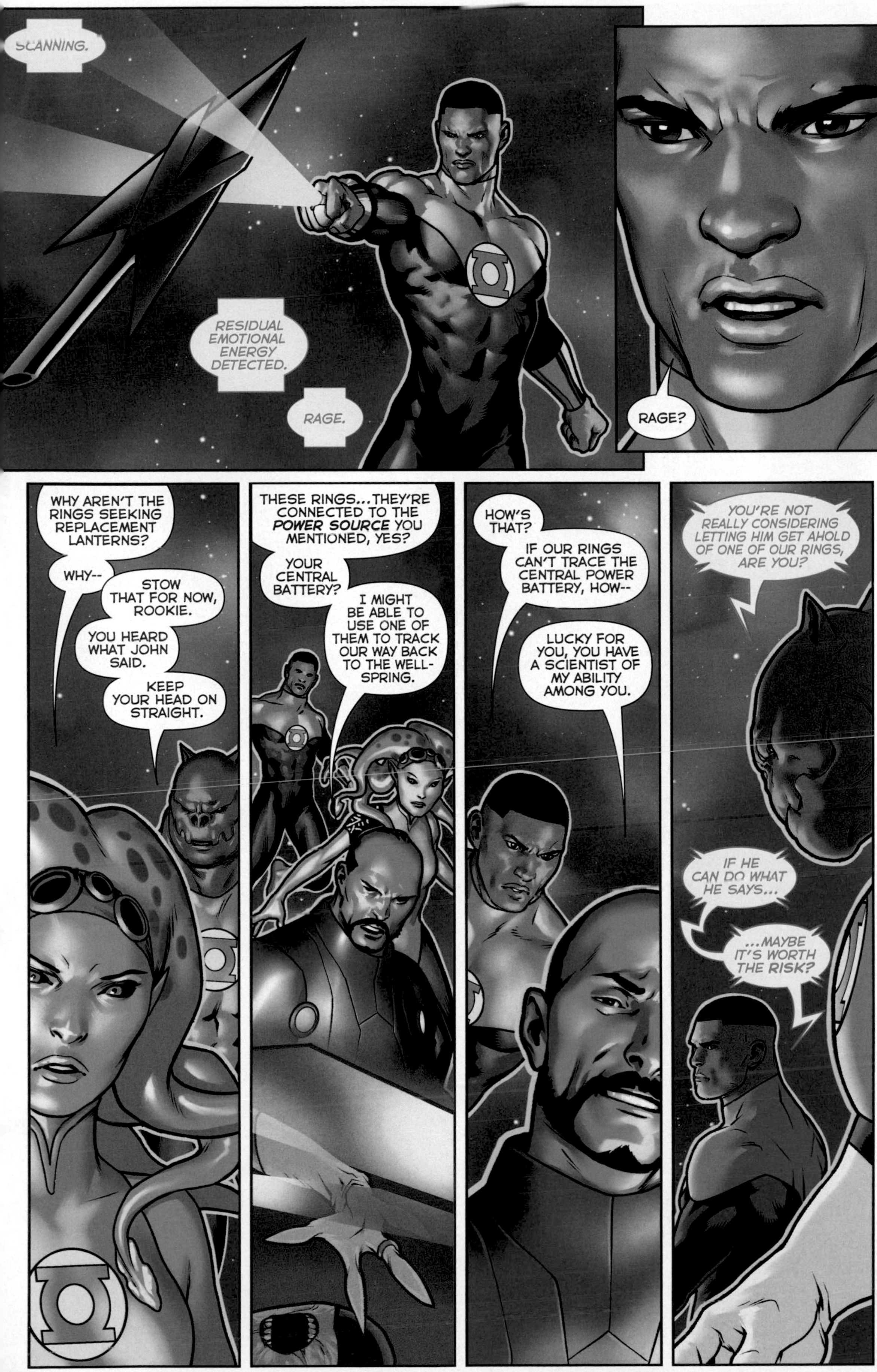
SCANNING.
RESIDUAL EMOTIONAL ENERGY DETECTED.
RAGE.
RAGE?
WHY AREN'T THE RINGS SEEKING REPLACEMENT LANTERNS?
WHY--
STOW THAT FOR NOW, ROOKIE.
YOU HEARD WHAT JOHN SAID.
KEEP YOUR HEAD ON STRAIGHT.
THESE RINGS...THEY'RE CONNECTED TO THE POWER SOURCE YOU MENTIONED, YES?
YOUR CENTRAL BATTERY?
I MIGHT BE ABLE TO USE ONE OF THEM TO TRACK OUR WAY BACK TO THE WELL-SPRING.
HOW'S THAT?
IF OUR RINGS CAN'T TRACE THE CENTRAL POWER BATTERY, HOW--
LUCKY FOR YOU, YOU HAVE A SCIENTIST OF MY ABILITY AMONG YOU.
YOU'RE NOT REALLY CONSIDERING LETTING HIM GET AHOLD OF ONE OF OUR RINGS, ARE YOU?
IF HE CAN DO WHAT HE SAYS...
...MAYBE IT'S WORTH THE RISK?

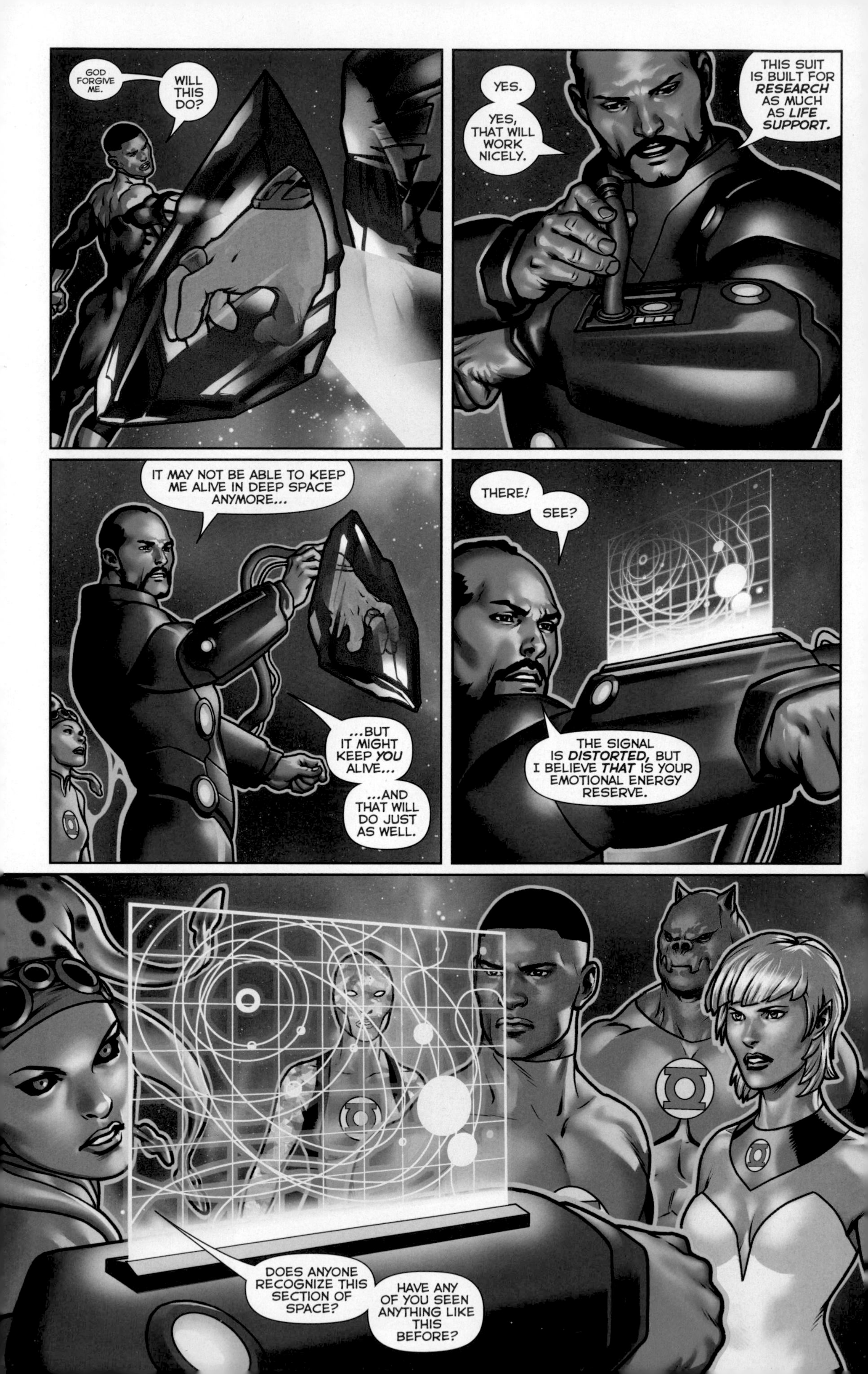
GOD FORGIVE ME.
WILL THIS DO?
YES.
YES, THAT WILL WORK NICELY.
THIS SUIT IS BUILT FOR *RESEARCH* AS MUCH AS *LIFE SUPPORT.*
IT MAY NOT BE ABLE TO KEEP ME ALIVE IN DEEP SPACE ANYMORE...
...BUT IT MIGHT KEEP *YOU* ALIVE...
...AND THAT WILL DO JUST AS WELL.
THERE!
SEE?
THE SIGNAL IS *DISTORTED,* BUT I BELIEVE *THAT* IS YOUR EMOTIONAL ENERGY RESERVE.
DOES ANYONE RECOGNIZE THIS SECTION OF SPACE?
HAVE ANY OF YOU SEEN ANYTHING LIKE THIS BEFORE?

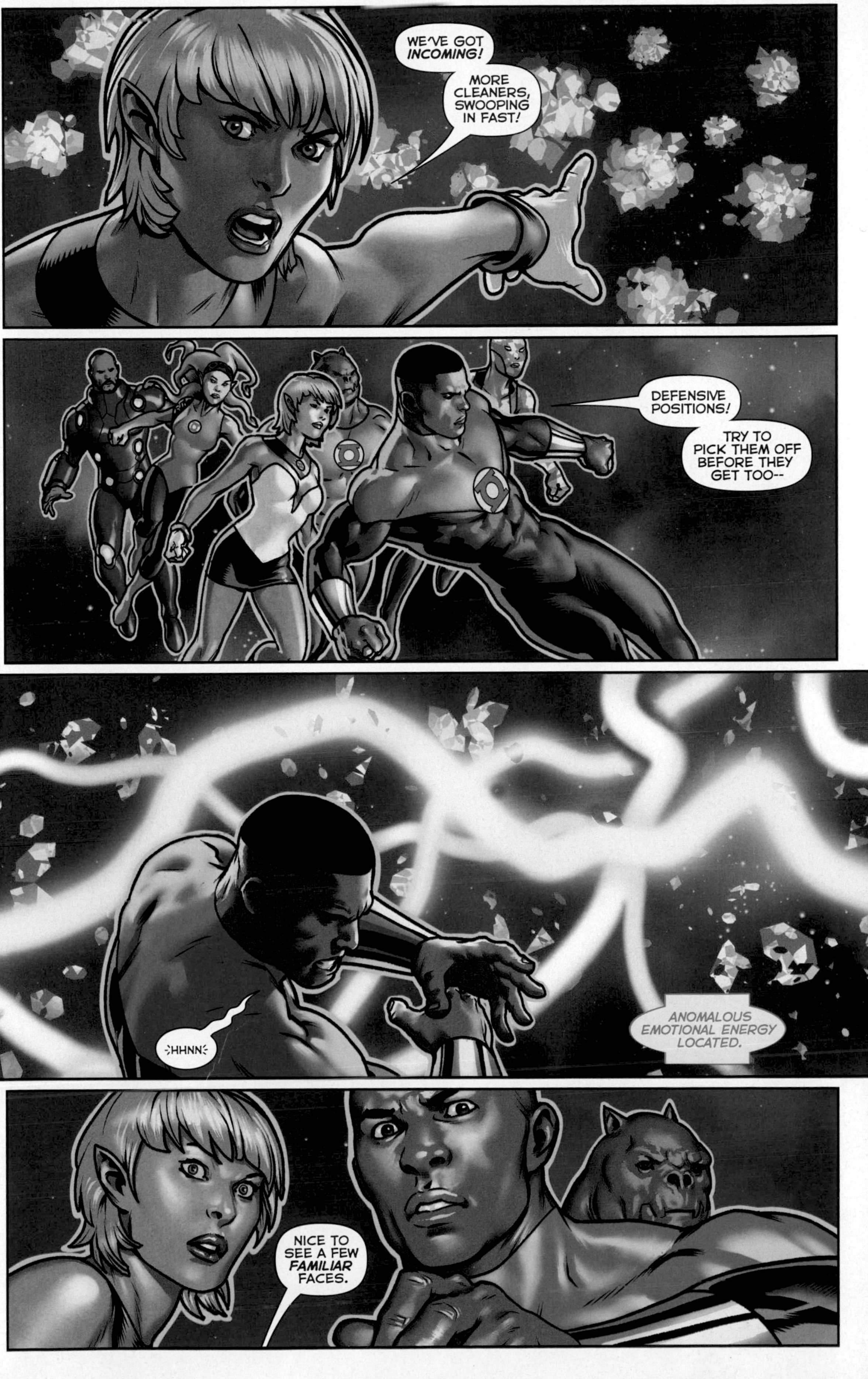

WE'VE GOT *INCOMING!*
MORE CLEANERS, SWOOPING IN FAST!
DEFENSIVE POSITIONS!
TRY TO PICK THEM OFF BEFORE THEY GET TOO--
HHNN
ANOMALOUS EMOTIONAL ENERGY LOCATED.
NICE TO SEE A FEW ***FAMILIAR*** FACES.

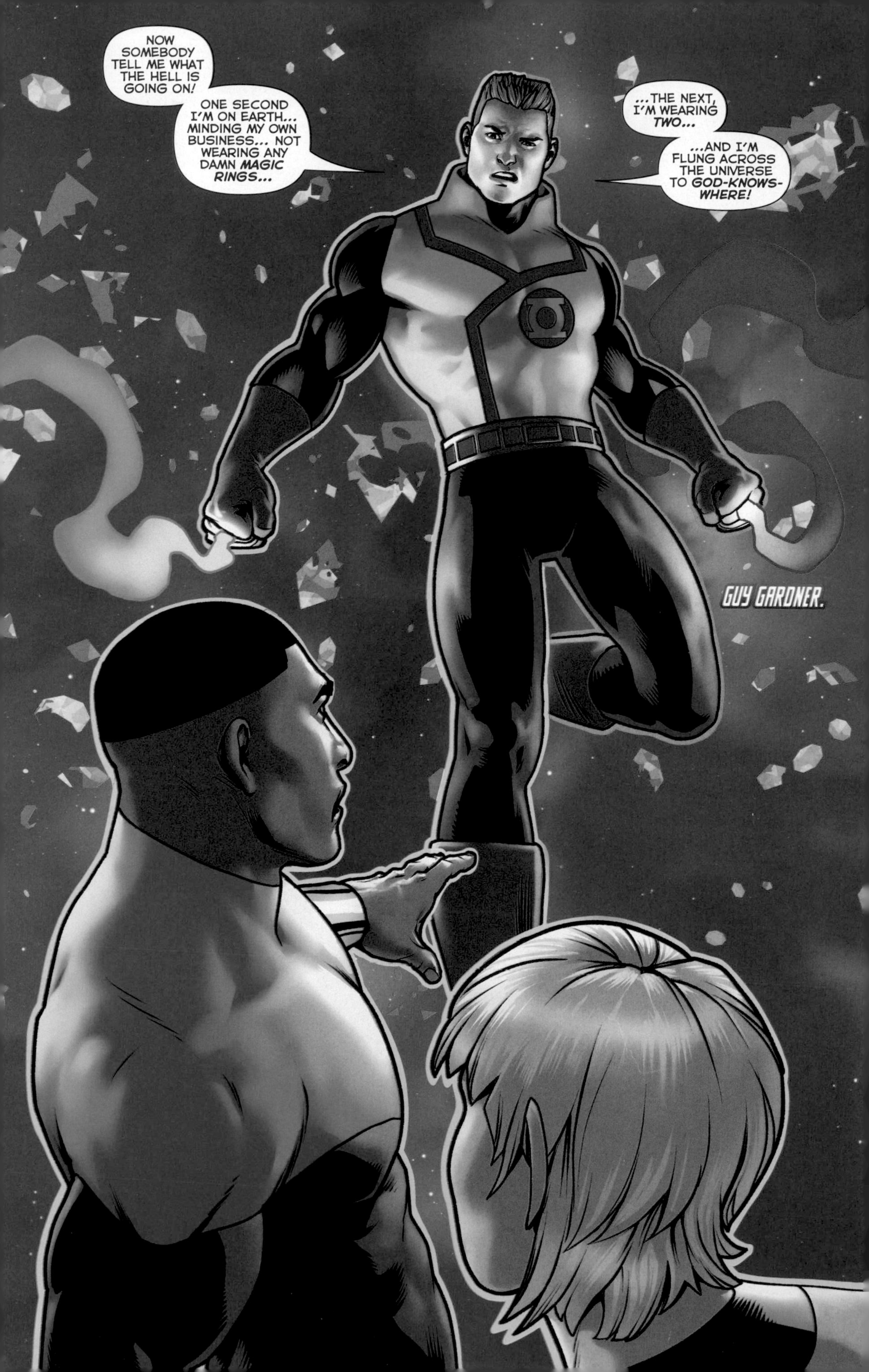
NOW SOMEBODY TELL ME WHAT THE HELL IS GOING ON!
ONE SECOND I'M ON EARTH... MINDING MY OWN BUSINESS... NOT WEARING ANY DAMN *MAGIC RINGS*...
...THE NEXT, I'M WEARING *TWO*...
...AND I'M FLUNG ACROSS THE UNIVERSE TO *GOD-KNOWS-WHERE!*
GUY GARDNER.

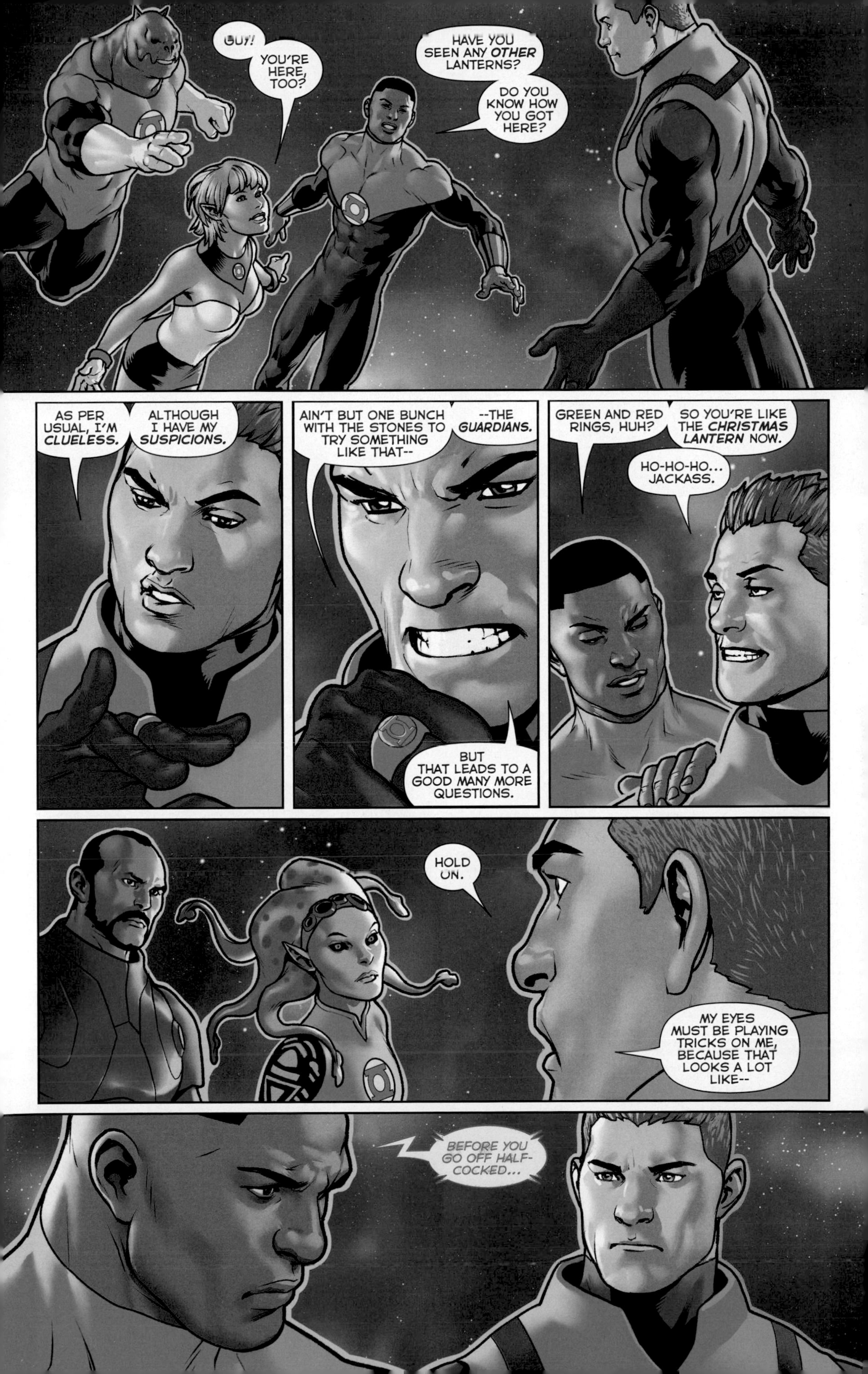
GUY!
YOU'RE HERE, TOO?
HAVE YOU SEEN ANY OTHER LANTERNS?
DO YOU KNOW HOW YOU GOT HERE?
AS PER USUAL, I'M CLUELESS.
ALTHOUGH I HAVE MY SUSPICIONS.
AIN'T BUT ONE BUNCH WITH THE STONES TO TRY SOMETHING LIKE THAT--
--THE GUARDIANS.
BUT THAT LEADS TO A GOOD MANY MORE QUESTIONS.
GREEN AND RED RINGS, HUH?
SO YOU'RE LIKE THE CHRISTMAS LANTERN NOW.
HO-HO-HO... JACKASS.
HOLD ON.
MY EYES MUST BE PLAYING TRICKS ON ME, BECAUSE THAT LOOKS A LOT LIKE--
BEFORE YOU GO OFF HALF-COCKED...

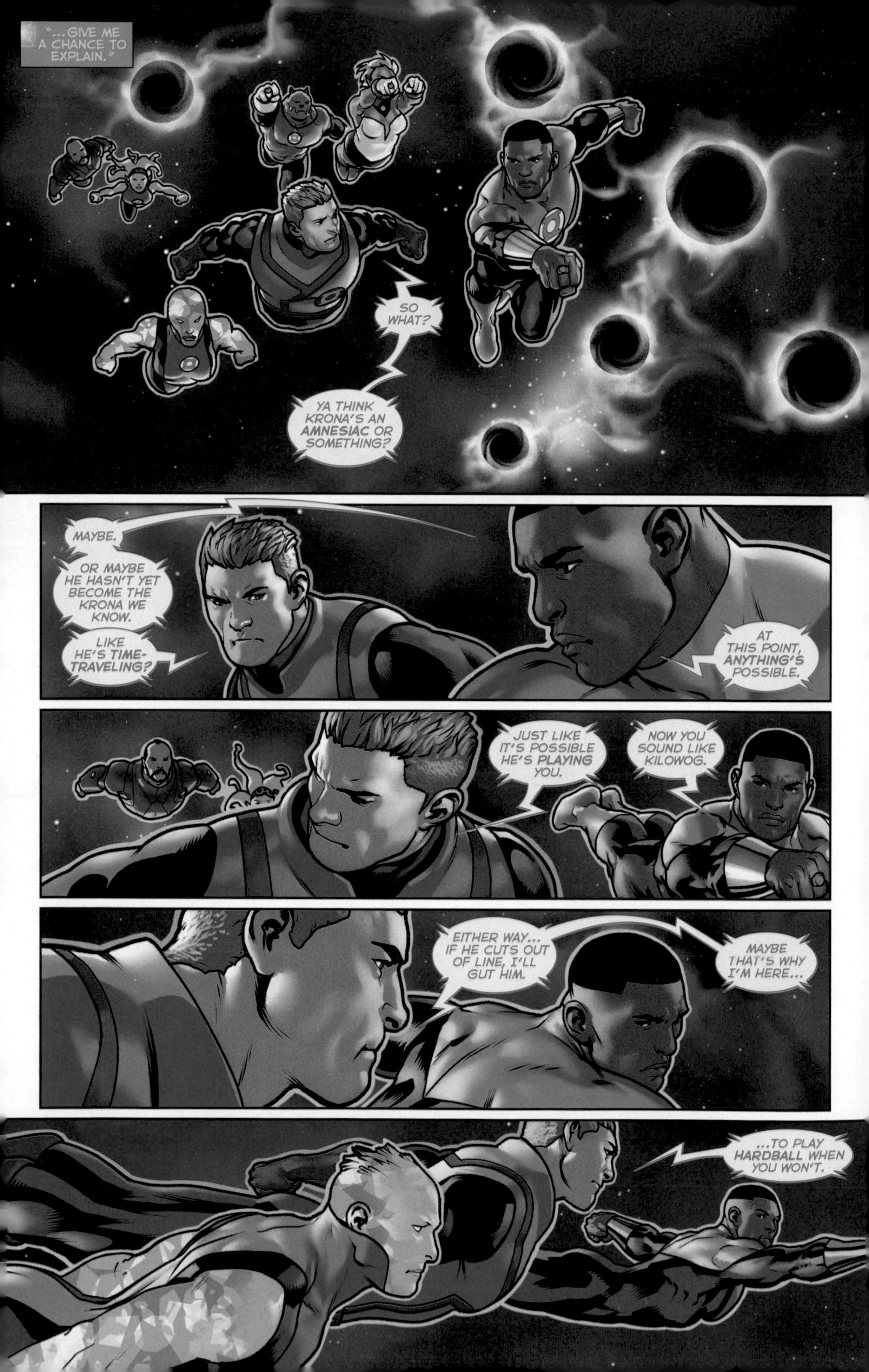
"...GIVE ME A CHANCE TO EXPLAIN."
SO WHAT?
YA THINK KRONA'S AN AMNESIAC OR SOMETHING?
MAYBE.
OR MAYBE HE HASN'T YET BECOME THE KRONA WE KNOW.
LIKE HE'S TIME-TRAVELING?
AT THIS POINT, ANYTHING'S POSSIBLE.
JUST LIKE IT'S POSSIBLE HE'S PLAYING YOU.
NOW YOU SOUND LIKE KILOWOG.
EITHER WAY... IF HE CUTS OUT OF LINE, I'LL GUT HIM.
MAYBE THAT'S WHY I'M HERE...
...TO PLAY HARDBALL WHEN YOU WON'T.

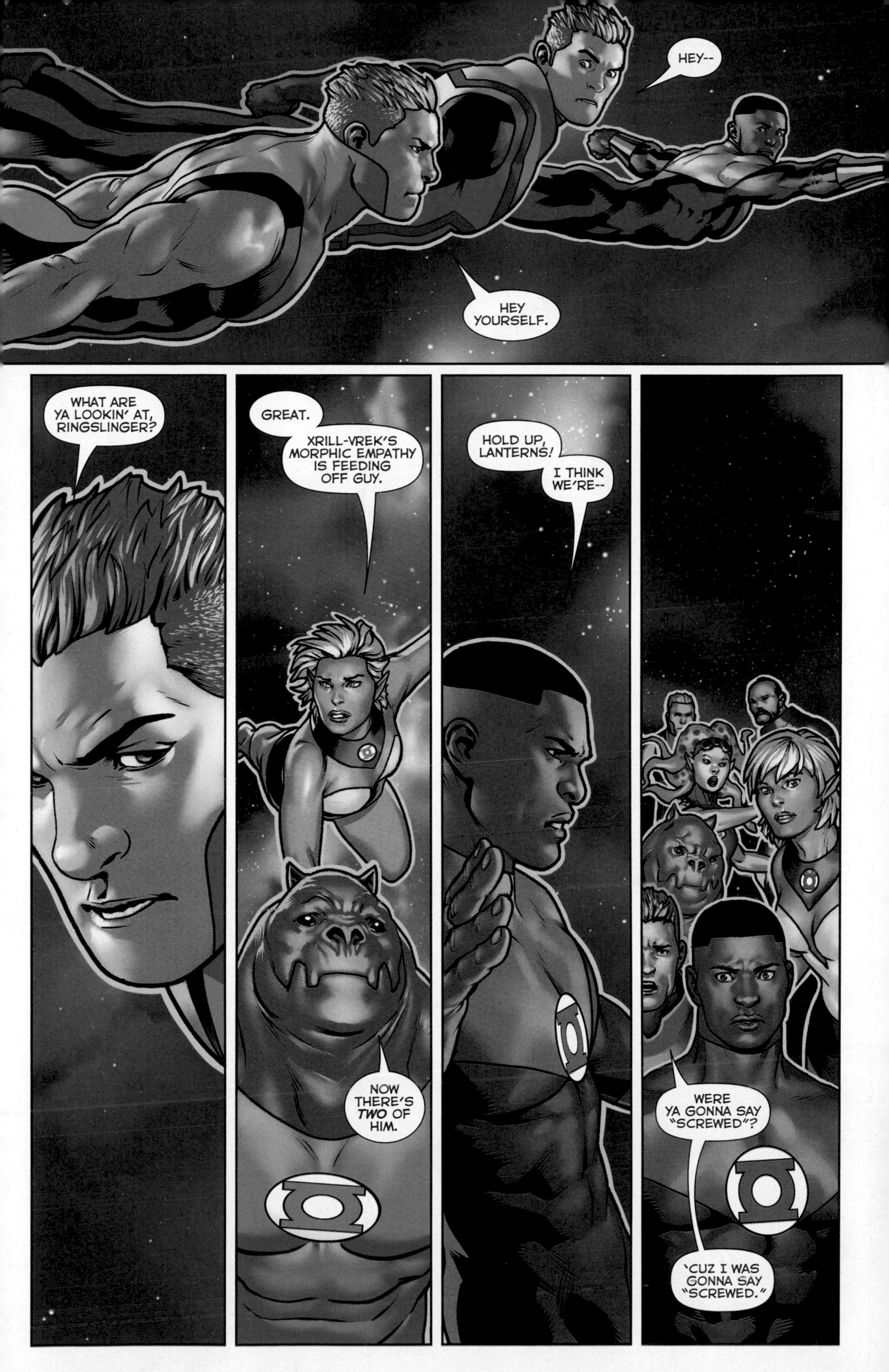
HEY--
HEY YOURSELF.
WHAT ARE YA LOOKIN' AT, RINGSLINGER?
GREAT.
XRILL-VREK'S MORPHIC EMPATHY IS FEEDING OFF GUY.
NOW THERE'S *TWO* OF HIM.
HOLD UP, LANTERNS!
I THINK WE'RE--
WERE YA GONNA SAY "SCREWED"?
'CUZ I WAS GONNA SAY "SCREWED."

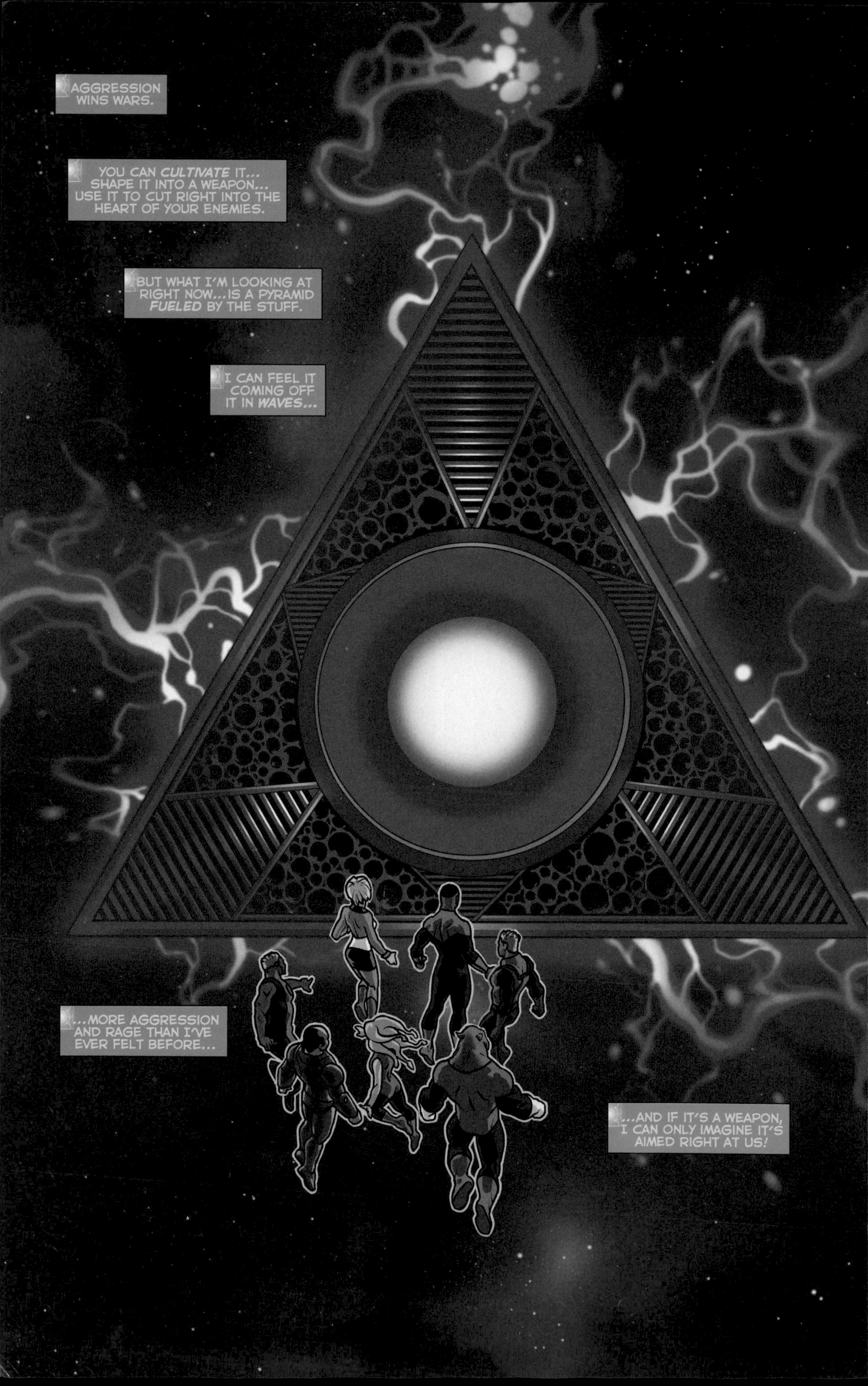

AGGRESSION WINS WARS.
YOU CAN CULTIVATE IT... SHAPE IT INTO A WEAPON... USE IT TO CUT RIGHT INTO THE HEART OF YOUR ENEMIES.
BUT WHAT I'M LOOKING AT RIGHT NOW...IS A PYRAMID FUELED BY THE STUFF.
I CAN FEEL IT COMING OFF IT IN WAVES...
...MORE AGGRESSION AND RAGE THAN I'VE EVER FELT BEFORE...
...AND IF IT'S A WEAPON, I CAN ONLY IMAGINE IT'S AIMED RIGHT AT US!

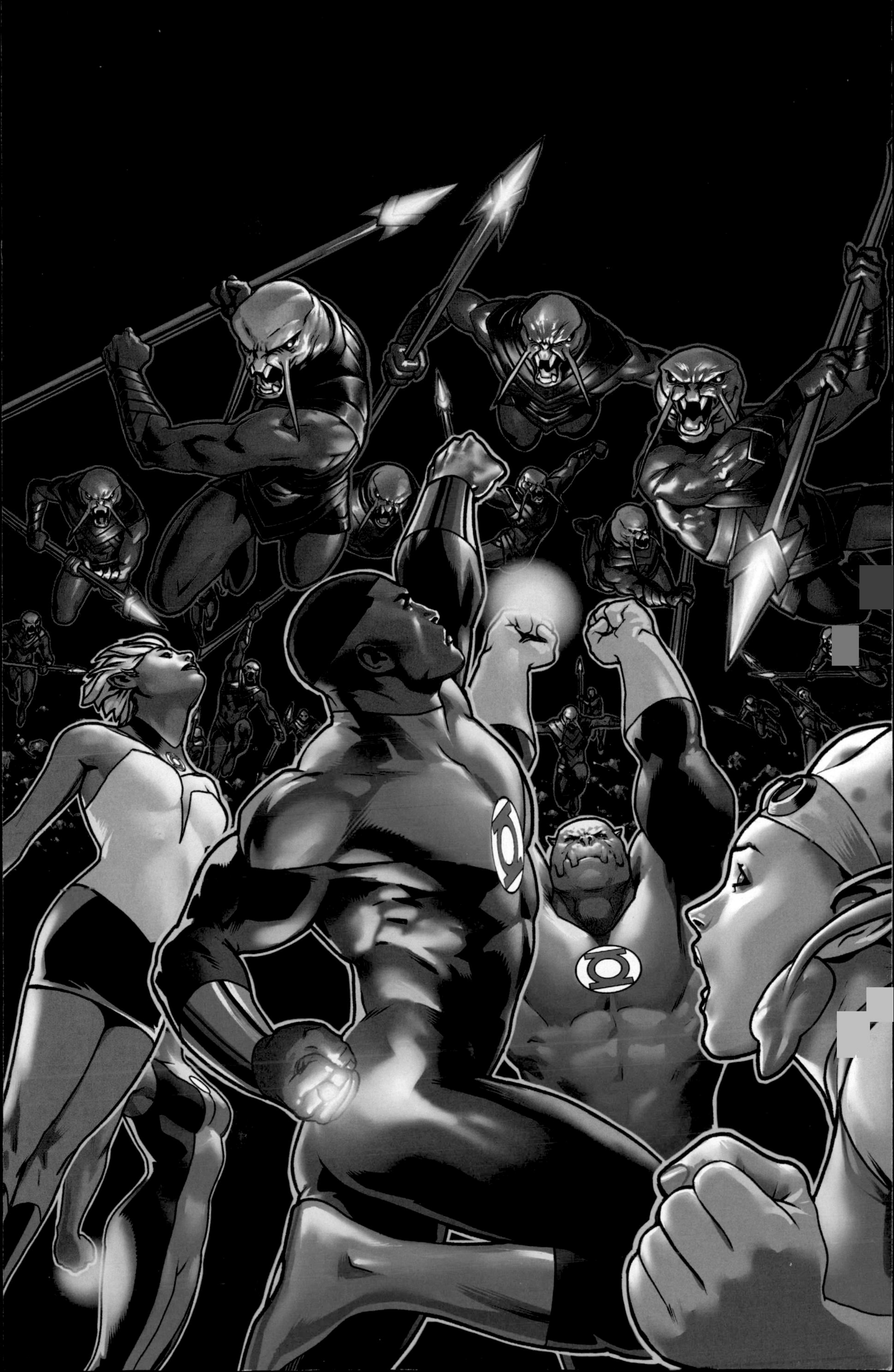

CULLEN BUNN writer **JESUS SAIZ** artist, colorist & cover **DAVE SHARPE** letterer

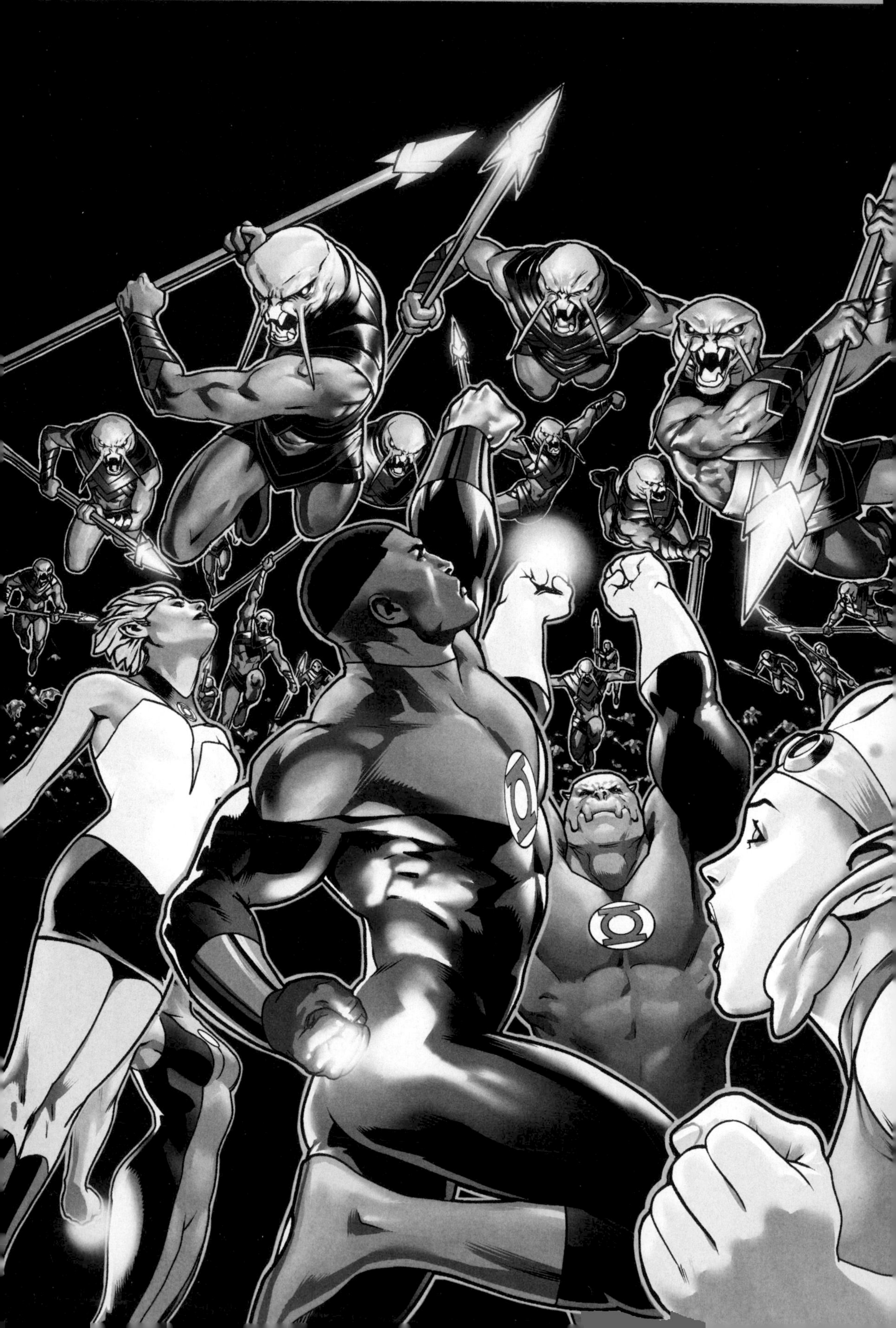

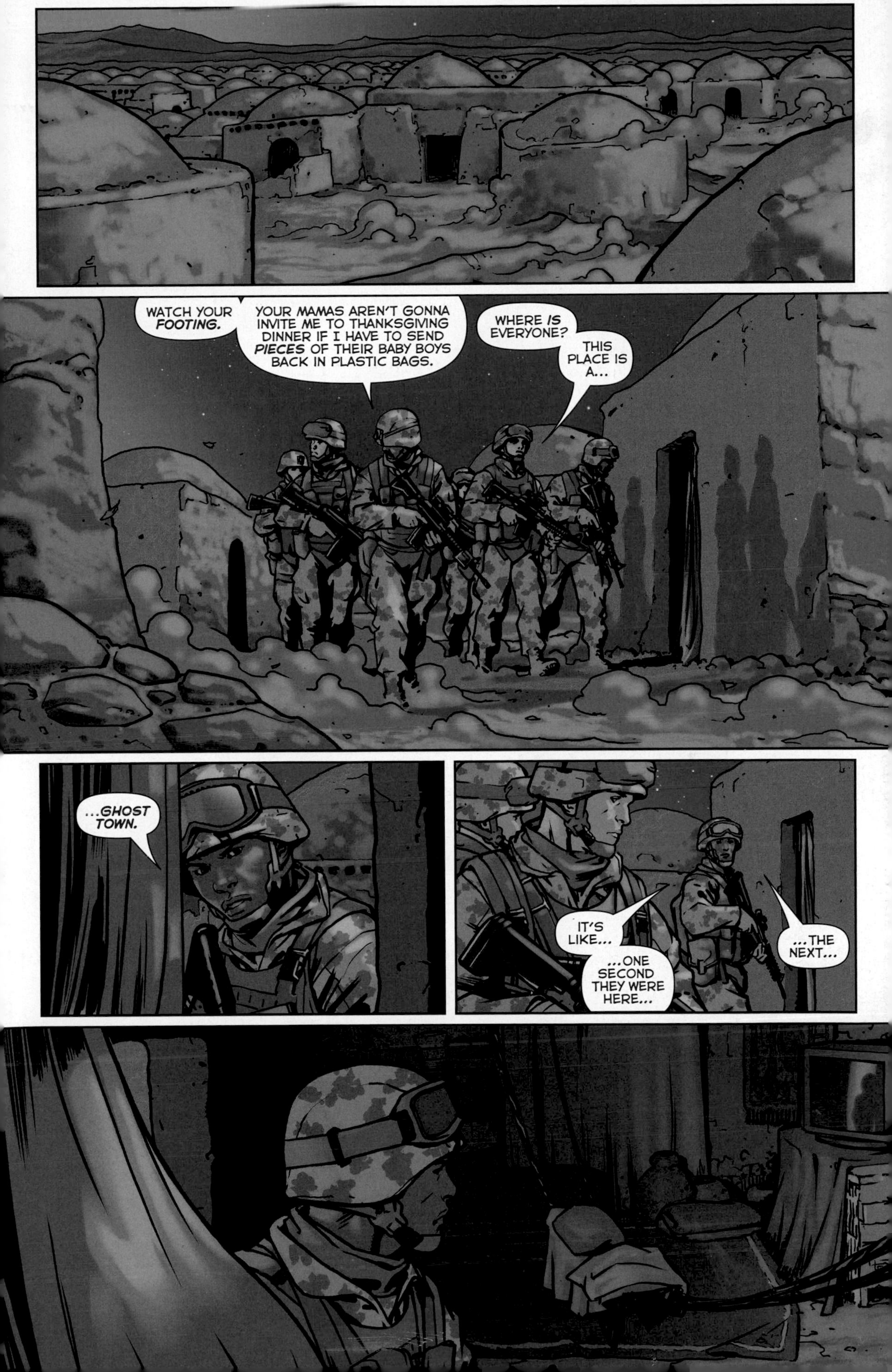
WATCH YOUR FOOTING.
YOUR MAMAS AREN'T GONNA INVITE ME TO THANKSGIVING DINNER IF I HAVE TO SEND PIECES OF THEIR BABY BOYS BACK IN PLASTIC BAGS.
WHERE IS EVERYONE?
THIS PLACE IS A...
...GHOST TOWN.
IT'S LIKE...
...ONE SECOND THEY WERE HERE...
...THE NEXT...

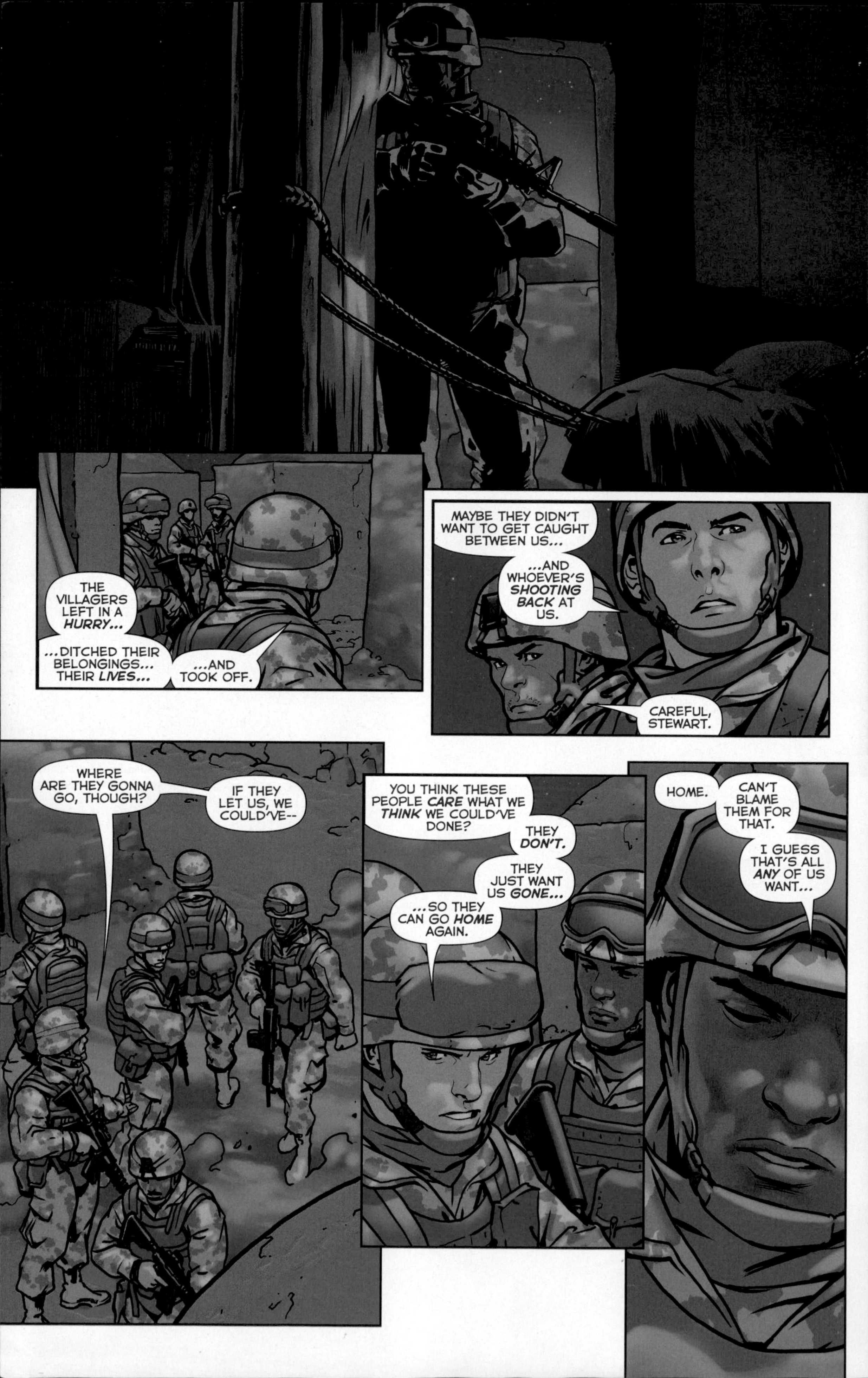
THE VILLAGERS LEFT IN A *HURRY*...
...DITCHED THEIR BELONGINGS... THEIR *LIVES*...
...AND TOOK OFF.
MAYBE THEY DIDN'T WANT TO GET CAUGHT BETWEEN US...
...AND WHOEVER'S *SHOOTING BACK* AT US.
CAREFUL, STEWART.
WHERE ARE THEY GONNA GO, THOUGH?
IF THEY LET US, WE COULD'VE--
YOU THINK THESE PEOPLE *CARE* WHAT WE *THINK* WE COULD'VE DONE?
THEY *DON'T.*
THEY JUST WANT US *GONE*...
...SO THEY CAN GO *HOME* AGAIN.
HOME.
CAN'T BLAME THEM FOR THAT.
I GUESS THAT'S ALL *ANY* OF US WANT...

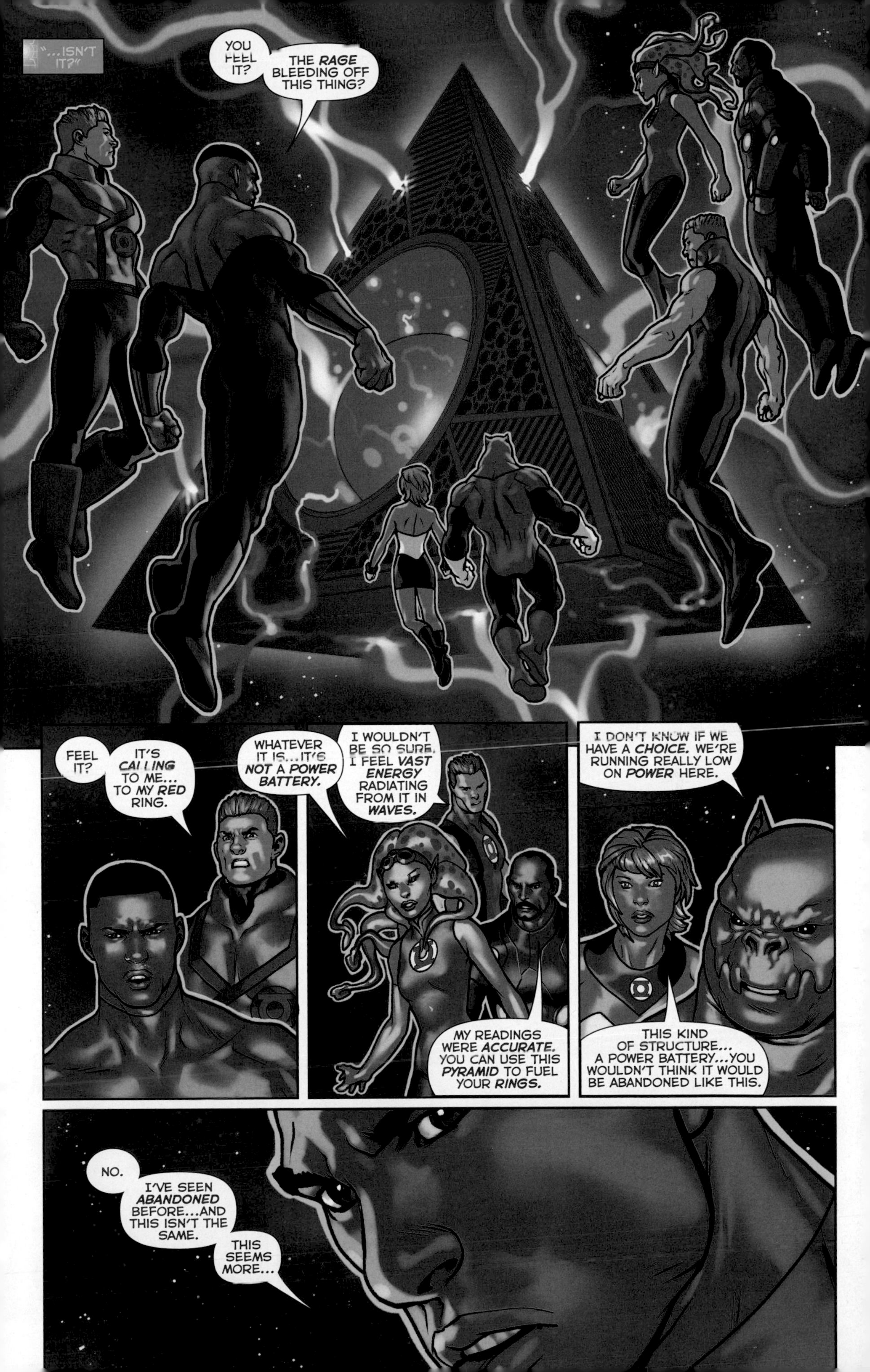

"...ISN'T IT?"
YOU FEEL IT?
THE RAGE BLEEDING OFF THIS THING?
FEEL IT?
IT'S CALLING TO ME... TO MY RED RING.
WHATEVER IT IS...IT'S NOT A POWER BATTERY.
I WOULDN'T BE SO SURE. I FEEL VAST ENERGY RADIATING FROM IT IN WAVES.
MY READINGS WERE ACCURATE. YOU CAN USE THIS PYRAMID TO FUEL YOUR RINGS.
I DON'T KNOW IF WE HAVE A CHOICE. WE'RE RUNNING REALLY LOW ON POWER HERE.
THIS KIND OF STRUCTURE... A POWER BATTERY...YOU WOULDN'T THINK IT WOULD BE ABANDONED LIKE THIS.
NO.
I'VE SEEN ABANDONED BEFORE...AND THIS ISN'T THE SAME.
THIS SEEMS MORE...

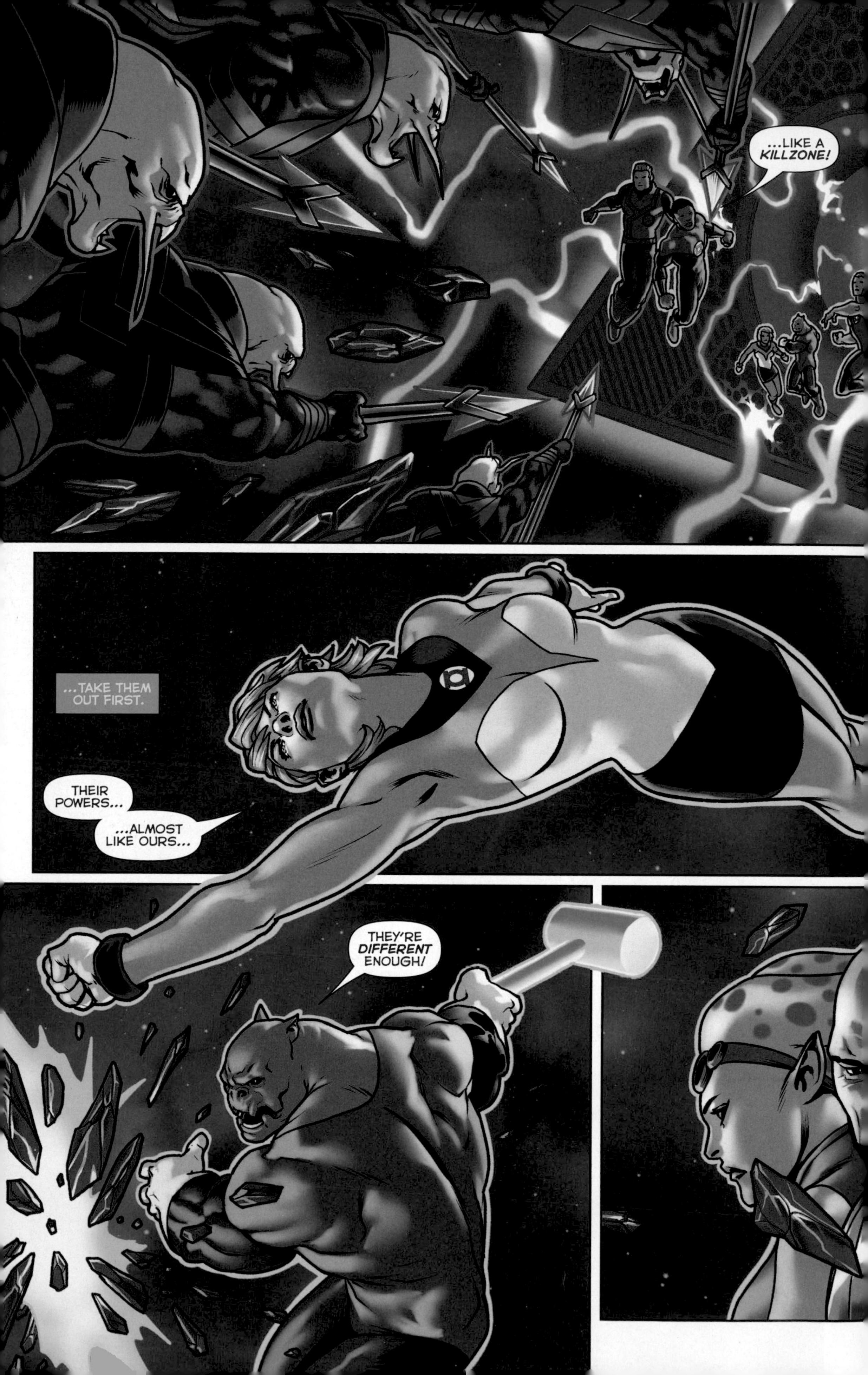
...LIKE A KILLZONE!
...TAKE THEM OUT FIRST.
THEIR POWERS...
...ALMOST LIKE OURS...
THEY'RE DIFFERENT ENOUGH!

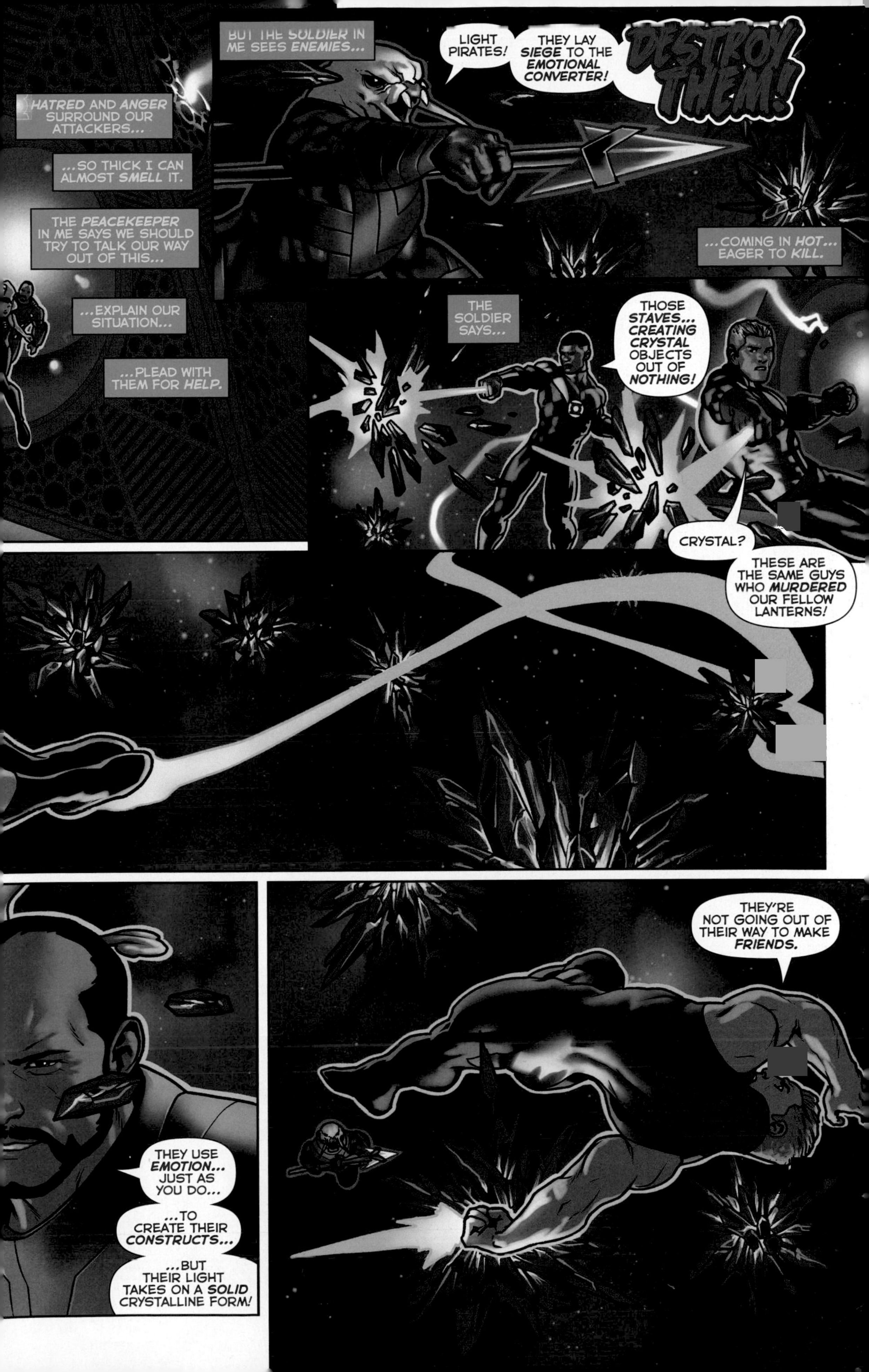

HATRED AND ANGER SURROUND OUR ATTACKERS...
...SO THICK I CAN ALMOST SMELL IT.
THE PEACEKEEPER IN ME SAYS WE SHOULD TRY TO TALK OUR WAY OUT OF THIS...
...EXPLAIN OUR SITUATION...
...PLEAD WITH THEM FOR HELP.
BUT THE SOLDIER IN ME SEES ENEMIES...
LIGHT PIRATES!
THEY LAY SIEGE TO THE EMOTIONAL CONVERTER!
DESTROY THEM!
...COMING IN HOT... EAGER TO KILL.
THE SOLDIER SAYS...
THOSE STAVES... CREATING CRYSTAL OBJECTS OUT OF NOTHING!
CRYSTAL?
THESE ARE THE SAME GUYS WHO MURDERED OUR FELLOW LANTERNS!
THEY USE EMOTION... JUST AS YOU DO...
...TO CREATE THEIR CONSTRUCTS...
...BUT THEIR LIGHT TAKES ON A SOLID CRYSTALLINE FORM!
THEY'RE NOT GOING OUT OF THEIR WAY TO MAKE FRIENDS.

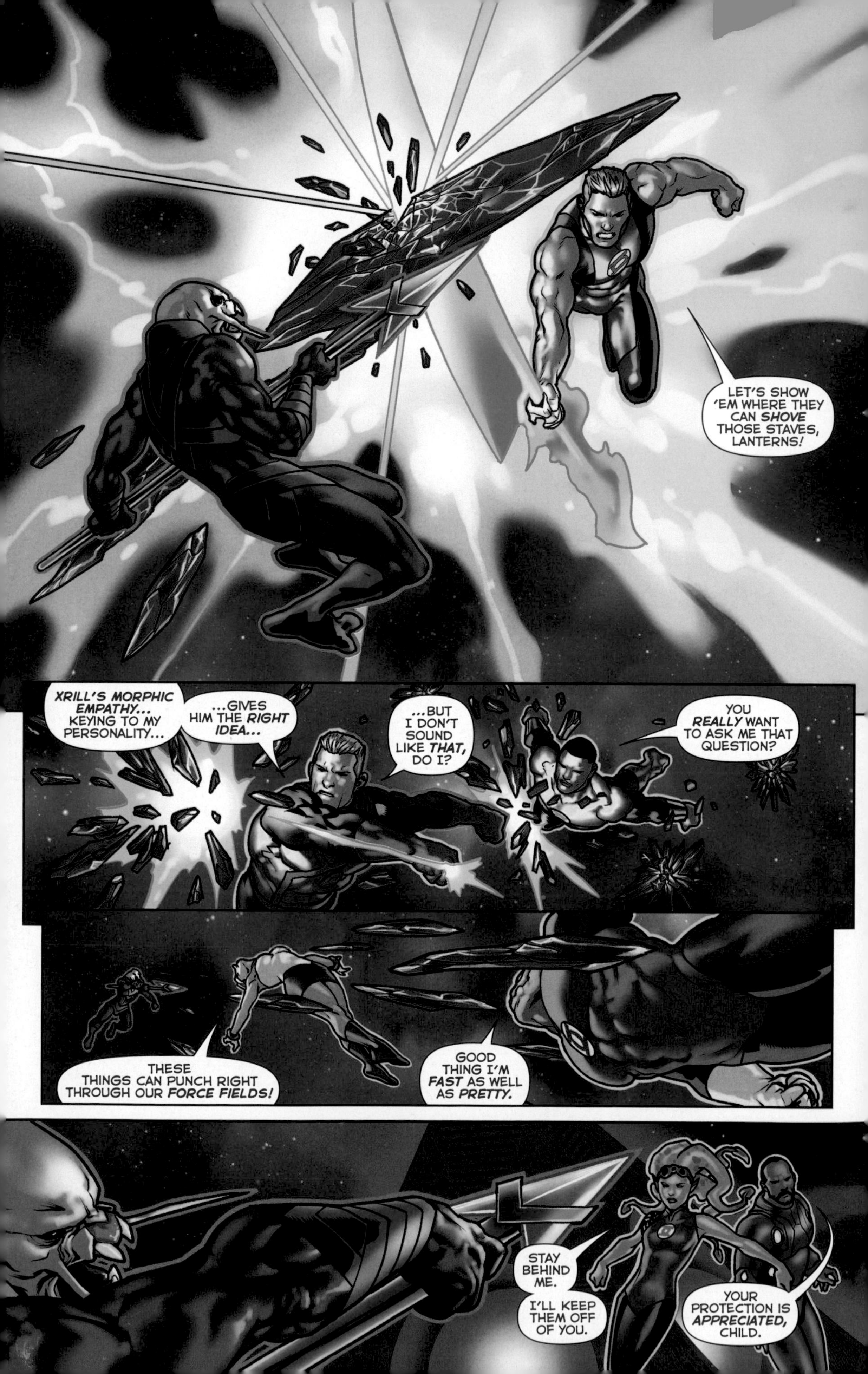

LET'S SHOW 'EM WHERE THEY CAN SHOVE THOSE STAVES, LANTERNS!
XRILL'S MORPHIC EMPATHY... KEYING TO MY PERSONALITY...
...GIVES HIM THE RIGHT IDEA...
...BUT I DON'T SOUND LIKE THAT, DO I?
YOU REALLY WANT TO ASK ME THAT QUESTION?
THESE THINGS CAN PUNCH RIGHT THROUGH OUR FORCE FIELDS!
GOOD THING I'M FAST AS WELL AS PRETTY.
STAY BEHIND ME.
I'LL KEEP THEM OFF OF YOU.
YOUR PROTECTION IS APPRECIATED, CHILD.

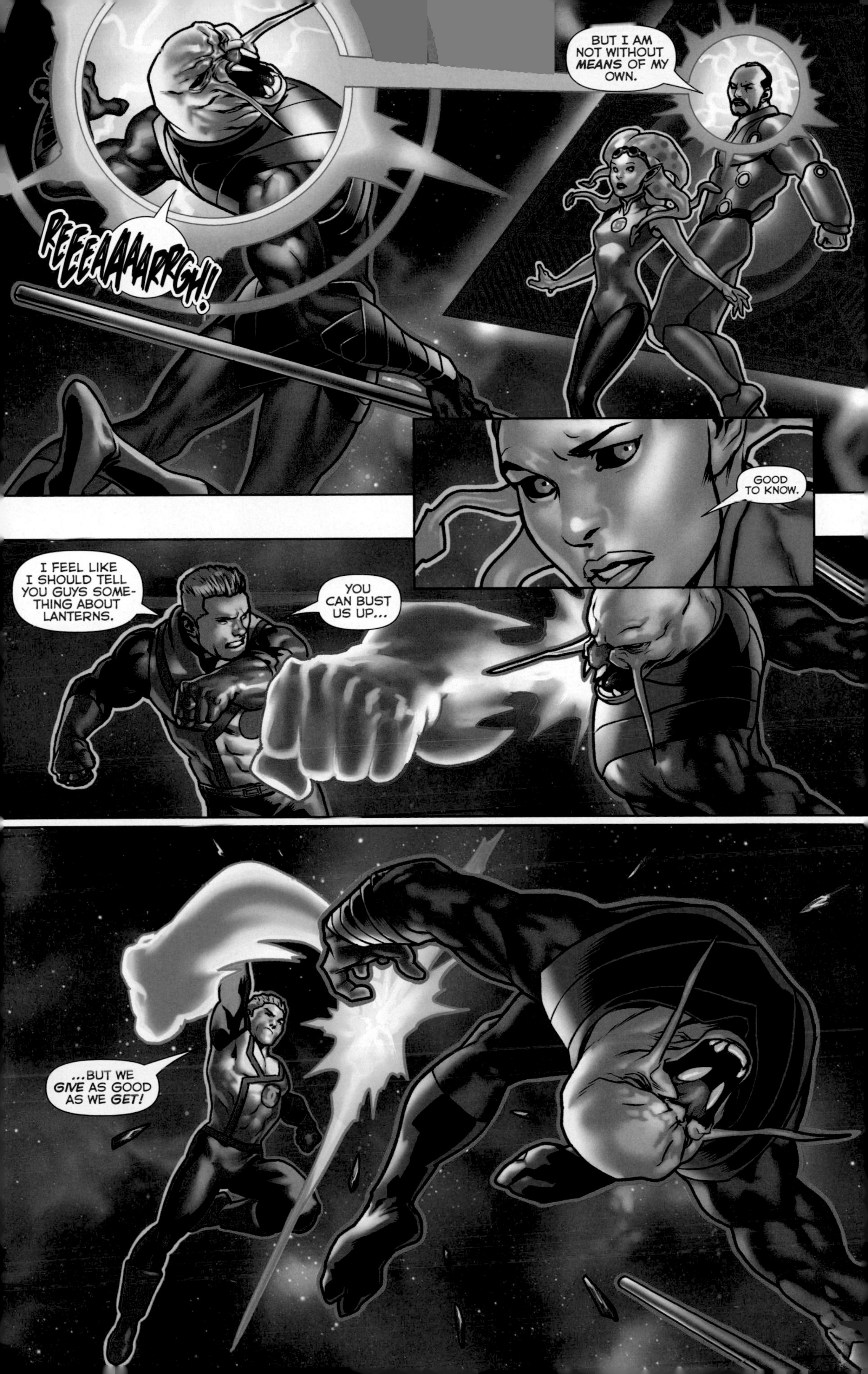

REEEAAAARRGH!!
BUT I AM NOT WITHOUT MEANS OF MY OWN.
GOOD TO KNOW.
I FEEL LIKE I SHOULD TELL YOU GUYS SOMETHING ABOUT LANTERNS.
YOU CAN BUST US UP...
...BUT WE GIVE AS GOOD AS WE GET!

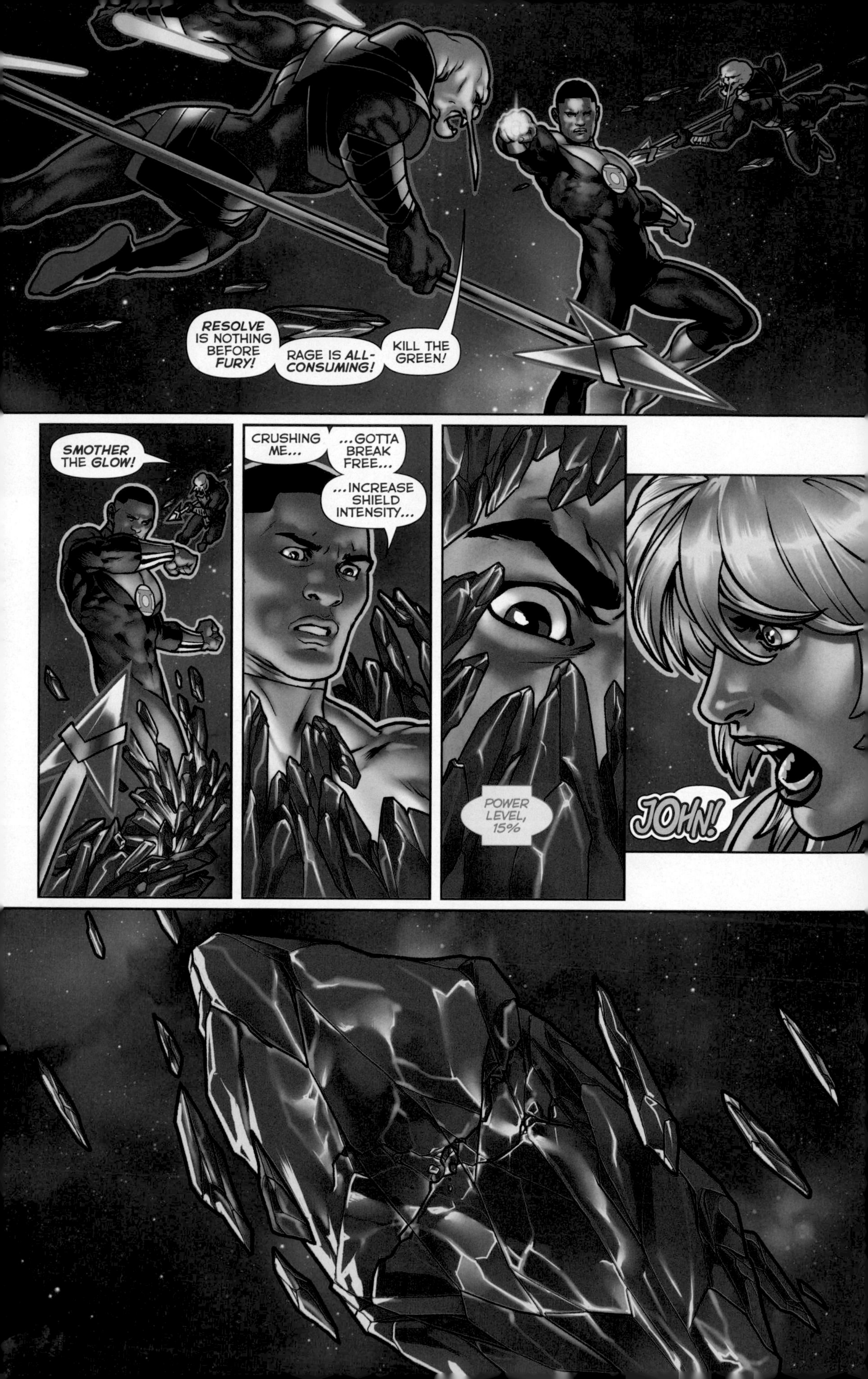

RESOLVE IS NOTHING BEFORE FURY!
RAGE IS ALL-CONSUMING!
KILL THE GREEN!
SMOTHER THE GLOW!
CRUSHING ME...
...GOTTA BREAK FREE...
...INCREASE SHIELD INTENSITY...
POWER LEVEL, 15%
JOHN!

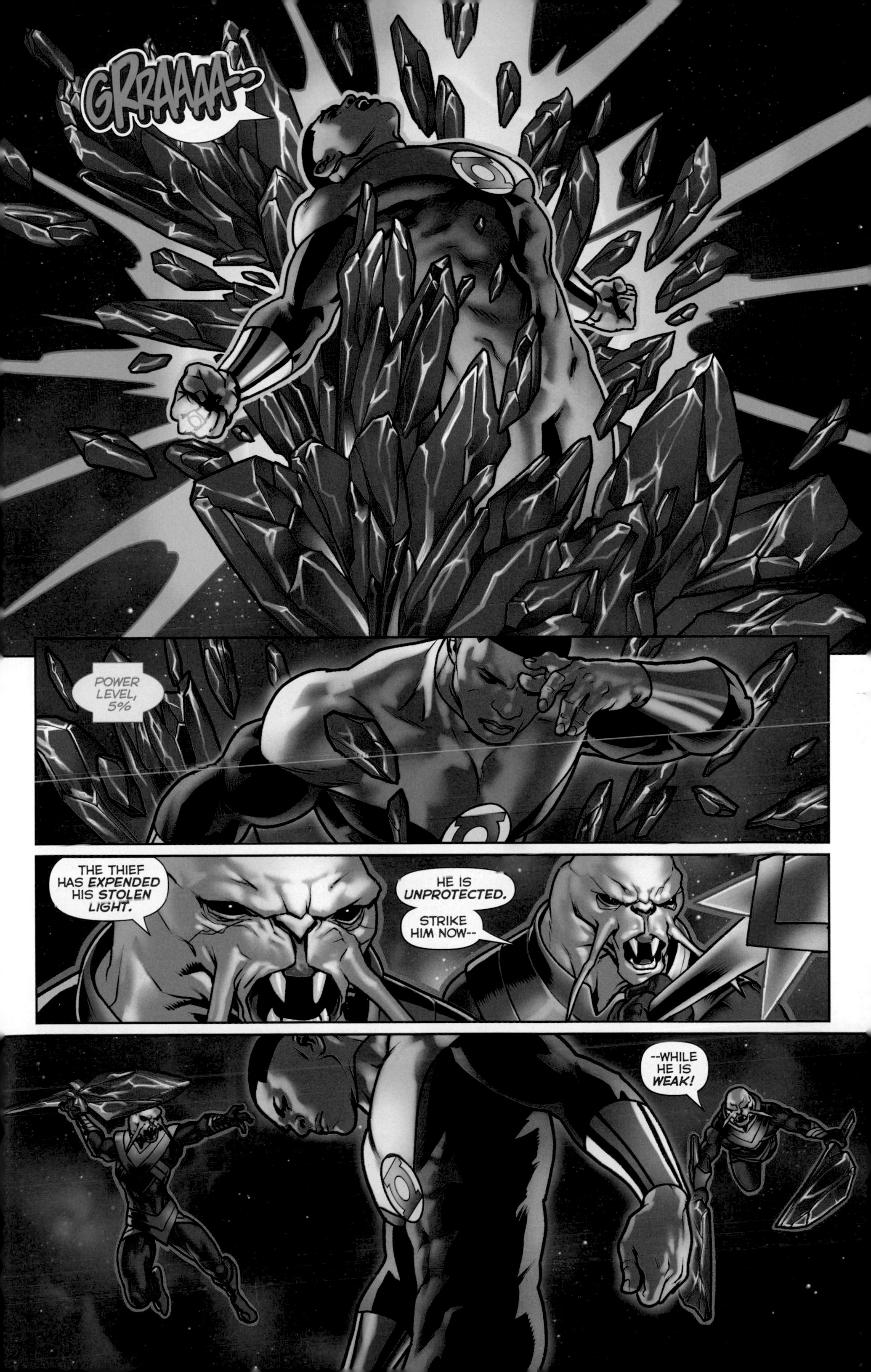
GRRAAAA--
POWER LEVEL, 5%
THE THIEF HAS EXPENDED HIS STOLEN LIGHT.
HE IS UNPROTECTED.
STRIKE HIM NOW--
--WHILE HE IS WEAK!

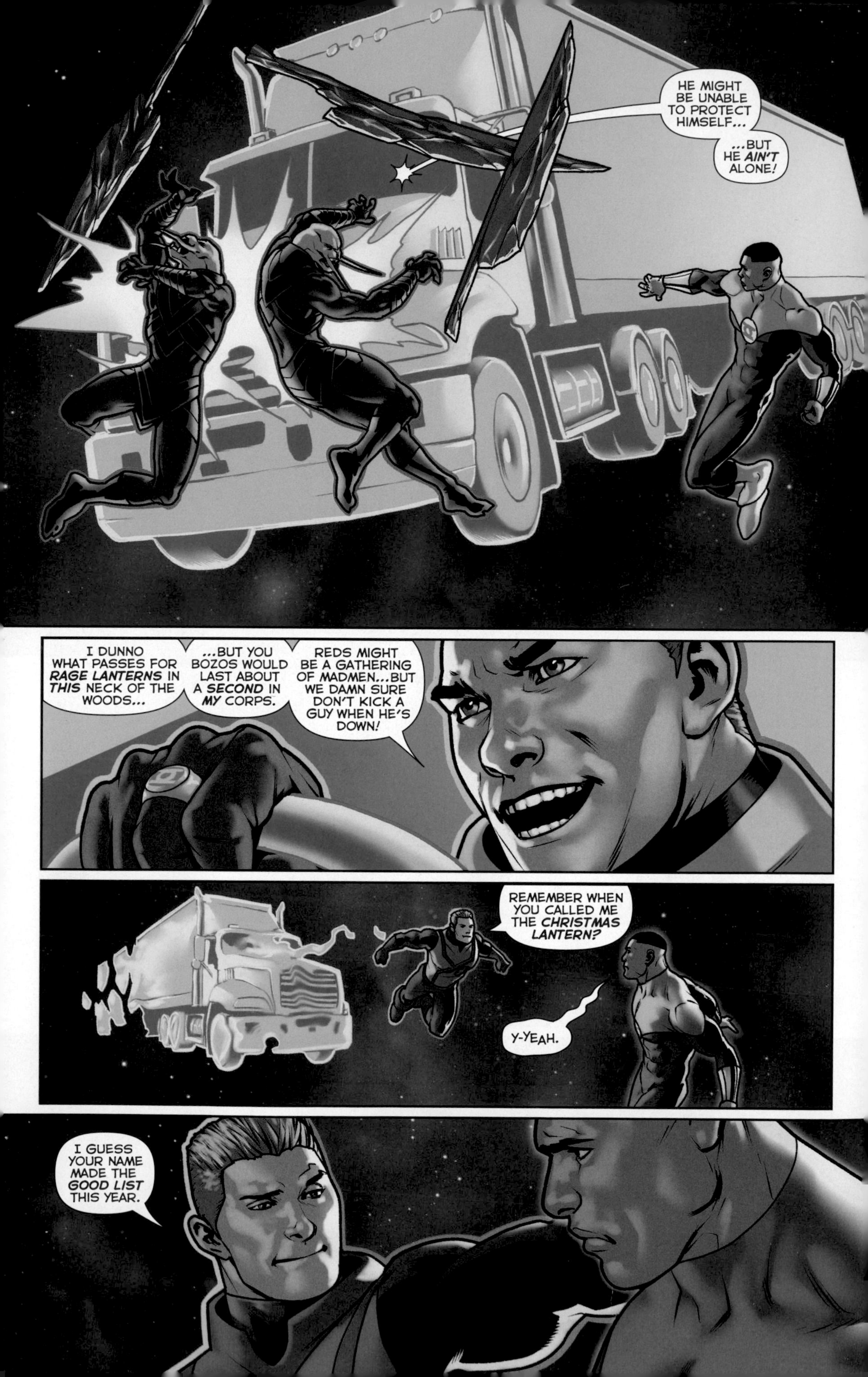
HE MIGHT BE UNABLE TO PROTECT HIMSELF...
...BUT HE AIN'T ALONE!
I DUNNO WHAT PASSES FOR RAGE LANTERNS IN THIS NECK OF THE WOODS...
...BUT YOU BOZOS WOULD LAST ABOUT A SECOND IN MY CORPS.
REDS MIGHT BE A GATHERING OF MADMEN...BUT WE DAMN SURE DON'T KICK A GUY WHEN HE'S DOWN!
REMEMBER WHEN YOU CALLED ME THE CHRISTMAS LANTERN?
Y-YEAH.
I GUESS YOUR NAME MADE THE GOOD LIST THIS YEAR.

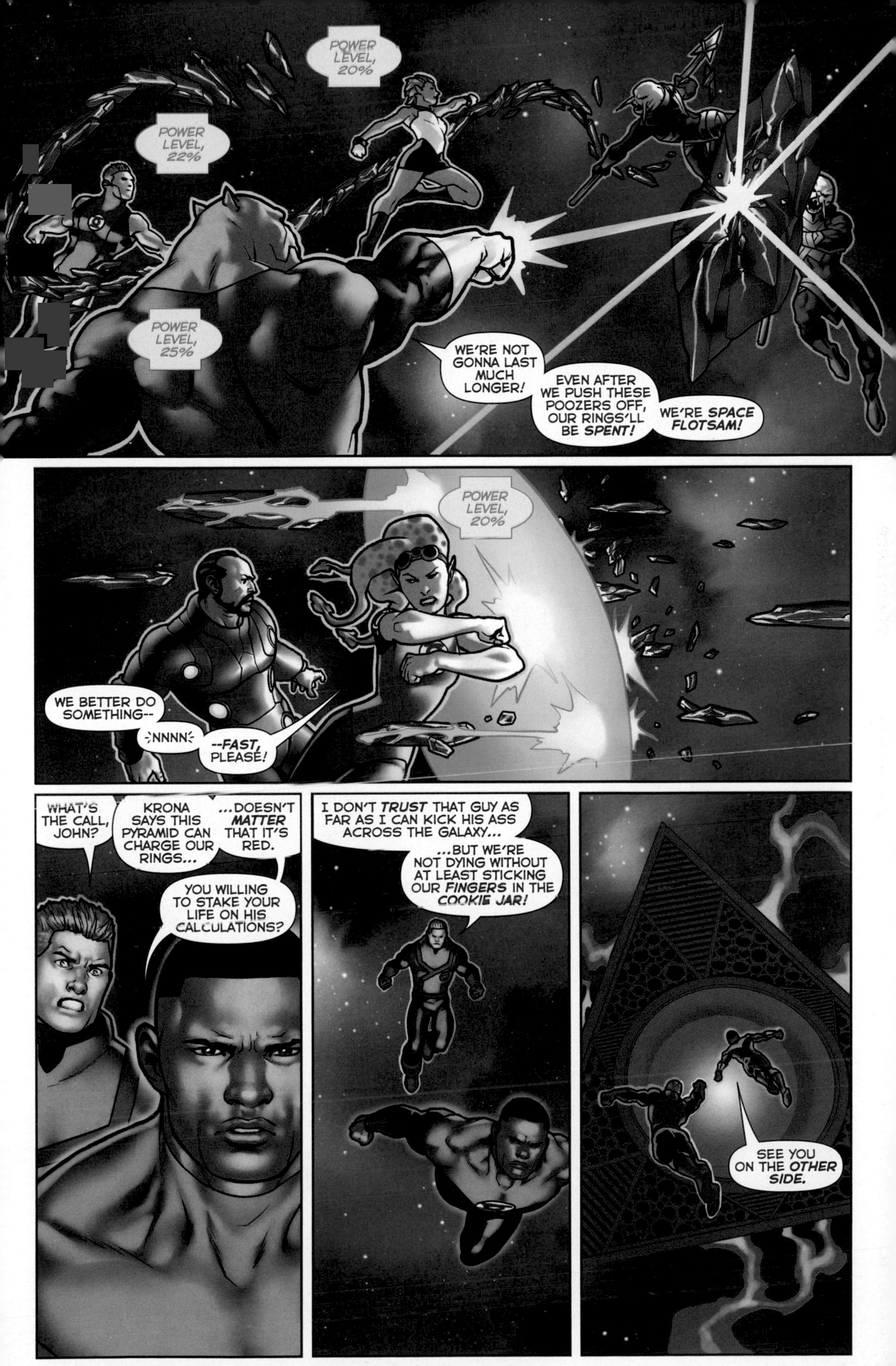

POWER LEVEL, 20%
POWER LEVEL, 22%
POWER LEVEL, 25%
WE'RE NOT GONNA LAST MUCH LONGER!
EVEN AFTER WE PUSH THESE POOZERS OFF, OUR RINGS'LL BE SPENT!
WE'RE SPACE FLOTSAM!
POWER LEVEL, 20%
WE BETTER DO SOMETHING--
NNNN
--FAST, PLEASE!
WHAT'S THE CALL, JOHN?
KRONA SAYS THIS PYRAMID CAN CHARGE OUR RINGS...
...DOESN'T MATTER THAT IT'S RED.
YOU WILLING TO STAKE YOUR LIFE ON HIS CALCULATIONS?
I DON'T TRUST THAT GUY AS FAR AS I CAN KICK HIS ASS ACROSS THE GALAXY...
...BUT WE'RE NOT DYING WITHOUT AT LEAST STICKING OUR FINGERS IN THE COOKIE JAR!
SEE YOU ON THE OTHER SIDE.

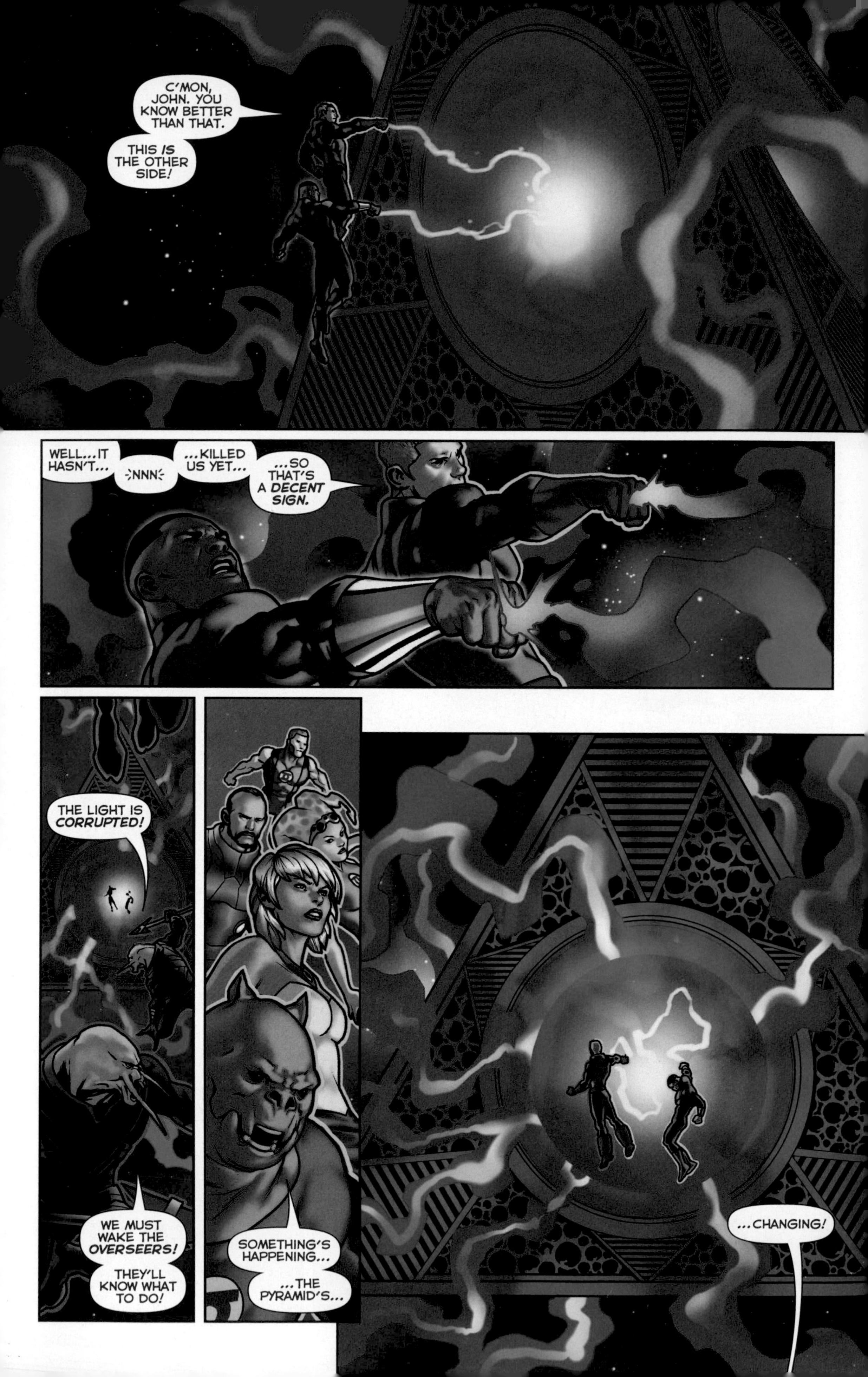
C'MON, JOHN. YOU KNOW BETTER THAN THAT.
THIS *IS* THE OTHER SIDE!
WELL...IT HASN'T...
NNN
...KILLED US YET...
...SO THAT'S A *DECENT SIGN.*
THE LIGHT IS *CORRUPTED!*
WE MUST WAKE THE *OVERSEERS!*
THEY'LL KNOW WHAT TO DO!
SOMETHING'S HAPPENING...
...THE PYRAMID'S...
...CHANGING!

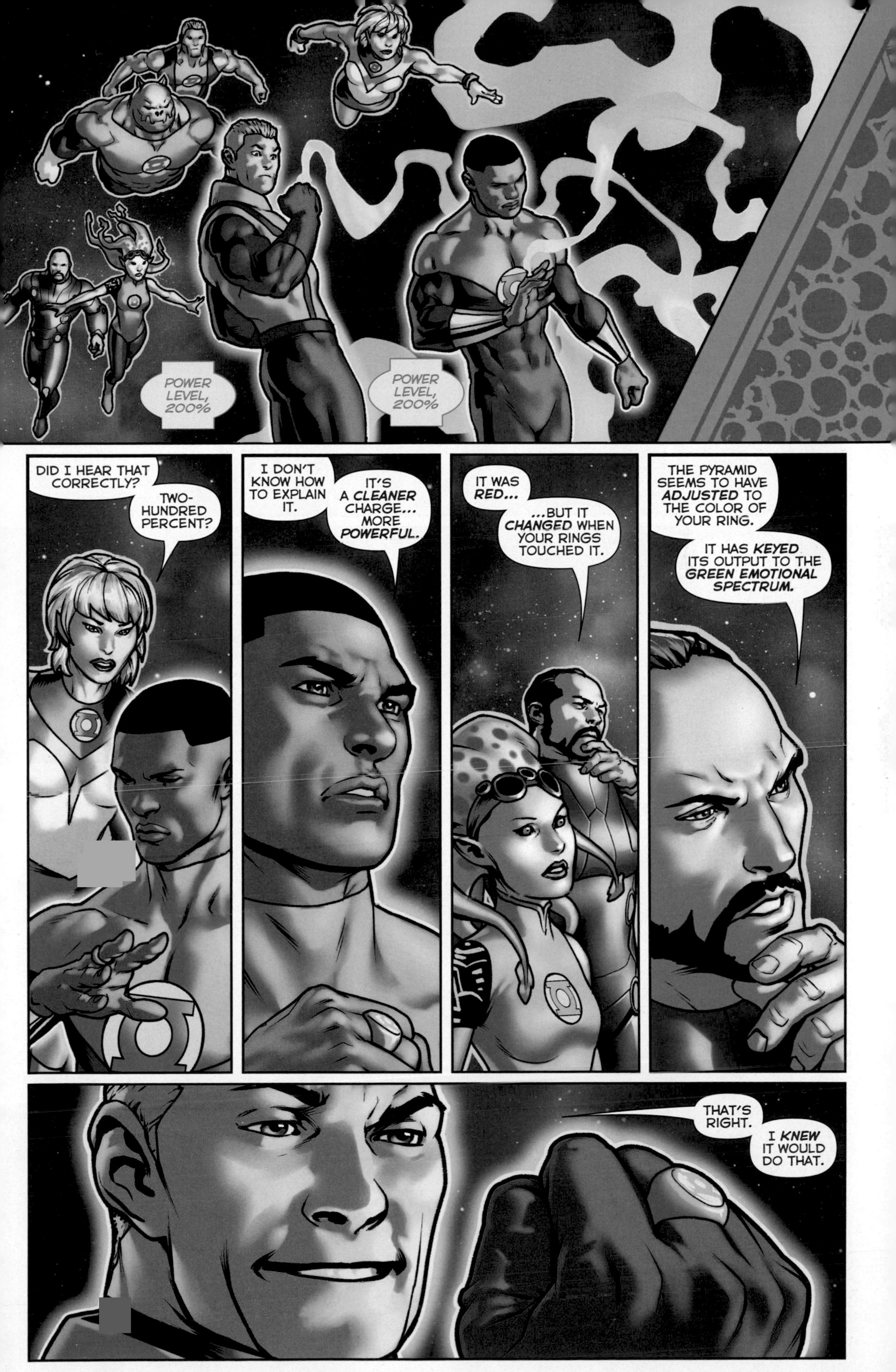
POWER LEVEL, 200%
POWER LEVEL, 200%
DID I HEAR THAT CORRECTLY?
TWO-HUNDRED PERCENT?
I DON'T KNOW HOW TO EXPLAIN IT.
IT'S A CLEANER CHARGE... MORE POWERFUL.
IT WAS RED...
...BUT IT CHANGED WHEN YOUR RINGS TOUCHED IT.
THE PYRAMID SEEMS TO HAVE ADJUSTED TO THE COLOR OF YOUR RING.
IT HAS KEYED ITS OUTPUT TO THE GREEN EMOTIONAL SPECTRUM.
THAT'S RIGHT.
I KNEW IT WOULD DO THAT.

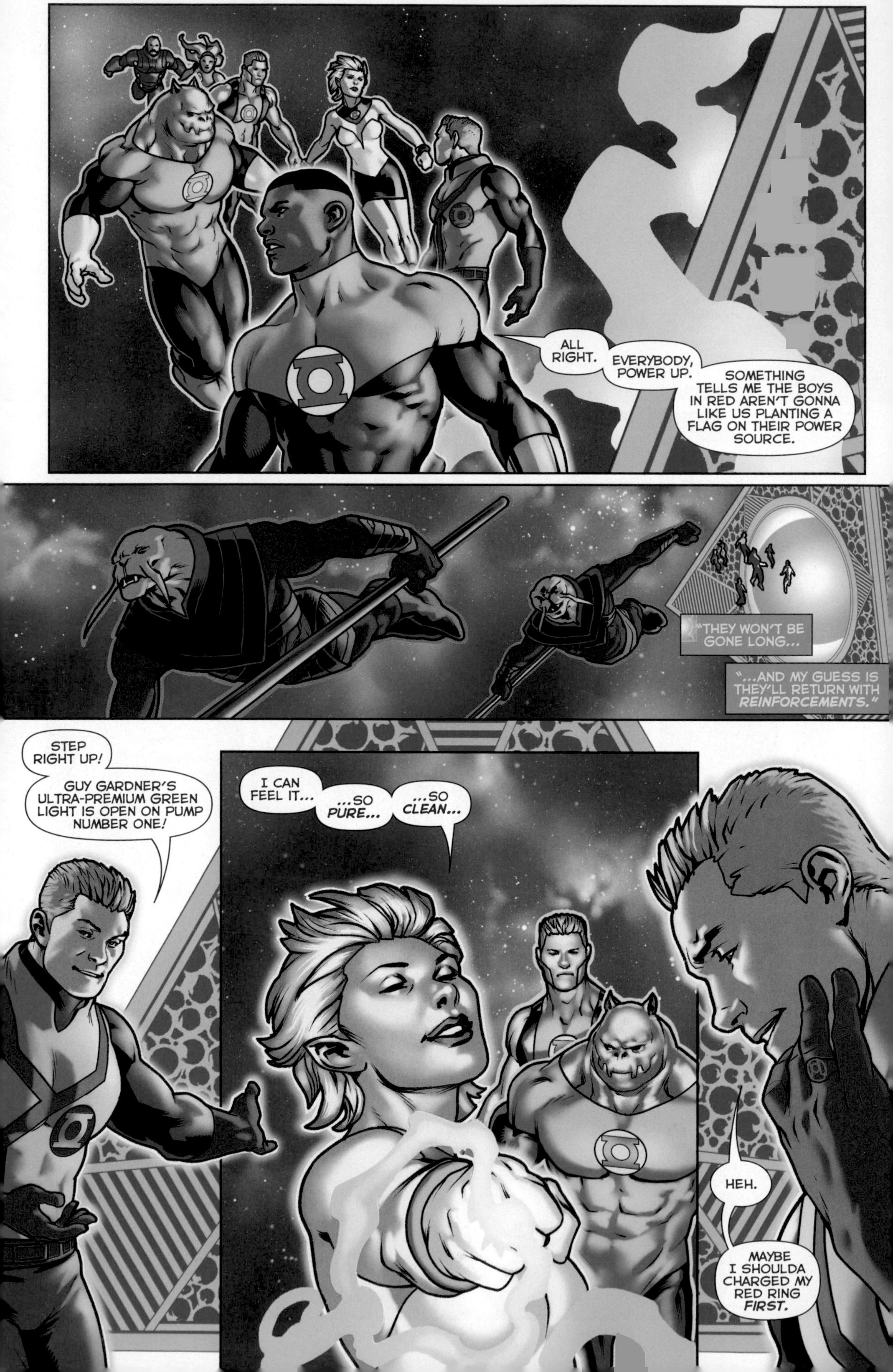
ALL RIGHT.
EVERYBODY, POWER UP.
SOMETHING TELLS ME THE BOYS IN RED AREN'T GONNA LIKE US PLANTING A FLAG ON THEIR POWER SOURCE.
"THEY WON'T BE GONE LONG...
"...AND MY GUESS IS THEY'LL RETURN WITH *REINFORCEMENTS.*"
STEP RIGHT UP!
GUY GARDNER'S ULTRA-PREMIUM GREEN LIGHT IS OPEN ON PUMP NUMBER ONE!
I CAN FEEL IT...
...SO *PURE*...
...SO *CLEAN*...
HEH.
MAYBE I SHOULDA CHARGED MY RED RING *FIRST.*

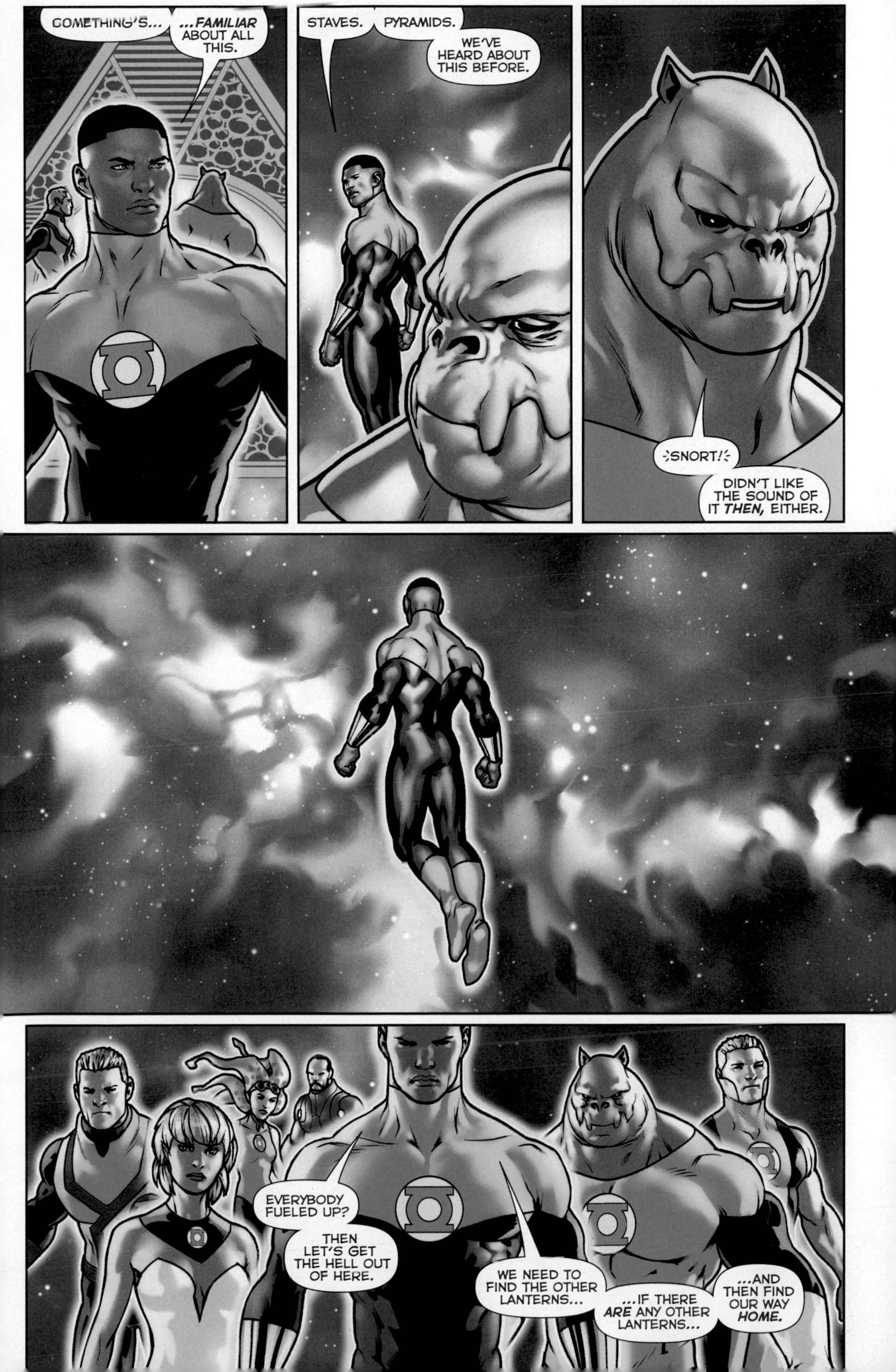
COMETHING'S...
...FAMILIAR ABOUT ALL THIS.
STAVES.
PYRAMIDS.
WE'VE HEARD ABOUT THIS BEFORE.
SNORT!
DIDN'T LIKE THE SOUND OF IT THEN, EITHER.
EVERYBODY FUELED UP?
THEN LET'S GET THE HELL OUT OF HERE.
WE NEED TO FIND THE OTHER LANTERNS...
...IF THERE ARE ANY OTHER LANTERNS...
...AND THEN FIND OUR WAY HOME.

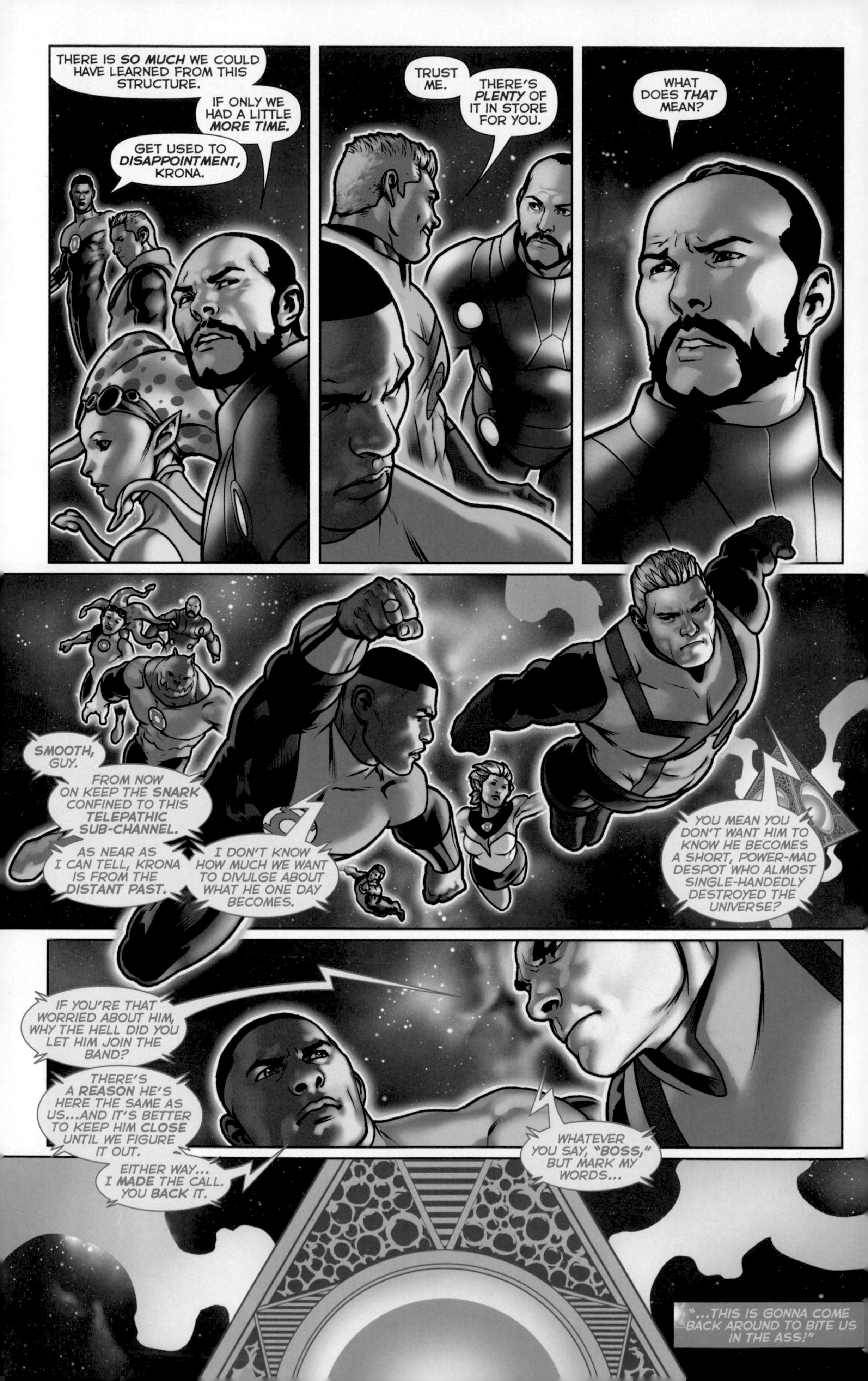
THERE IS SO MUCH WE COULD HAVE LEARNED FROM THIS STRUCTURE.
IF ONLY WE HAD A LITTLE MORE TIME.
GET USED TO DISAPPOINTMENT, KRONA.
TRUST ME.
THERE'S PLENTY OF IT IN STORE FOR YOU.
WHAT DOES THAT MEAN?
SMOOTH, GUY.
FROM NOW ON KEEP THE SNARK CONFINED TO THIS TELEPATHIC SUB-CHANNEL.
AS NEAR AS I CAN TELL, KRONA IS FROM THE DISTANT PAST.
I DON'T KNOW HOW MUCH WE WANT TO DIVULGE ABOUT WHAT HE ONE DAY BECOMES.
YOU MEAN YOU DON'T WANT HIM TO KNOW HE BECOMES A SHORT, POWER-MAD DESPOT WHO ALMOST SINGLE-HANDEDLY DESTROYED THE UNIVERSE?
IF YOU'RE THAT WORRIED ABOUT HIM, WHY THE HELL DID YOU LET HIM JOIN THE BAND?
THERE'S A REASON HE'S HERE THE SAME AS US...AND IT'S BETTER TO KEEP HIM CLOSE UNTIL WE FIGURE IT OUT.
EITHER WAY... I MADE THE CALL. YOU BACK IT.
WHATEVER YOU SAY, "BOSS," BUT MARK MY WORDS...
"...THIS IS GONNA COME BACK AROUND TO BITE US IN THE ASS!"

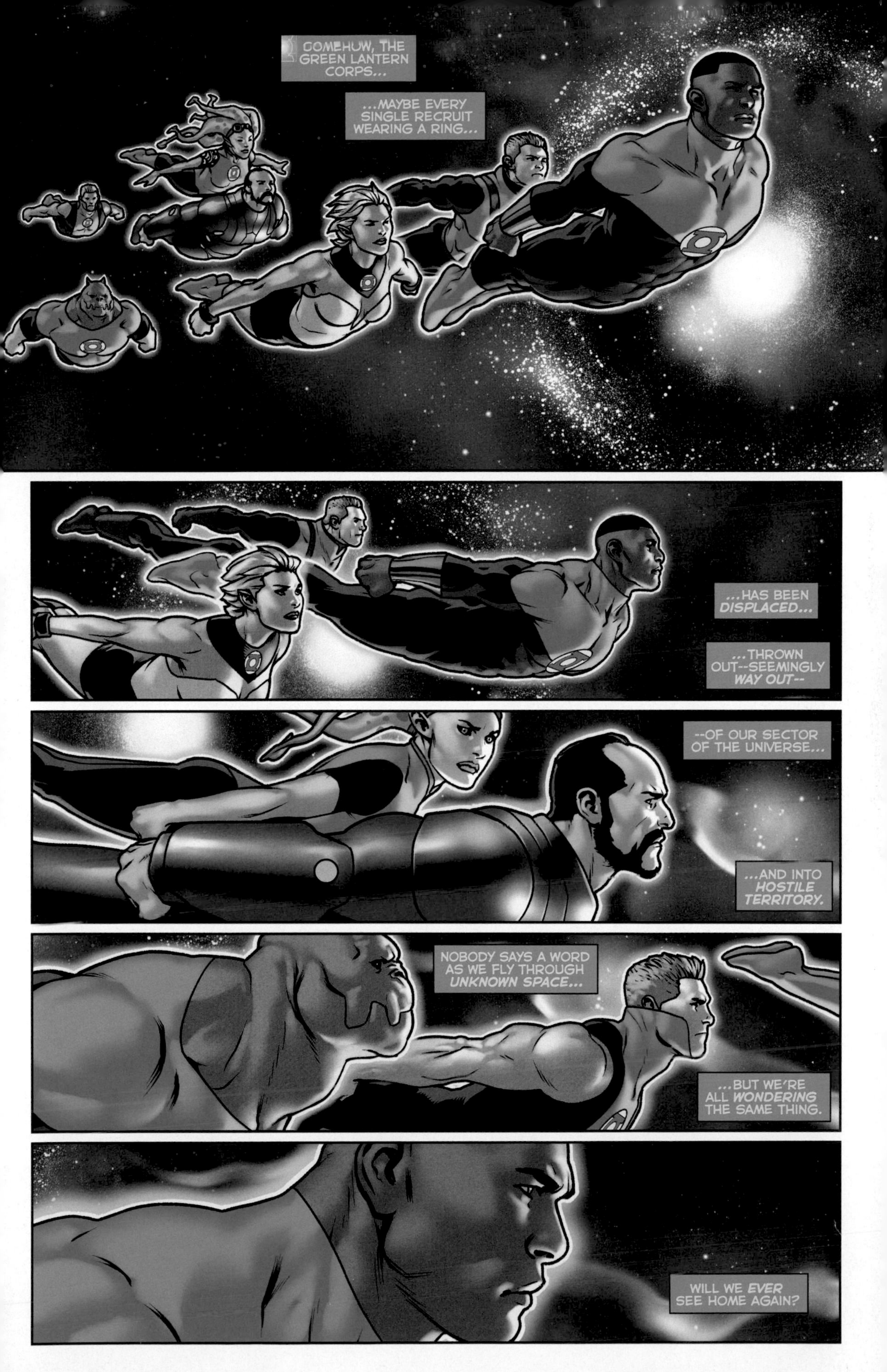
SOMEHOW, THE GREEN LANTERN CORPS...
...MAYBE EVERY SINGLE RECRUIT WEARING A RING...
...HAS BEEN DISPLACED...
...THROWN OUT--SEEMINGLY WAY OUT--
--OF OUR SECTOR OF THE UNIVERSE...
...AND INTO HOSTILE TERRITORY.
NOBODY SAYS A WORD AS WE FLY THROUGH UNKNOWN SPACE...
...BUT WE'RE ALL WONDERING THE SAME THING.
WILL WE EVER SEE HOME AGAIN?

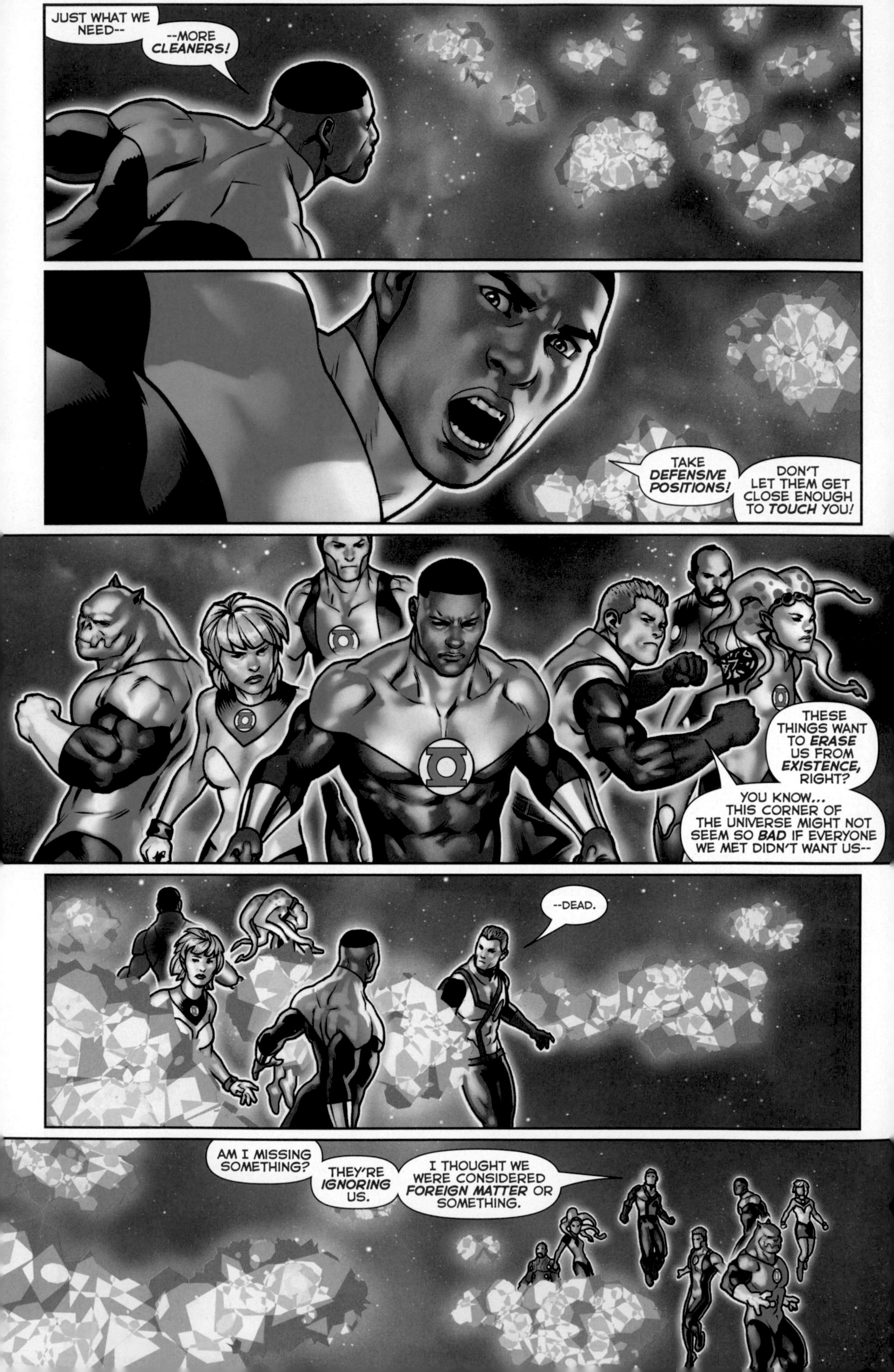

JUST WHAT WE NEED--
--MORE CLEANERS!
TAKE DEFENSIVE POSITIONS!
DON'T LET THEM GET CLOSE ENOUGH TO TOUCH YOU!
THESE THINGS WANT TO ERASE US FROM EXISTENCE, RIGHT?
YOU KNOW... THIS CORNER OF THE UNIVERSE MIGHT NOT SEEM SO BAD IF EVERYONE WE MET DIDN'T WANT US--
--DEAD.
AM I MISSING SOMETHING?
THEY'RE IGNORING US.
I THOUGHT WE WERE CONSIDERED FOREIGN MATTER OR SOMETHING.

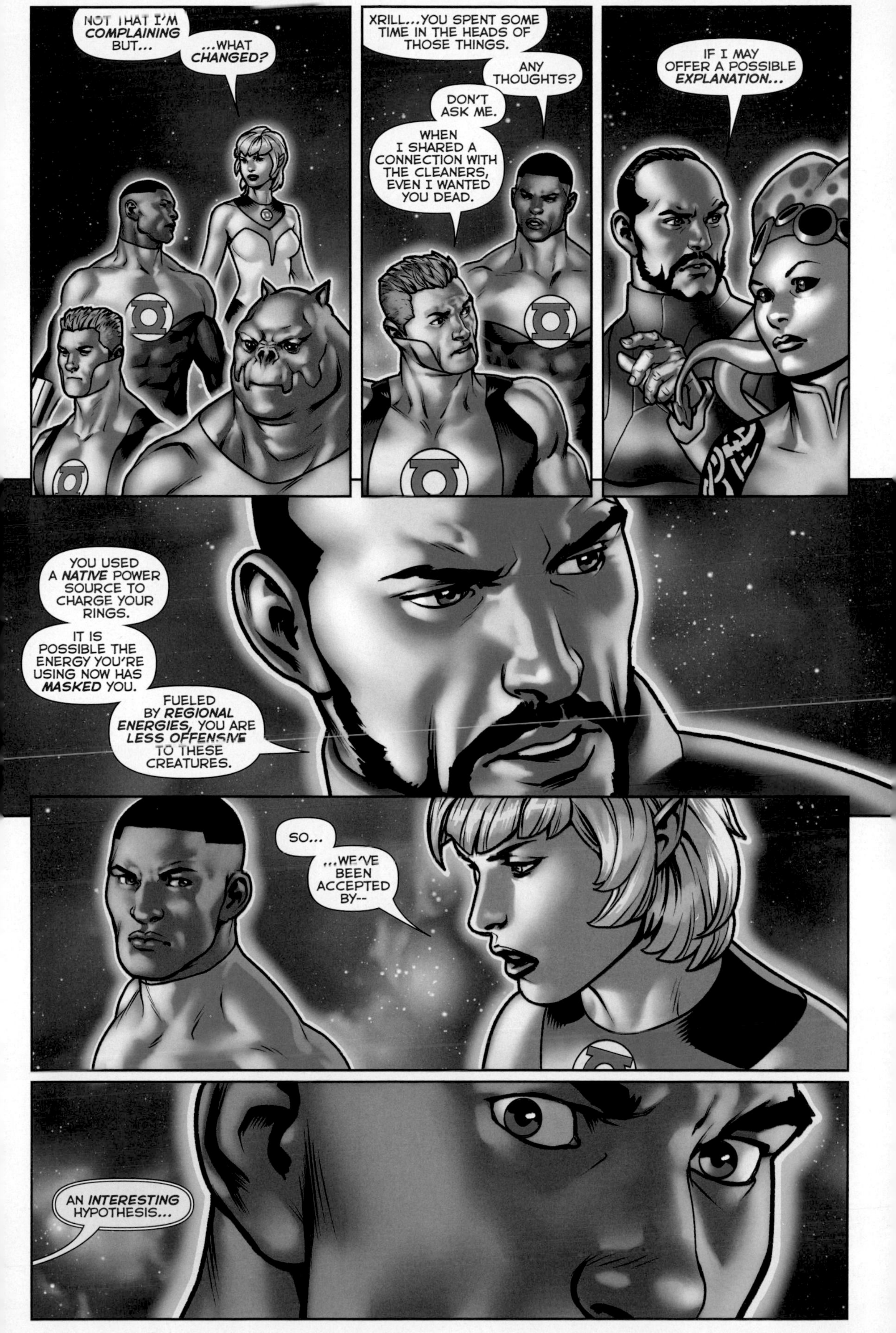
NOT THAT I'M COMPLAINING BUT...
...WHAT CHANGED?
XRILL...YOU SPENT SOME TIME IN THE HEADS OF THOSE THINGS.
ANY THOUGHTS?
DON'T ASK ME.
WHEN I SHARED A CONNECTION WITH THE CLEANERS, EVEN I WANTED YOU DEAD.
IF I MAY OFFER A POSSIBLE EXPLANATION...
YOU USED A NATIVE POWER SOURCE TO CHARGE YOUR RINGS.
IT IS POSSIBLE THE ENERGY YOU'RE USING NOW HAS MASKED YOU.
FUELED BY REGIONAL ENERGIES, YOU ARE LESS OFFENSIVE TO THESE CREATURES.
SO...
...WE'VE BEEN ACCEPTED BY--
AN INTERESTING HYPOTHESIS...

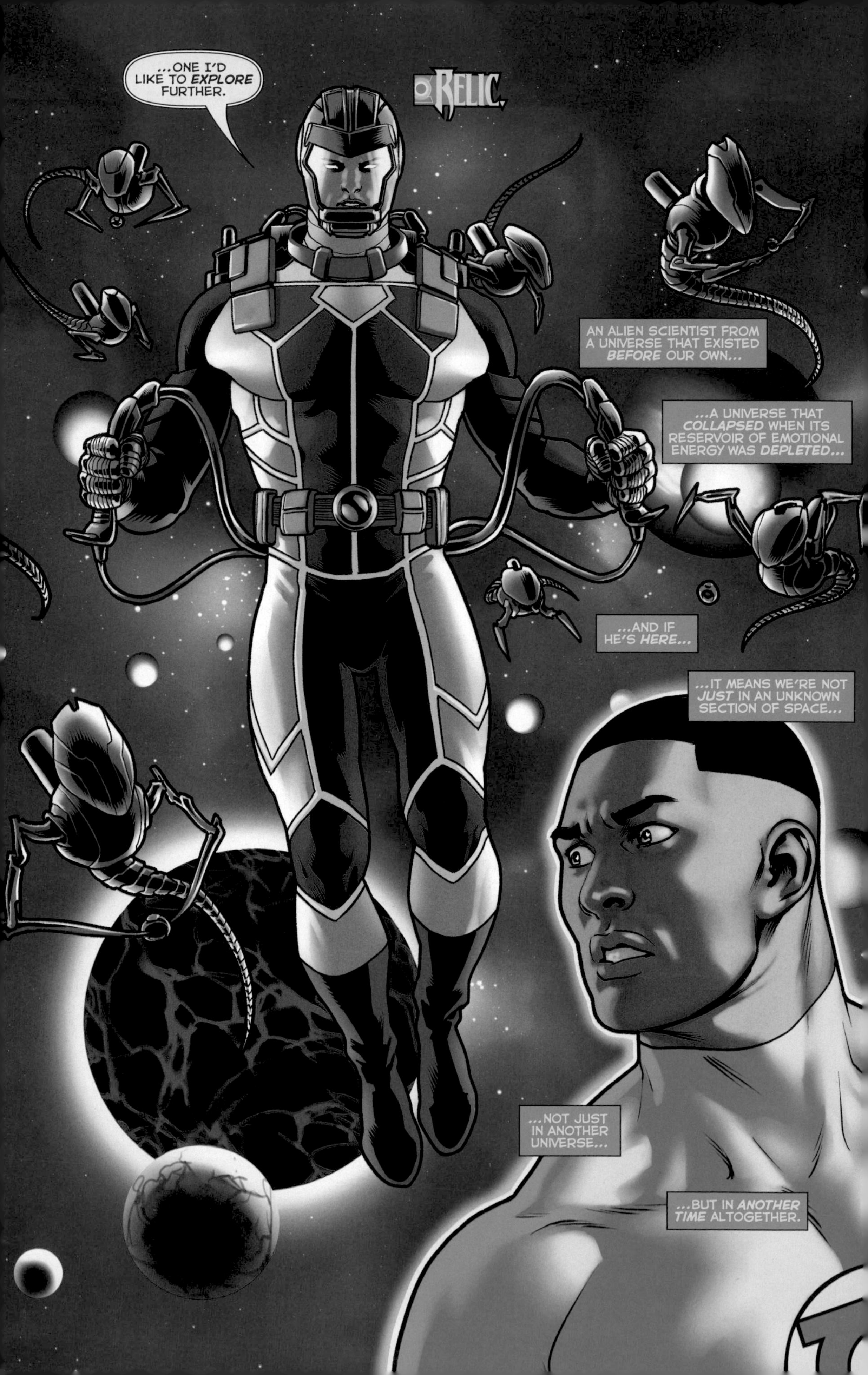
...ONE I'D LIKE TO EXPLORE FURTHER.
RELIC
AN ALIEN SCIENTIST FROM A UNIVERSE THAT EXISTED BEFORE OUR OWN...
...A UNIVERSE THAT COLLAPSED WHEN ITS RESERVOIR OF EMOTIONAL ENERGY WAS DEPLETED...
...AND IF HE'S HERE...
...IT MEANS WE'RE NOT JUST IN AN UNKNOWN SECTION OF SPACE...
...NOT JUST IN ANOTHER UNIVERSE...
...BUT IN ANOTHER TIME ALTOGETHER.

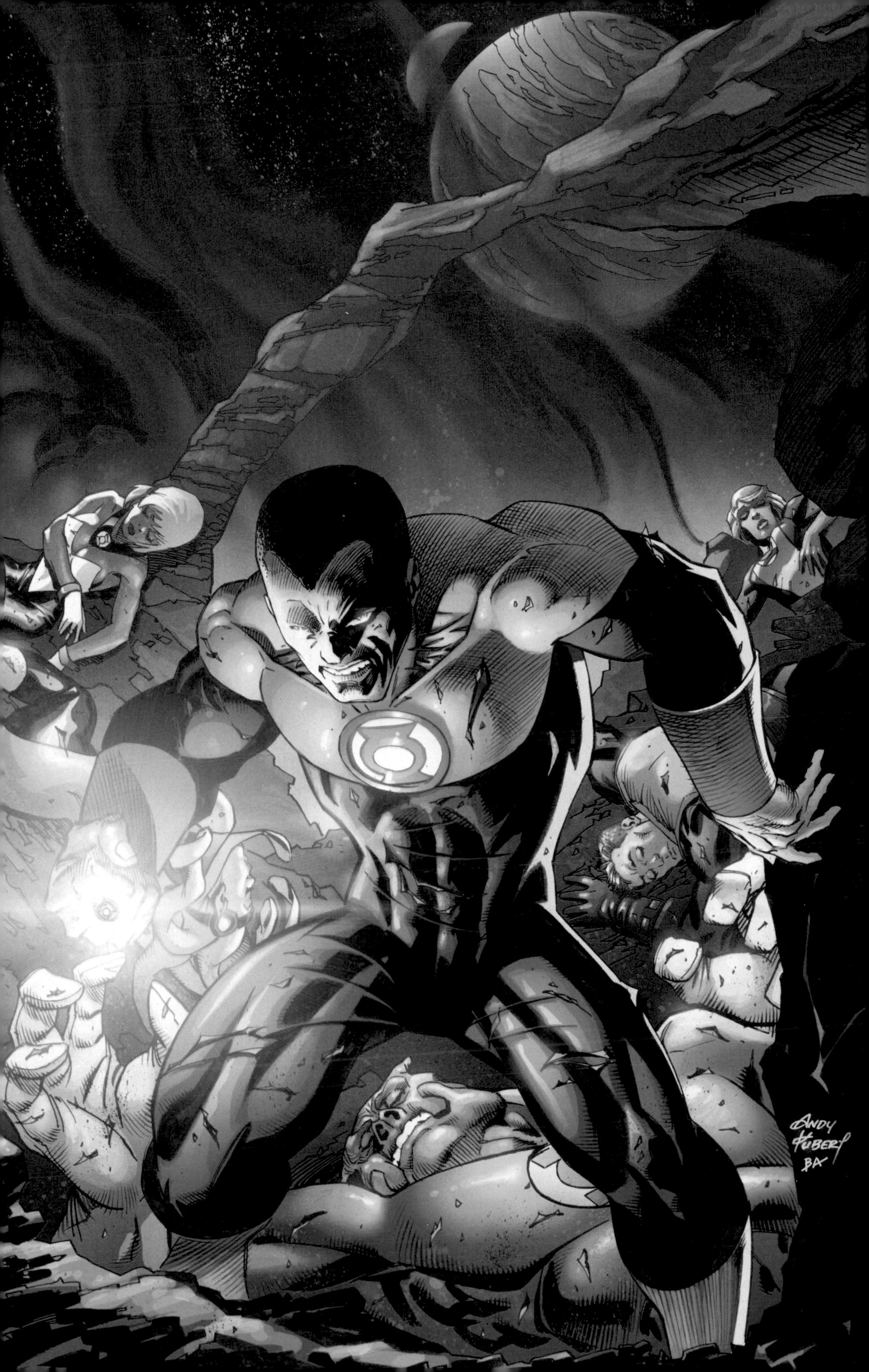
ANDY KUBERT BA

CULLEN BUNN writer **JESUS SAIZ & CLIFF RICHARDS** artists **JESUS SAIZ & MICHAEL ATIYEH** colorists **DAVE SHARPE** letterer **ANDY KUBERT & BRAD ANDERSON** cover

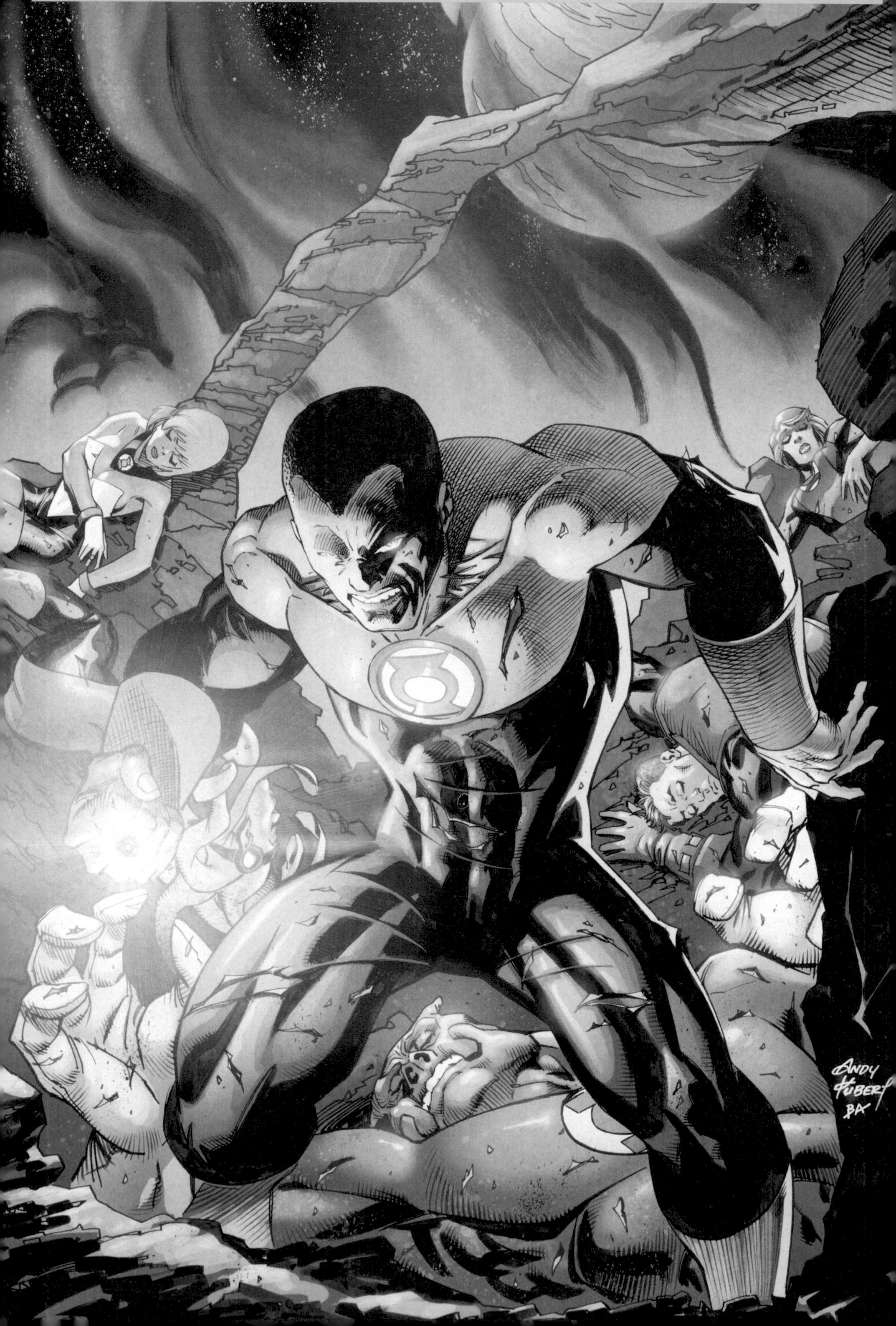
ANDY KUBERT BA

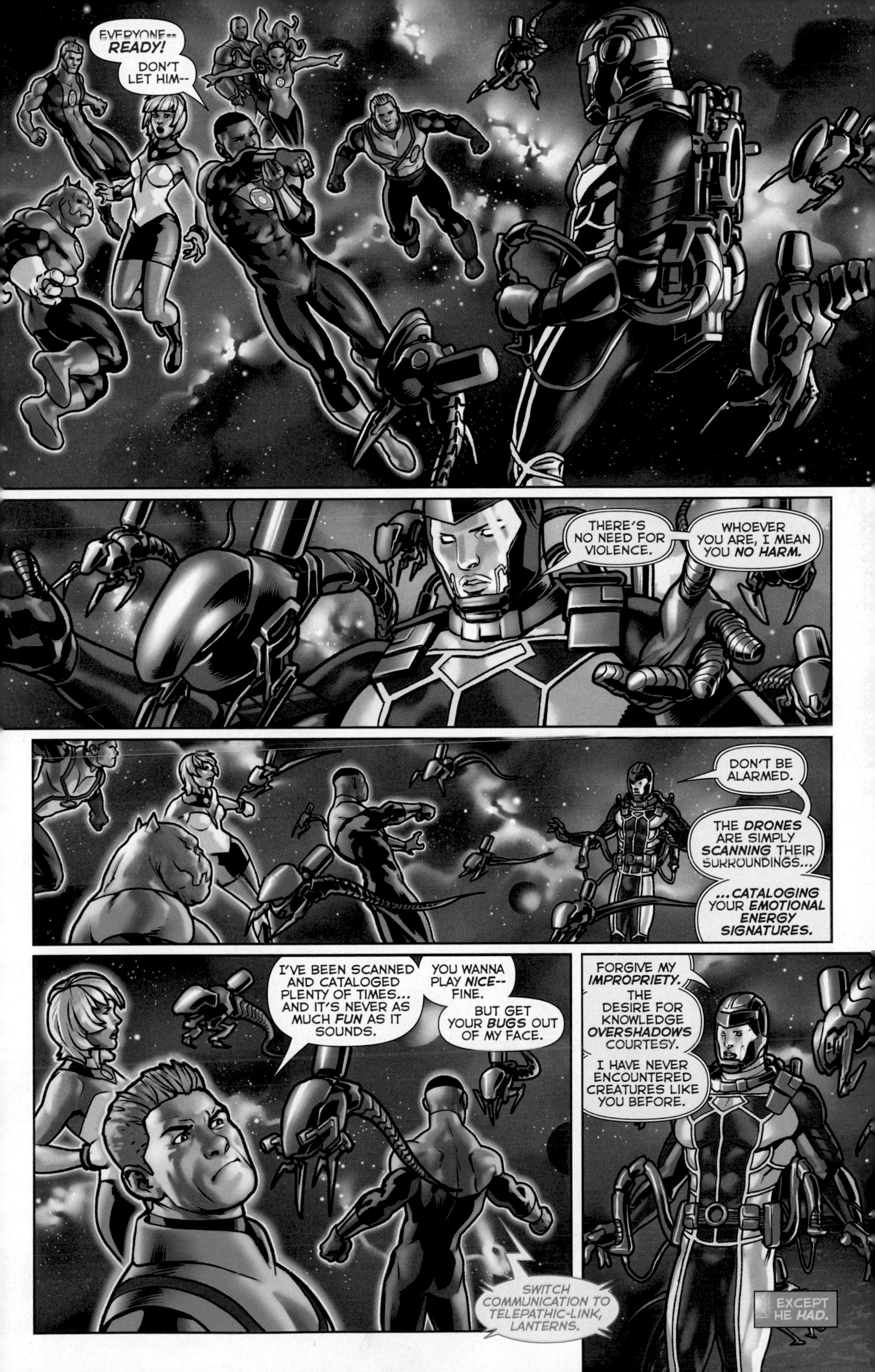
EVERYONE--
READY!
DON'T LET HIM--
THERE'S NO NEED FOR VIOLENCE.
WHOEVER YOU ARE, I MEAN YOU NO HARM.
DON'T BE ALARMED.
THE DRONES ARE SIMPLY SCANNING THEIR SURROUNDINGS...
...CATALOGING YOUR EMOTIONAL ENERGY SIGNATURES.
I'VE BEEN SCANNED AND CATALOGED PLENTY OF TIMES... AND IT'S NEVER AS MUCH FUN AS IT SOUNDS.
YOU WANNA PLAY NICE-- FINE.
BUT GET YOUR BUGS OUT OF MY FACE.
SWITCH COMMUNICATION TO TELEPATHIC-LINK, LANTERNS.
FORGIVE MY IMPROPRIETY.
THE DESIRE FOR KNOWLEDGE OVERSHADOWS COURTESY.
I HAVE NEVER ENCOUNTERED CREATURES LIKE YOU BEFORE.
EXCEPT HE HAD.

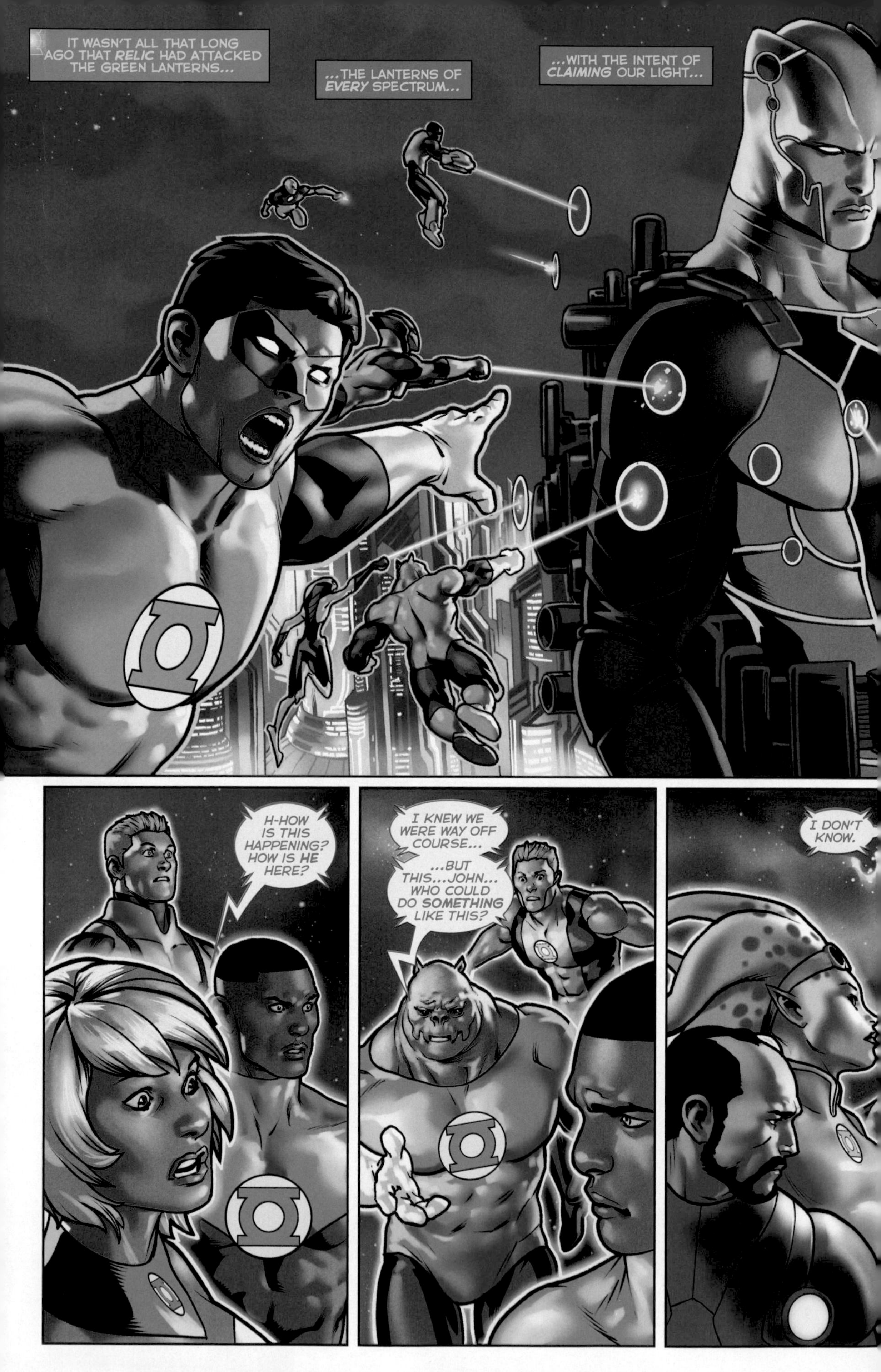
IT WASN'T ALL THAT LONG AGO THAT RELIC HAD ATTACKED THE GREEN LANTERNS...
...THE LANTERNS OF EVERY SPECTRUM...
...WITH THE INTENT OF CLAIMING OUR LIGHT...
H-HOW IS THIS HAPPENING? HOW IS HE HERE?
I KNEW WE WERE WAY OFF COURSE...
...BUT THIS...JOHN... WHO COULD DO SOMETHING LIKE THIS?
I DON'T KNOW.

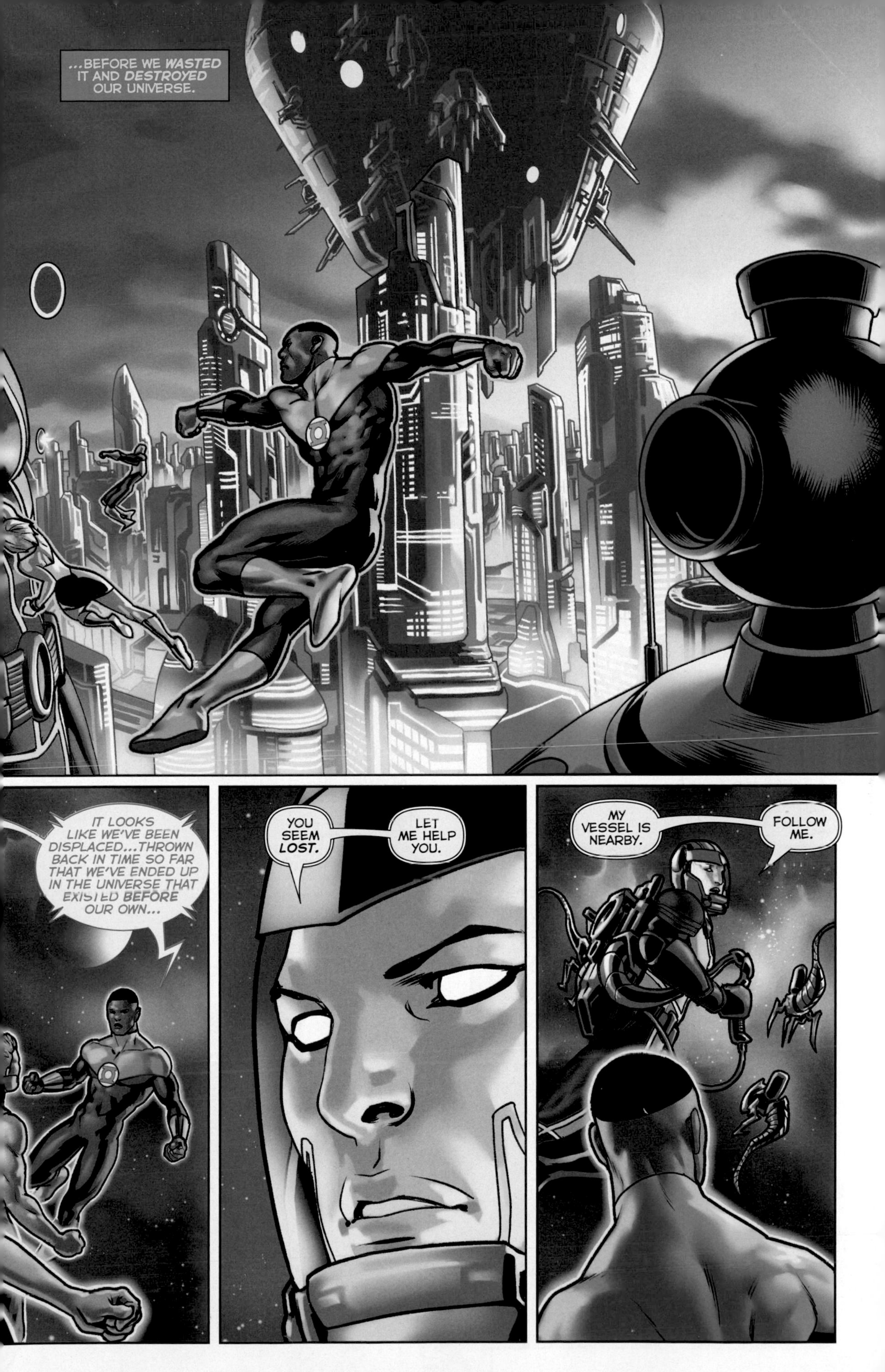
...BEFORE WE WASTED IT AND DESTROYED OUR UNIVERSE.
IT LOOKS LIKE WE'VE BEEN DISPLACED...THROWN BACK IN TIME SO FAR THAT WE'VE ENDED UP IN THE UNIVERSE THAT EXISTED BEFORE OUR OWN...
YOU SEEM LOST.
LET ME HELP YOU.
MY VESSEL IS NEARBY.
FOLLOW ME.

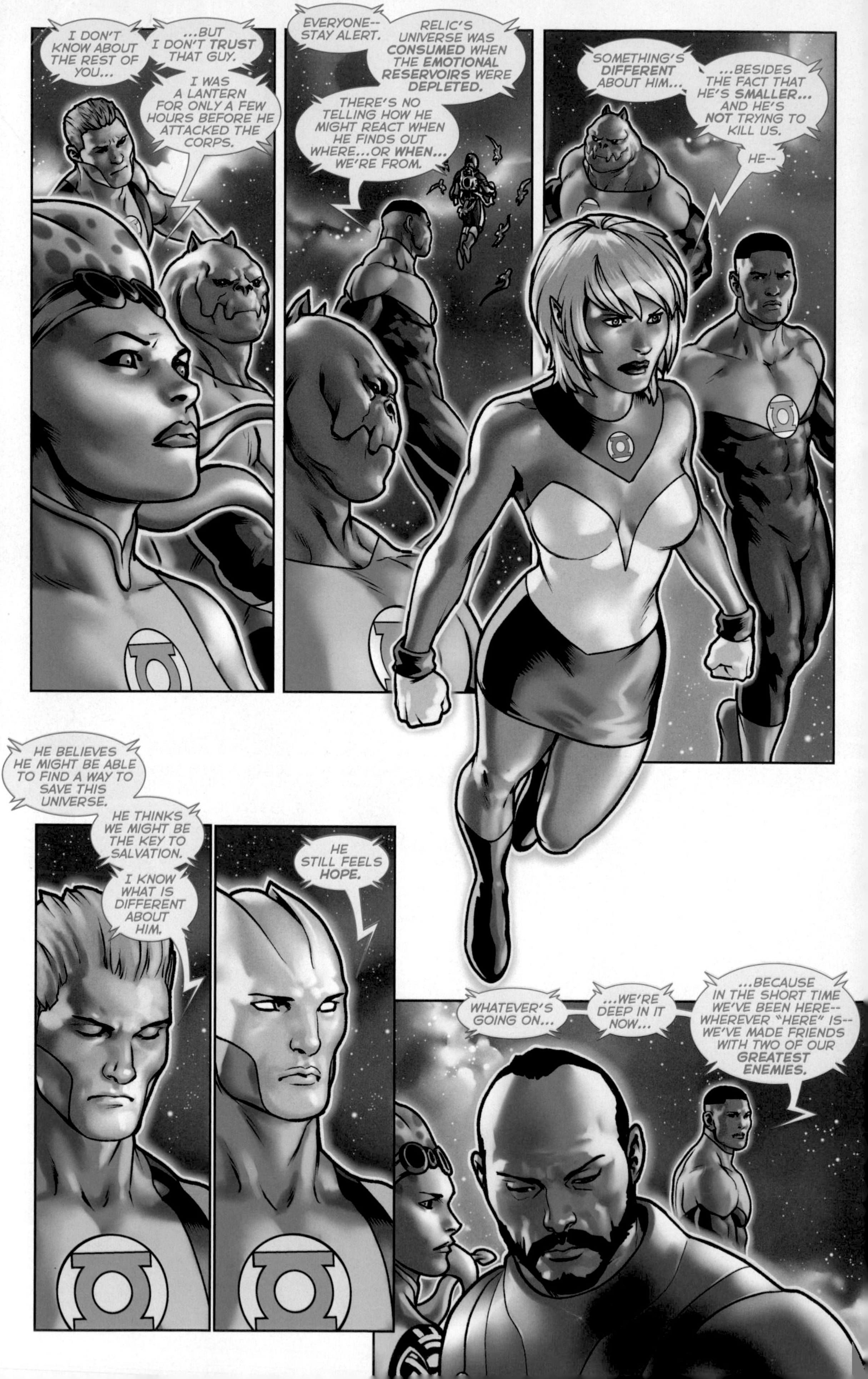

I DON'T KNOW ABOUT THE REST OF YOU...
...BUT I DON'T **TRUST** THAT GUY.
I WAS A LANTERN FOR ONLY A FEW HOURS BEFORE HE ATTACKED THE CORPS.
EVERYONE-- STAY ALERT.
RELIC'S UNIVERSE WAS **CONSUMED** WHEN THE **EMOTIONAL RESERVOIRS** WERE **DEPLETED.**
THERE'S NO TELLING HOW HE MIGHT REACT WHEN HE FINDS OUT WHERE...OR **WHEN...** WE'RE FROM.
SOMETHING'S **DIFFERENT** ABOUT HIM...
...BESIDES THE FACT THAT HE'S **SMALLER...** AND HE'S **NOT** TRYING TO KILL US.
HE--
HE BELIEVES HE MIGHT BE ABLE TO FIND A WAY TO SAVE THIS UNIVERSE.
HE THINKS WE MIGHT BE THE KEY TO SALVATION.
I KNOW WHAT IS DIFFERENT ABOUT HIM.
HE STILL FEELS **HOPE.**
WHATEVER'S GOING ON...
...WE'RE DEEP IN IT NOW...
...BECAUSE IN THE SHORT TIME WE'VE BEEN HERE-- WHEREVER "HERE" IS-- WE'VE MADE FRIENDS WITH TWO OF OUR **GREATEST ENEMIES.**

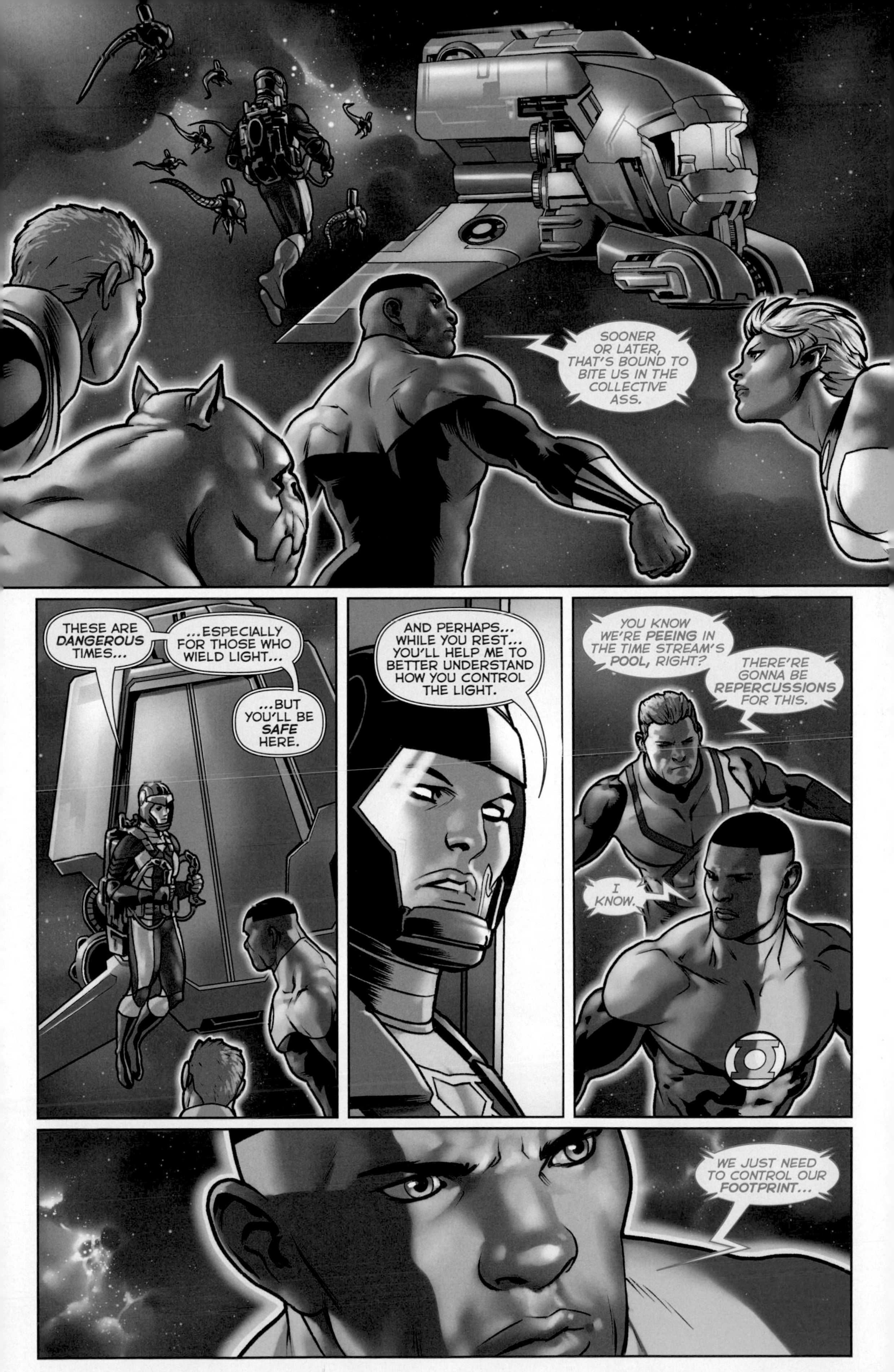
SOONER OR LATER, THAT'S BOUND TO BITE US IN THE COLLECTIVE ASS.
THESE ARE *DANGEROUS* TIMES...
...ESPECIALLY FOR THOSE WHO WIELD LIGHT...
...BUT YOU'LL BE *SAFE* HERE.
AND PERHAPS... WHILE YOU REST... YOU'LL HELP ME TO BETTER UNDERSTAND HOW YOU CONTROL THE LIGHT.
YOU KNOW WE'RE *PEEING* IN THE TIME STREAM'S *POOL*, RIGHT?
THERE'RE GONNA BE *REPERCUSSIONS* FOR THIS.
I KNOW.
WE JUST NEED TO CONTROL OUR *FOOTPRINT*...

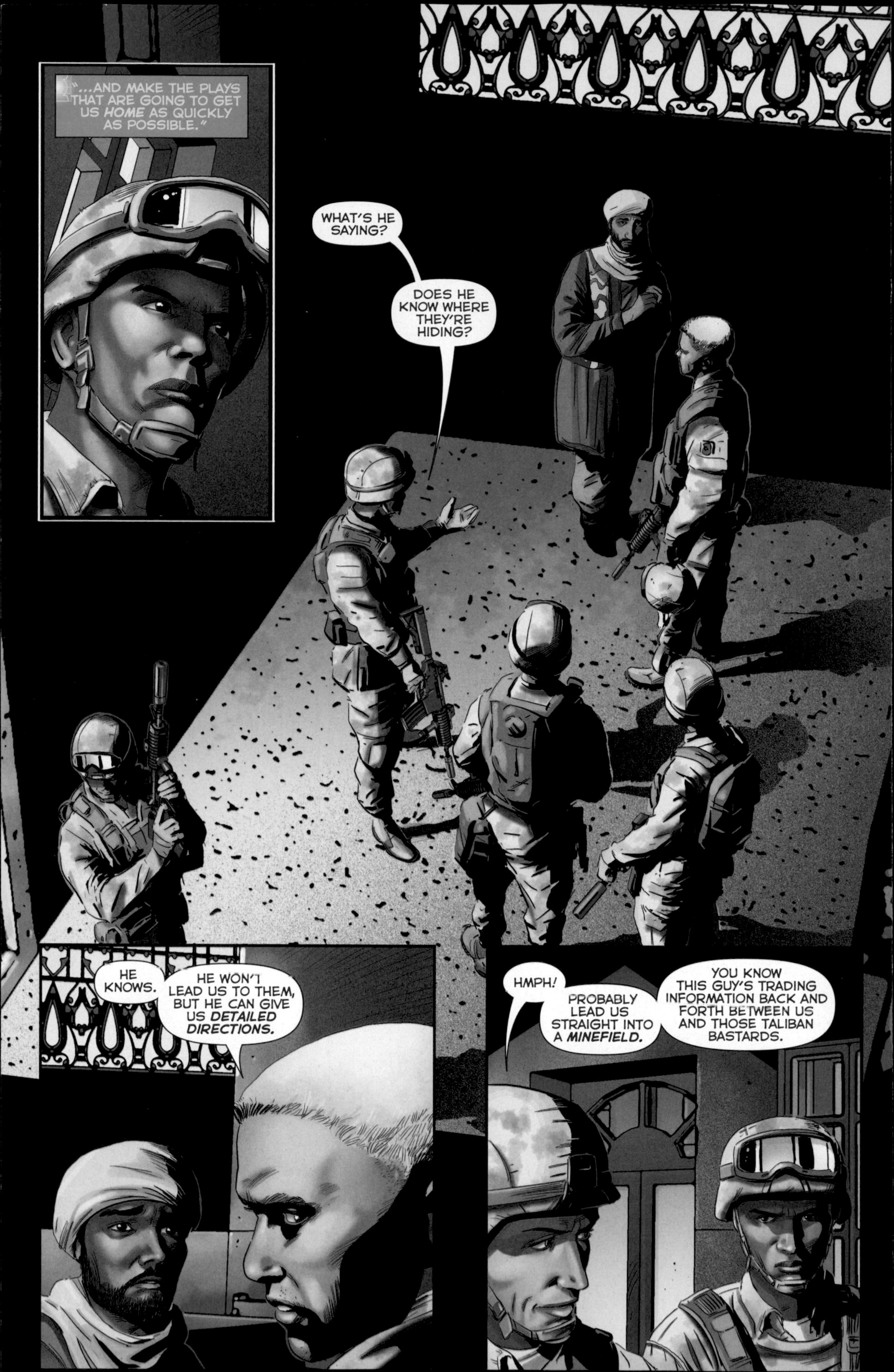
"...AND MAKE THE PLAYS THAT ARE GOING TO GET US *HOME* AS QUICKLY AS POSSIBLE."
WHAT'S HE SAYING?
DOES HE KNOW WHERE THEY'RE HIDING?
HE KNOWS.
HE WON'T LEAD US TO THEM, BUT HE CAN GIVE US *DETAILED DIRECTIONS.*
HMPH!
PROBABLY LEAD US STRAIGHT INTO A *MINEFIELD.*
YOU KNOW THIS GUY'S TRADING INFORMATION BACK AND FORTH BETWEEN US AND THOSE TALIBAN BASTARDS.

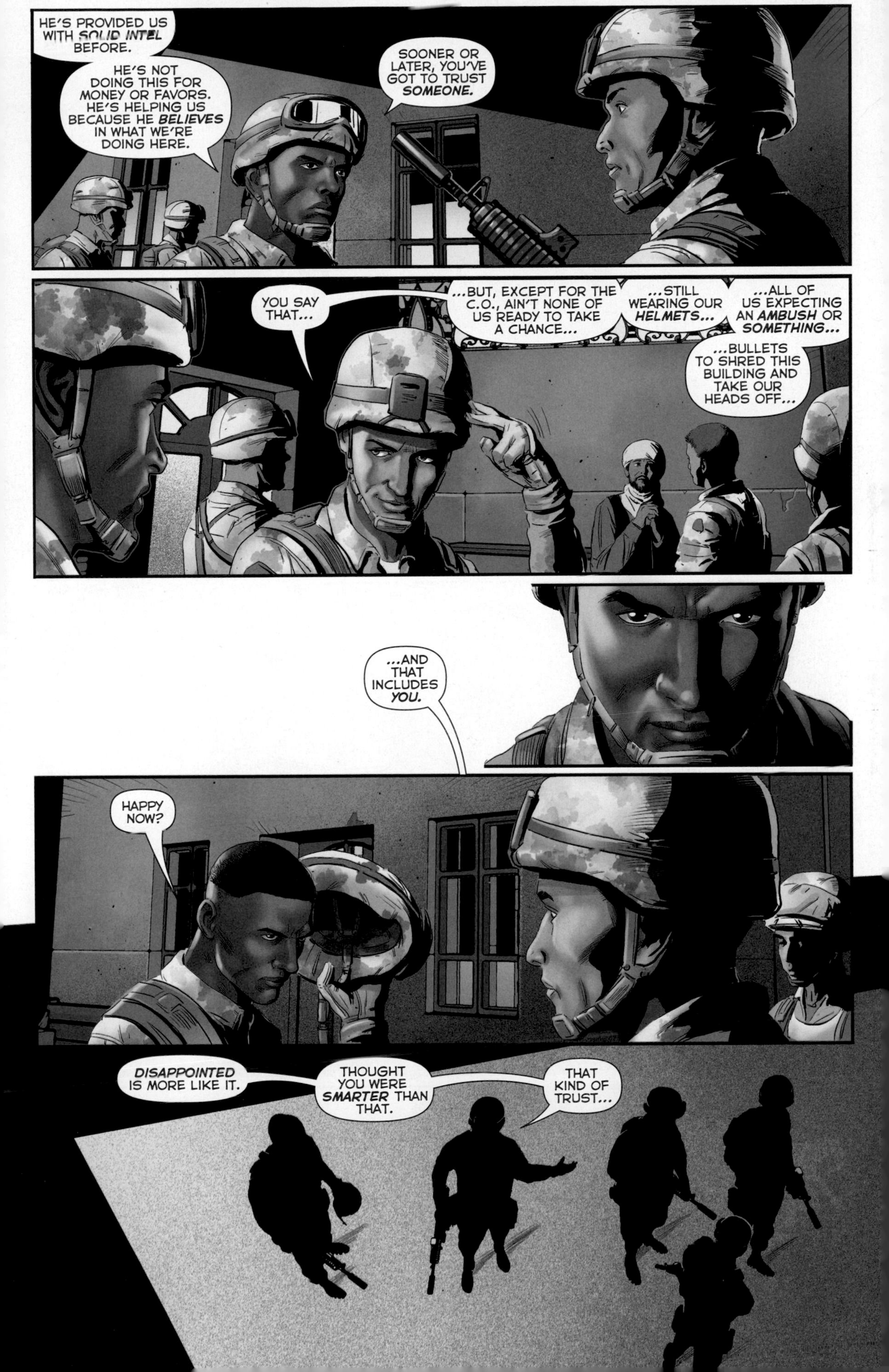
HE'S PROVIDED US WITH SOLID INTEL BEFORE.
HE'S NOT DOING THIS FOR MONEY OR FAVORS. HE'S HELPING US BECAUSE HE BELIEVES IN WHAT WE'RE DOING HERE.
SOONER OR LATER, YOU'VE GOT TO TRUST SOMEONE.
YOU SAY THAT...
...BUT, EXCEPT FOR THE C.O., AIN'T NONE OF US READY TO TAKE A CHANCE...
...STILL WEARING OUR HELMETS...
...ALL OF US EXPECTING AN AMBUSH OR SOMETHING...
...BULLETS TO SHRED THIS BUILDING AND TAKE OUR HEADS OFF...
...AND THAT INCLUDES YOU.
HAPPY NOW?
DISAPPOINTED IS MORE LIKE IT.
THOUGHT YOU WERE SMARTER THAN THAT.
THAT KIND OF TRUST...

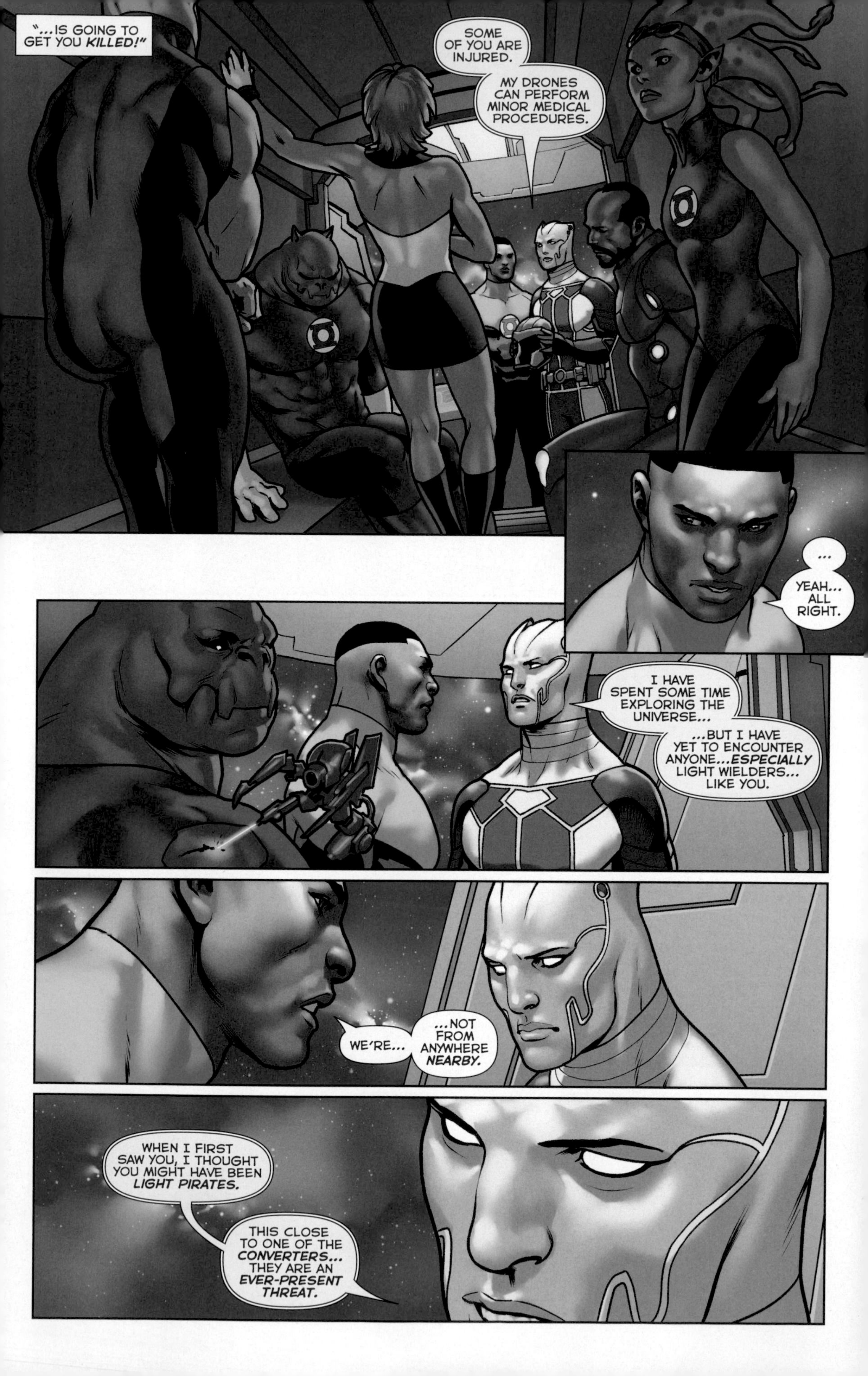
"...IS GOING TO GET YOU KILLED!"
SOME OF YOU ARE INJURED.
MY DRONES CAN PERFORM MINOR MEDICAL PROCEDURES.
...
YEAH... ALL RIGHT.
I HAVE SPENT SOME TIME EXPLORING THE UNIVERSE...
...BUT I HAVE YET TO ENCOUNTER ANYONE...ESPECIALLY LIGHT WIELDERS... LIKE YOU.
WE'RE...
...NOT FROM ANYWHERE NEARBY.
WHEN I FIRST SAW YOU, I THOUGHT YOU MIGHT HAVE BEEN LIGHT PIRATES.
THIS CLOSE TO ONE OF THE CONVERTERS... THEY ARE AN EVER-PRESENT THREAT.

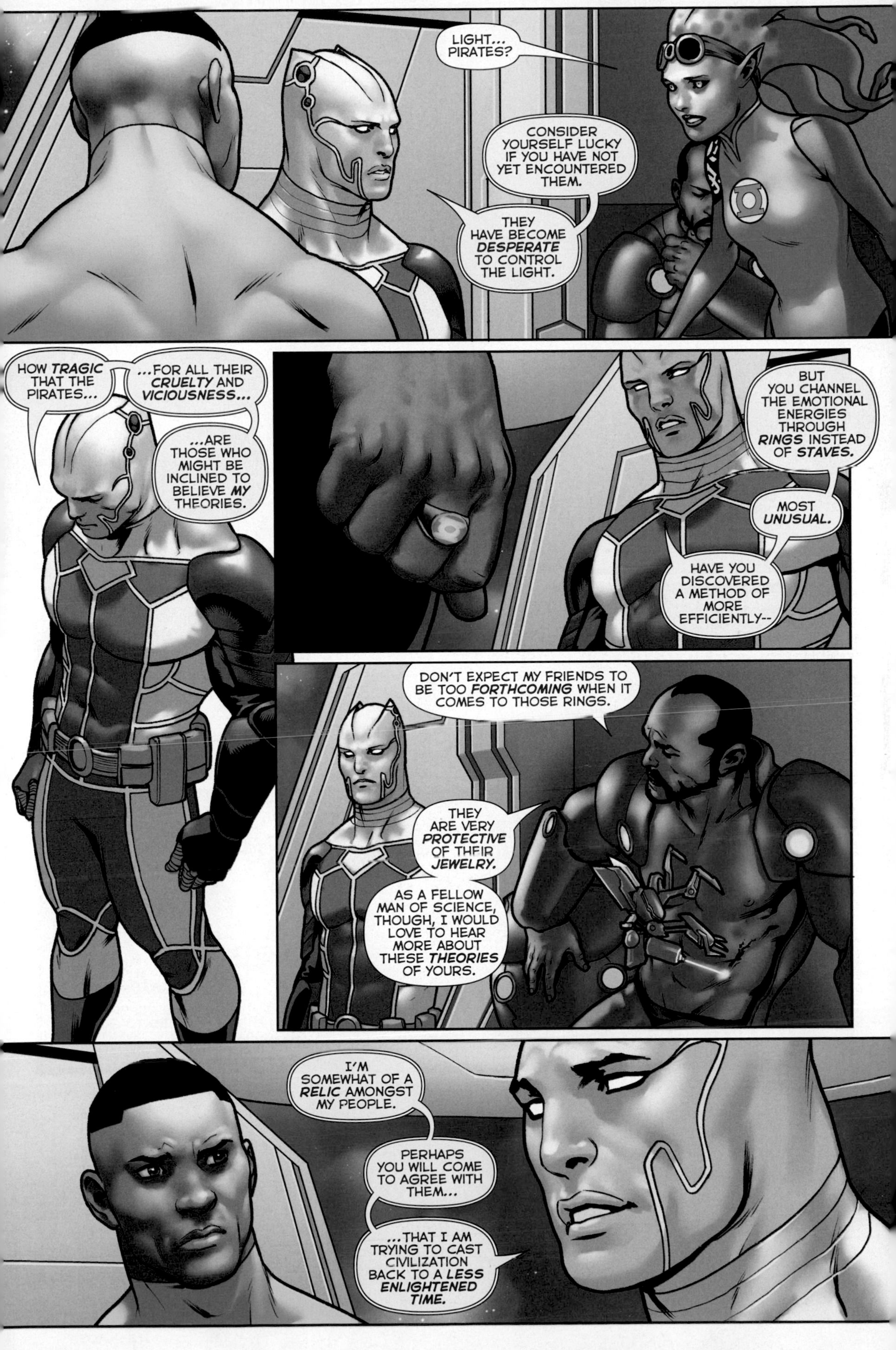
LIGHT... PIRATES?
CONSIDER YOURSELF LUCKY IF YOU HAVE NOT YET ENCOUNTERED THEM.
THEY HAVE BECOME DESPERATE TO CONTROL THE LIGHT.
HOW TRAGIC THAT THE PIRATES...
...FOR ALL THEIR CRUELTY AND VICIOUSNESS...
...ARE THOSE WHO MIGHT BE INCLINED TO BELIEVE MY THEORIES.
BUT YOU CHANNEL THE EMOTIONAL ENERGIES THROUGH RINGS INSTEAD OF STAVES.
MOST UNUSUAL.
HAVE YOU DISCOVERED A METHOD OF MORE EFFICIENTLY--
DON'T EXPECT MY FRIENDS TO BE TOO FORTHCOMING WHEN IT COMES TO THOSE RINGS.
THEY ARE VERY PROTECTIVE OF THEIR JEWELRY.
AS A FELLOW MAN OF SCIENCE, THOUGH, I WOULD LOVE TO HEAR MORE ABOUT THESE THEORIES OF YOURS.
I'M SOMEWHAT OF A RELIC AMONGST MY PEOPLE.
PERHAPS YOU WILL COME TO AGREE WITH THEM...
...THAT I AM TRYING TO CAST CIVILIZATION BACK TO A LESS ENLIGHTENED TIME.

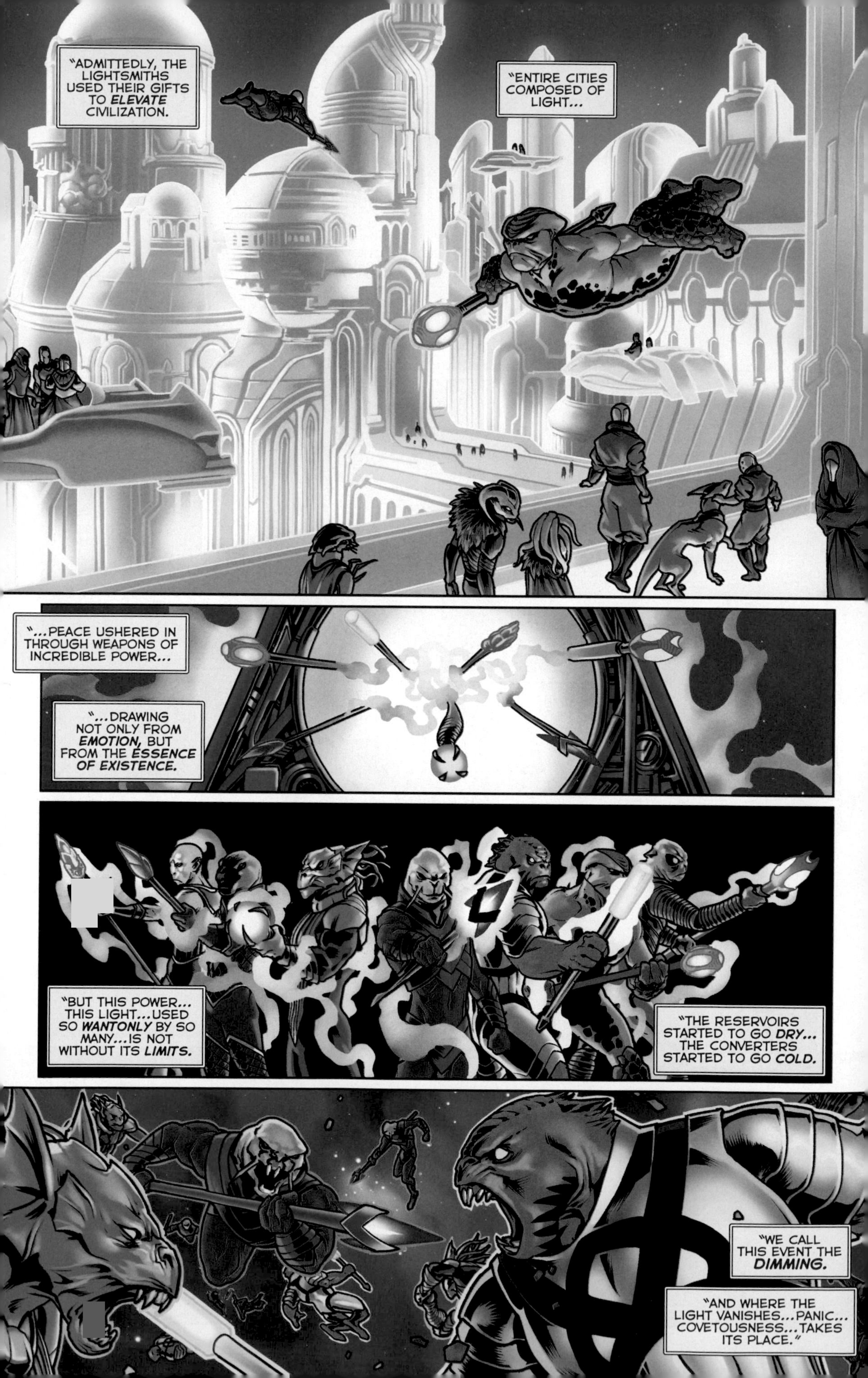
"ADMITTEDLY, THE LIGHTSMITHS USED THEIR GIFTS TO *ELEVATE* CIVILIZATION.
"ENTIRE CITIES COMPOSED OF LIGHT...
"...PEACE USHERED IN THROUGH WEAPONS OF INCREDIBLE POWER...
"...DRAWING NOT ONLY FROM *EMOTION,* BUT FROM THE *ESSENCE OF EXISTENCE.*
"BUT THIS POWER... THIS LIGHT...USED SO *WANTONLY* BY SO MANY...IS NOT WITHOUT ITS *LIMITS.*
"THE RESERVOIRS STARTED TO GO *DRY...* THE CONVERTERS STARTED TO GO *COLD.*
"WE CALL THIS EVENT THE *DIMMING.*
"AND WHERE THE LIGHT VANISHES...PANIC... COVETOUSNESS...TAKES ITS PLACE."

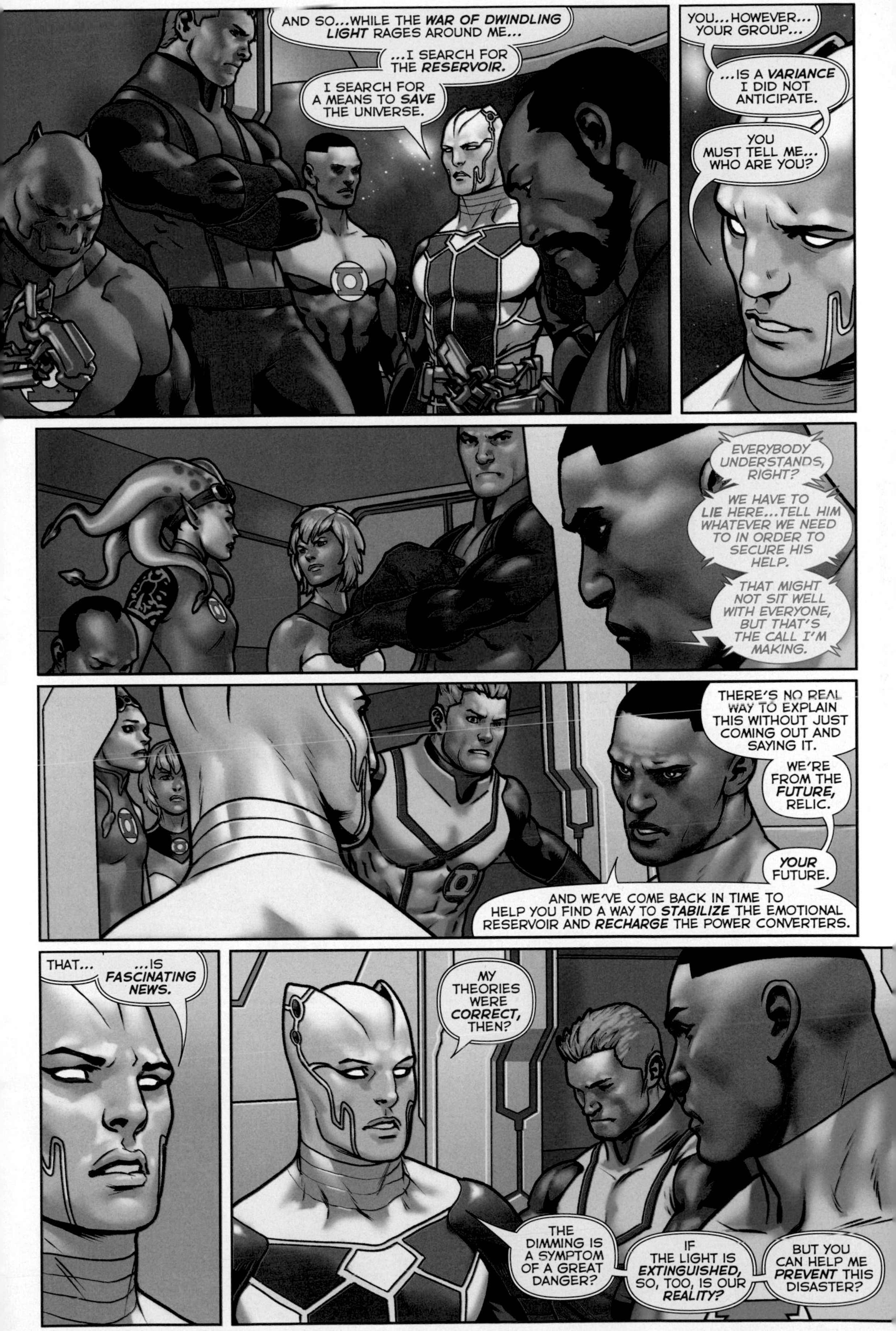
AND SO...WHILE THE WAR OF DWINDLING LIGHT RAGES AROUND ME...
...I SEARCH FOR THE RESERVOIR.
I SEARCH FOR A MEANS TO SAVE THE UNIVERSE.
YOU...HOWEVER... YOUR GROUP...
...IS A VARIANCE I DID NOT ANTICIPATE.
YOU MUST TELL ME... WHO ARE YOU?
EVERYBODY UNDERSTANDS, RIGHT?
WE HAVE TO LIE HERE...TELL HIM WHATEVER WE NEED TO IN ORDER TO SECURE HIS HELP.
THAT MIGHT NOT SIT WELL WITH EVERYONE, BUT THAT'S THE CALL I'M MAKING.
THERE'S NO REAL WAY TO EXPLAIN THIS WITHOUT JUST COMING OUT AND SAYING IT.
WE'RE FROM THE FUTURE, RELIC.
YOUR FUTURE.
AND WE'VE COME BACK IN TIME TO HELP YOU FIND A WAY TO STABILIZE THE EMOTIONAL RESERVOIR AND RECHARGE THE POWER CONVERTERS.
THAT...
...IS FASCINATING NEWS.
MY THEORIES WERE CORRECT, THEN?
THE DIMMING IS A SYMPTOM OF A GREAT DANGER?
IF THE LIGHT IS EXTINGUISHED, SO, TOO, IS OUR REALITY?
BUT YOU CAN HELP ME PREVENT THIS DISASTER?

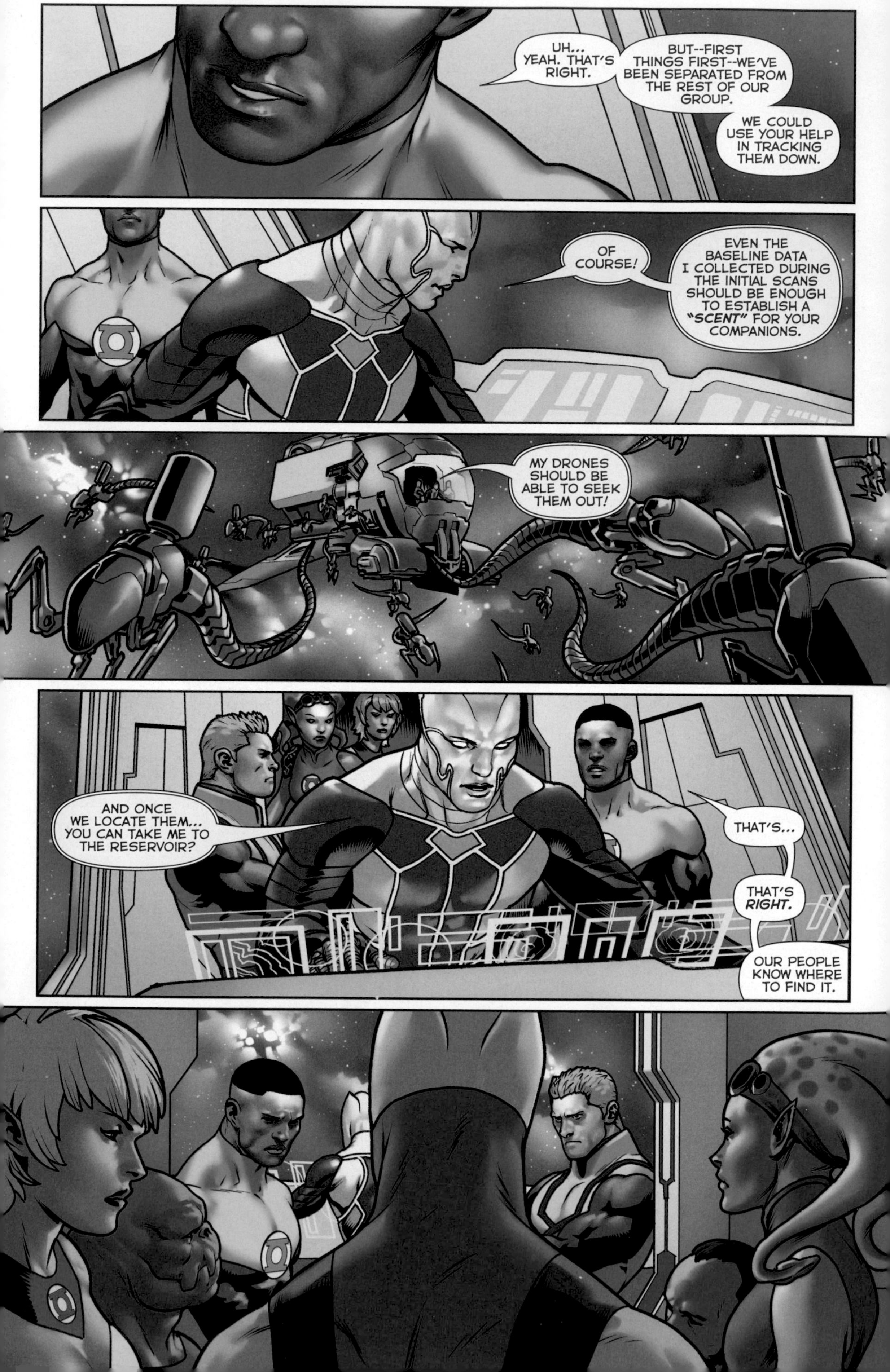
UH... YEAH. THAT'S RIGHT.
BUT--FIRST THINGS FIRST--WE'VE BEEN SEPARATED FROM THE REST OF OUR GROUP.
WE COULD USE YOUR HELP IN TRACKING THEM DOWN.
OF COURSE!
EVEN THE BASELINE DATA I COLLECTED DURING THE INITIAL SCANS SHOULD BE ENOUGH TO ESTABLISH A "SCENT" FOR YOUR COMPANIONS.
MY DRONES SHOULD BE ABLE TO SEEK THEM OUT!
AND ONCE WE LOCATE THEM... YOU CAN TAKE ME TO THE RESERVOIR?
THAT'S...
THAT'S RIGHT.
OUR PEOPLE KNOW WHERE TO FIND IT.

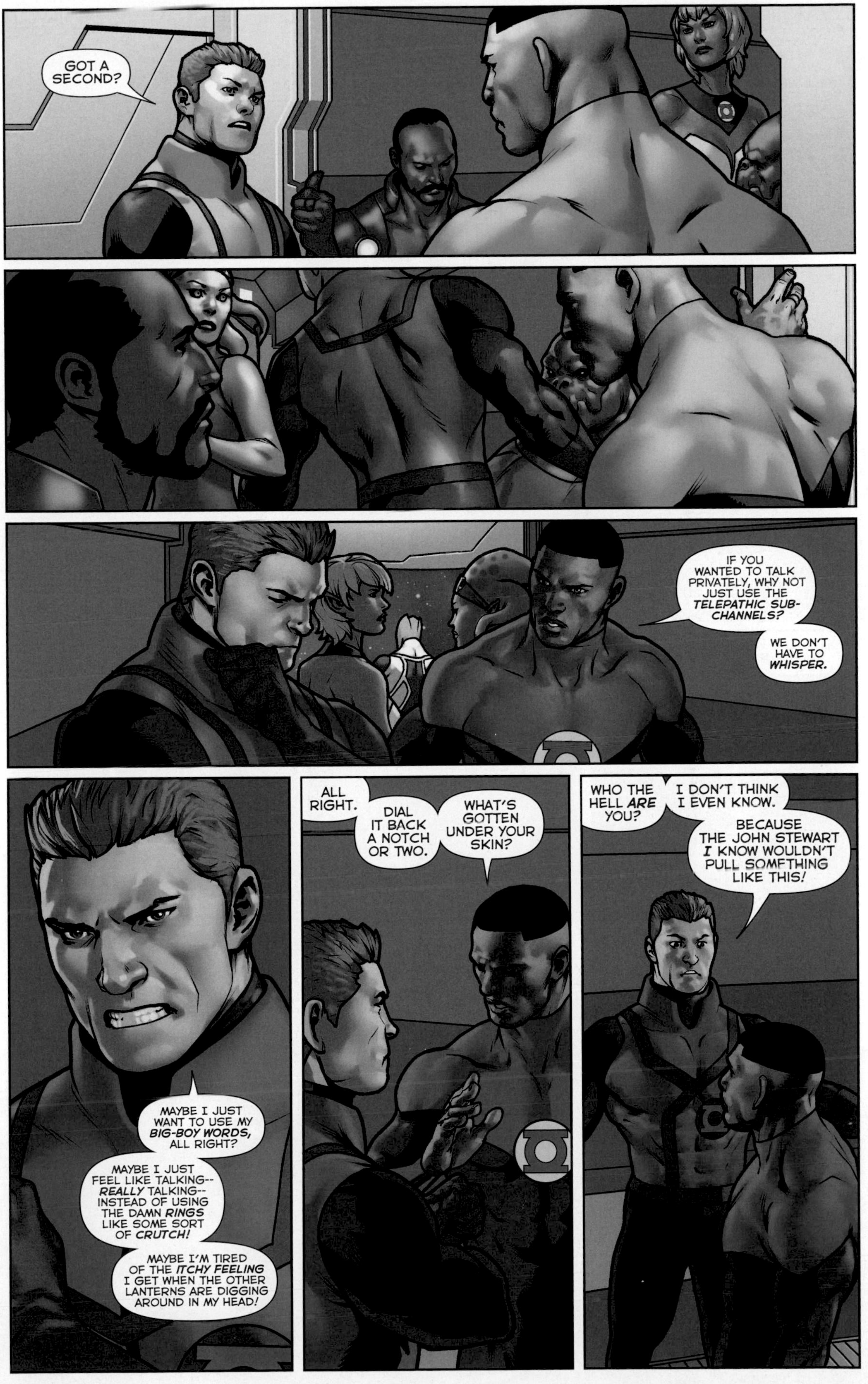
GOT A SECOND?
IF YOU WANTED TO TALK PRIVATELY, WHY NOT JUST USE THE TELEPATHIC SUB-CHANNELS?
WE DON'T HAVE TO WHISPER.
MAYBE I JUST WANT TO USE MY BIG-BOY WORDS, ALL RIGHT?
MAYBE I JUST FEEL LIKE TALKING--REALLY TALKING--INSTEAD OF USING THE DAMN RINGS LIKE SOME SORT OF CRUTCH!
MAYBE I'M TIRED OF THE ITCHY FEELING I GET WHEN THE OTHER LANTERNS ARE DIGGING AROUND IN MY HEAD!
ALL RIGHT.
DIAL IT BACK A NOTCH OR TWO.
WHAT'S GOTTEN UNDER YOUR SKIN?
WHO THE HELL ARE YOU?
I DON'T THINK I EVEN KNOW.
BECAUSE THE JOHN STEWART I KNOW WOULDN'T PULL SOMFTHING LIKE THIS!

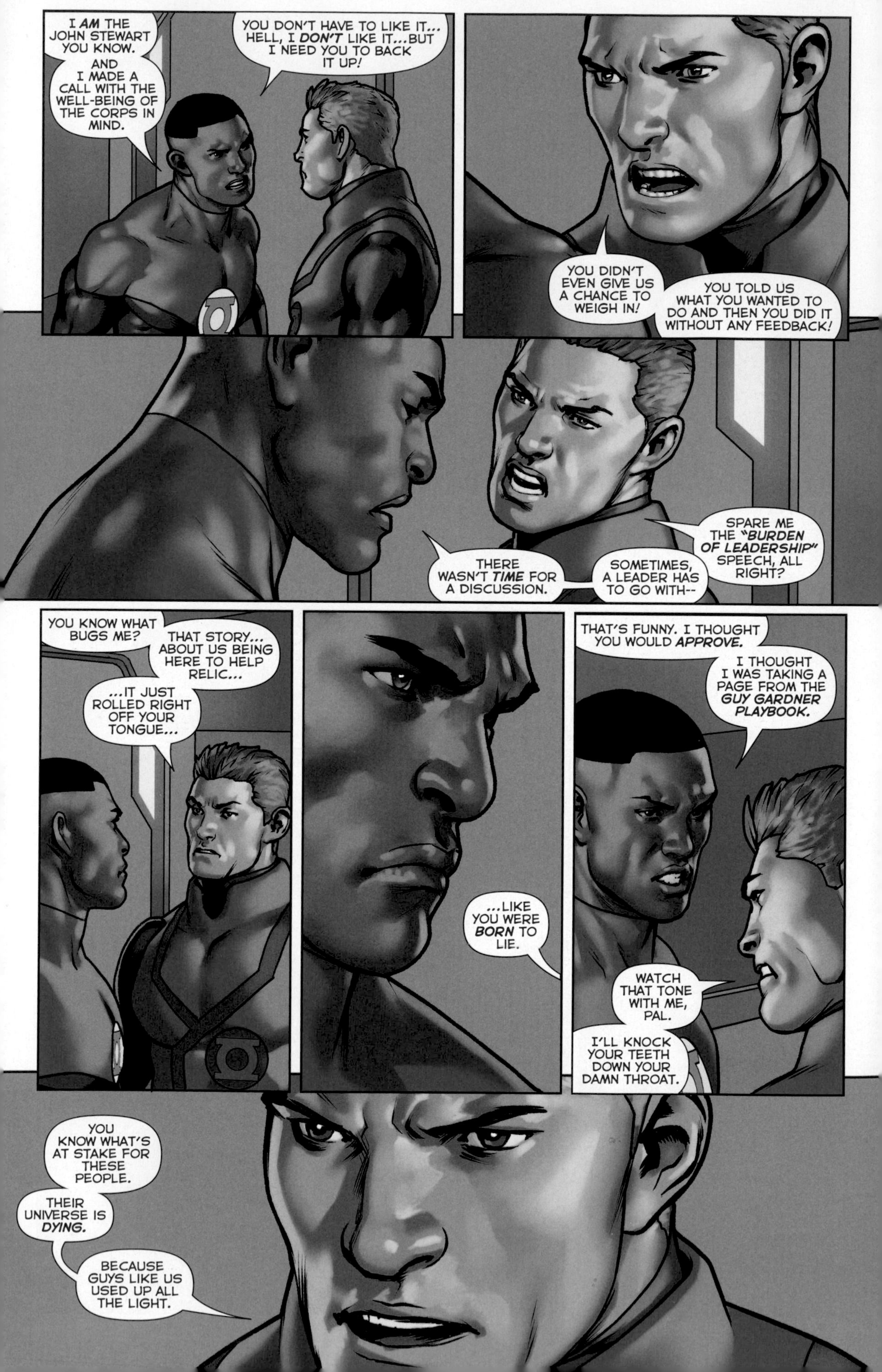
I AM THE JOHN STEWART YOU KNOW.
AND I MADE A CALL WITH THE WELL-BEING OF THE CORPS IN MIND.
YOU DON'T HAVE TO LIKE IT... HELL, I DON'T LIKE IT...BUT I NEED YOU TO BACK IT UP!
YOU DIDN'T EVEN GIVE US A CHANCE TO WEIGH IN!
YOU TOLD US WHAT YOU WANTED TO DO AND THEN YOU DID IT WITHOUT ANY FEEDBACK!
THERE WASN'T TIME FOR A DISCUSSION.
SOMETIMES, A LEADER HAS TO GO WITH--
SPARE ME THE "BURDEN OF LEADERSHIP" SPEECH, ALL RIGHT?
YOU KNOW WHAT BUGS ME?
THAT STORY... ABOUT US BEING HERE TO HELP RELIC...
...IT JUST ROLLED RIGHT OFF YOUR TONGUE...
...LIKE YOU WERE BORN TO LIE.
THAT'S FUNNY. I THOUGHT YOU WOULD APPROVE.
I THOUGHT I WAS TAKING A PAGE FROM THE GUY GARDNER PLAYBOOK.
WATCH THAT TONE WITH ME, PAL.
I'LL KNOCK YOUR TEETH DOWN YOUR DAMN THROAT.
YOU KNOW WHAT'S AT STAKE FOR THESE PEOPLE.
THEIR UNIVERSE IS DYING.
BECAUSE GUYS LIKE US USED UP ALL THE LIGHT.

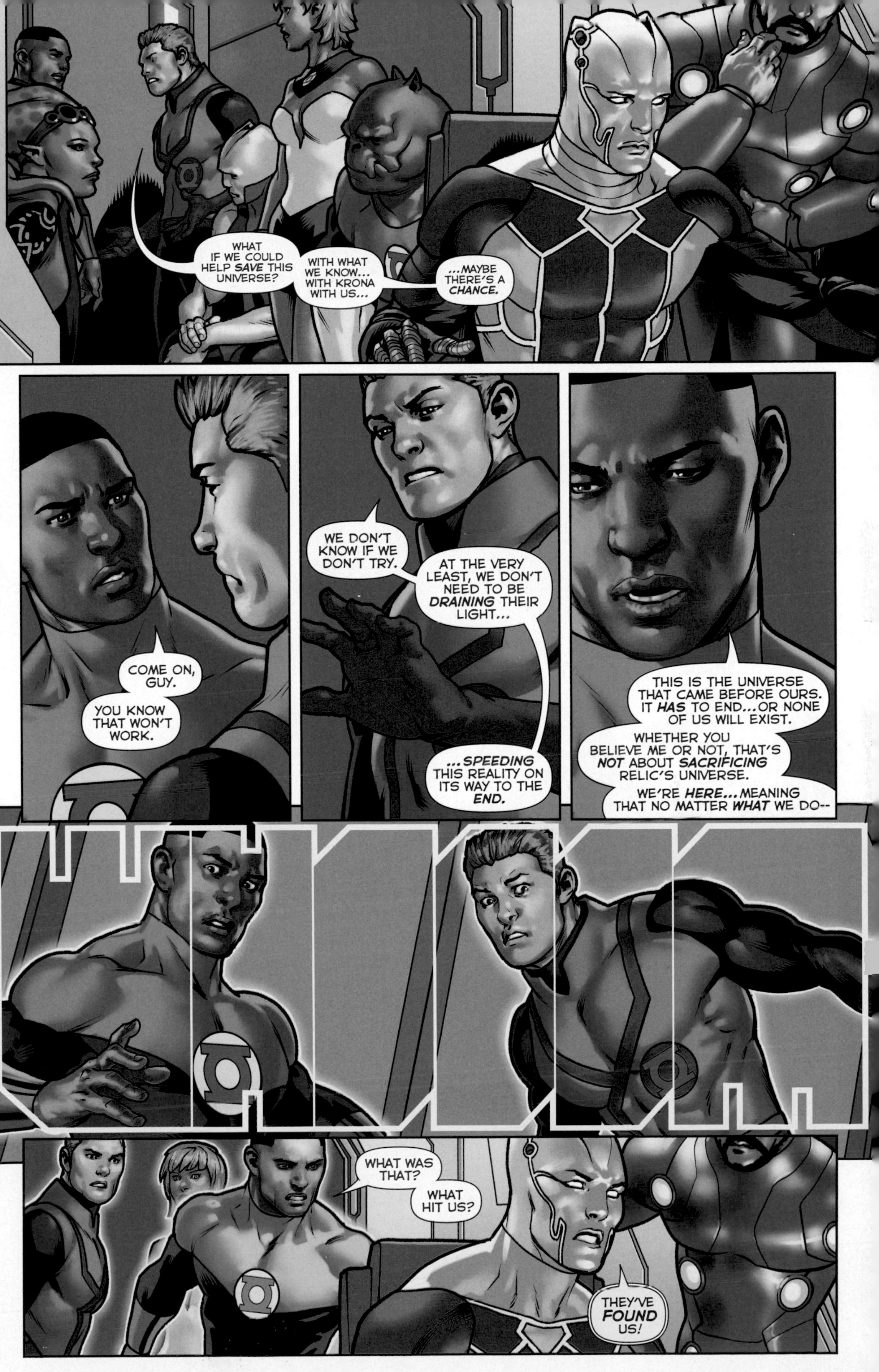
WHAT IF WE COULD HELP SAVE THIS UNIVERSE?
WITH WHAT WE KNOW... WITH KRONA WITH US...
...MAYBE THERE'S A CHANCE.
COME ON, GUY.
YOU KNOW THAT WON'T WORK.
WE DON'T KNOW IF WE DON'T TRY.
AT THE VERY LEAST, WE DON'T NEED TO BE DRAINING THEIR LIGHT...
...SPEEDING THIS REALITY ON ITS WAY TO THE END.
THIS IS THE UNIVERSE THAT CAME BEFORE OURS. IT HAS TO END...OR NONE OF US WILL EXIST.
WHETHER YOU BELIEVE ME OR NOT, THAT'S NOT ABOUT SACRIFICING RELIC'S UNIVERSE.
WE'RE HERE... MEANING THAT NO MATTER WHAT WE DO--
WHAT WAS THAT?
WHAT HIT US?
THEY'VE FOUND US!

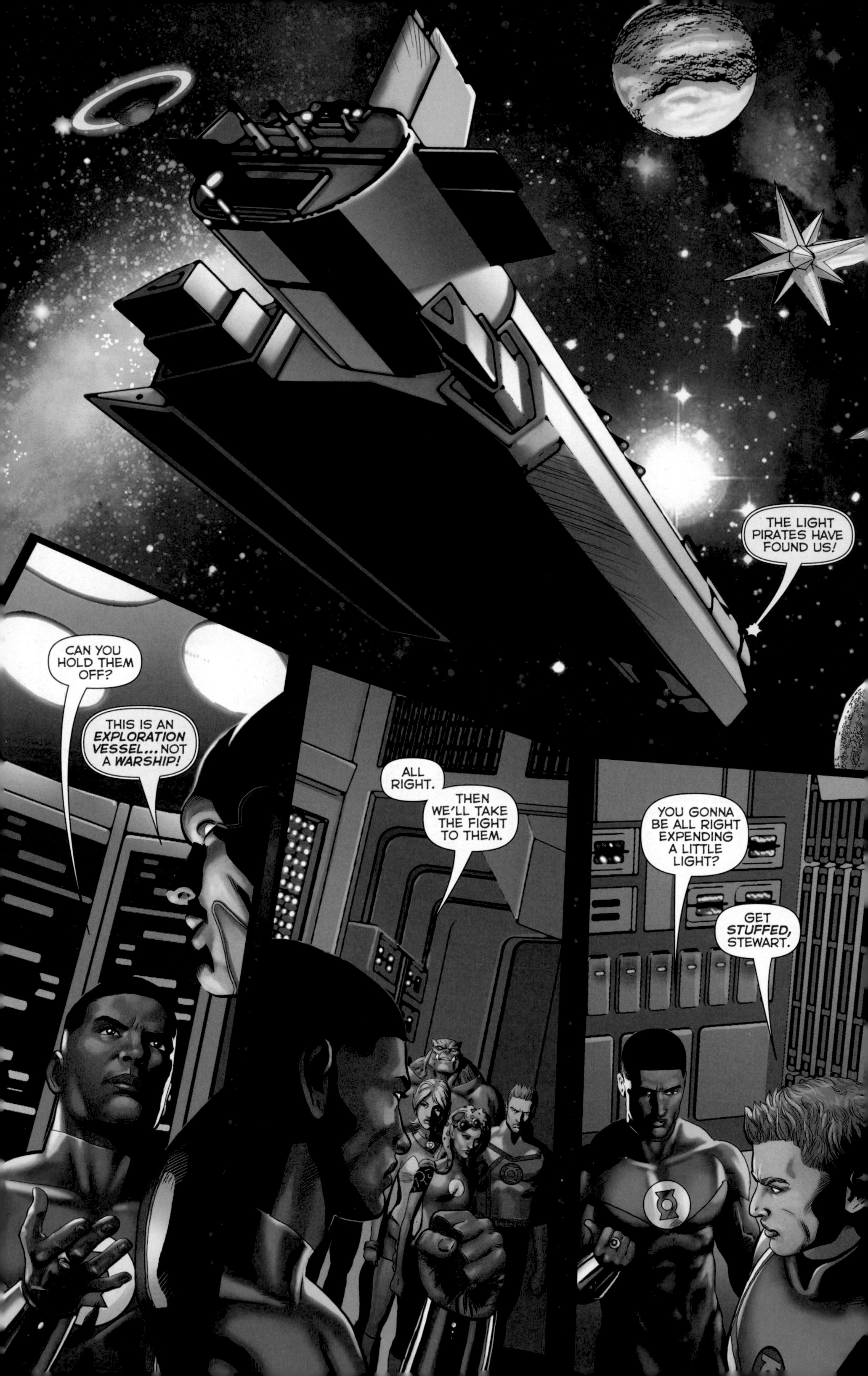
THE LIGHT PIRATES HAVE FOUND US!
CAN YOU HOLD THEM OFF?
THIS IS AN *EXPLORATION VESSEL*... NOT A *WARSHIP!*
ALL RIGHT.
THEN WE'LL TAKE THE FIGHT TO THEM.
YOU GONNA BE ALL RIGHT EXPENDING A LITTLE LIGHT?
GET *STUFFED,* STEWART.

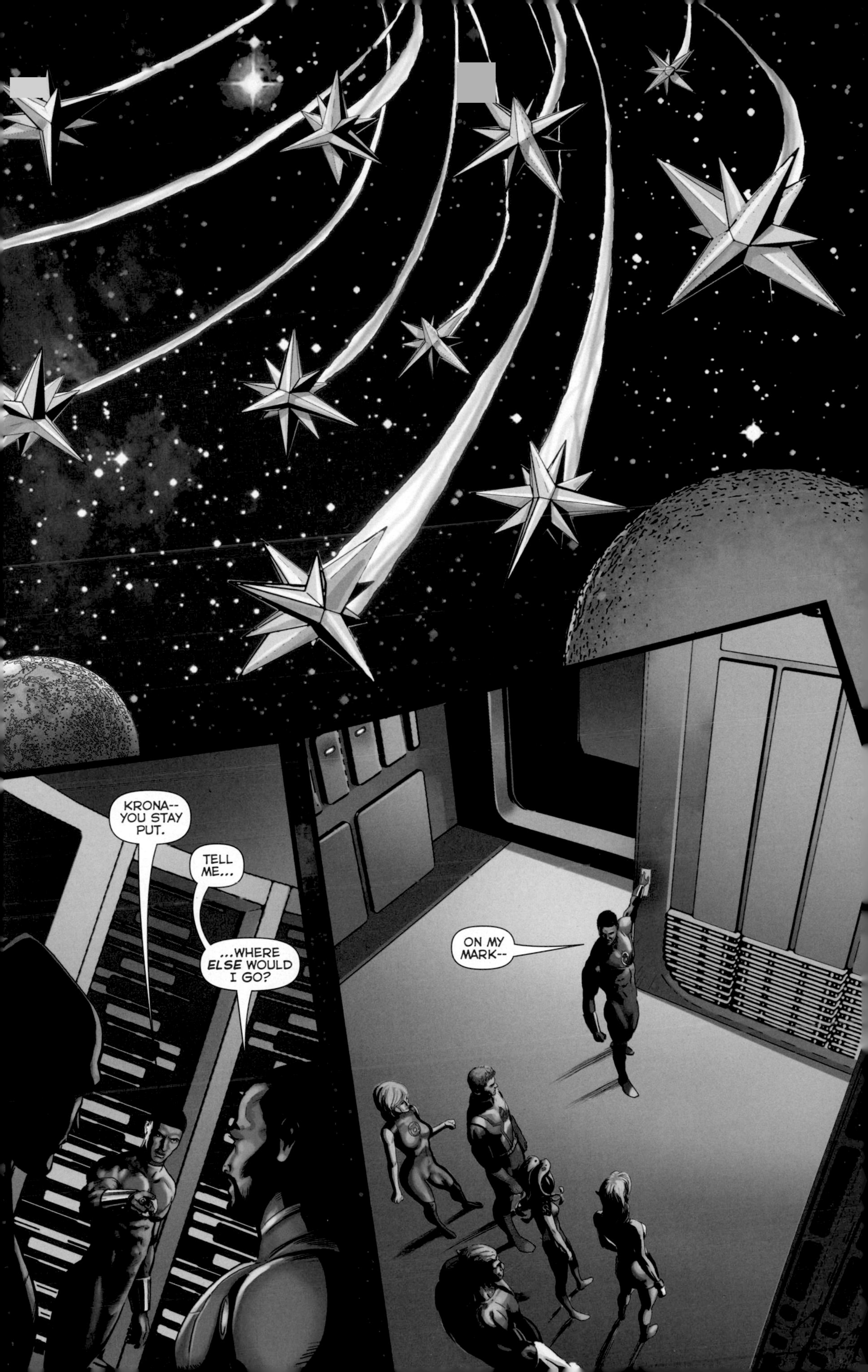
KRONA--
YOU STAY
PUT.
TELL
ME...
...WHERE
ELSE WOULD
I GO?
ON MY
MARK--

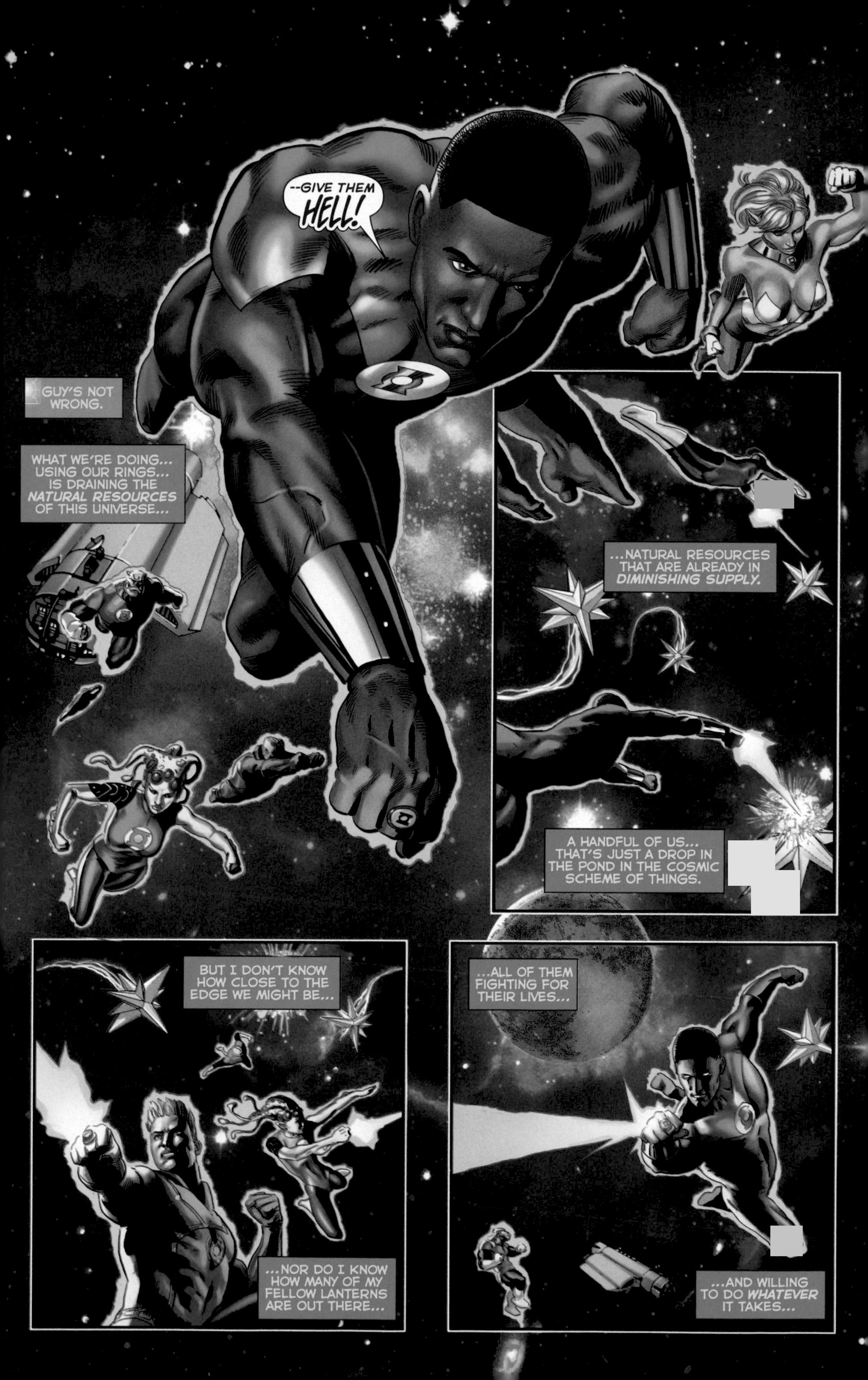
--GIVE THEM HELL!
GUY'S NOT WRONG.
WHAT WE'RE DOING... USING OUR RINGS... IS DRAINING THE NATURAL RESOURCES OF THIS UNIVERSE...
...NATURAL RESOURCES THAT ARE ALREADY IN DIMINISHING SUPPLY.
A HANDFUL OF US... THAT'S JUST A DROP IN THE POND IN THE COSMIC SCHEME OF THINGS.
BUT I DON'T KNOW HOW CLOSE TO THE EDGE WE MIGHT BE...
...NOR DO I KNOW HOW MANY OF MY FELLOW LANTERNS ARE OUT THERE...
...ALL OF THEM FIGHTING FOR THEIR LIVES...
...AND WILLING TO DO WHATEVER IT TAKES...

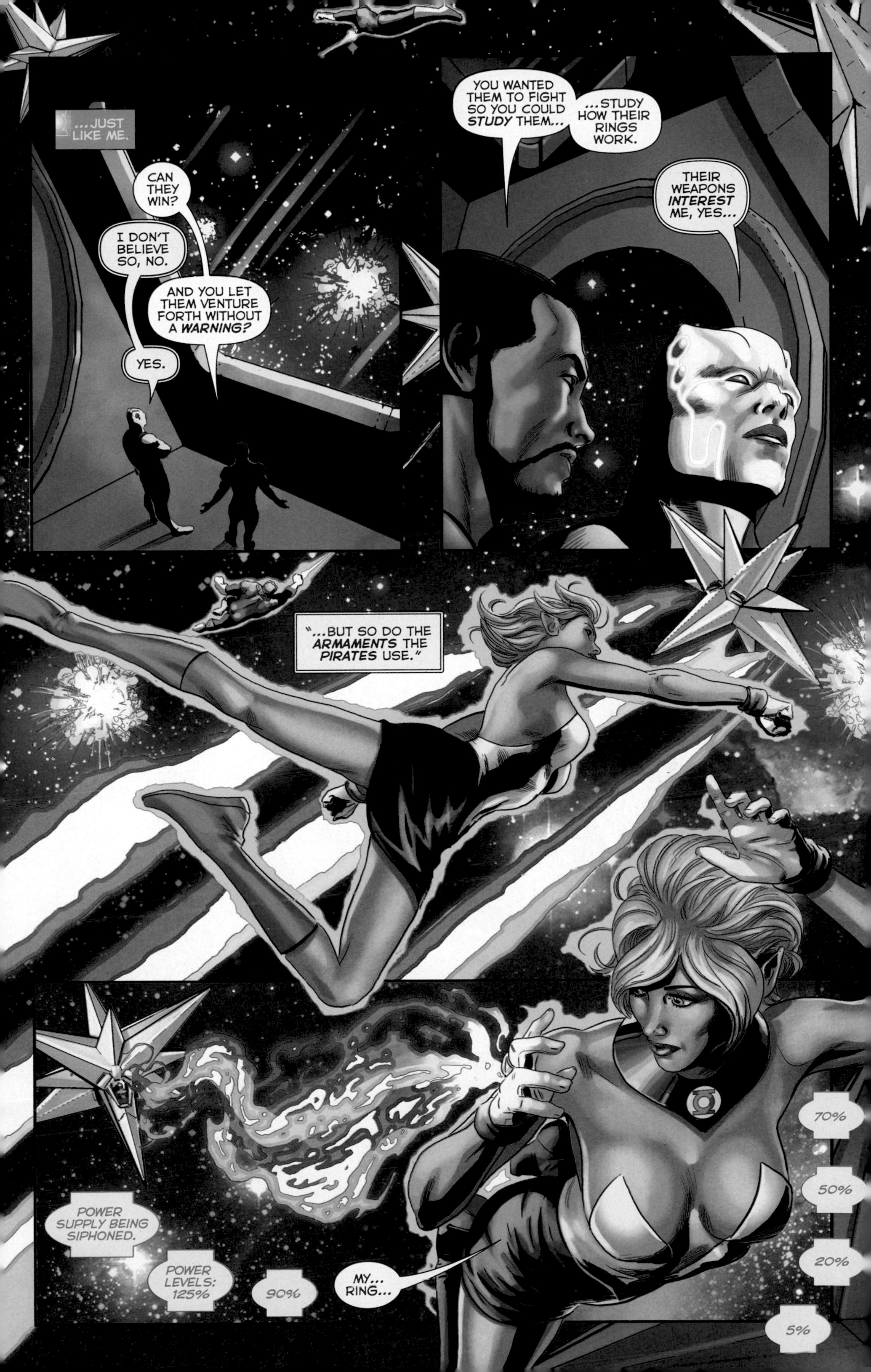
...JUST LIKE ME.
CAN THEY WIN?
I DON'T BELIEVE SO, NO.
AND YOU LET THEM VENTURE FORTH WITHOUT A WARNING?
YES.
YOU WANTED THEM TO FIGHT SO YOU COULD STUDY THEM...
...STUDY HOW THEIR RINGS WORK.
THEIR WEAPONS INTEREST ME, YES...
"...BUT SO DO THE ARMAMENTS THE PIRATES USE."
POWER SUPPLY BEING SIPHONED.
POWER LEVELS: 125%
90%
MY... RING...
70%
50%
20%
5%

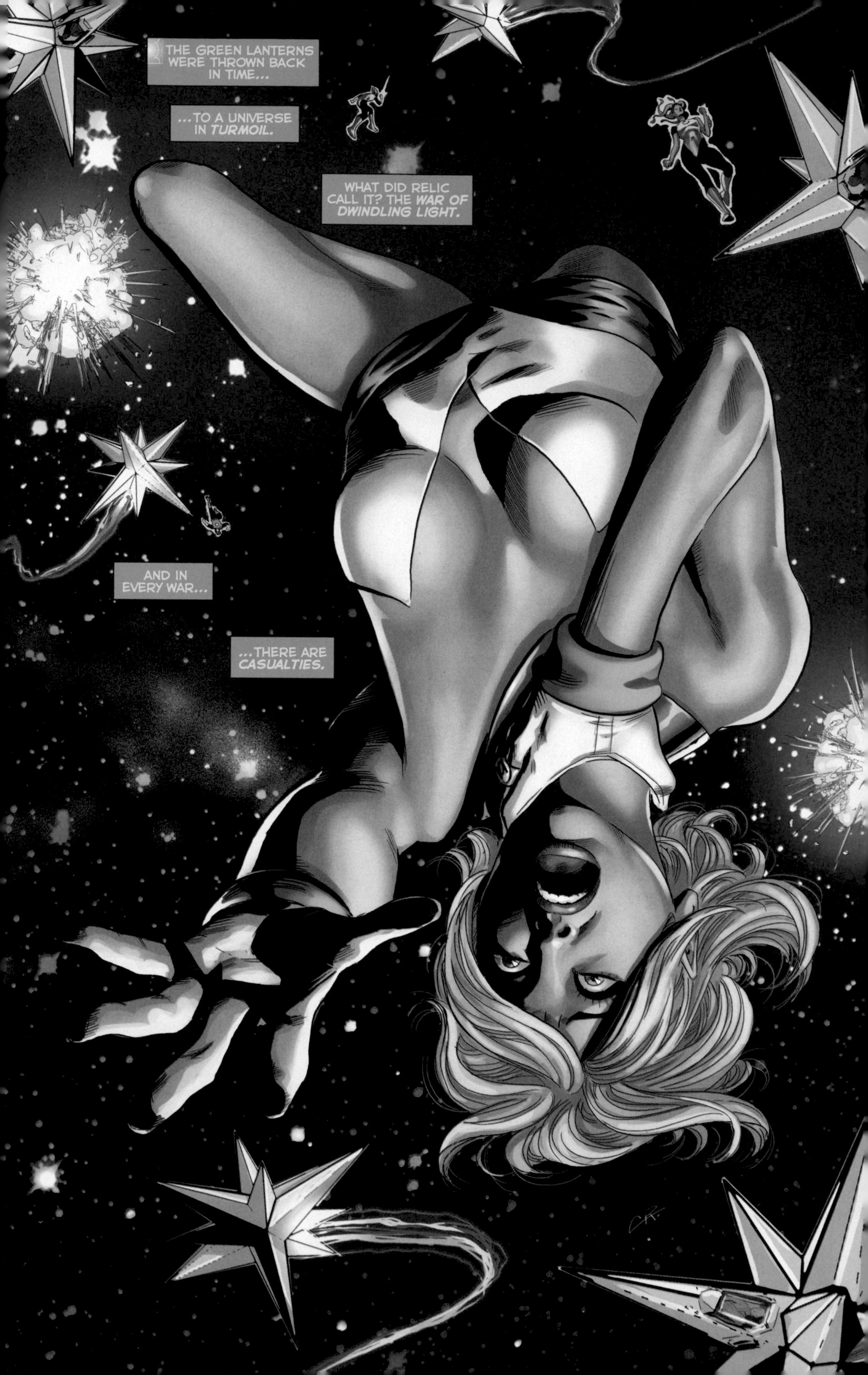
THE GREEN LANTERNS WERE THROWN BACK IN TIME...
...TO A UNIVERSE IN TURMOIL.
WHAT DID RELIC CALL IT? THE WAR OF DWINDLING LIGHT.
AND IN EVERY WAR...
...THERE ARE CASUALTIES.

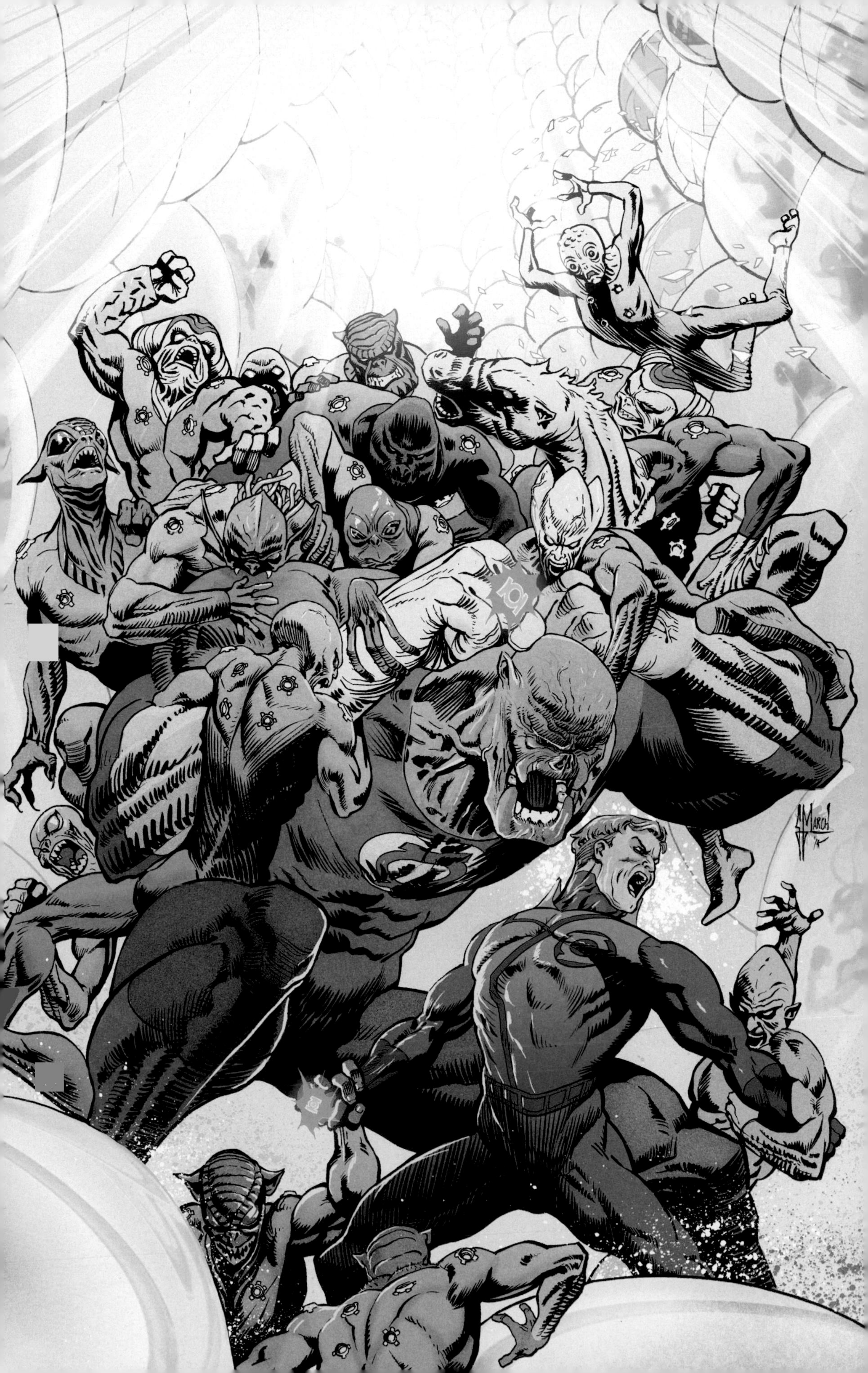

CULLEN BUNN writer JAVIER PIÑA artist CHRIS SOTOMAYOR colorist DAVE SHARPE letterer GUILLEM MARCH cover

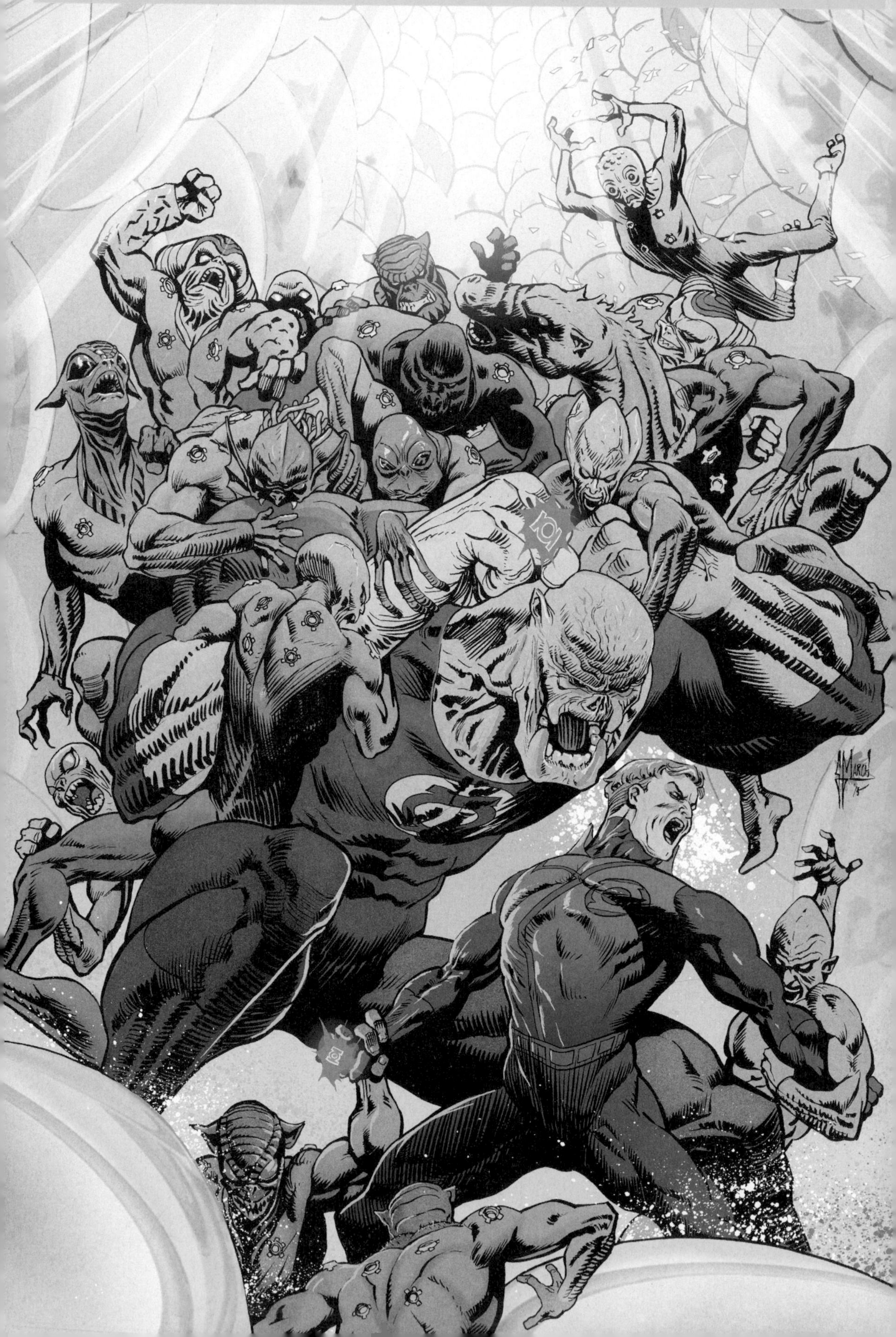

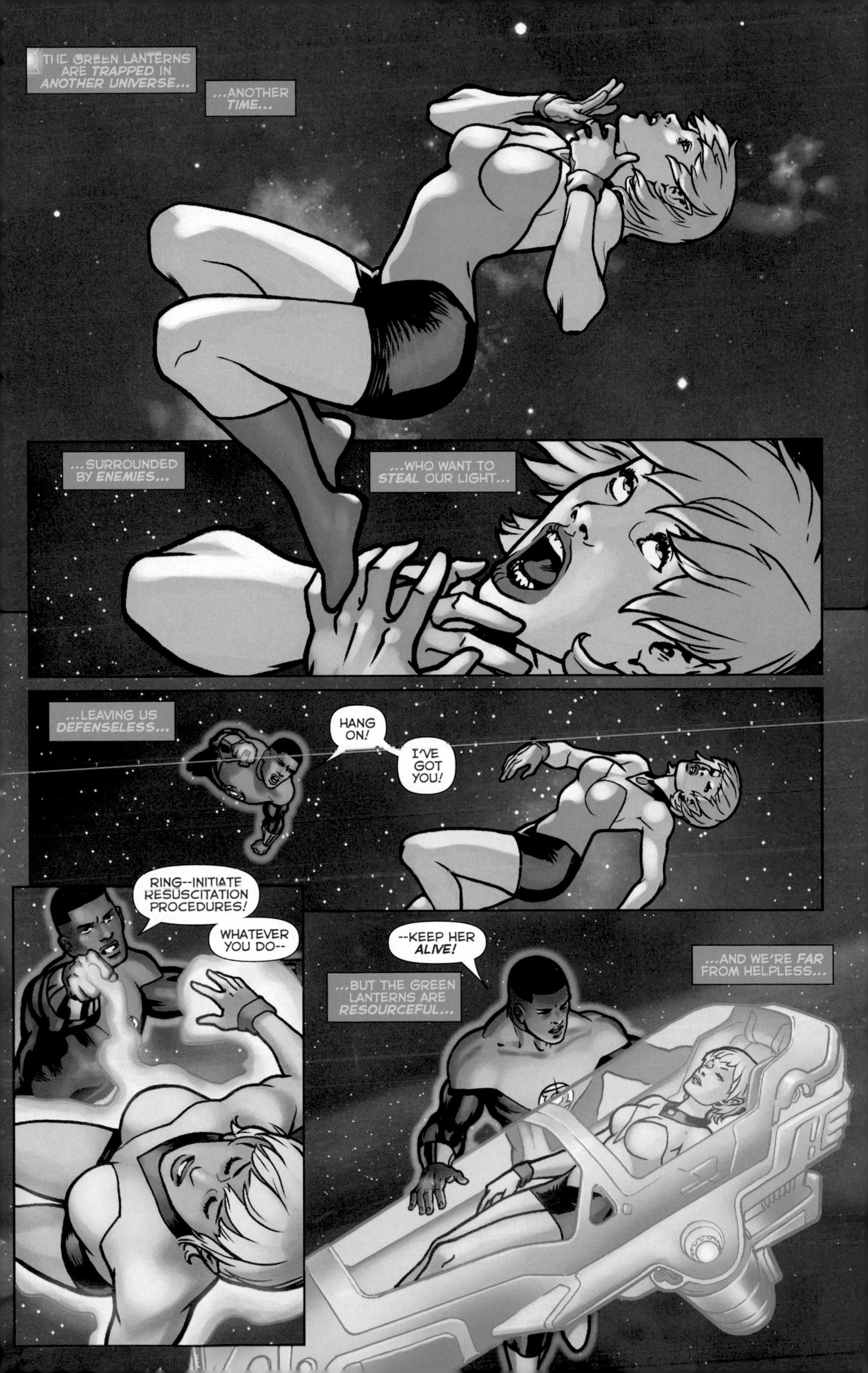
THE GREEN LANTERNS ARE TRAPPED IN ANOTHER UNIVERSE...
...ANOTHER TIME...
...SURROUNDED BY ENEMIES...
...WHO WANT TO STEAL OUR LIGHT...
...LEAVING US DEFENSELESS...
HANG ON!
I'VE GOT YOU!
RING--INITIATE RESUSCITATION PROCEDURES!
WHATEVER YOU DO--
--KEEP HER ALIVE!
...BUT THE GREEN LANTERNS ARE RESOURCEFUL...
...AND WE'RE FAR FROM HELPLESS...

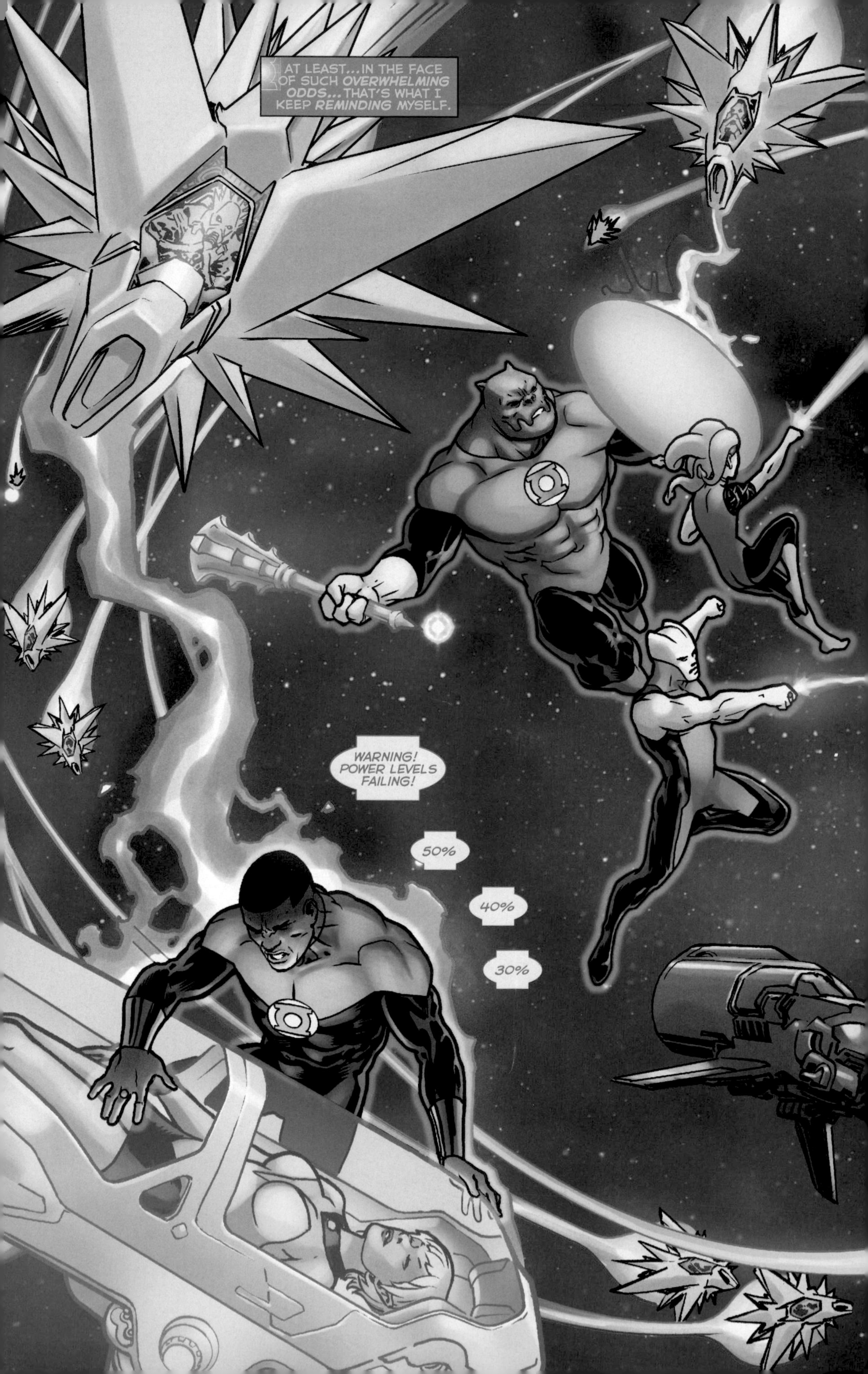
AT LEAST...IN THE FACE OF SUCH OVERWHELMING ODDS...THAT'S WHAT I KEEP REMINDING MYSELF.
WARNING! POWER LEVELS FAILING!
50%
40%
30%

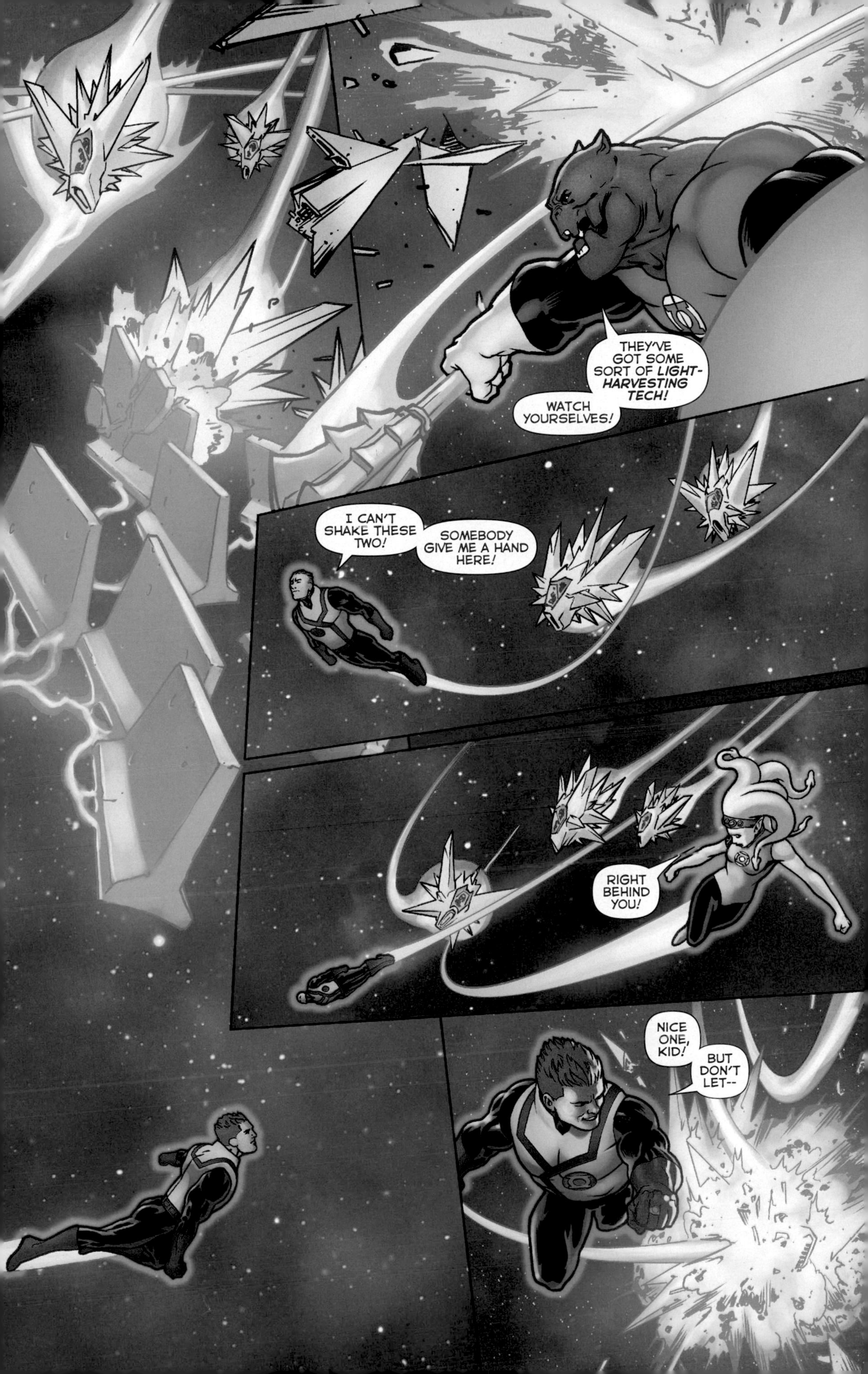

THEY'VE GOT SOME SORT OF LIGHT-HARVESTING TECH!
WATCH YOURSELVES!
I CAN'T SHAKE THESE TWO!
SOMEBODY GIVE ME A HAND HERE!
RIGHT BEHIND YOU!
NICE ONE, KID!
BUT DON'T LET--

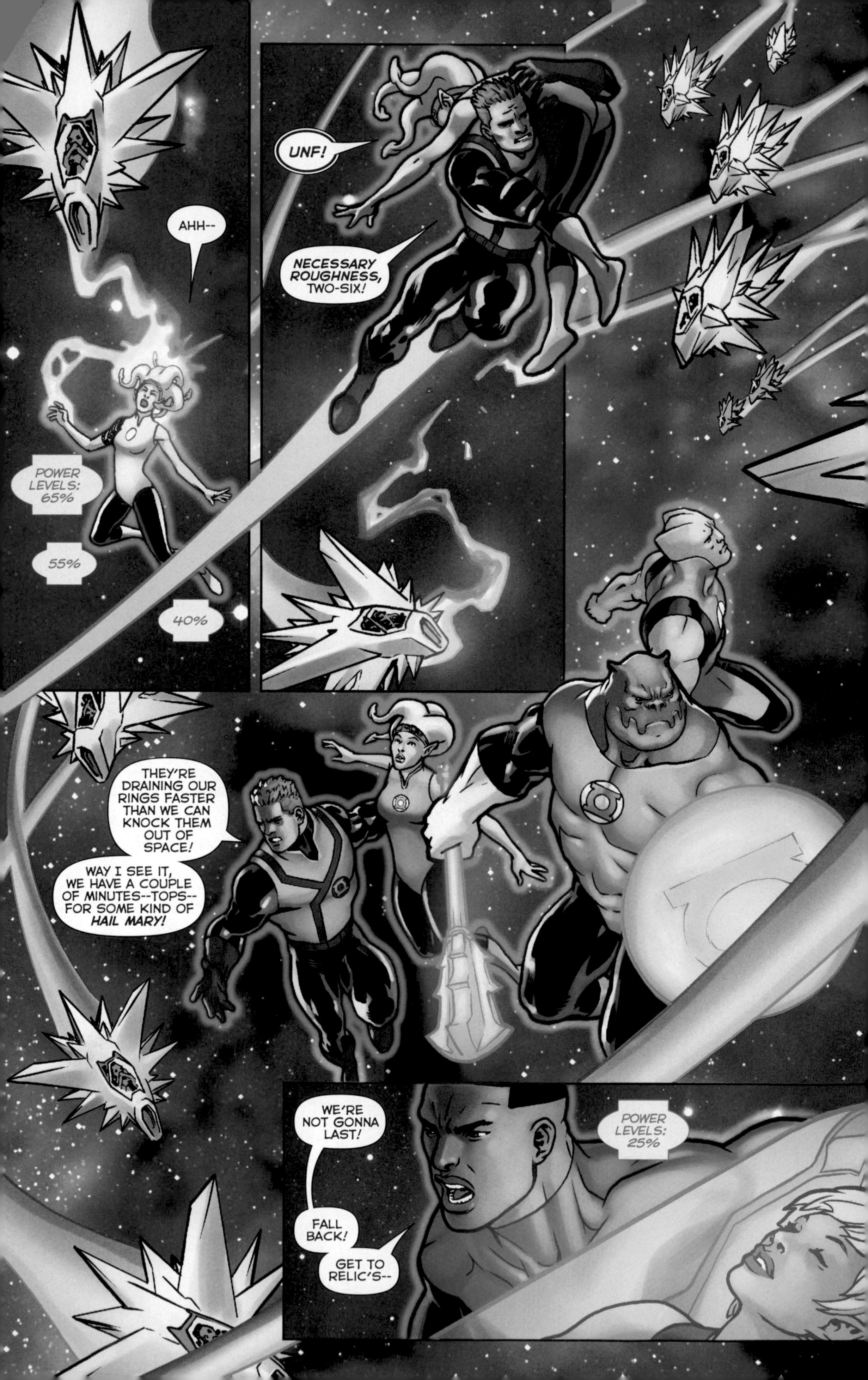
AHH--
POWER LEVELS: 65%
55%
40%
UNF!
NECESSARY ROUGHNESS, TWO-SIX!
THEY'RE DRAINING OUR RINGS FASTER THAN WE CAN KNOCK THEM OUT OF SPACE!
WAY I SEE IT, WE HAVE A COUPLE OF MINUTES--TOPS--FOR SOME KIND OF HAIL MARY!
WE'RE NOT GONNA LAST!
FALL BACK!
GET TO RELIC'S--
POWER LEVELS: 25%

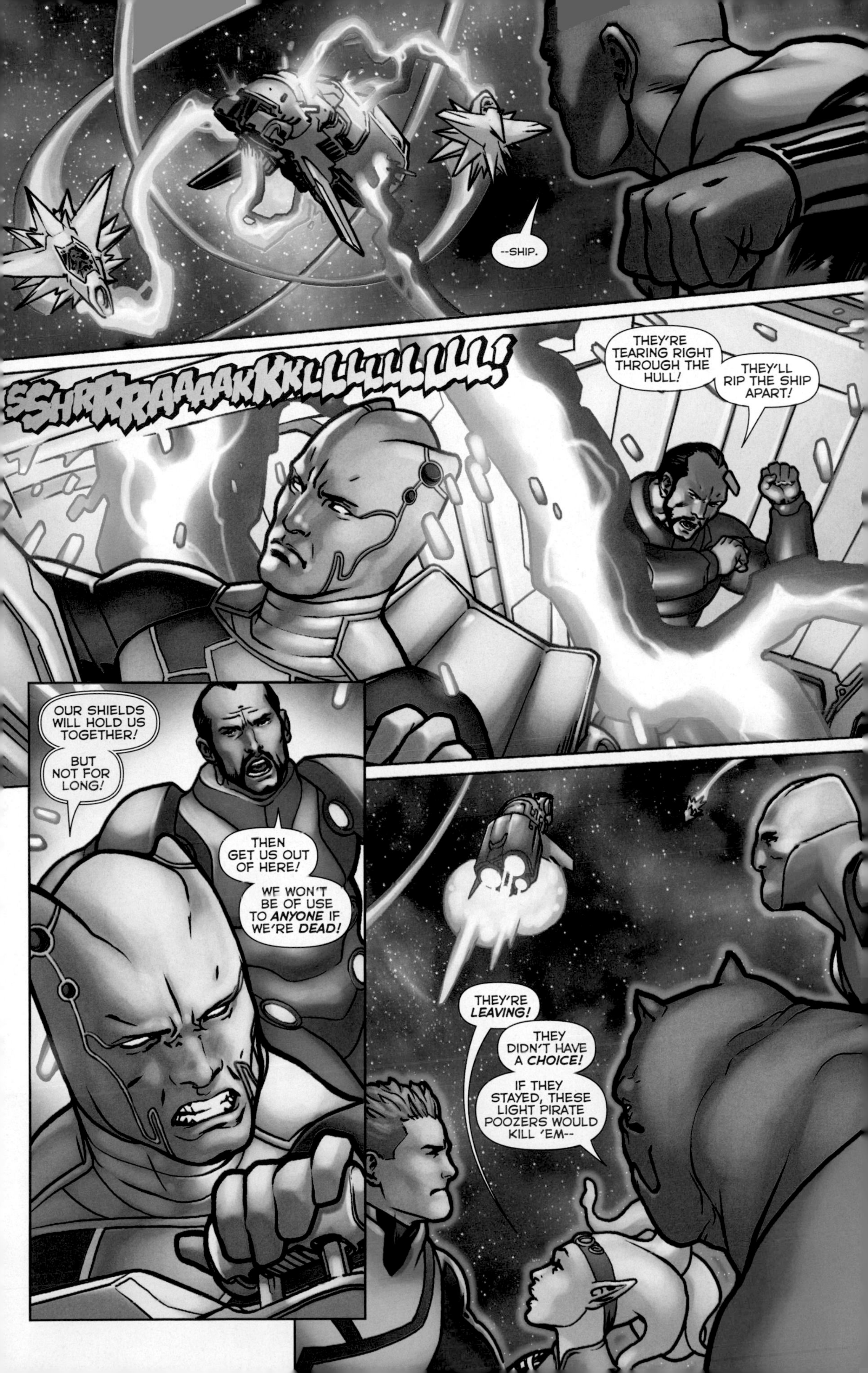
--SHIP.
SSHRRRAAAAKKKLLLLLLLLL!
THEY'RE TEARING RIGHT THROUGH THE HULL!
THEY'LL RIP THE SHIP APART!
OUR SHIELDS WILL HOLD US TOGETHER!
BUT NOT FOR LONG!
THEN GET US OUT OF HERE!
WE WON'T BE OF USE TO ANYONE IF WE'RE DEAD!
THEY'RE LEAVING!
THEY DIDN'T HAVE A CHOICE!
IF THEY STAYED, THESE LIGHT PIRATE POOZERS WOULD KILL 'EM--

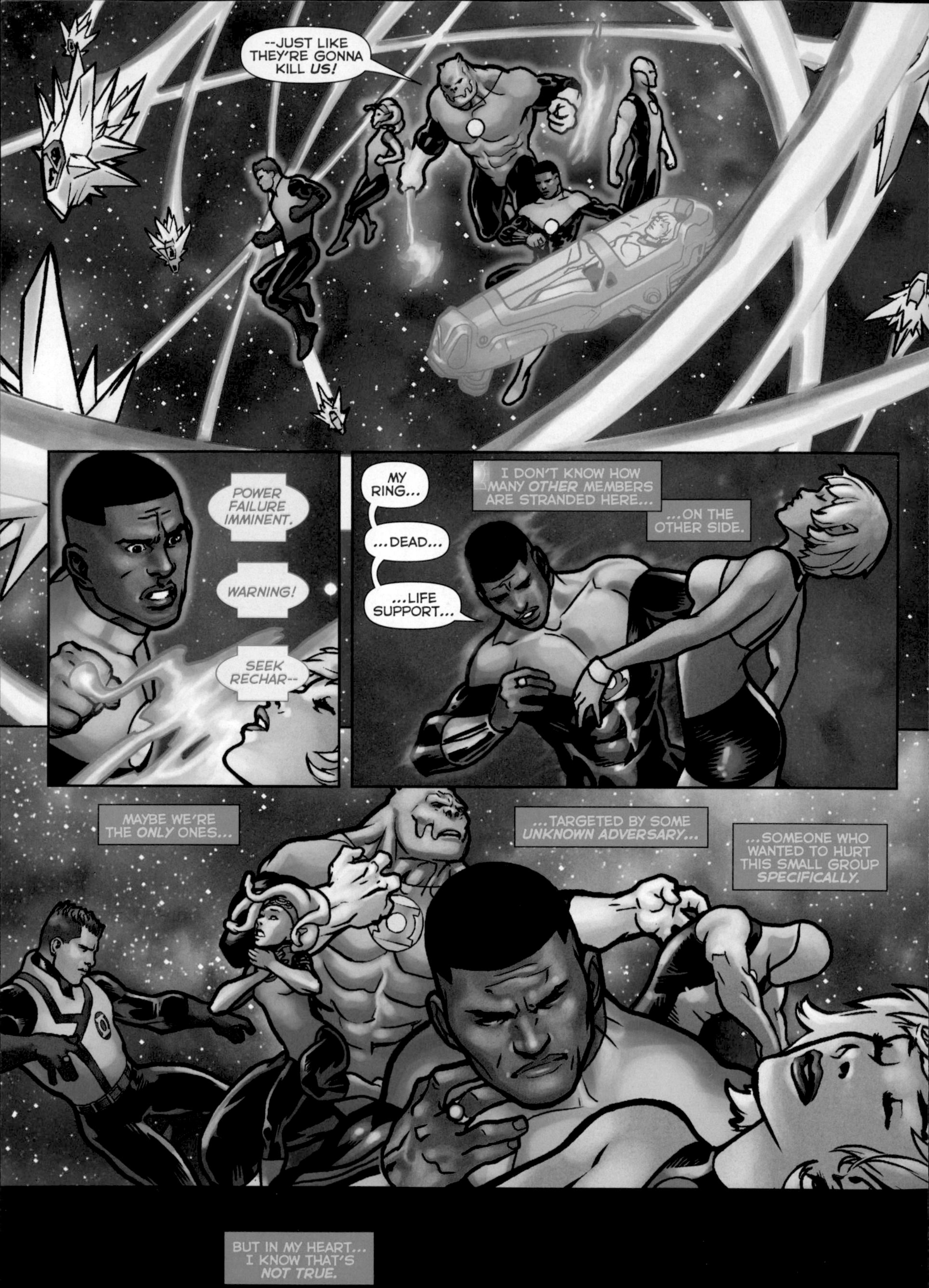

--JUST LIKE THEY'RE GONNA KILL *US!*
POWER FAILURE IMMINENT.
WARNING!
SEEK RECHAR--
MY RING...
...DEAD...
...LIFE SUPPORT...
I DON'T KNOW HOW MANY *OTHER* MEMBERS ARE STRANDED HERE...
...ON THE OTHER SIDE.
MAYBE WE'RE THE *ONLY* ONES...
...TARGETED BY SOME *UNKNOWN ADVERSARY...*
...SOMEONE WHO WANTED TO HURT THIS SMALL GROUP *SPECIFICALLY.*
BUT IN MY HEART... I KNOW THAT'S *NOT TRUE.*

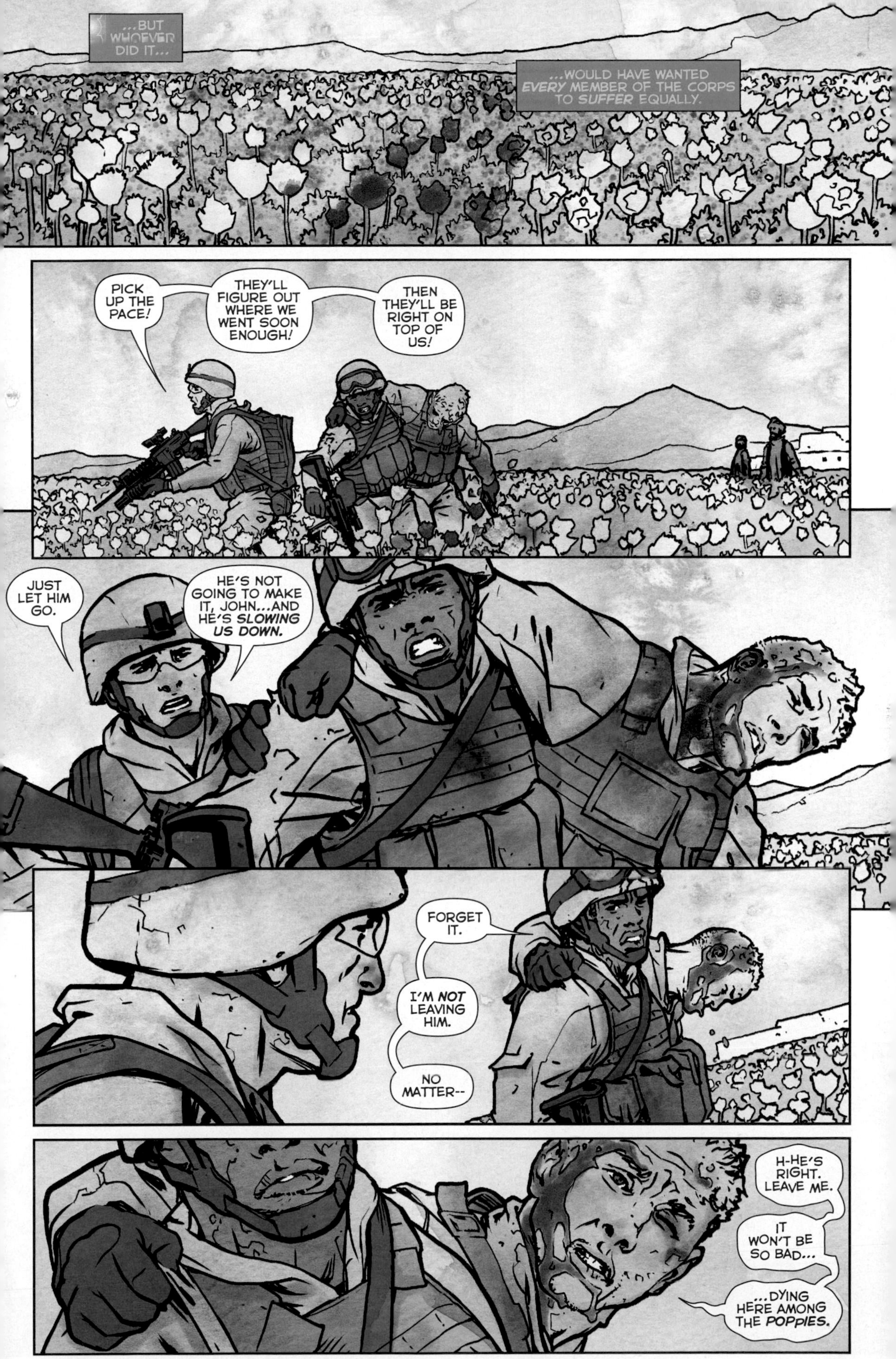
...BUT WHOEVER DID IT...
...WOULD HAVE WANTED EVERY MEMBER OF THE CORPS TO SUFFER EQUALLY.
PICK UP THE PACE!
THEY'LL FIGURE OUT WHERE WE WENT SOON ENOUGH!
THEN THEY'LL BE RIGHT ON TOP OF US!
JUST LET HIM GO.
HE'S NOT GOING TO MAKE IT, JOHN...AND HE'S SLOWING US DOWN.
FORGET IT.
I'M NOT LEAVING HIM.
NO MATTER--
H-HE'S RIGHT. LEAVE ME.
IT WON'T BE SO BAD...
...DYING HERE AMONG THE POPPIES.

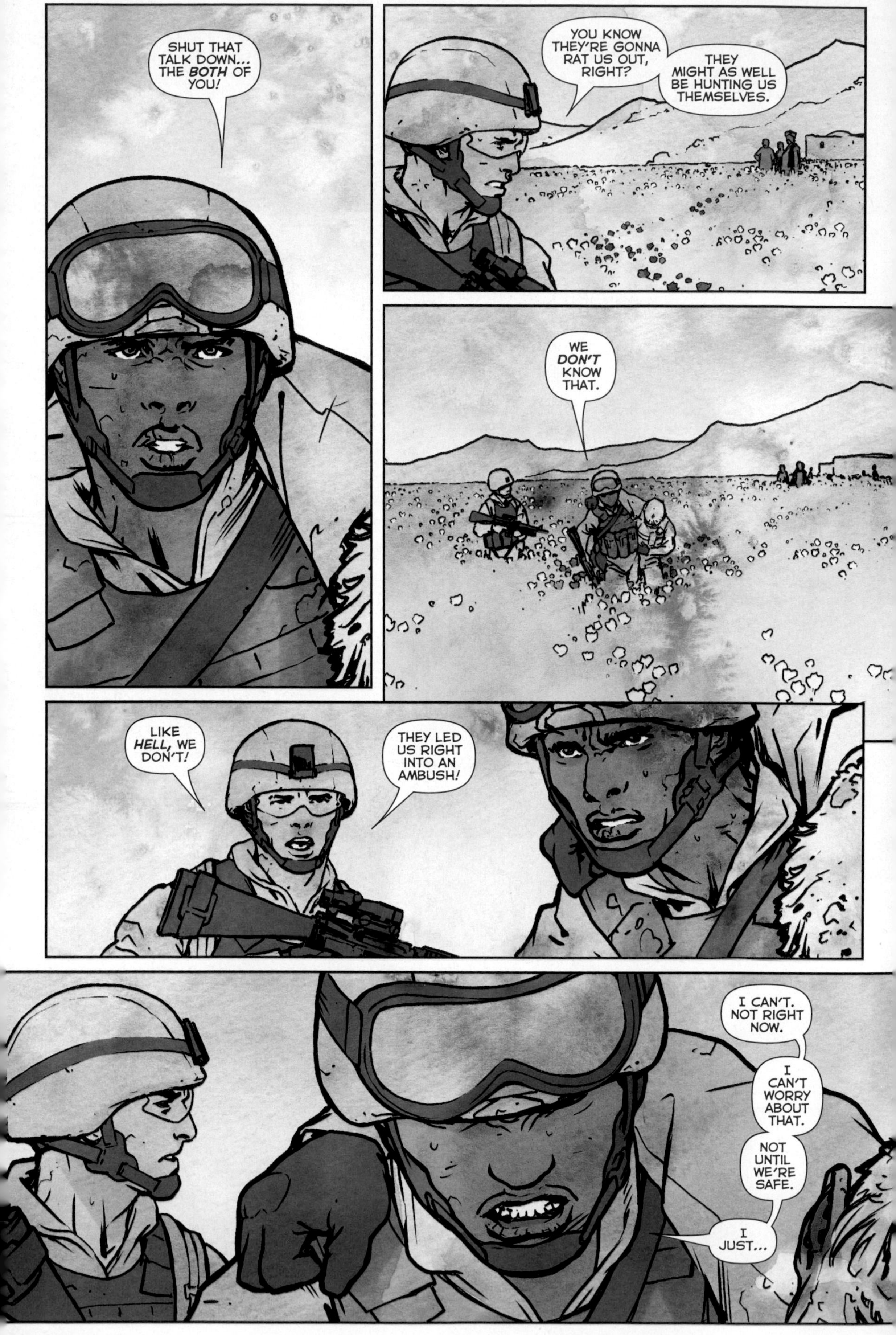
SHUT THAT TALK DOWN... THE *BOTH* OF YOU!
YOU KNOW THEY'RE GONNA RAT US OUT, RIGHT?
THEY MIGHT AS WELL BE HUNTING US THEMSELVES.
WE *DON'T* KNOW THAT.
LIKE *HELL*, WE DON'T!
THEY LED US RIGHT INTO AN AMBUSH!
I CAN'T. NOT RIGHT NOW.
I CAN'T WORRY ABOUT THAT.
NOT UNTIL WE'RE SAFE.
I JUST...

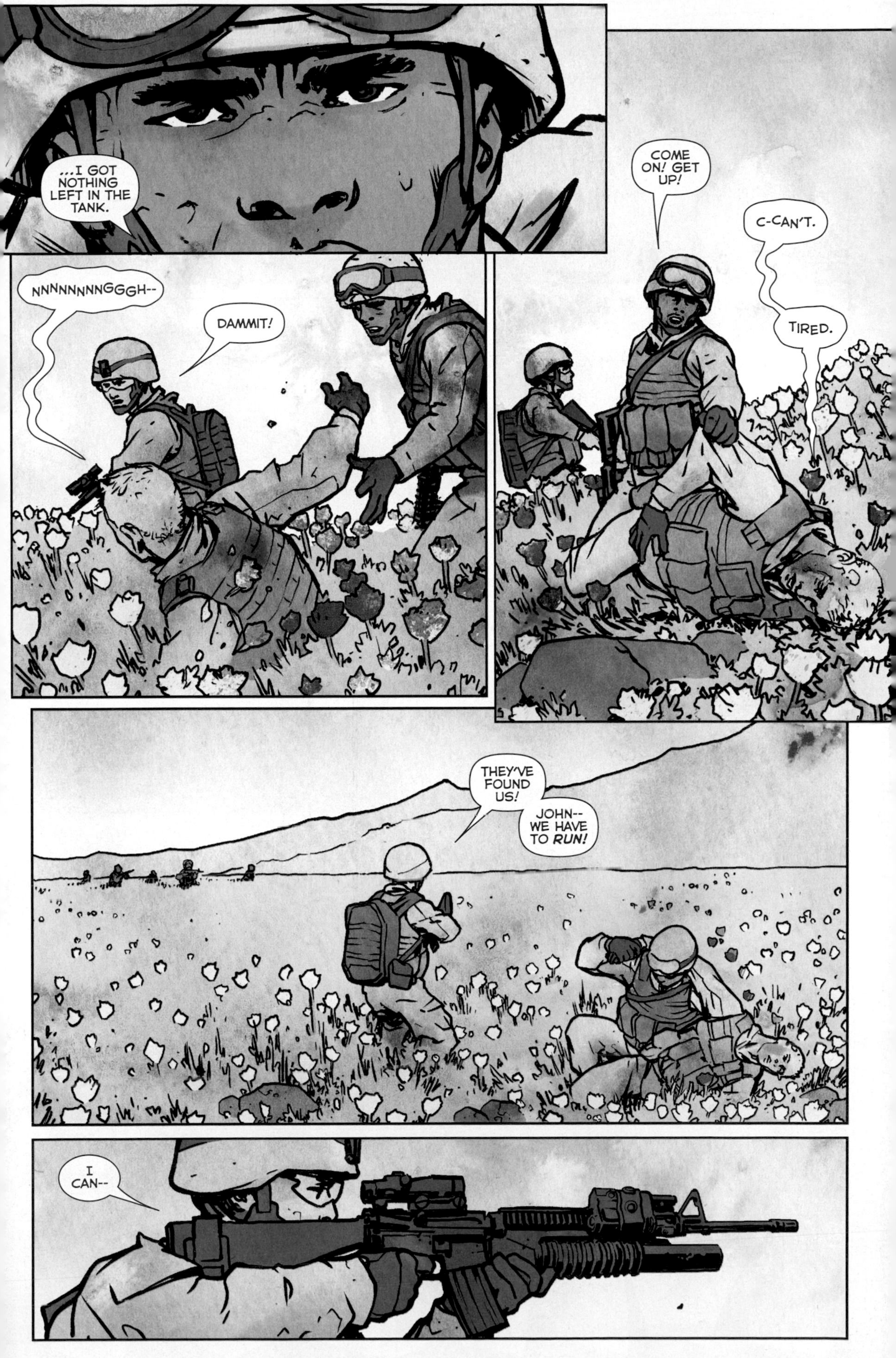
...I GOT NOTHING LEFT IN THE TANK.
NNNNNNNNGGGH--
DAMMIT!
COME ON! GET UP!
C-CAN'T.
TIRED.
THEY'VE FOUND US!
JOHN-- WE HAVE TO *RUN!*
I CAN--

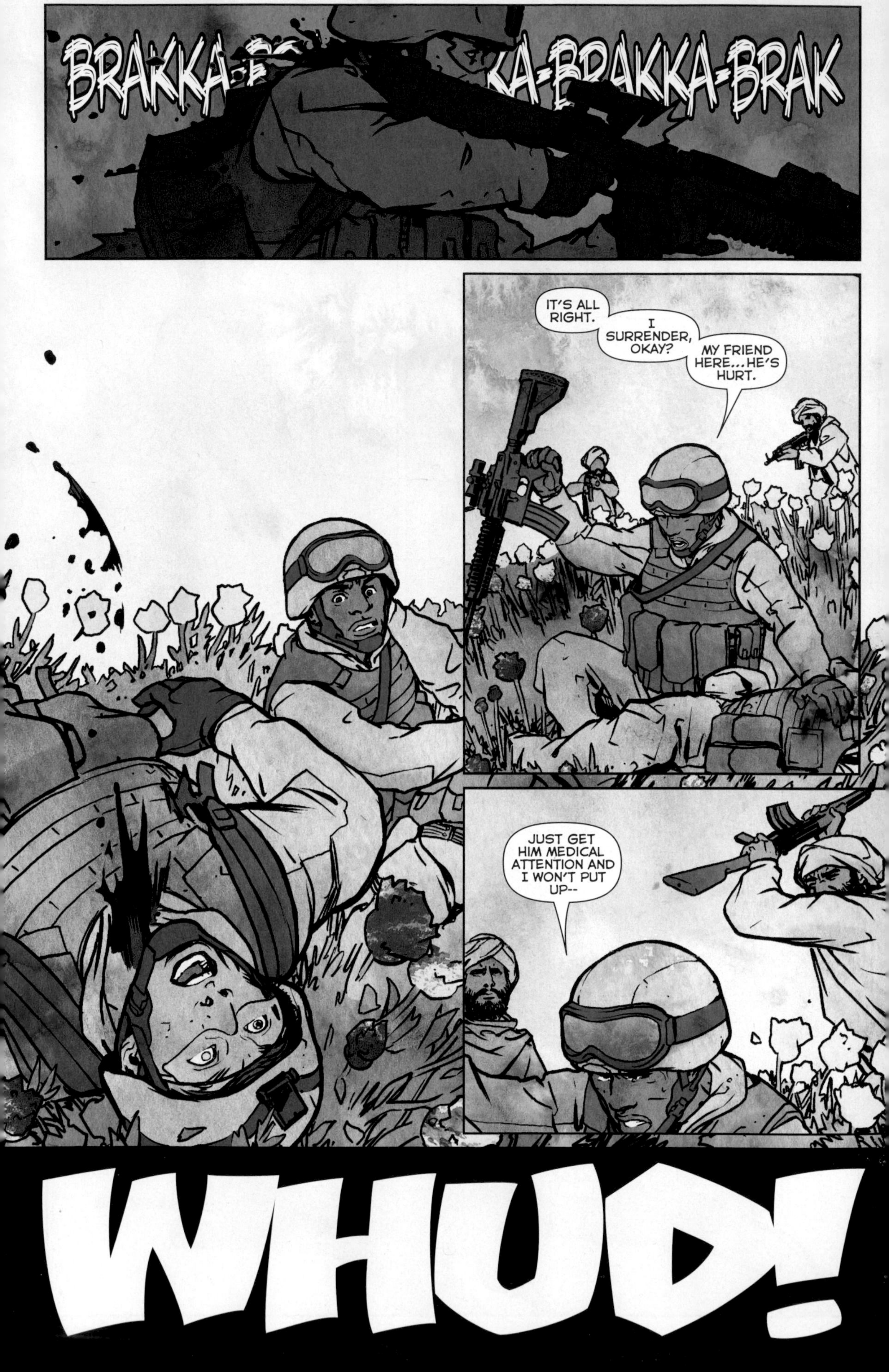
BRAKKA-BR
KA-BRAKKA-BRAK
IT'S ALL RIGHT.
I SURRENDER, OKAY?
MY FRIEND HERE...HE'S HURT.
JUST GET HIM MEDICAL ATTENTION AND I WON'T PUT UP--
WHUD!

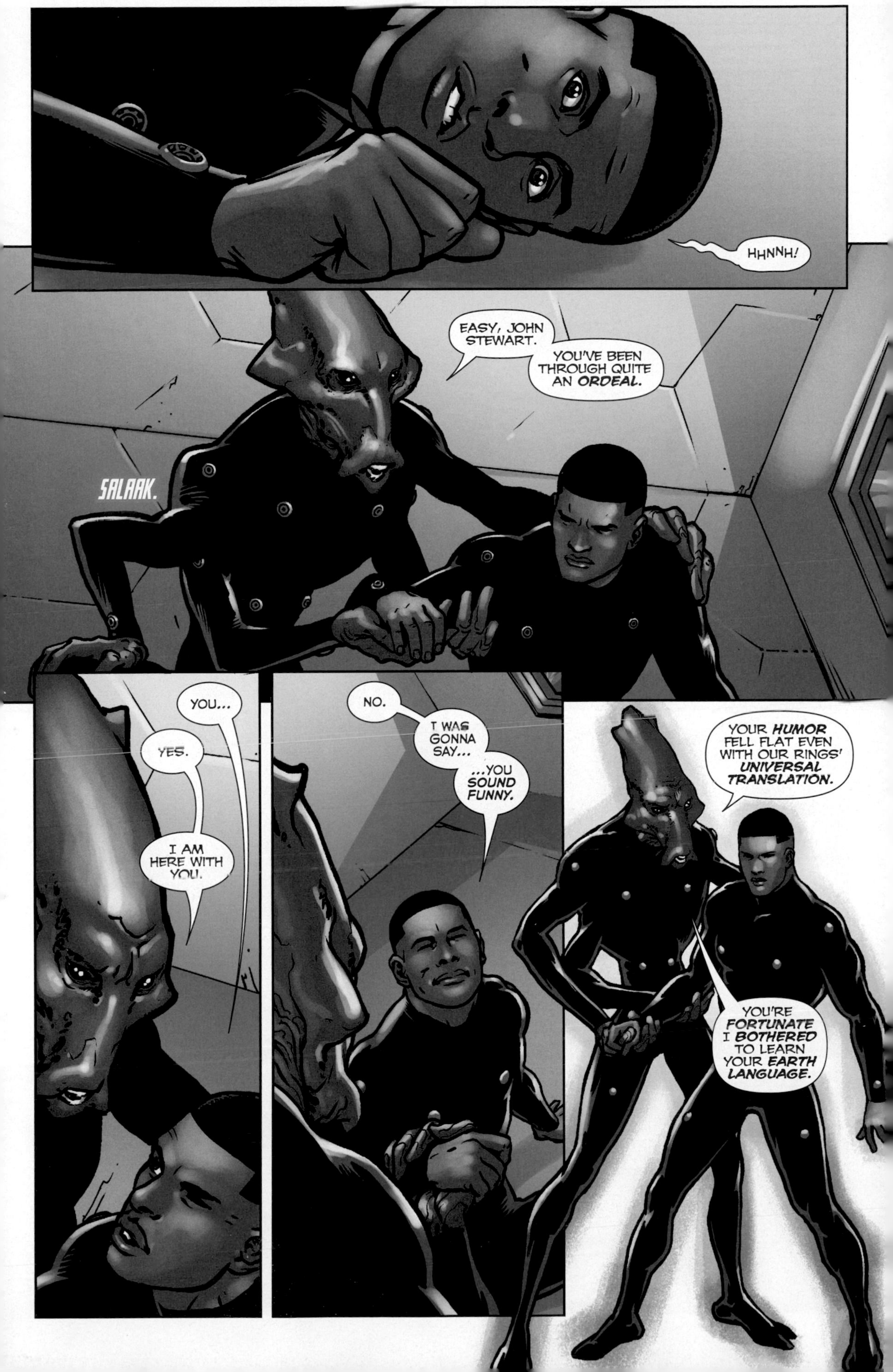
HHNNH!
EASY, JOHN STEWART.
YOU'VE BEEN THROUGH QUITE AN ORDEAL.
SALAAK.
YOU...
YES.
I AM HERE WITH YOU.
NO.
I WAS GONNA SAY...
...YOU SOUND FUNNY.
YOUR HUMOR FELL FLAT EVEN WITH OUR RINGS' UNIVERSAL TRANSLATION.
YOU'RE FORTUNATE I BOTHERED TO LEARN YOUR EARTH LANGUAGE.

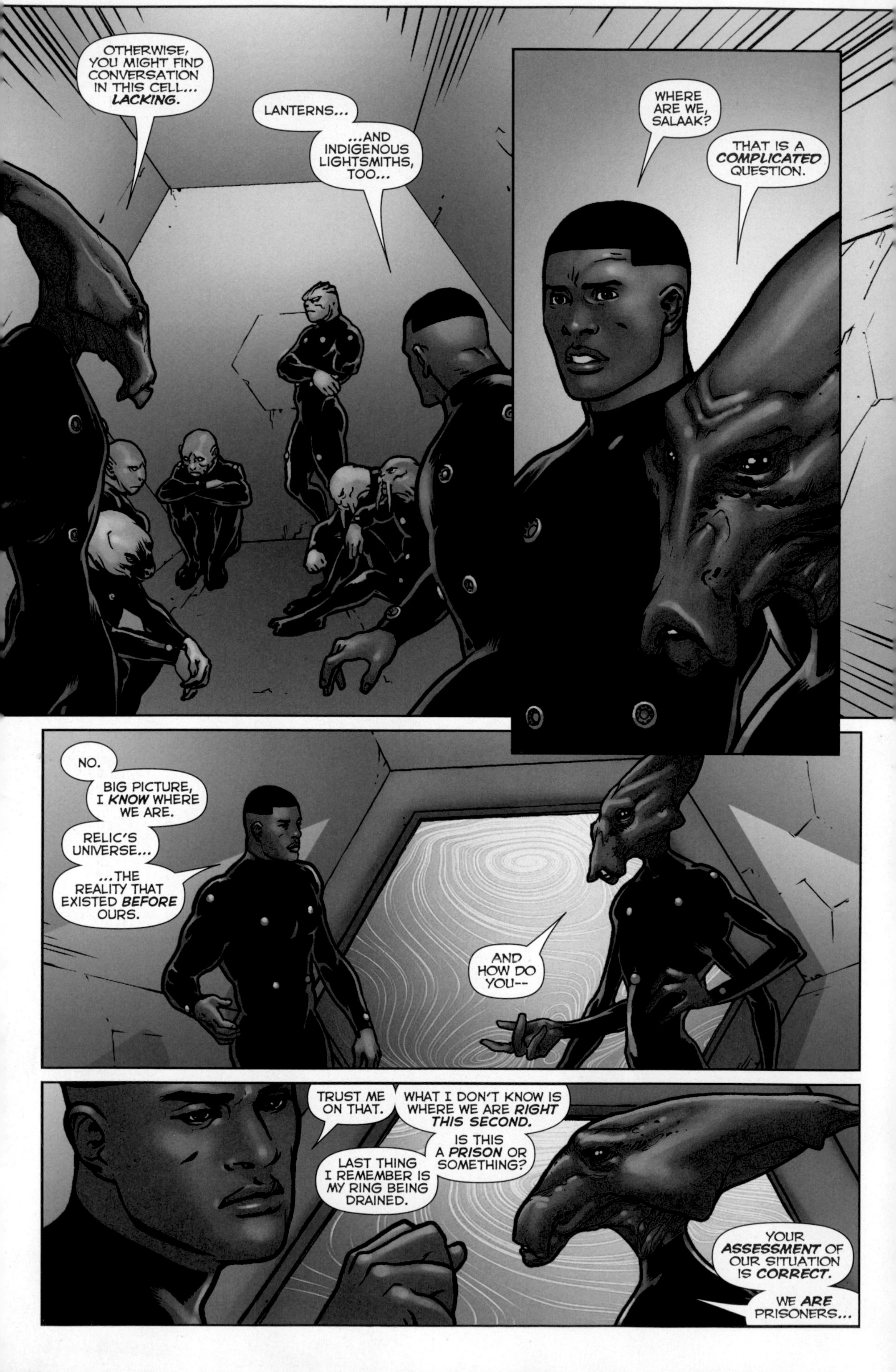
OTHERWISE, YOU MIGHT FIND CONVERSATION IN THIS CELL... LACKING.
LANTERNS...
...AND INDIGENOUS LIGHTSMITHS, TOO...
WHERE ARE WE, SALAAK?
THAT IS A COMPLICATED QUESTION.
NO.
BIG PICTURE, I KNOW WHERE WE ARE.
RELIC'S UNIVERSE...
...THE REALITY THAT EXISTED BEFORE OURS.
AND HOW DO YOU--
TRUST ME ON THAT.
WHAT I DON'T KNOW IS WHERE WE ARE RIGHT THIS SECOND.
IS THIS A PRISON OR SOMETHING?
LAST THING I REMEMBER IS MY RING BEING DRAINED.
YOUR ASSESSMENT OF OUR SITUATION IS CORRECT.
WE ARE PRISONERS...

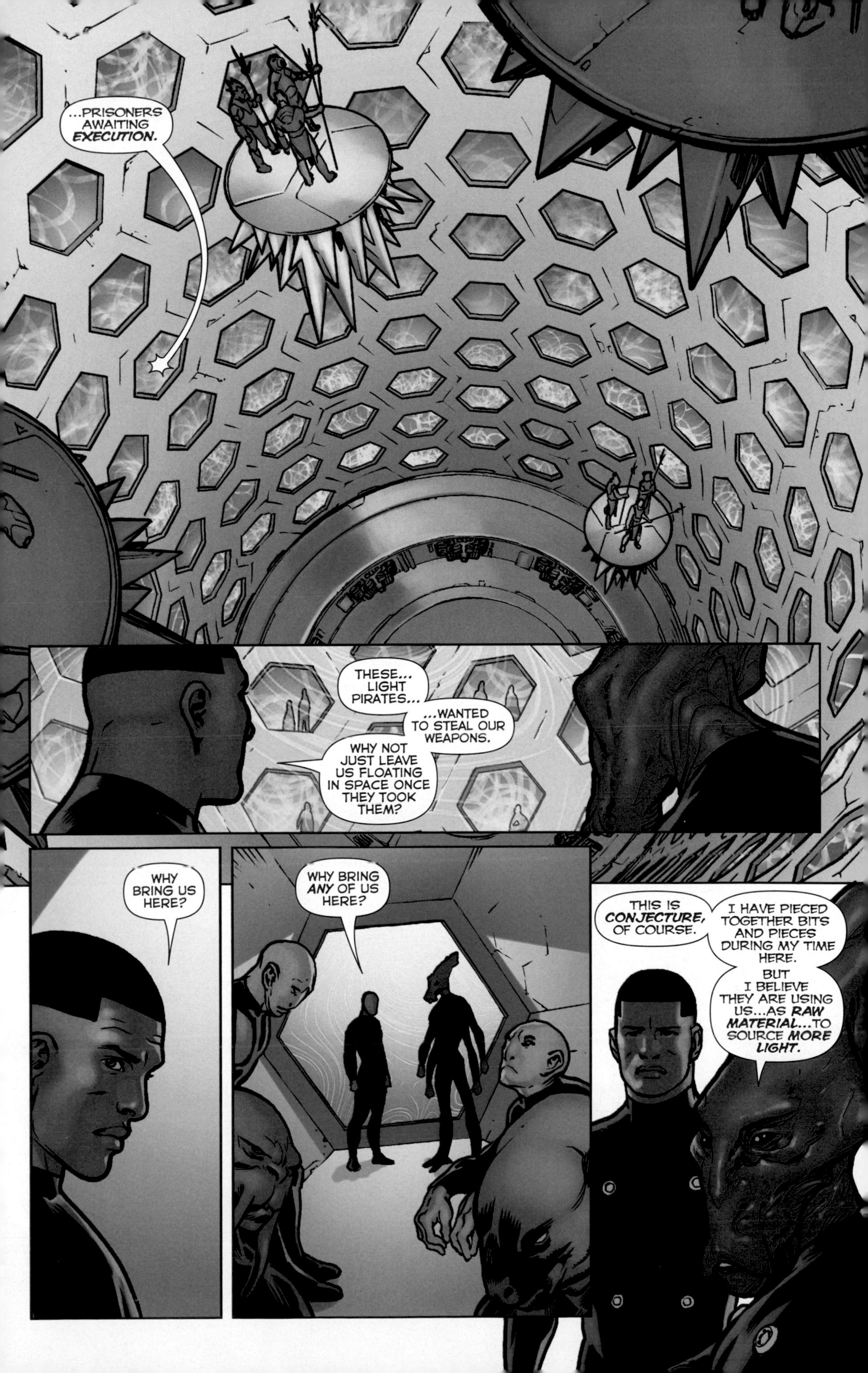
...PRISONERS AWAITING EXECUTION.
THESE... LIGHT PIRATES...
...WANTED TO STEAL OUR WEAPONS.
WHY NOT JUST LEAVE US FLOATING IN SPACE ONCE THEY TOOK THEM?
WHY BRING US HERE?
WHY BRING ANY OF US HERE?
THIS IS CONJECTURE, OF COURSE.
I HAVE PIECED TOGETHER BITS AND PIECES DURING MY TIME HERE.
BUT I BELIEVE THEY ARE USING US...AS RAW MATERIAL...TO SOURCE MORE LIGHT.

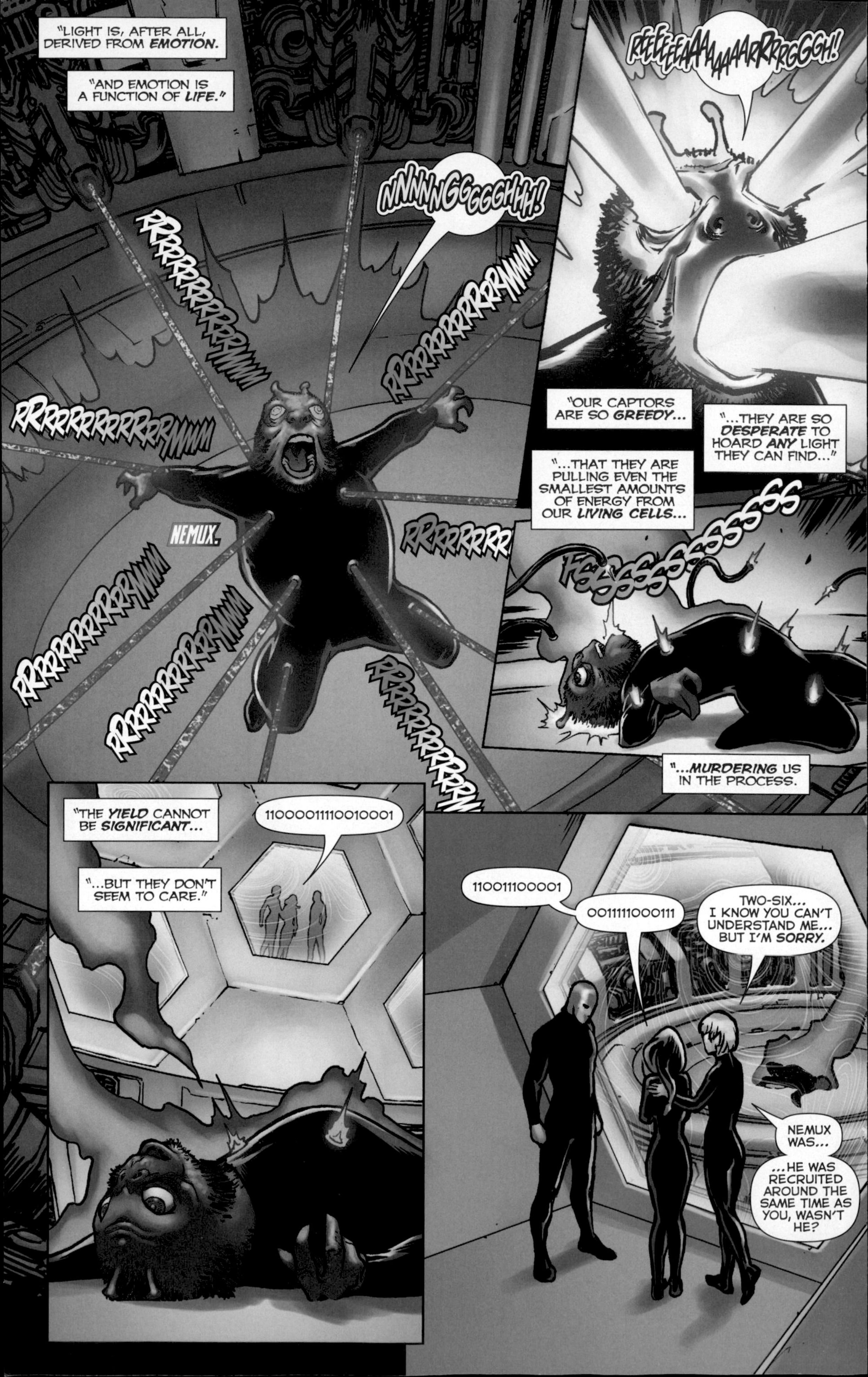
"LIGHT IS, AFTER ALL, DERIVED FROM EMOTION.
"AND EMOTION IS A FUNCTION OF LIFE."
NNNNNGGGGGHHH!
RRRRRRRRRRRRRMMMM
RRRRRRRRRRRRRMMMM
RRRRRRRRRRRRRMMMM
NEMUX.
RRRRRRRR
RRRRRRRRRRRRMMMM
RRRRRRRRRRRRMMMM
RRRRRRRRRRRRRMMMM
RRRRRRRRRRRRRMMMM
REEEEEEAAAAAAAARRRRGGGH!
"OUR CAPTORS ARE SO GREEDY...
"...THAT THEY ARE PULLING EVEN THE SMALLEST AMOUNTS OF ENERGY FROM OUR LIVING CELLS...
"...THEY ARE SO DESPERATE TO HOARD ANY LIGHT THEY CAN FIND..."
FSSSSSSSSSSSSSSSS
"...MURDERING US IN THE PROCESS.
"THE YIELD CANNOT BE SIGNIFICANT...
"...BUT THEY DON'T SEEM TO CARE."
11000011110010001
110011100001
0011111000111
TWO-SIX... I KNOW YOU CAN'T UNDERSTAND ME... BUT I'M SORRY.
NEMUX WAS...
...HE WAS RECRUITED AROUND THE SAME TIME AS YOU, WASN'T HE?

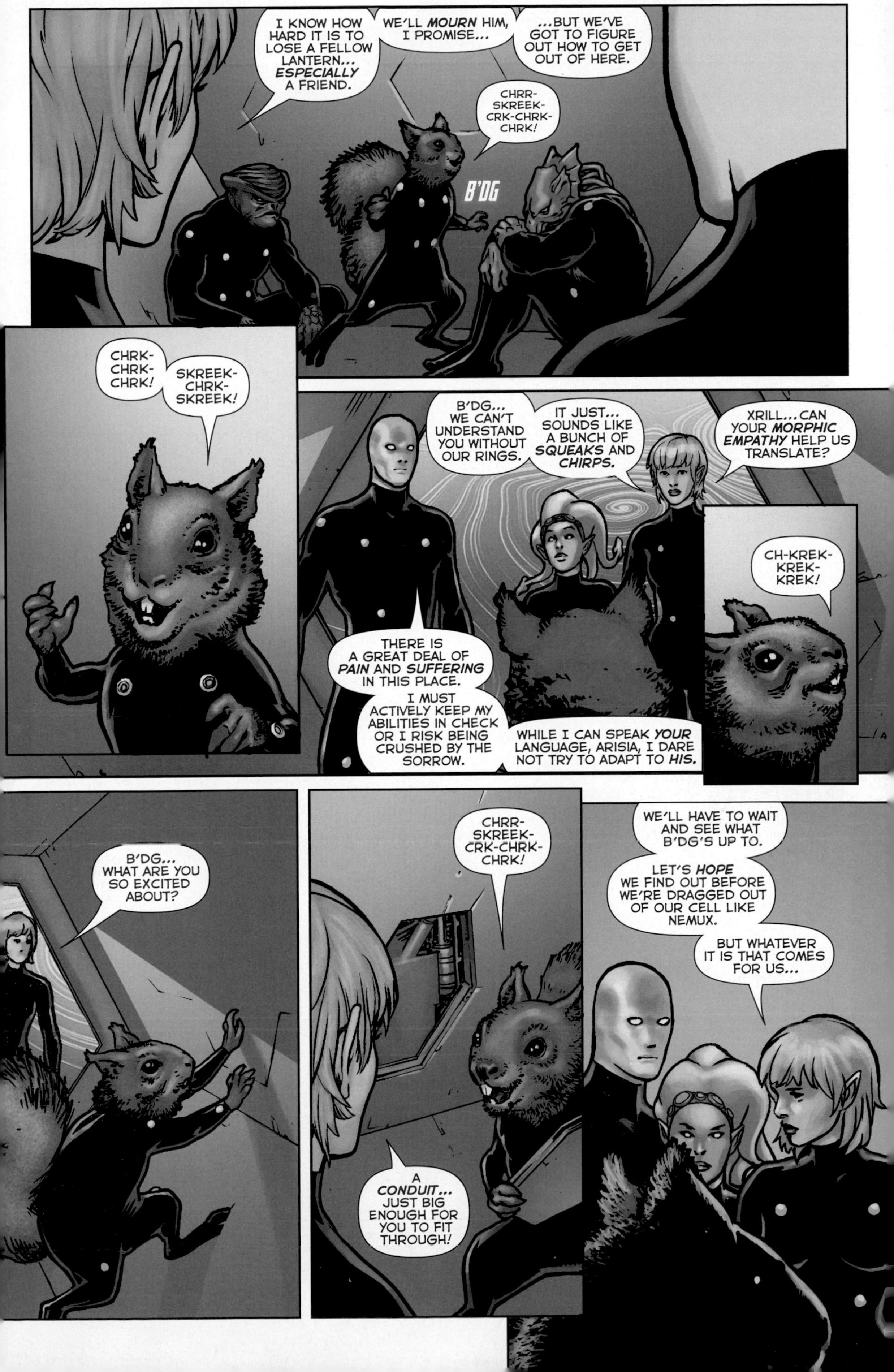
I KNOW HOW HARD IT IS TO LOSE A FELLOW LANTERN... ESPECIALLY A FRIEND.
WE'LL MOURN HIM, I PROMISE...
...BUT WE'VE GOT TO FIGURE OUT HOW TO GET OUT OF HERE.
CHRR-SKREEK-CRK-CHRK-CHRK!
B'DG
CHRK-CHRK-CHRK!
SKREEK-CHRK-SKREEK!
B'DG... WE CAN'T UNDERSTAND YOU WITHOUT OUR RINGS.
IT JUST... SOUNDS LIKE A BUNCH OF SQUEAKS AND CHIRPS.
XRILL... CAN YOUR MORPHIC EMPATHY HELP US TRANSLATE?
CH-KREK-KREK-KREK!
THERE IS A GREAT DEAL OF PAIN AND SUFFERING IN THIS PLACE.
I MUST ACTIVELY KEEP MY ABILITIES IN CHECK OR I RISK BEING CRUSHED BY THE SORROW.
WHILE I CAN SPEAK YOUR LANGUAGE, ARISIA, I DARE NOT TRY TO ADAPT TO HIS.
B'DG... WHAT ARE YOU SO EXCITED ABOUT?
CHRR-SKREEK-CRK-CHRK-CHRK!
A CONDUIT... JUST BIG ENOUGH FOR YOU TO FIT THROUGH!
WE'LL HAVE TO WAIT AND SEE WHAT B'DG'S UP TO.
LET'S HOPE WE FIND OUT BEFORE WE'RE DRAGGED OUT OF OUR CELL LIKE NEMUX.
BUT WHATEVER IT IS THAT COMES FOR US...

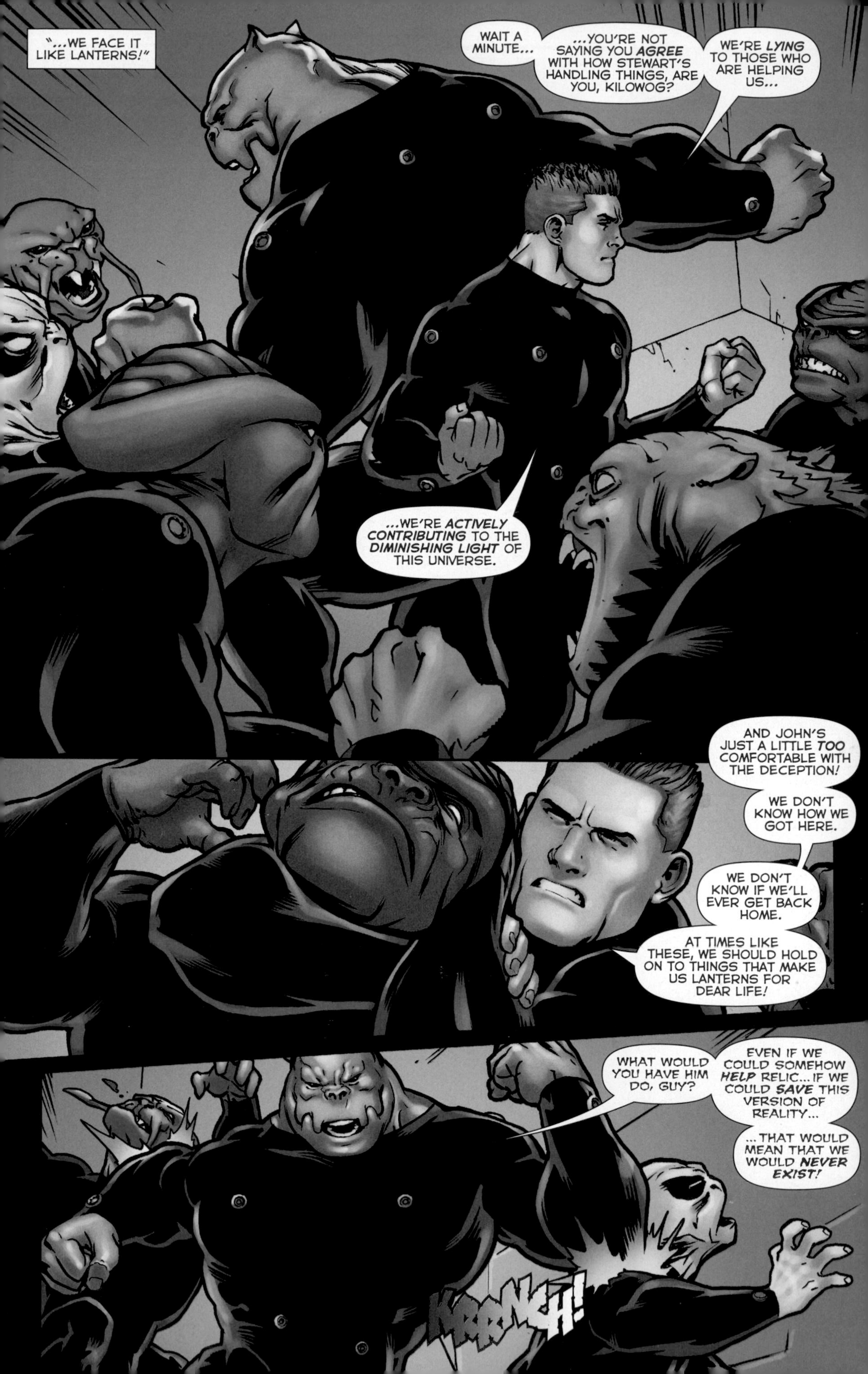
"...WE FACE IT LIKE LANTERNS!"
WAIT A MINUTE...
...YOU'RE NOT SAYING YOU AGREE WITH HOW STEWART'S HANDLING THINGS, ARE YOU, KILOWOG?
WE'RE LYING TO THOSE WHO ARE HELPING US...
...WE'RE ACTIVELY CONTRIBUTING TO THE DIMINISHING LIGHT OF THIS UNIVERSE.
AND JOHN'S JUST A LITTLE TOO COMFORTABLE WITH THE DECEPTION!
WE DON'T KNOW HOW WE GOT HERE.
WE DON'T KNOW IF WE'LL EVER GET BACK HOME.
AT TIMES LIKE THESE, WE SHOULD HOLD ON TO THINGS THAT MAKE US LANTERNS FOR DEAR LIFE!
WHAT WOULD YOU HAVE HIM DO, GUY?
EVEN IF WE COULD SOMEHOW HELP RELIC...IF WE COULD SAVE THIS VERSION OF REALITY...
...THAT WOULD MEAN THAT WE WOULD NEVER EXIST!
KRRNCH!

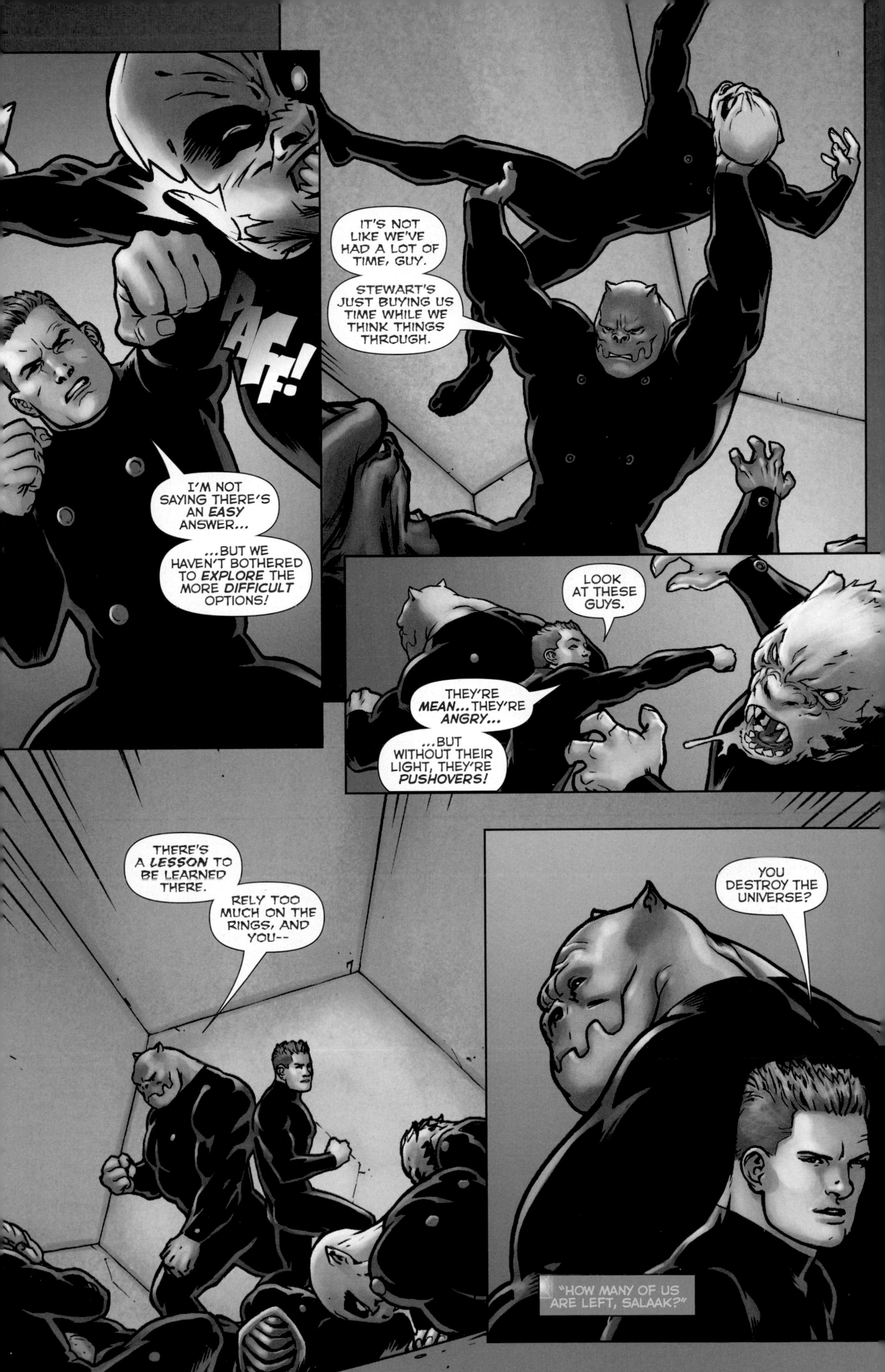
PAFF!
I'M NOT SAYING THERE'S AN EASY ANSWER...
...BUT WE HAVEN'T BOTHERED TO EXPLORE THE MORE DIFFICULT OPTIONS!
IT'S NOT LIKE WE'VE HAD A LOT OF TIME, GUY.
STEWART'S JUST BUYING US TIME WHILE WE THINK THINGS THROUGH.
LOOK AT THESE GUYS.
THEY'RE MEAN...THEY'RE ANGRY...
...BUT WITHOUT THEIR LIGHT, THEY'RE PUSHOVERS!
THERE'S A LESSON TO BE LEARNED THERE.
RELY TOO MUCH ON THE RINGS, AND YOU--
YOU DESTROY THE UNIVERSE?
"HOW MANY OF US ARE LEFT, SALAAK?"

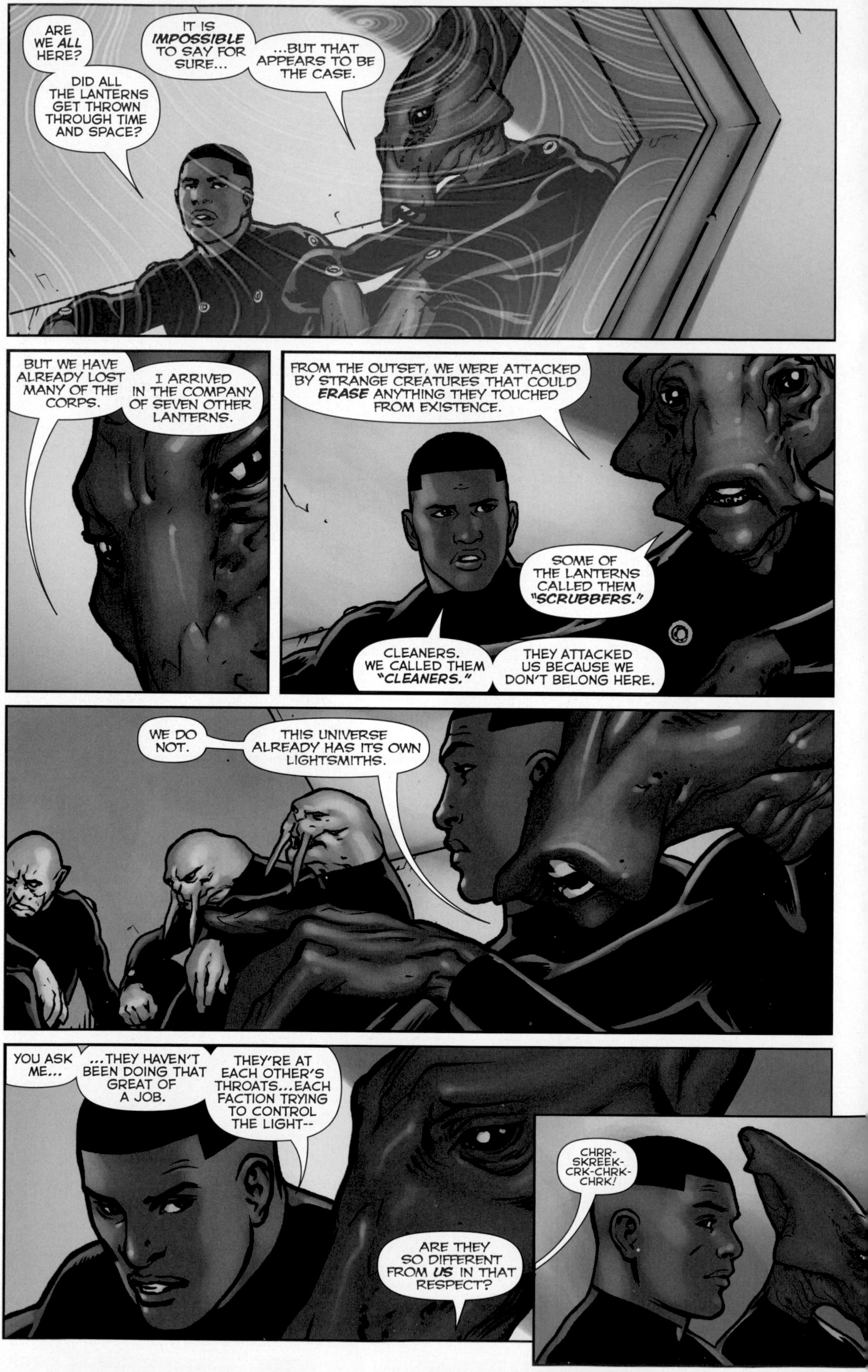

ARE WE *ALL* HERE?
DID ALL THE LANTERNS GET THROWN THROUGH TIME AND SPACE?
IT IS *IMPOSSIBLE* TO SAY FOR SURE...
...BUT THAT APPEARS TO BE THE CASE.
BUT WE HAVE ALREADY LOST MANY OF THE CORPS.
I ARRIVED IN THE COMPANY OF SEVEN OTHER LANTERNS.
FROM THE OUTSET, WE WERE ATTACKED BY STRANGE CREATURES THAT COULD *ERASE* ANYTHING THEY TOUCHED FROM EXISTENCE.
SOME OF THE LANTERNS CALLED THEM "*SCRUBBERS.*"
CLEANERS. WE CALLED THEM "*CLEANERS.*"
THEY ATTACKED US BECAUSE WE DON'T BELONG HERE.
WE DO NOT.
THIS UNIVERSE ALREADY HAS ITS OWN LIGHTSMITHS.
YOU ASK ME...
...THEY HAVEN'T BEEN DOING THAT GREAT OF A JOB.
THEY'RE AT EACH OTHER'S THROATS...EACH FACTION TRYING TO CONTROL THE LIGHT--
ARE THEY SO DIFFERENT FROM *US* IN THAT RESPECT?
CHRR-SKREEK-CRK-CHRK-CHRK!

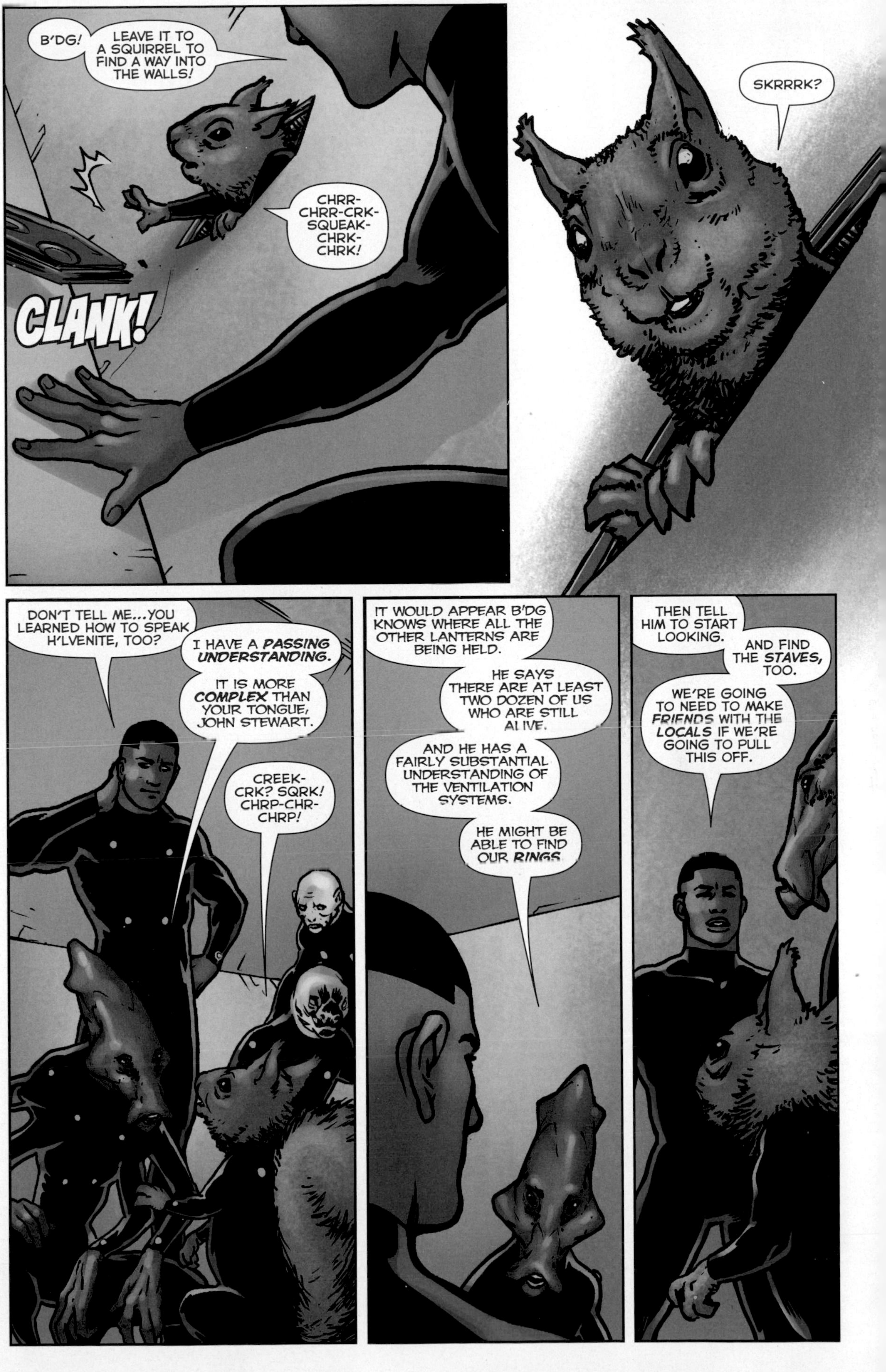
B'DG!
LEAVE IT TO A SQUIRREL TO FIND A WAY INTO THE WALLS!
CHRR-CHRR-CRK-SQUEAK-CHRK-CHRK!
CLANK!
SKRRRK?
DON'T TELL ME...YOU LEARNED HOW TO SPEAK H'LVENITE, TOO?
I HAVE A PASSING UNDERSTANDING.
IT IS MORE COMPLEX THAN YOUR TONGUE, JOHN STEWART.
CREEK-CRK? SQRK! CHRP-CHR-CHRP!
IT WOULD APPEAR B'DG KNOWS WHERE ALL THE OTHER LANTERNS ARE BEING HELD.
HE SAYS THERE ARE AT LEAST TWO DOZEN OF US WHO ARE STILL ALIVE.
AND HE HAS A FAIRLY SUBSTANTIAL UNDERSTANDING OF THE VENTILATION SYSTEMS.
HE MIGHT BE ABLE TO FIND OUR RINGS.
THEN TELL HIM TO START LOOKING.
AND FIND THE STAVES, TOO.
WE'RE GOING TO NEED TO MAKE FRIENDS WITH THE LOCALS IF WE'RE GOING TO PULL THIS OFF.

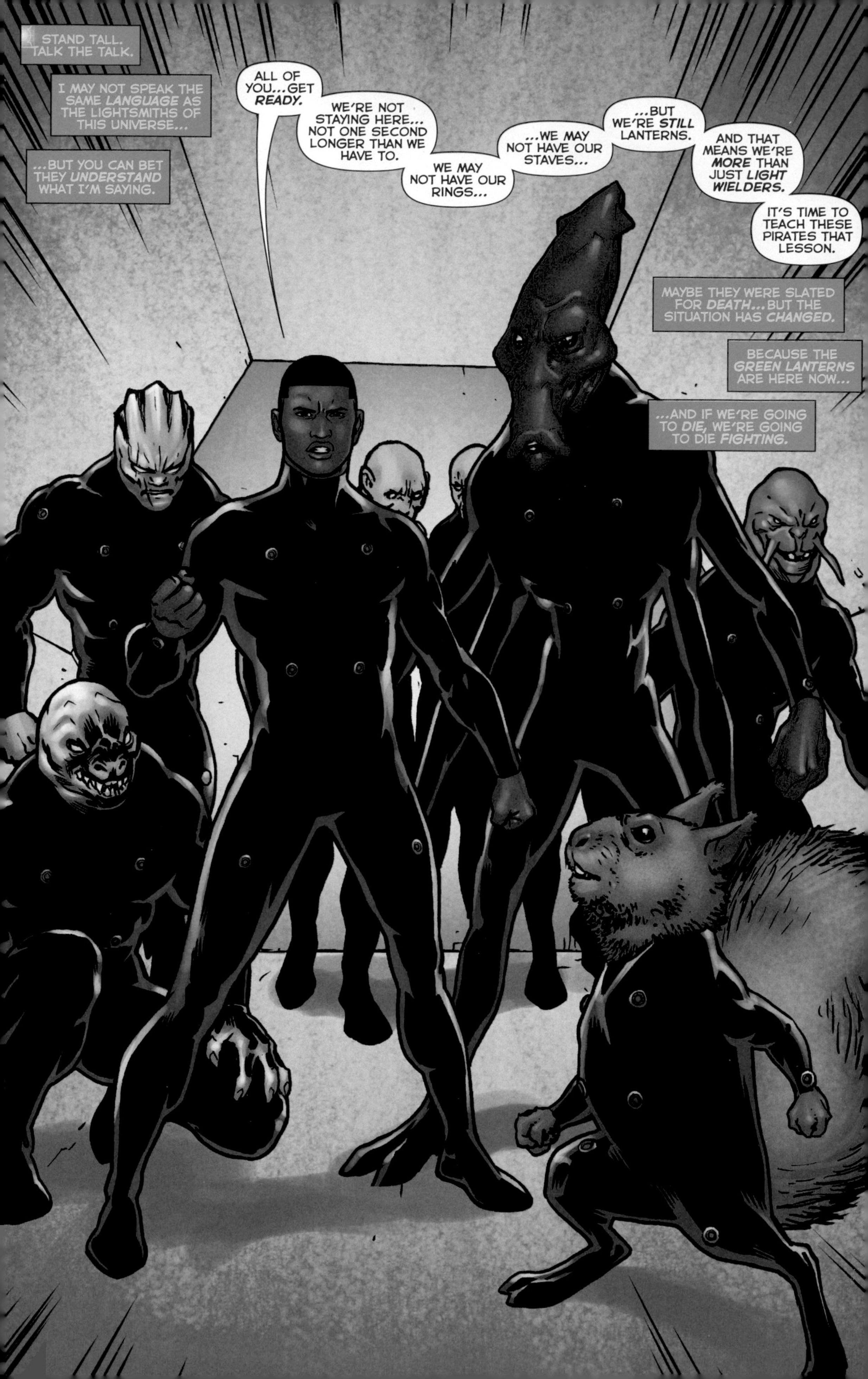
STAND TALL. TALK THE TALK.
I MAY NOT SPEAK THE SAME LANGUAGE AS THE LIGHTSMITHS OF THIS UNIVERSE...
...BUT YOU CAN BET THEY UNDERSTAND WHAT I'M SAYING.
ALL OF YOU...GET READY.
WE'RE NOT STAYING HERE... NOT ONE SECOND LONGER THAN WE HAVE TO.
WE MAY NOT HAVE OUR RINGS...
...WE MAY NOT HAVE OUR STAVES...
...BUT WE'RE STILL LANTERNS.
AND THAT MEANS WE'RE MORE THAN JUST LIGHT WIELDERS.
IT'S TIME TO TEACH THESE PIRATES THAT LESSON.
MAYBE THEY WERE SLATED FOR DEATH...BUT THE SITUATION HAS CHANGED.
BECAUSE THE GREEN LANTERNS ARE HERE NOW...
...AND IF WE'RE GOING TO DIE, WE'RE GOING TO DIE FIGHTING.

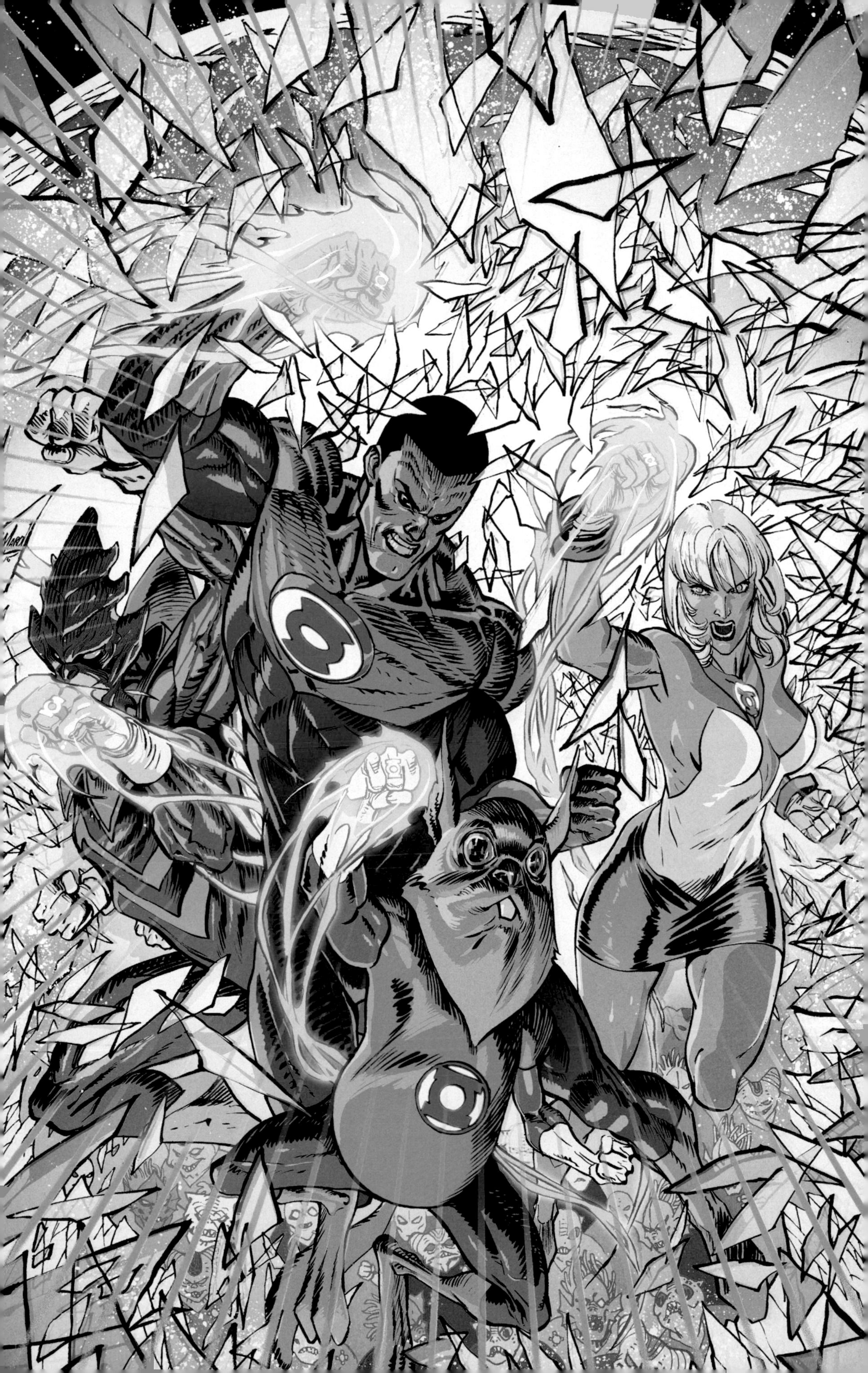

CULLEN BUNN writer JESUS SAIZ artist & colorist DAVE SHARPE letterer GUILLEM MARCH cover

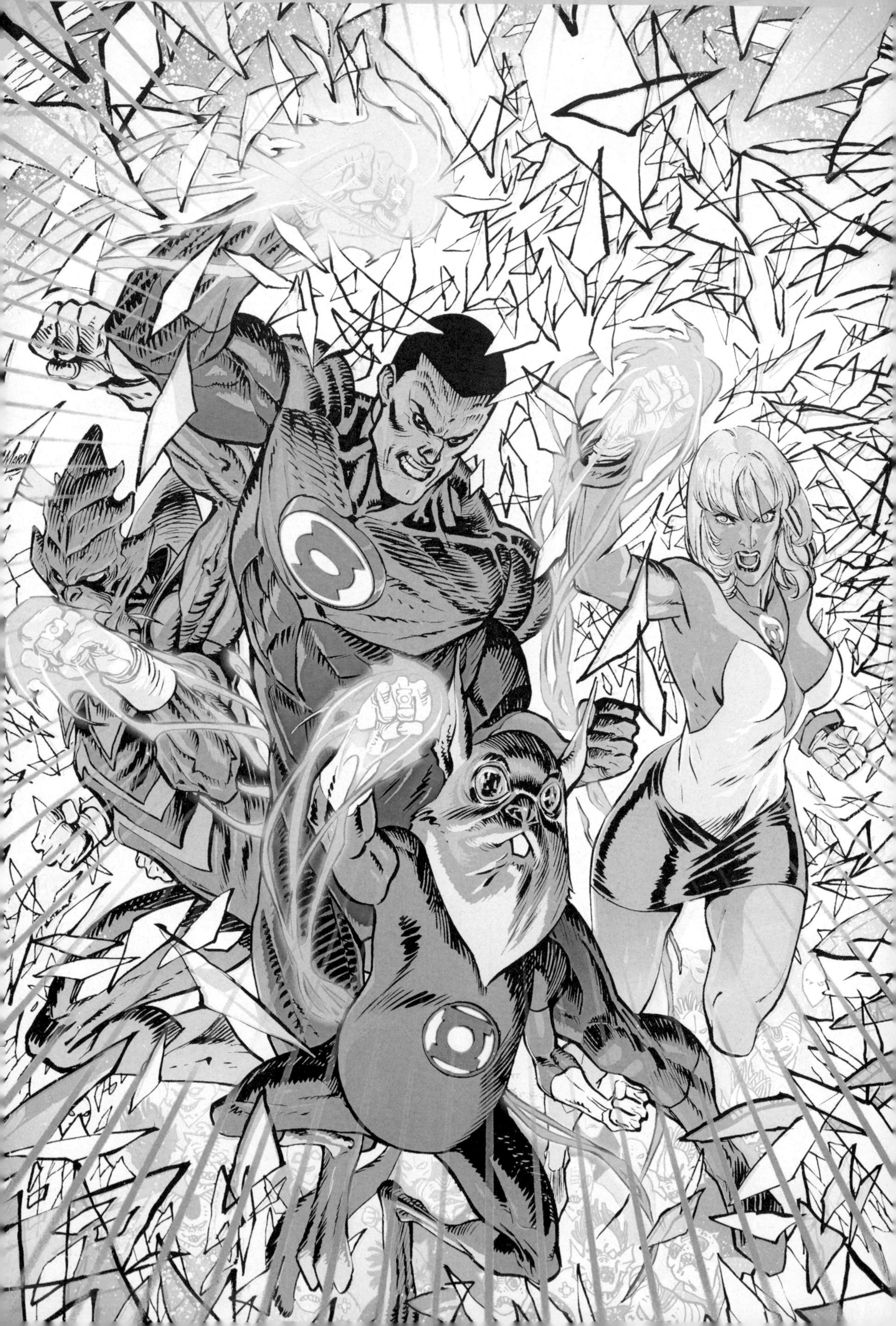

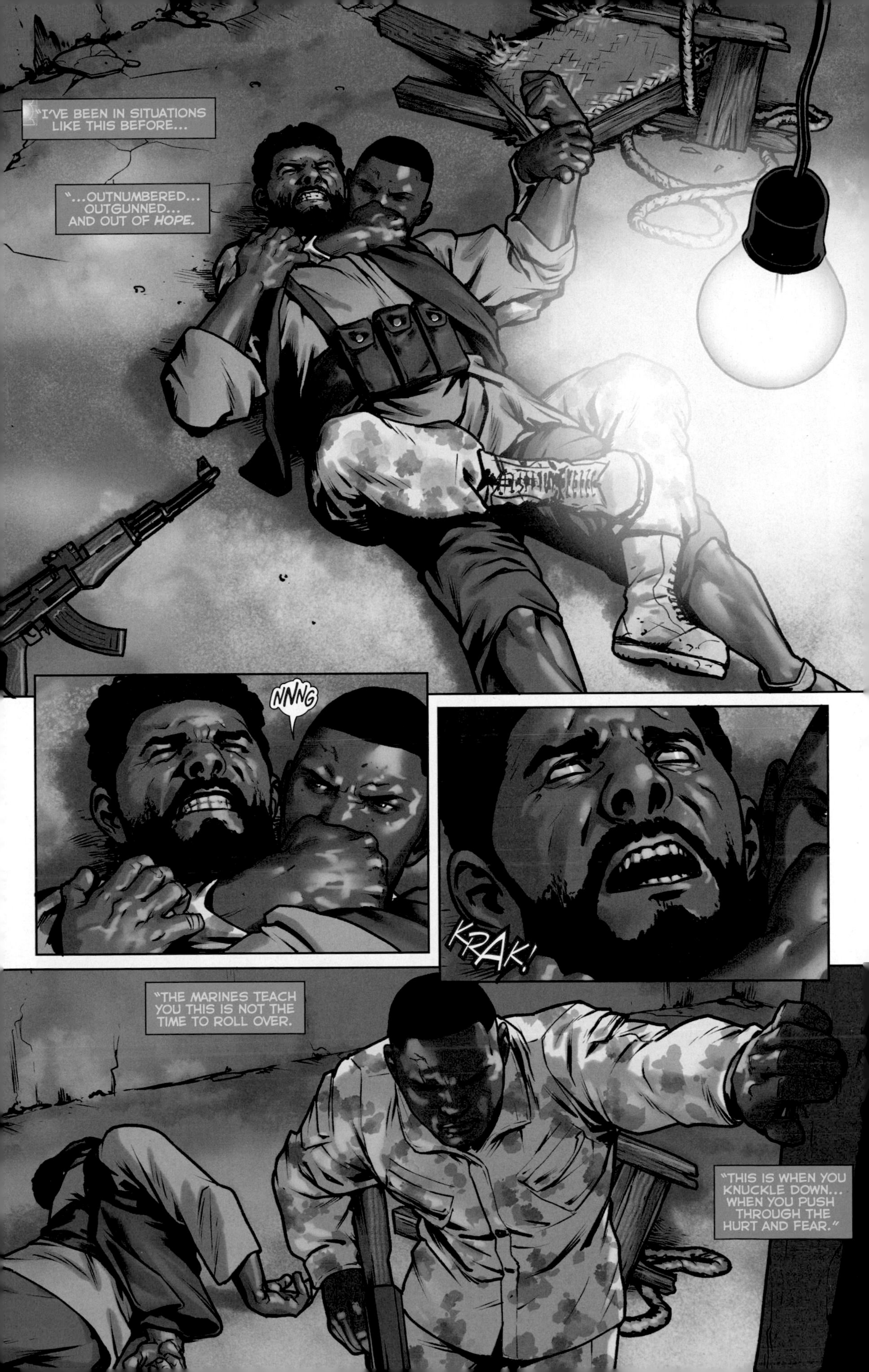
"I'VE BEEN IN SITUATIONS LIKE THIS BEFORE...
"...OUTNUMBERED... OUTGUNNED... AND OUT OF HOPE.
NNNG
KRAK!
"THE MARINES TEACH YOU THIS IS NOT THE TIME TO ROLL OVER.
"THIS IS WHEN YOU KNUCKLE DOWN... WHEN YOU PUSH THROUGH THE HURT AND FEAR."

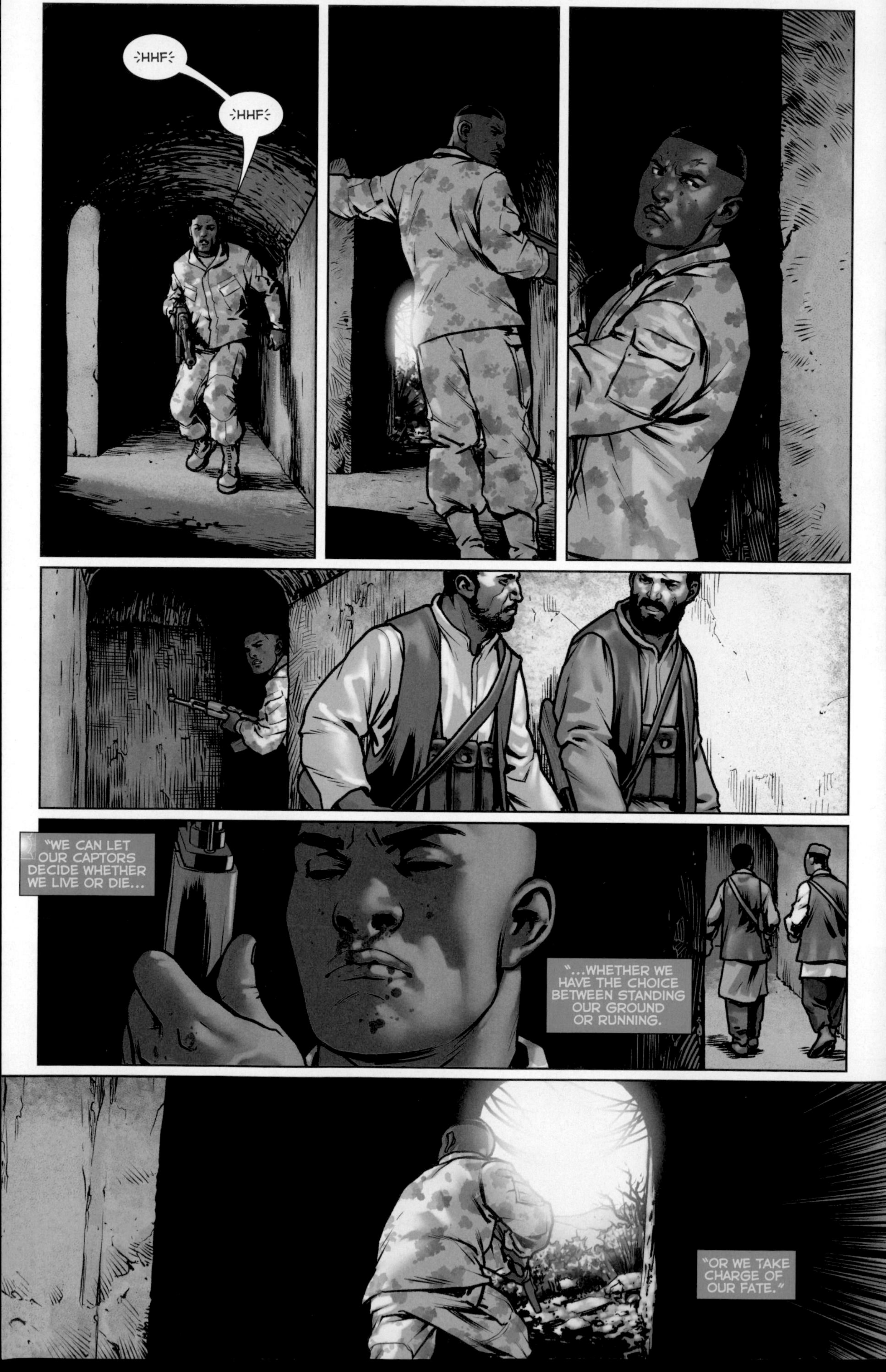
HHF
HHF
"WE CAN LET OUR CAPTORS DECIDE WHETHER WE LIVE OR DIE...
"...WHETHER WE HAVE THE CHOICE BETWEEN STANDING OUR GROUND OR RUNNING.
"OR WE TAKE CHARGE OF OUR FATE."

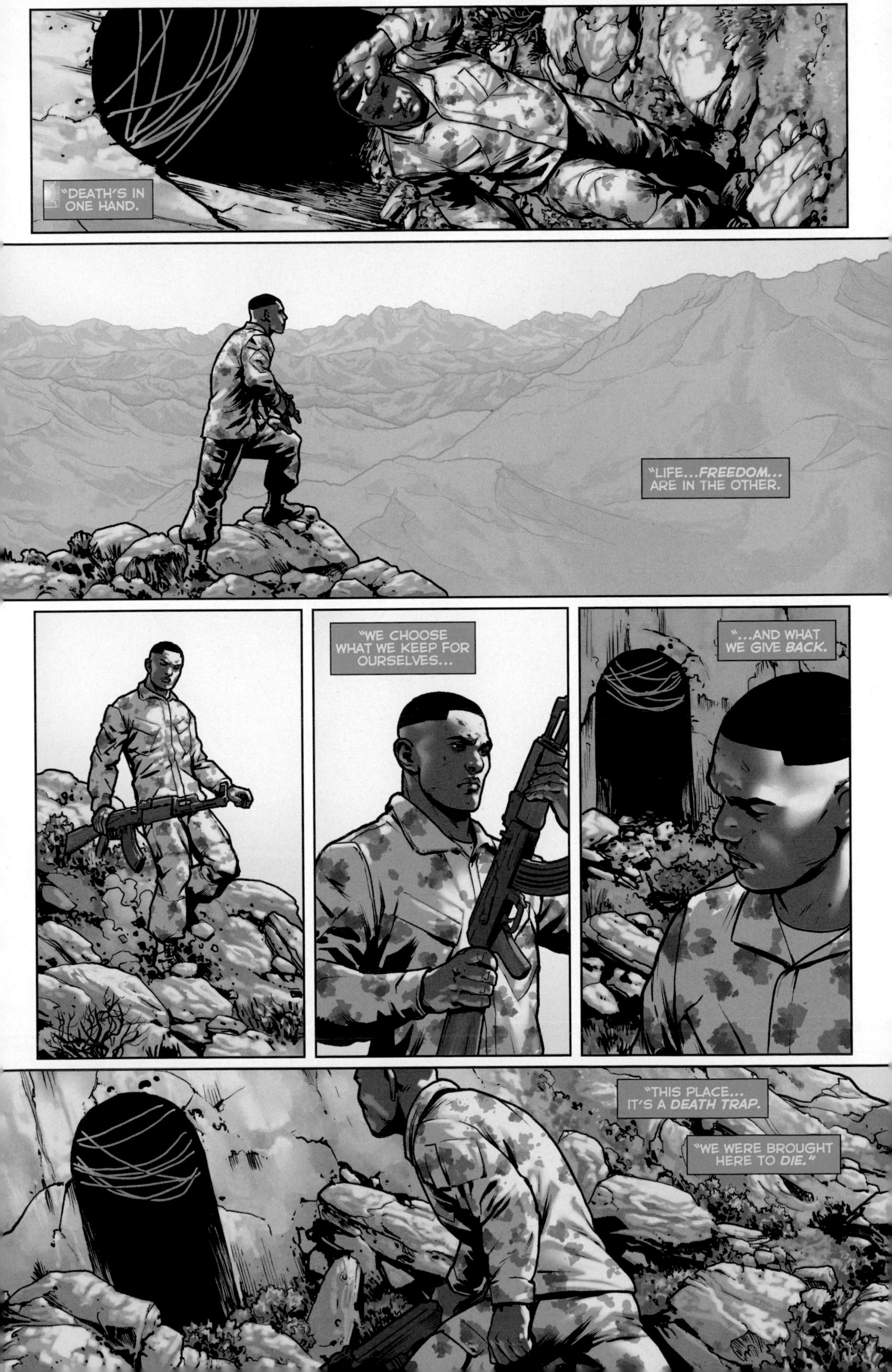
"DEATH'S IN ONE HAND.
"LIFE...FREEDOM... ARE IN THE OTHER.
"WE CHOOSE WHAT WE KEEP FOR OURSELVES...
"...AND WHAT WE GIVE BACK.
"THIS PLACE... IT'S A DEATH TRAP.
"WE WERE BROUGHT HERE TO DIE."

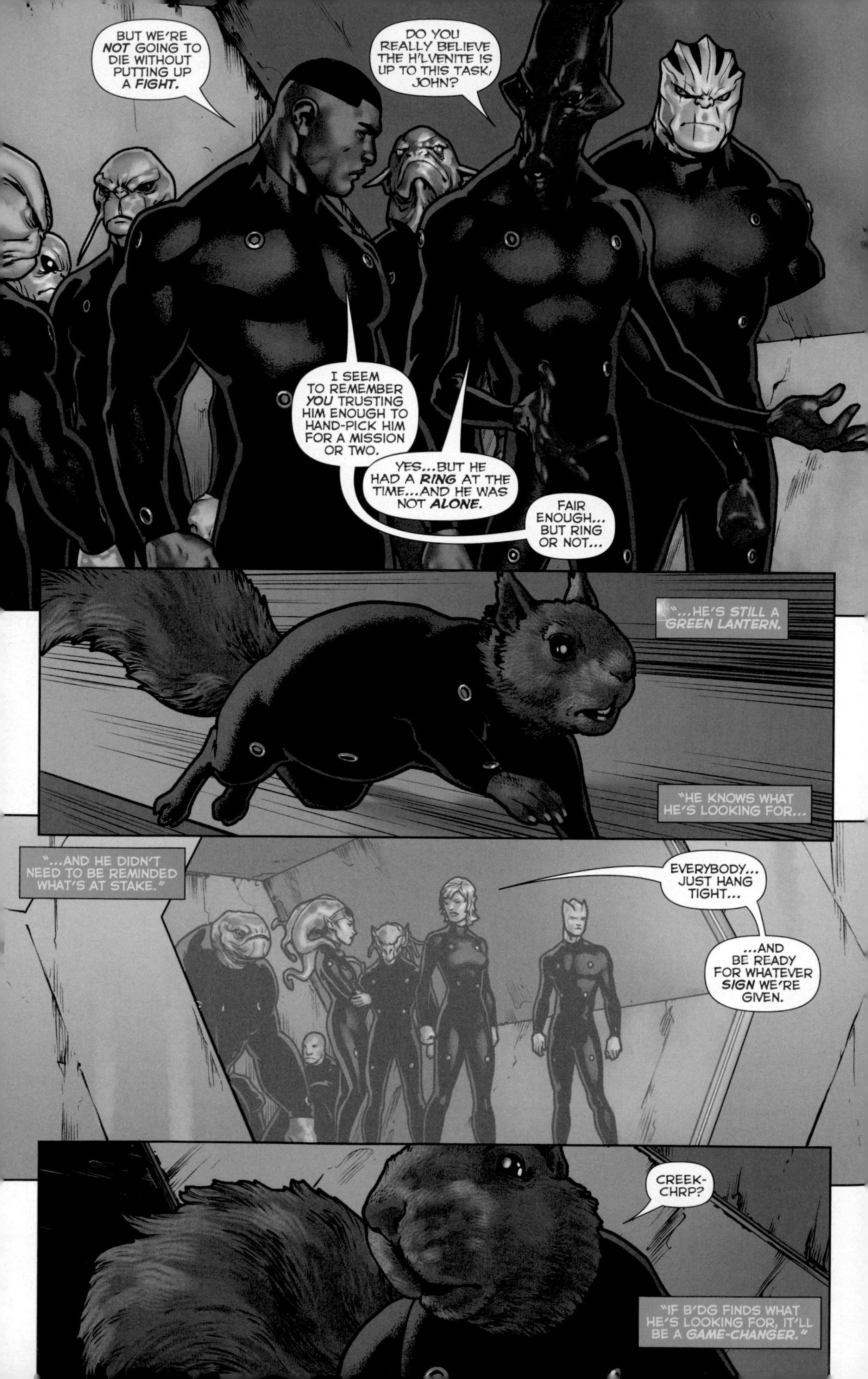
BUT WE'RE NOT GOING TO DIE WITHOUT PUTTING UP A FIGHT.
DO YOU REALLY BELIEVE THE H'LVENITE IS UP TO THIS TASK, JOHN?
I SEEM TO REMEMBER YOU TRUSTING HIM ENOUGH TO HAND-PICK HIM FOR A MISSION OR TWO.
YES...BUT HE HAD A RING AT THE TIME...AND HE WAS NOT ALONE.
FAIR ENOUGH... BUT RING OR NOT...
"...HE'S STILL A GREEN LANTERN.
"HE KNOWS WHAT HE'S LOOKING FOR...
"...AND HE DIDN'T NEED TO BE REMINDED WHAT'S AT STAKE."
EVERYBODY... JUST HANG TIGHT...
...AND BE READY FOR WHATEVER SIGN WE'RE GIVEN.
CREEK-CHRP?
"IF B'DG FINDS WHAT HE'S LOOKING FOR, IT'LL BE A GAME-CHANGER."

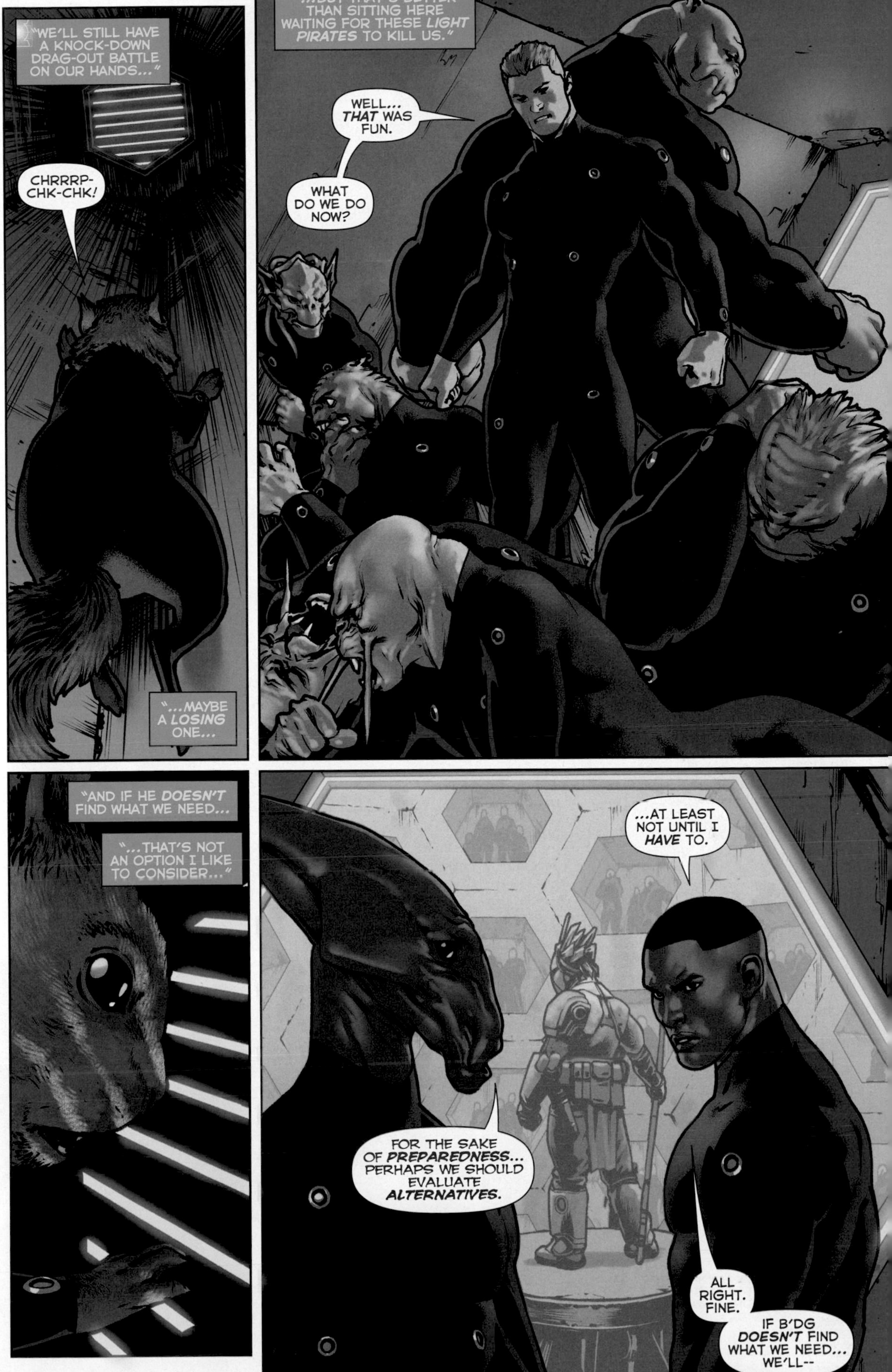
"WE'LL STILL HAVE A KNOCK-DOWN DRAG-OUT BATTLE ON OUR HANDS..."
CHRRRP-CHK-CHK!
"...MAYBE A LOSING ONE...
"...BUT THAT'S BETTER THAN SITTING HERE WAITING FOR THESE LIGHT PIRATES TO KILL US."
WELL... THAT WAS FUN.
WHAT DO WE DO NOW?
"AND IF HE DOESN'T FIND WHAT WE NEED...
"...THAT'S NOT AN OPTION I LIKE TO CONSIDER..."
...AT LEAST NOT UNTIL I HAVE TO.
FOR THE SAKE OF PREPAREDNESS... PERHAPS WE SHOULD EVALUATE ALTERNATIVES.
ALL RIGHT. FINE.
IF B'DG DOESN'T FIND WHAT WE NEED... WE'LL--

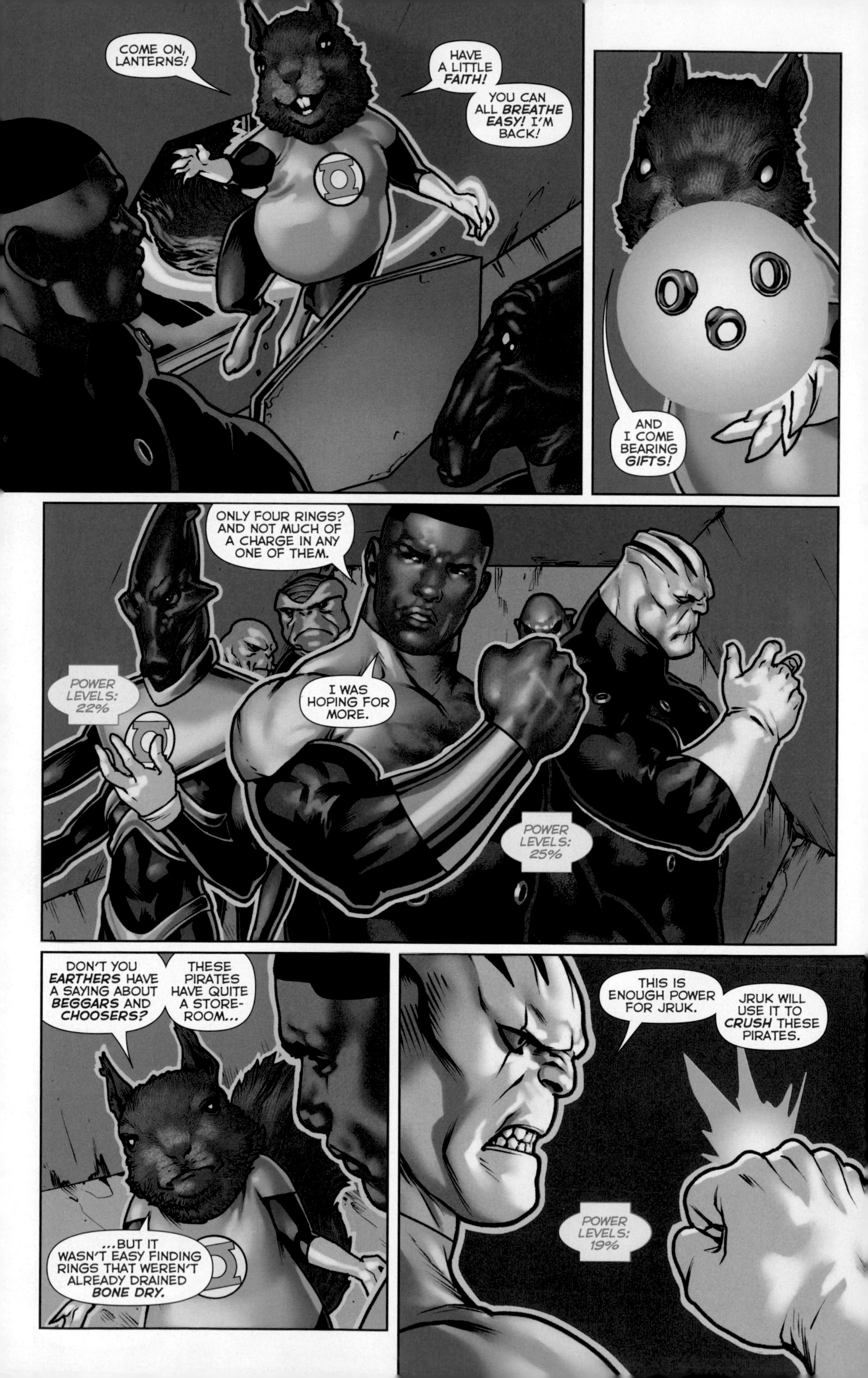
COME ON, LANTERNS!
HAVE A LITTLE FAITH!
YOU CAN ALL BREATHE EASY! I'M BACK!
AND I COME BEARING GIFTS!
ONLY FOUR RINGS? AND NOT MUCH OF A CHARGE IN ANY ONE OF THEM.
POWER LEVELS: 22%
I WAS HOPING FOR MORE.
POWER LEVELS: 25%
DON'T YOU EARTHERS HAVE A SAYING ABOUT BEGGARS AND CHOOSERS?
THESE PIRATES HAVE QUITE A STORE-ROOM...
...BUT IT WASN'T EASY FINDING RINGS THAT WEREN'T ALREADY DRAINED BONE DRY.
THIS IS ENOUGH POWER FOR JRUK.
JRUK WILL USE IT TO CRUSH THESE PIRATES.
POWER LEVELS: 19%

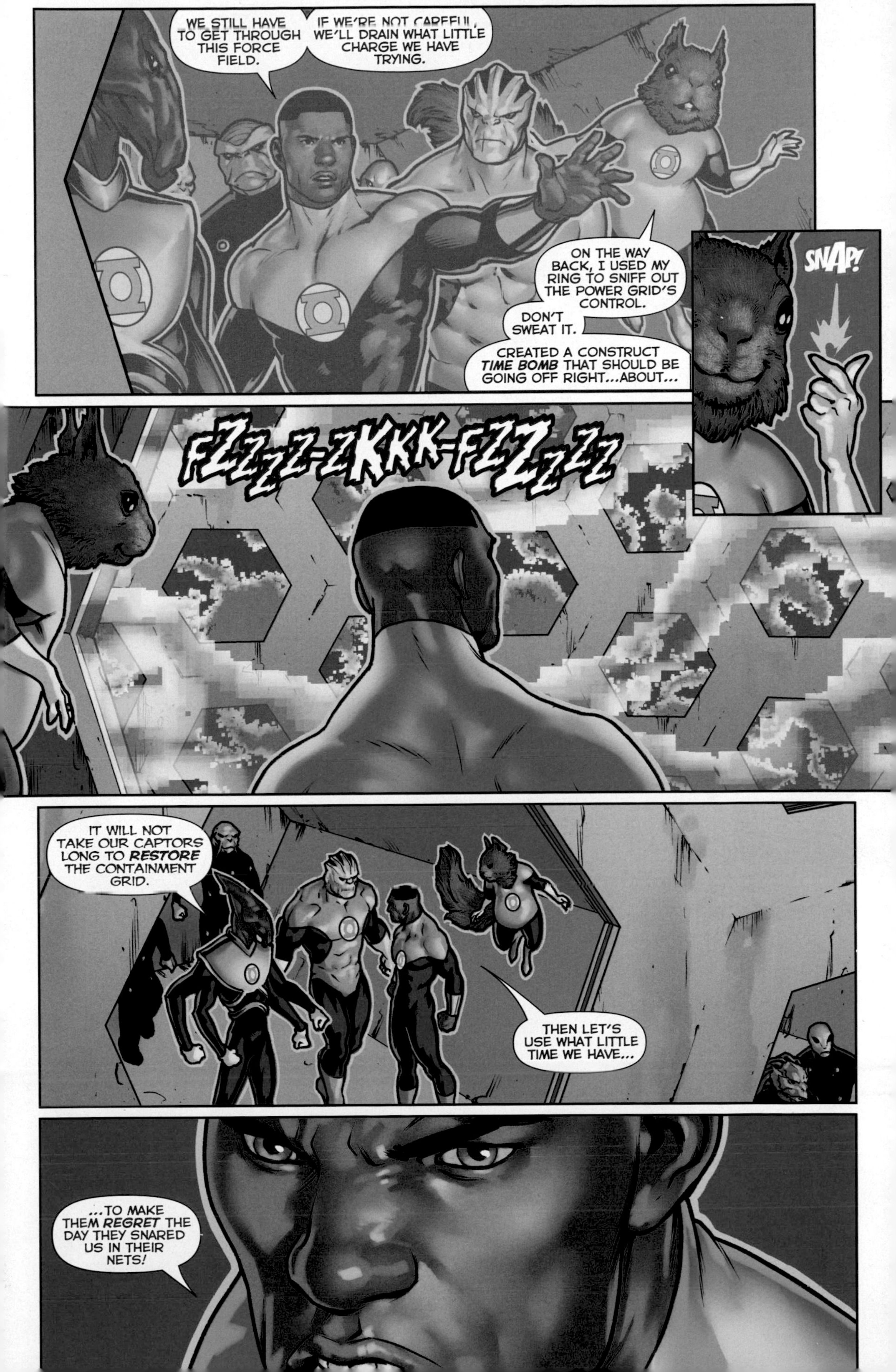
WE STILL HAVE TO GET THROUGH THIS FORCE FIELD.
IF WE'RE NOT CAREFUL, WE'LL DRAIN WHAT LITTLE CHARGE WE HAVE TRYING.
ON THE WAY BACK, I USED MY RING TO SNIFF OUT THE POWER GRID'S CONTROL.
DON'T SWEAT IT.
CREATED A CONSTRUCT TIME BOMB THAT SHOULD BE GOING OFF RIGHT...ABOUT...
SNAP!
FZZZZ-ZKKK-FZZZZZ
IT WILL NOT TAKE OUR CAPTORS LONG TO RESTORE THE CONTAINMENT GRID.
THEN LET'S USE WHAT LITTLE TIME WE HAVE...
...TO MAKE THEM REGRET THE DAY THEY SNARED US IN THEIR NETS!

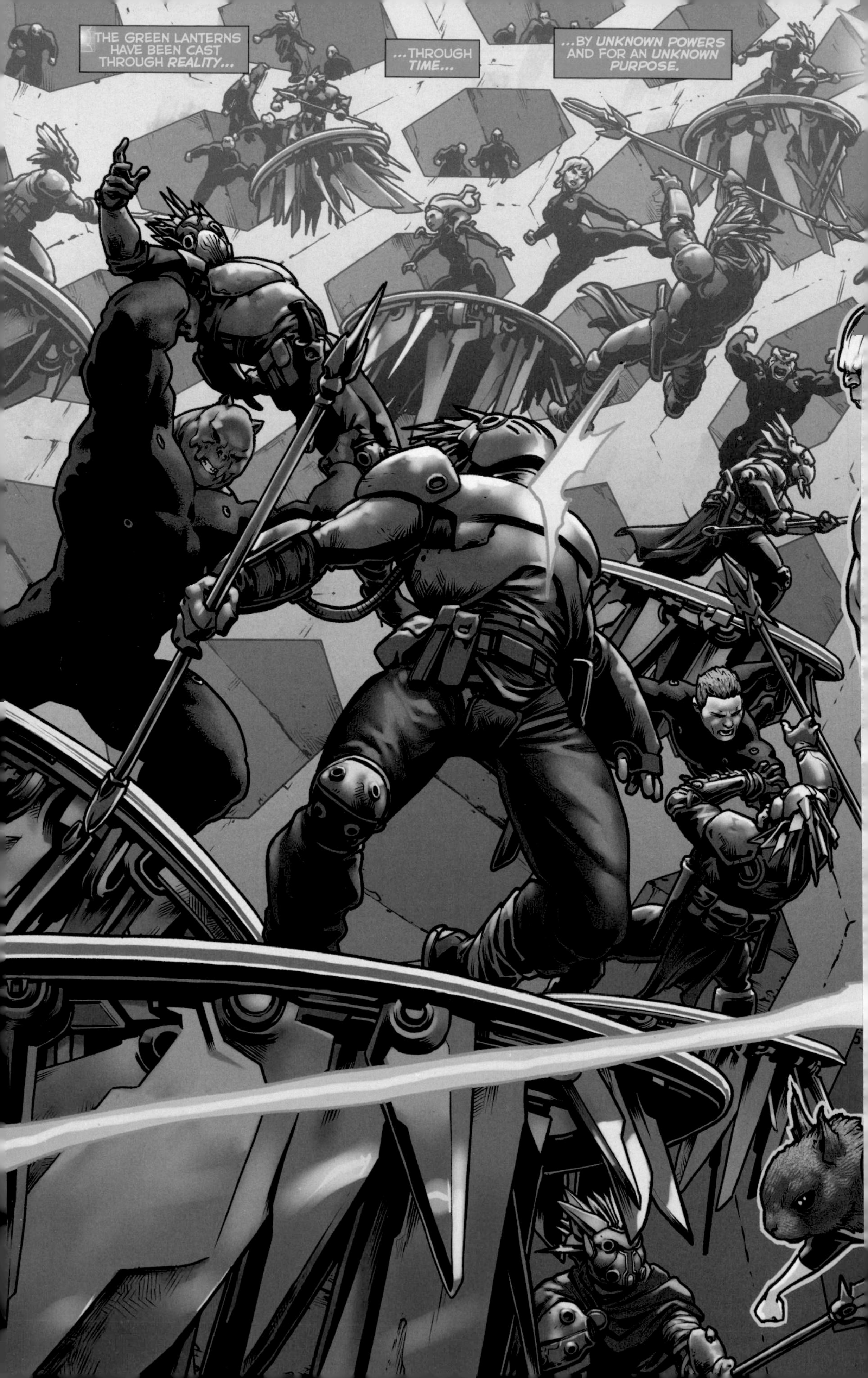
THE GREEN LANTERNS HAVE BEEN CAST THROUGH REALITY...
...THROUGH TIME...
...BY UNKNOWN POWERS AND FOR AN UNKNOWN PURPOSE.

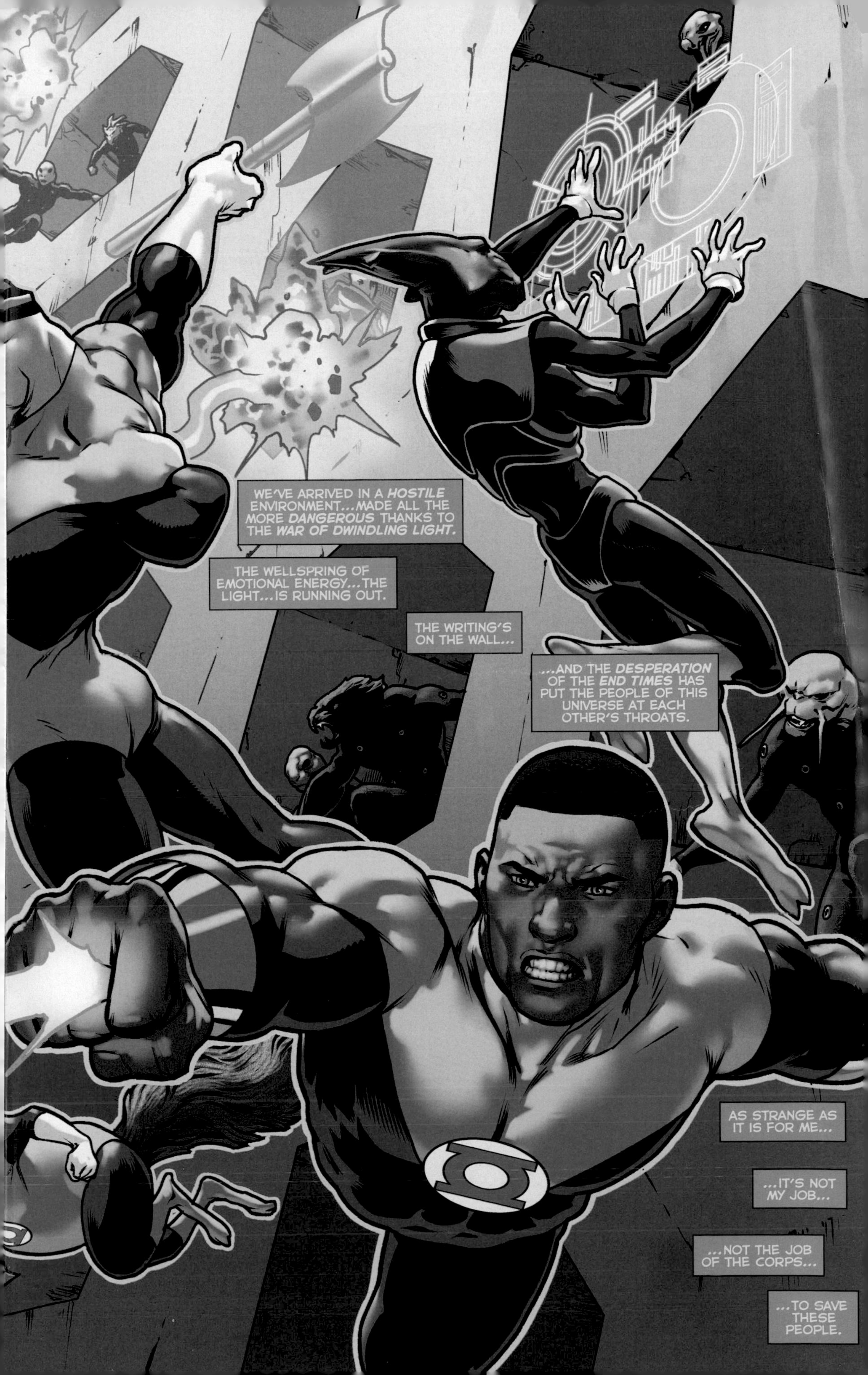

WE'VE ARRIVED IN A *HOSTILE* ENVIRONMENT...MADE ALL THE MORE *DANGEROUS* THANKS TO THE *WAR OF DWINDLING LIGHT.*
THE WELLSPRING OF EMOTIONAL ENERGY...THE LIGHT...IS RUNNING OUT.
THE WRITING'S ON THE WALL...
...AND THE *DESPERATION* OF THE *END TIMES* HAS PUT THE PEOPLE OF THIS UNIVERSE AT EACH OTHER'S THROATS.
AS STRANGE AS IT IS FOR ME...
...IT'S NOT MY JOB...
...NOT THE JOB OF THE CORPS...
...TO SAVE THESE PEOPLE.

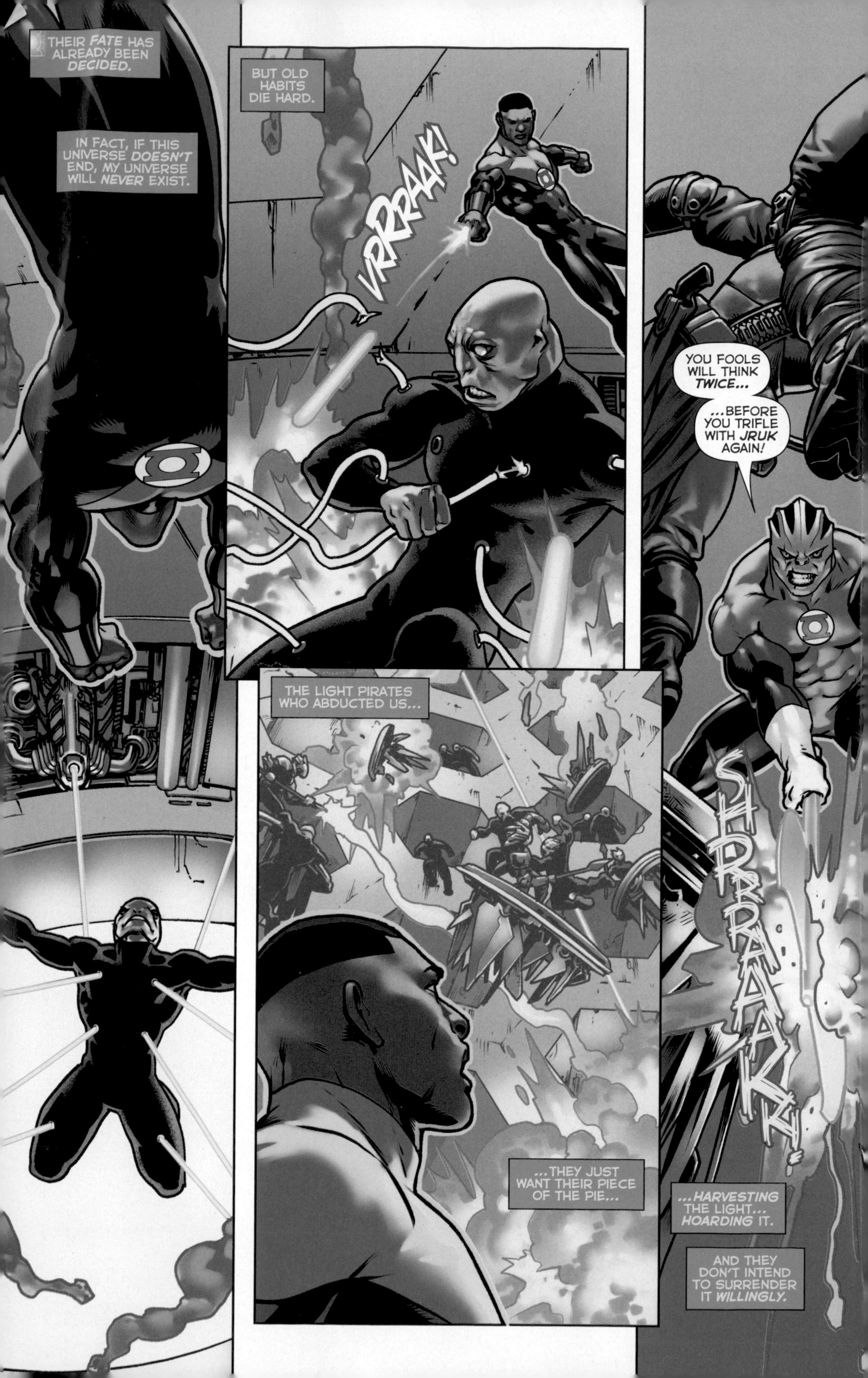

THEIR FATE HAS ALREADY BEEN DECIDED.
IN FACT, IF THIS UNIVERSE DOESN'T END, MY UNIVERSE WILL NEVER EXIST.
BUT OLD HABITS DIE HARD.
VRRRAAK!
YOU FOOLS WILL THINK TWICE...
...BEFORE YOU TRIFLE WITH JRUK AGAIN!
THE LIGHT PIRATES WHO ABDUCTED US...
...THEY JUST WANT THEIR PIECE OF THE PIE...
SHRRRAAAK!
...HARVESTING THE LIGHT... HOARDING IT.
AND THEY DON'T INTEND TO SURRENDER IT WILLINGLY.

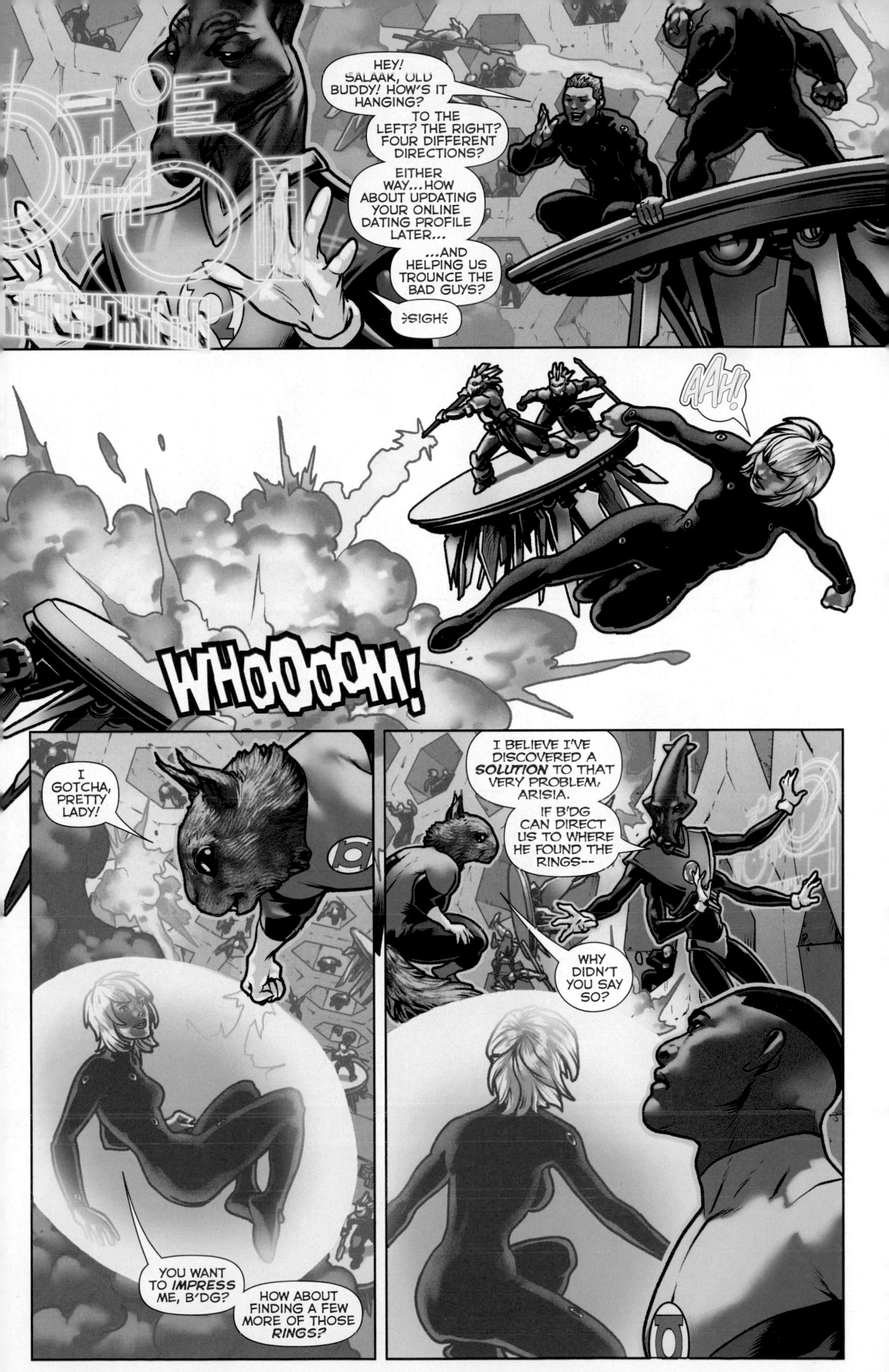
HEY! SALAAK, OLD BUDDY! HOW'S IT HANGING?
TO THE LEFT? THE RIGHT? FOUR DIFFERENT DIRECTIONS?
EITHER WAY...HOW ABOUT UPDATING YOUR ONLINE DATING PROFILE LATER...
...AND HELPING US TROUNCE THE BAD GUYS?
SIGH
AAH!
WHOOOOOM!
I GOTCHA, PRETTY LADY!
YOU WANT TO *IMPRESS* ME, B'DG?
HOW ABOUT FINDING A FEW MORE OF THOSE *RINGS?*
I BELIEVE I'VE DISCOVERED A *SOLUTION* TO THAT VERY PROBLEM, ARISIA.
IF B'DG CAN DIRECT US TO WHERE HE FOUND THE RINGS--
WHY DIDN'T YOU SAY SO?

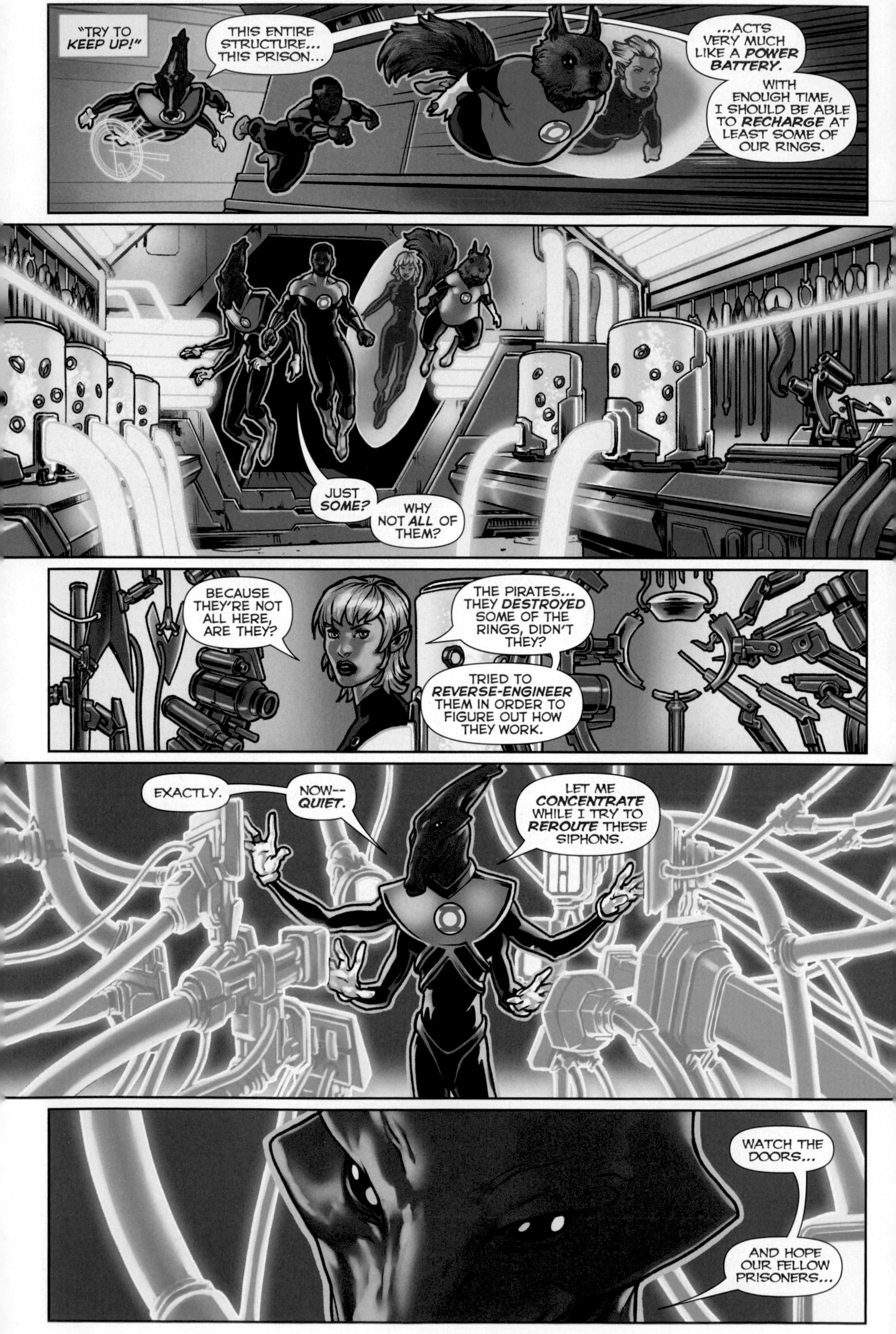
"TRY TO KEEP UP!"
THIS ENTIRE STRUCTURE... THIS PRISON...
...ACTS VERY MUCH LIKE A POWER BATTERY.
WITH ENOUGH TIME, I SHOULD BE ABLE TO RECHARGE AT LEAST SOME OF OUR RINGS.
JUST SOME?
WHY NOT ALL OF THEM?
BECAUSE THEY'RE NOT ALL HERE, ARE THEY?
THE PIRATES... THEY DESTROYED SOME OF THE RINGS, DIDN'T THEY?
TRIED TO REVERSE-ENGINEER THEM IN ORDER TO FIGURE OUT HOW THEY WORK.
EXACTLY.
NOW-- QUIET.
LET ME CONCENTRATE WHILE I TRY TO REROUTE THESE SIPHONS.
WATCH THE DOORS...
AND HOPE OUR FELLOW PRISONERS...

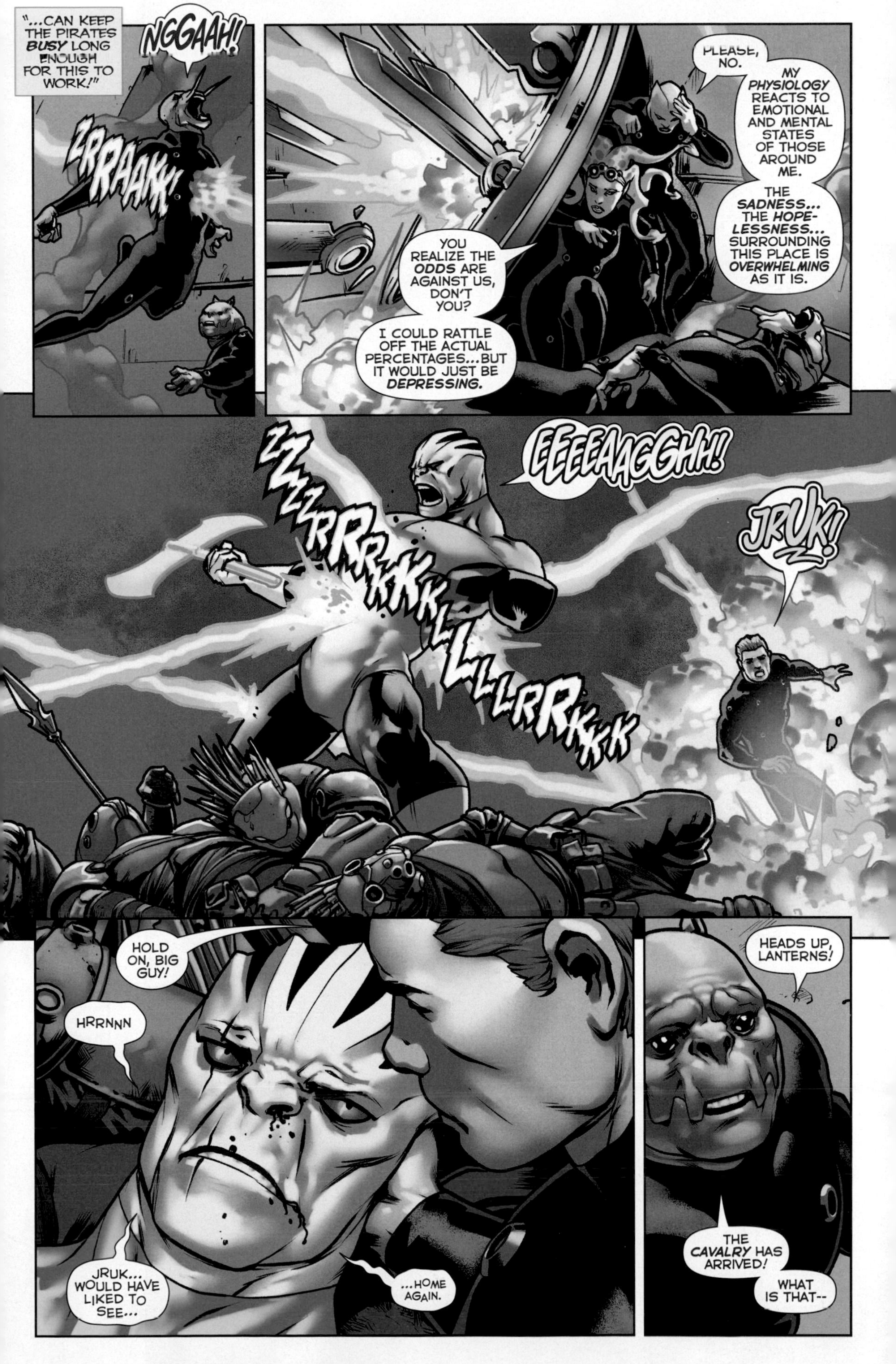
"...CAN KEEP THE PIRATES BUSY LONG ENOUGH FOR THIS TO WORK!"
NGGAAH!
ZRRAAKK!
PLEASE, NO.
MY PHYSIOLOGY REACTS TO EMOTIONAL AND MENTAL STATES OF THOSE AROUND ME.
THE SADNESS... THE HOPELESSNESS... SURROUNDING THIS PLACE IS OVERWHELMING AS IT IS.
YOU REALIZE THE ODDS ARE AGAINST US, DON'T YOU?
I COULD RATTLE OFF THE ACTUAL PERCENTAGES...BUT IT WOULD JUST BE DEPRESSING.
ZZZZRRRKKKLLLLRRKKK
EEEEAAGGHH!
JRUK!
HOLD ON, BIG GUY!
HRRNNN
JRUK... WOULD HAVE LIKED TO SEE...
...HOME AGAIN.
HEADS UP, LANTERNS!
THE CAVALRY HAS ARRIVED!
WHAT IS THAT--

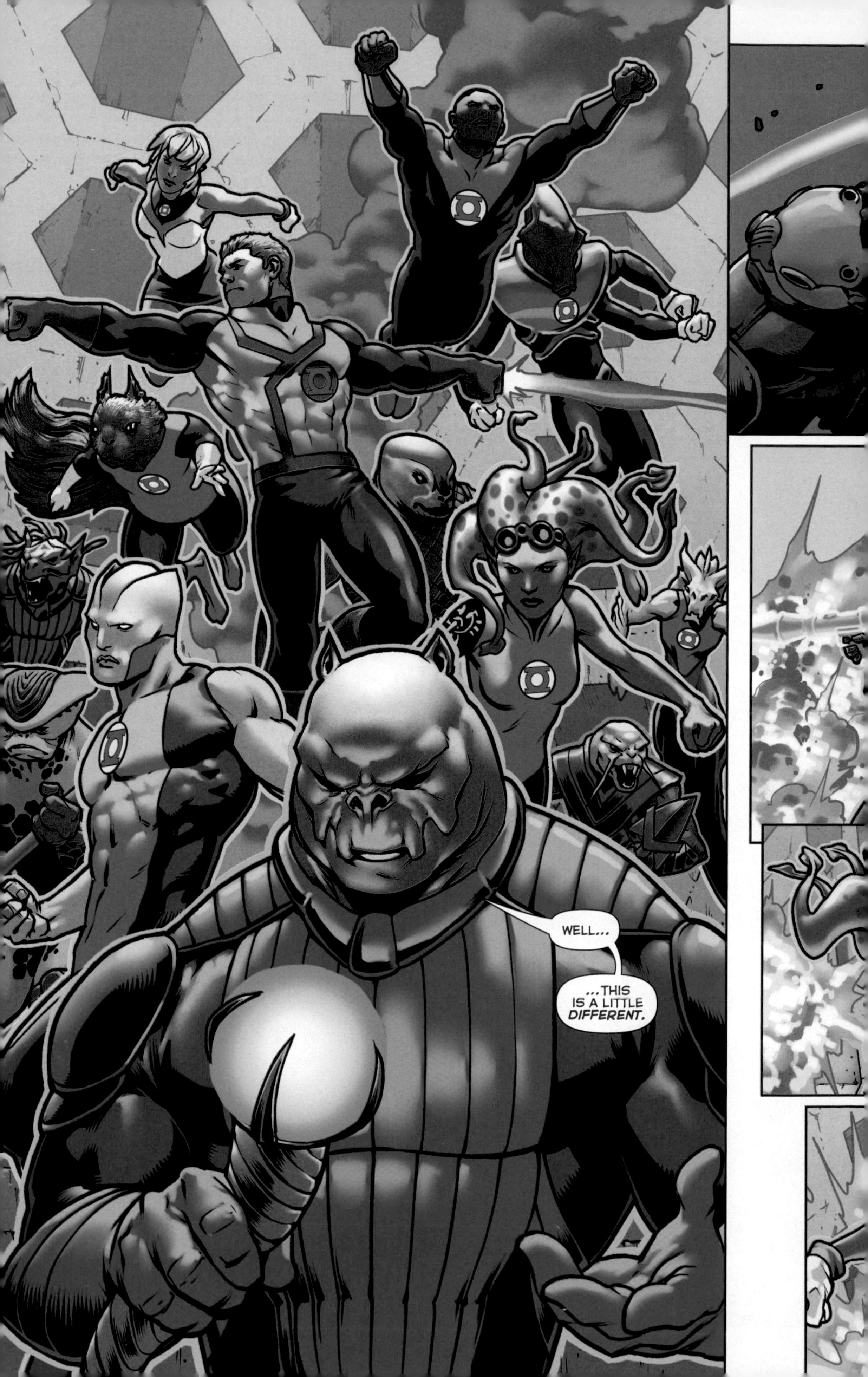
WELL...
...THIS IS A LITTLE DIFFERENT.

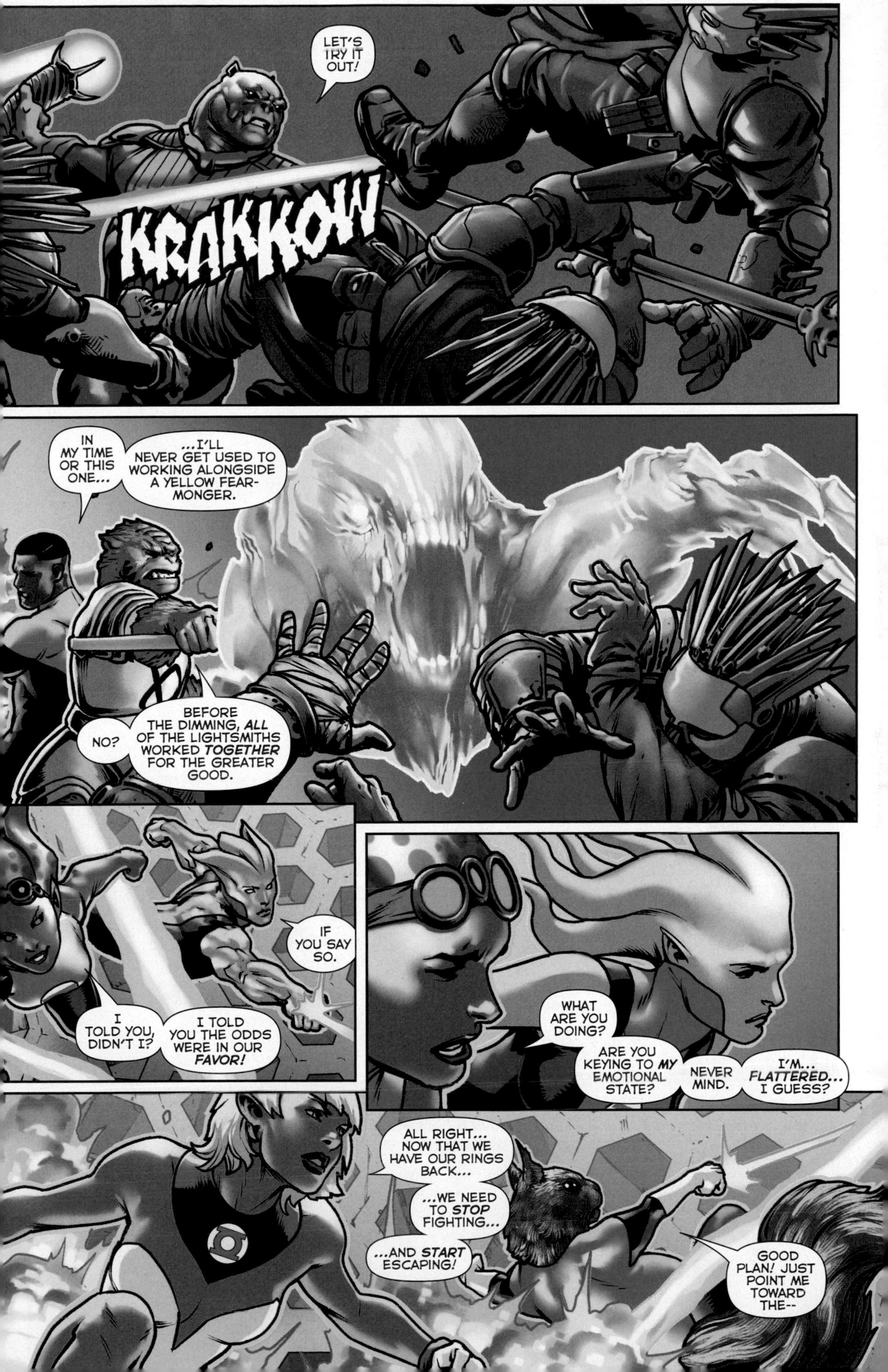
LET'S TRY IT OUT!
KRAKKOW
IN MY TIME OR THIS ONE...
...I'LL NEVER GET USED TO WORKING ALONGSIDE A YELLOW FEAR-MONGER.
NO?
BEFORE THE DIMMING, ALL OF THE LIGHTSMITHS WORKED TOGETHER FOR THE GREATER GOOD.
IF YOU SAY SO.
I TOLD YOU, DIDN'T I?
I TOLD YOU THE ODDS WERE IN OUR FAVOR!
WHAT ARE YOU DOING?
ARE YOU KEYING TO MY EMOTIONAL STATE?
NEVER MIND.
I'M... FLATTERED... I GUESS?
ALL RIGHT... NOW THAT WE HAVE OUR RINGS BACK...
...WE NEED TO STOP FIGHTING...
...AND START ESCAPING!
GOOD PLAN! JUST POINT ME TOWARD THE--

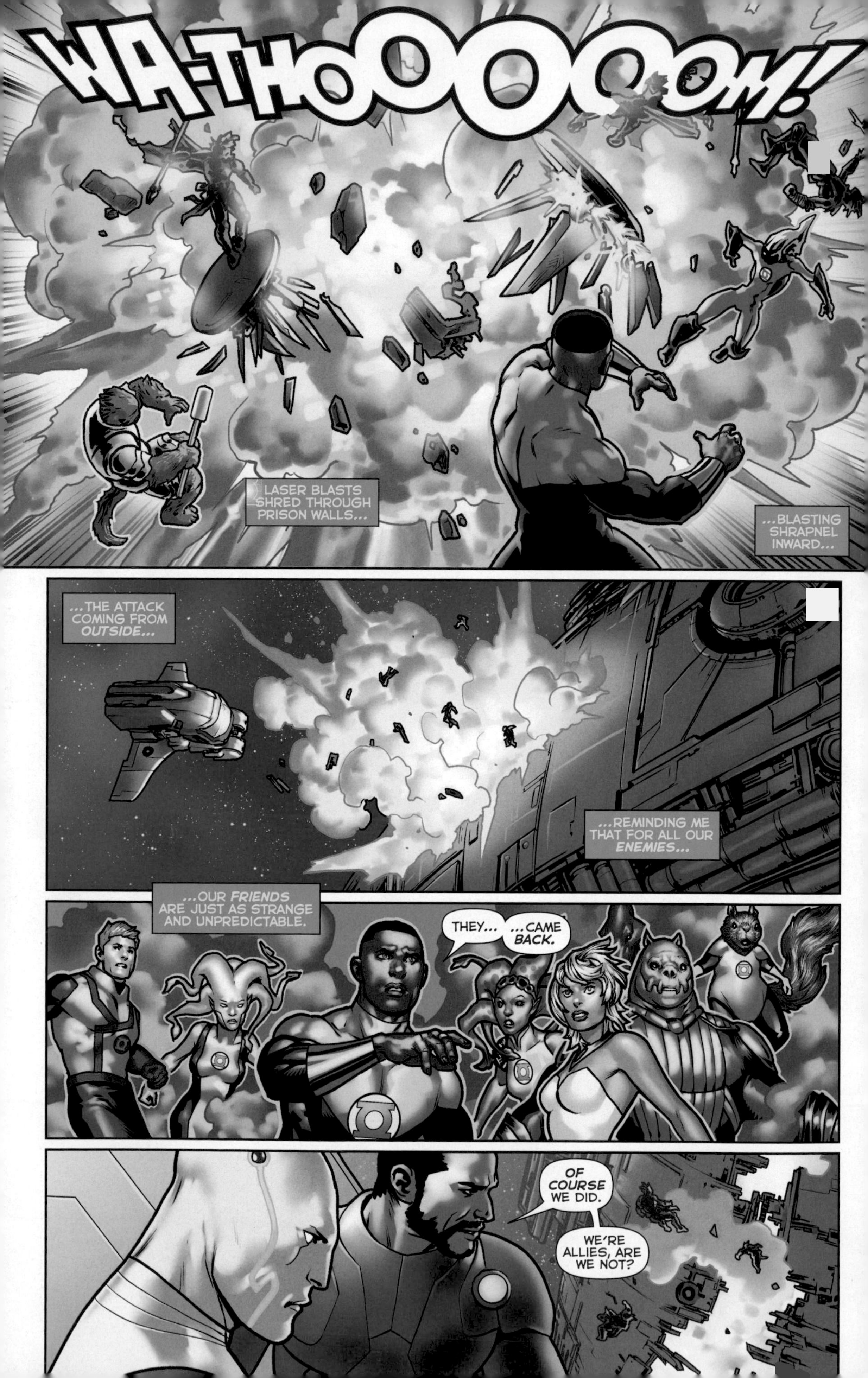
WA-THOOOOOOM!
LASER BLASTS SHRED THROUGH PRISON WALLS...
...BLASTING SHRAPNEL INWARD...
...THE ATTACK COMING FROM OUTSIDE...
...REMINDING ME THAT FOR ALL OUR ENEMIES...
...OUR FRIENDS ARE JUST AS STRANGE AND UNPREDICTABLE.
THEY... ...CAME BACK.
OF COURSE WE DID.
WE'RE ALLIES, ARE WE NOT?

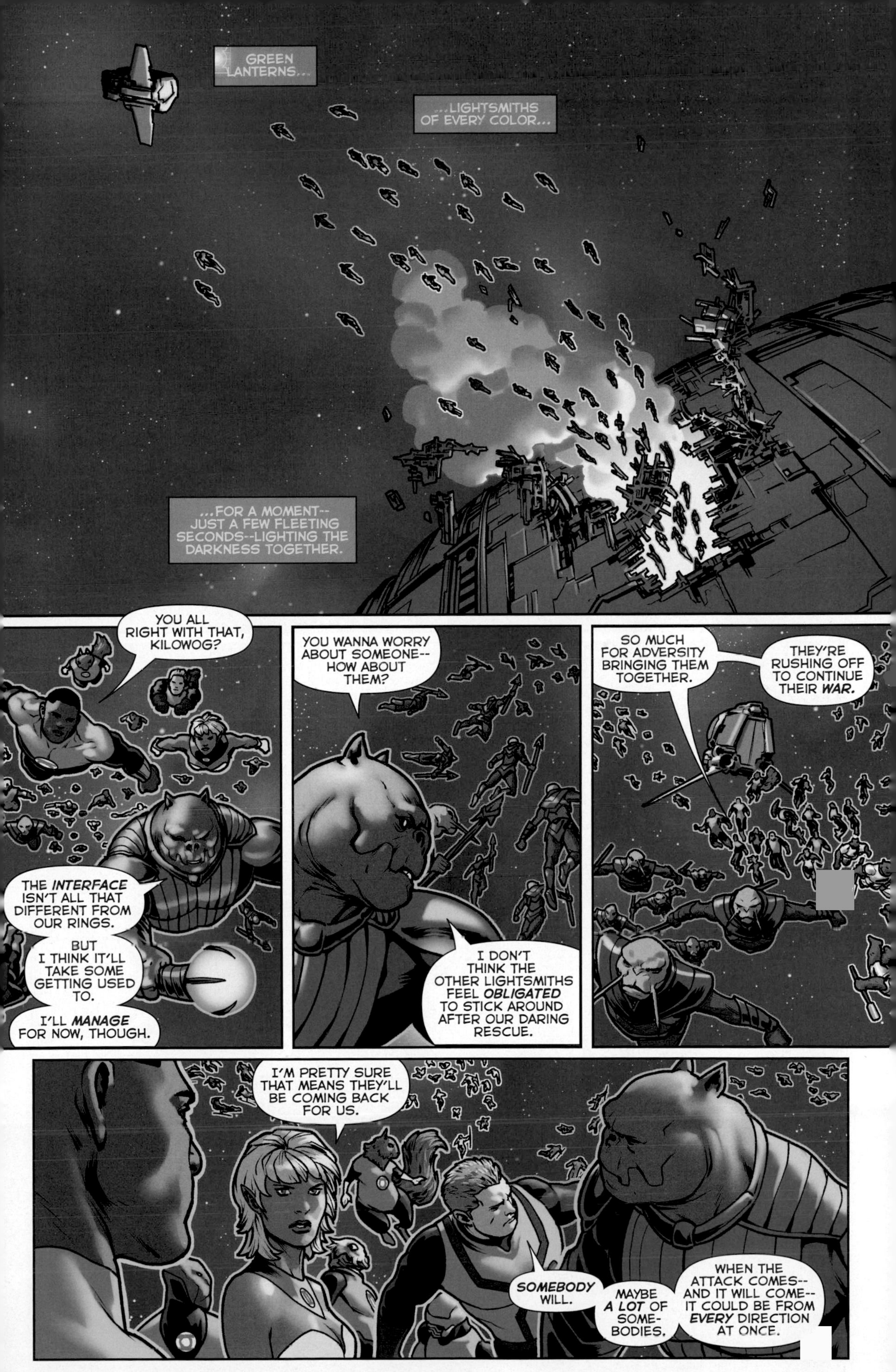
GREEN LANTERNS...
...LIGHTSMITHS OF EVERY COLOR...
...FOR A MOMENT-- JUST A FEW FLEETING SECONDS--LIGHTING THE DARKNESS TOGETHER.
YOU ALL RIGHT WITH THAT, KILOWOG?
THE INTERFACE ISN'T ALL THAT DIFFERENT FROM OUR RINGS.
BUT I THINK IT'LL TAKE SOME GETTING USED TO.
I'LL MANAGE FOR NOW, THOUGH.
YOU WANNA WORRY ABOUT SOMEONE-- HOW ABOUT THEM?
I DON'T THINK THE OTHER LIGHTSMITHS FEEL OBLIGATED TO STICK AROUND AFTER OUR DARING RESCUE.
SO MUCH FOR ADVERSITY BRINGING THEM TOGETHER.
THEY'RE RUSHING OFF TO CONTINUE THEIR WAR.
I'M PRETTY SURE THAT MEANS THEY'LL BE COMING BACK FOR US.
SOMEBODY WILL.
MAYBE A LOT OF SOME-BODIES.
WHEN THE ATTACK COMES-- AND IT WILL COME-- IT COULD BE FROM EVERY DIRECTION AT ONCE.

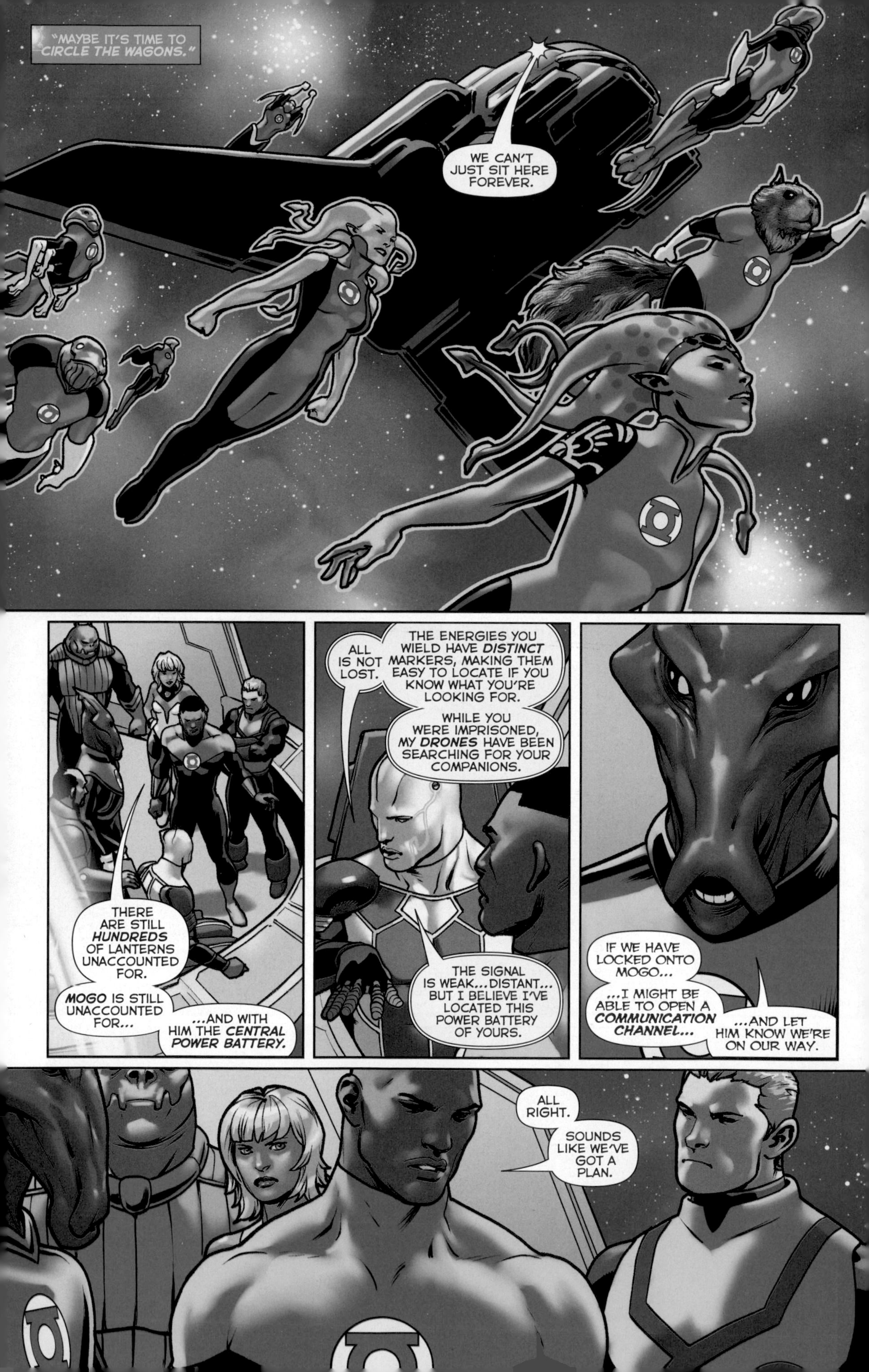
"MAYBE IT'S TIME TO CIRCLE THE WAGONS."
WE CAN'T JUST SIT HERE FOREVER.
THERE ARE STILL HUNDREDS OF LANTERNS UNACCOUNTED FOR.
MOGO IS STILL UNACCOUNTED FOR...
...AND WITH HIM THE CENTRAL POWER BATTERY.
ALL IS NOT LOST.
THE ENERGIES YOU WIELD HAVE DISTINCT MARKERS, MAKING THEM EASY TO LOCATE IF YOU KNOW WHAT YOU'RE LOOKING FOR.
WHILE YOU WERE IMPRISONED, MY DRONES HAVE BEEN SEARCHING FOR YOUR COMPANIONS.
THE SIGNAL IS WEAK...DISTANT... BUT I BELIEVE I'VE LOCATED THIS POWER BATTERY OF YOURS.
IF WE HAVE LOCKED ONTO MOGO...
...I MIGHT BE ABLE TO OPEN A COMMUNICATION CHANNEL...
...AND LET HIM KNOW WE'RE ON OUR WAY.
ALL RIGHT.
SOUNDS LIKE WE'VE GOT A PLAN.

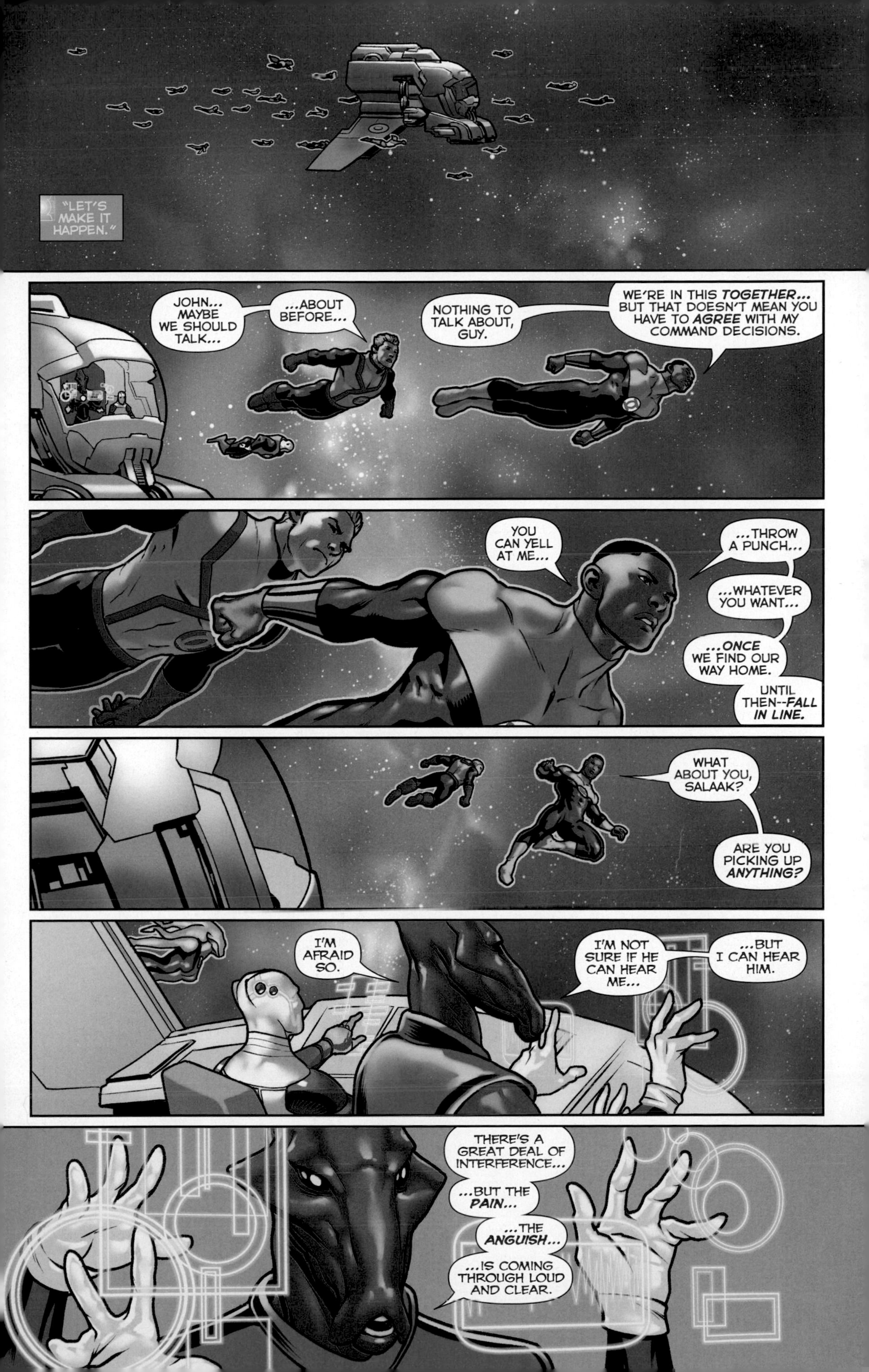
"LET'S MAKE IT HAPPEN."
JOHN... MAYBE WE SHOULD TALK...
...ABOUT BEFORE...
NOTHING TO TALK ABOUT, GUY.
WE'RE IN THIS TOGETHER... BUT THAT DOESN'T MEAN YOU HAVE TO AGREE WITH MY COMMAND DECISIONS.
YOU CAN YELL AT ME...
...THROW A PUNCH...
...WHATEVER YOU WANT...
...ONCE WE FIND OUR WAY HOME.
UNTIL THEN--FALL IN LINE.
WHAT ABOUT YOU, SALAAK?
ARE YOU PICKING UP ANYTHING?
I'M AFRAID SO.
I'M NOT SURE IF HE CAN HEAR ME...
...BUT I CAN HEAR HIM.
THERE'S A GREAT DEAL OF INTERFERENCE...
...BUT THE PAIN...
...THE ANGUISH...
...IS COMING THROUGH LOUD AND CLEAR.

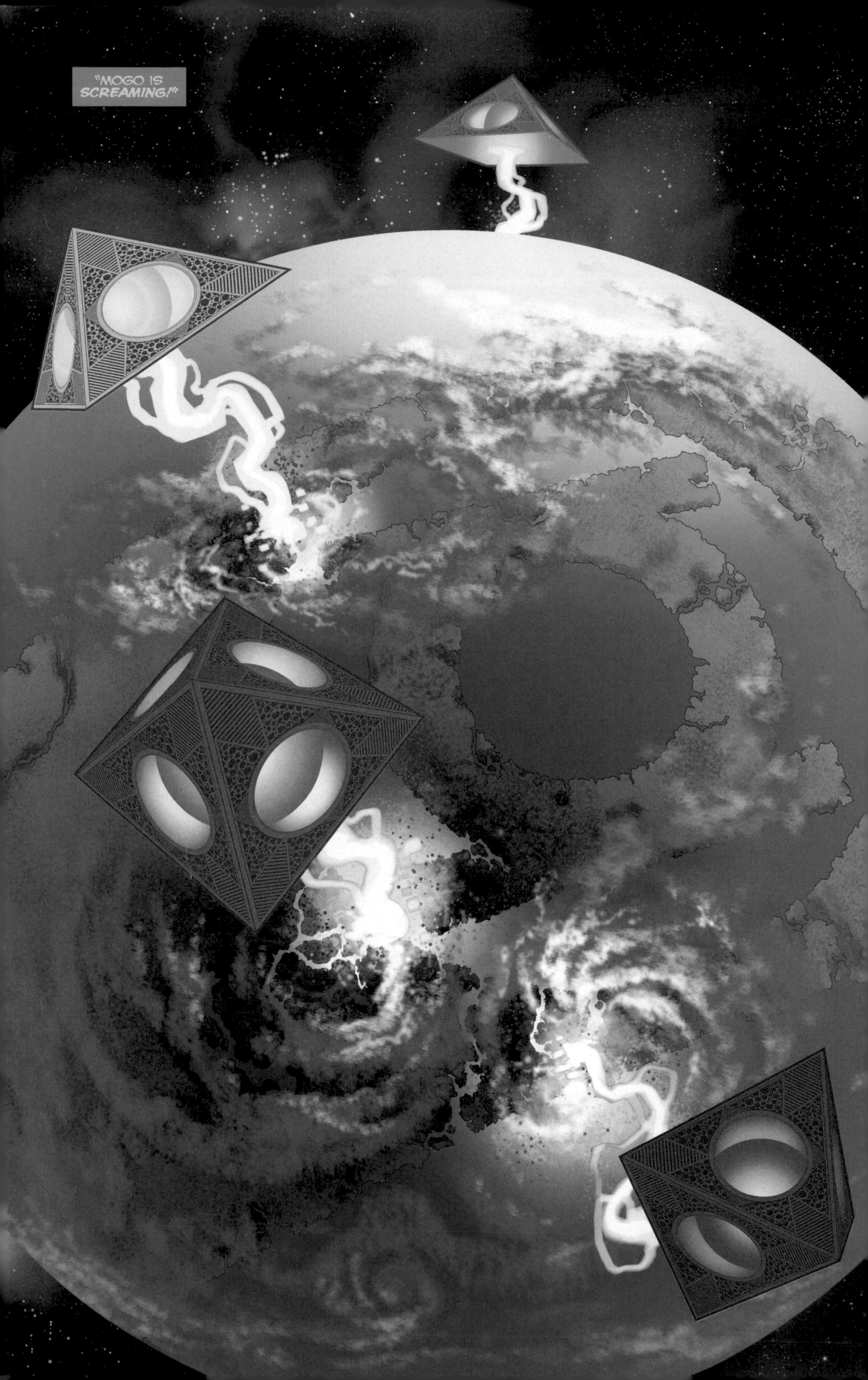
"MOGO IS SCREAMING!"

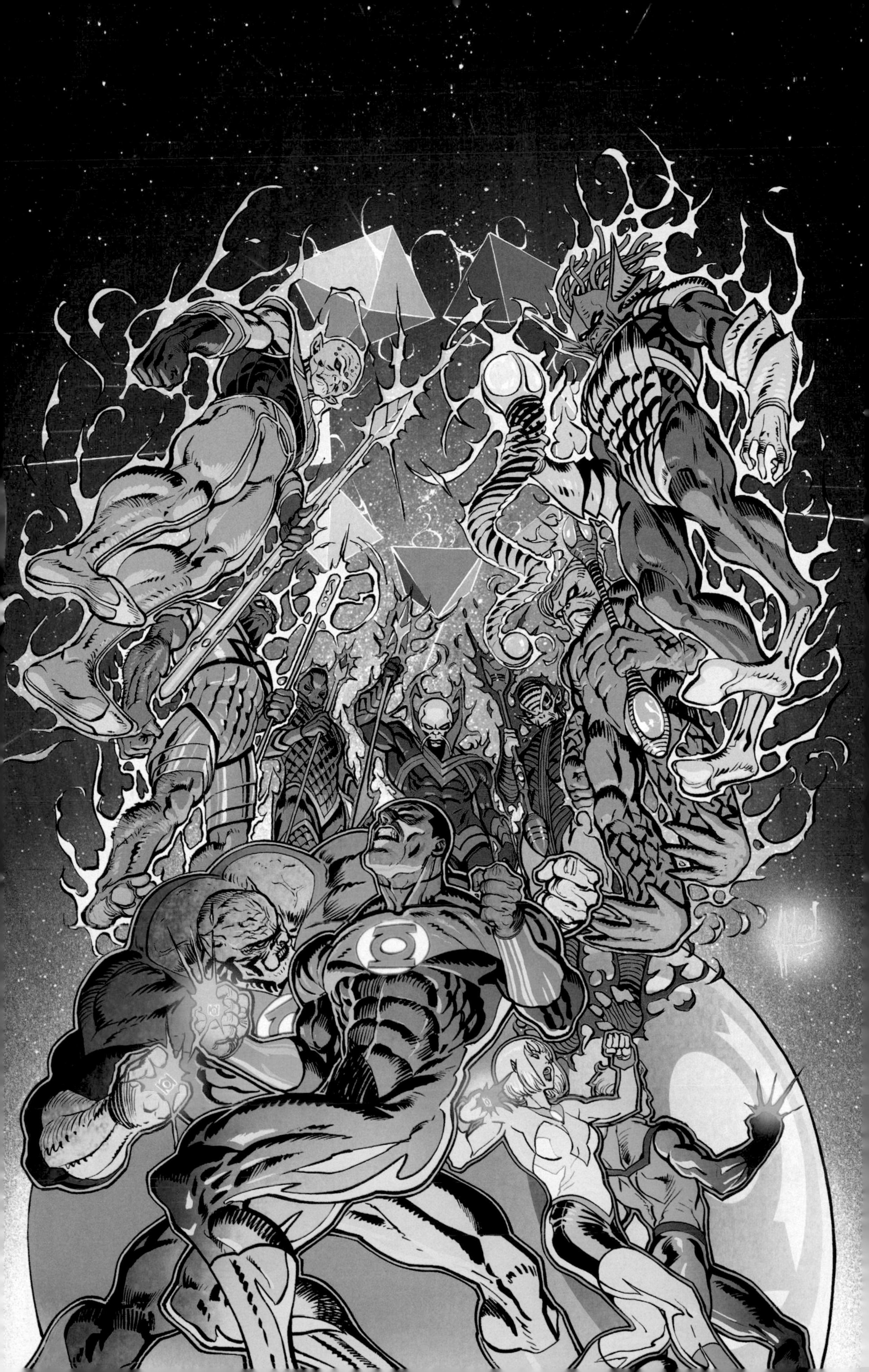

CULLEN BUNN writer **JESUS SAIZ** artist & colorist **DAVE SHARPE** letterer **GUILLEM MARCH** cover

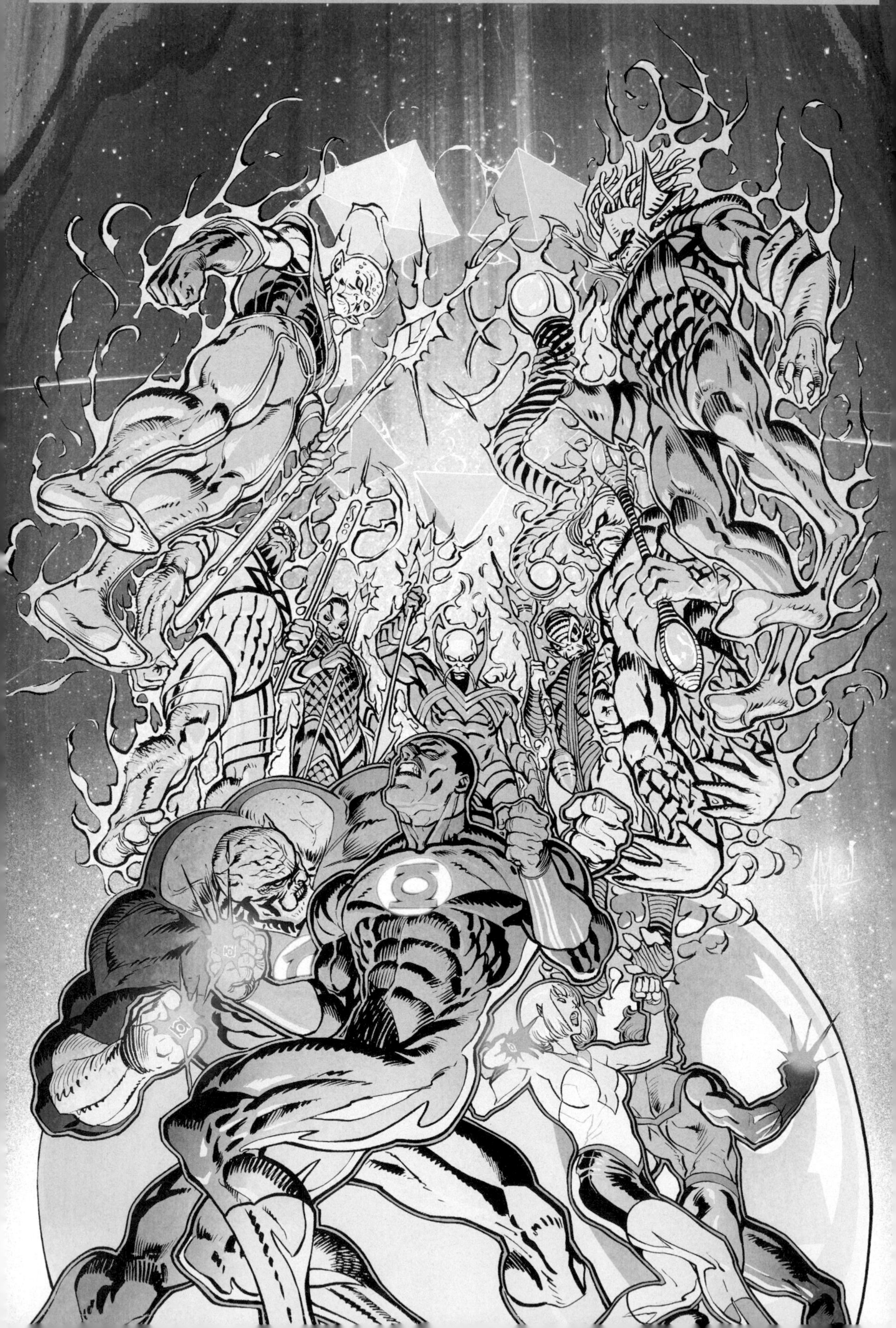

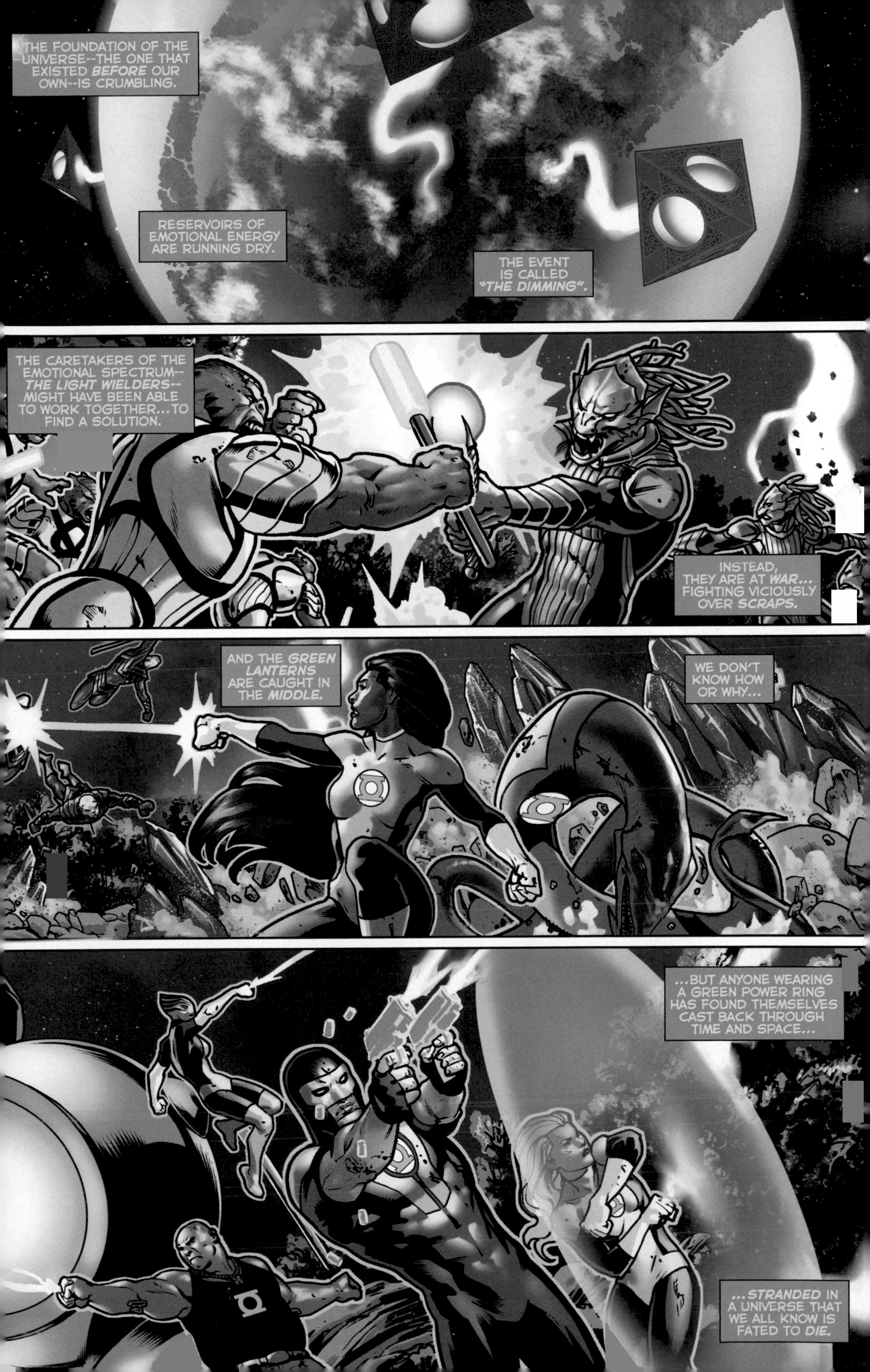
THE FOUNDATION OF THE UNIVERSE--THE ONE THAT EXISTED *BEFORE* OUR OWN--IS CRUMBLING.
RESERVOIRS OF EMOTIONAL ENERGY ARE RUNNING DRY.
THE EVENT IS CALLED *"THE DIMMING"*.
THE CARETAKERS OF THE EMOTIONAL SPECTRUM--*THE LIGHT WIELDERS*--MIGHT HAVE BEEN ABLE TO WORK TOGETHER...TO FIND A SOLUTION.
INSTEAD, THEY ARE AT *WAR*... FIGHTING VICIOUSLY OVER *SCRAPS*.
AND THE *GREEN LANTERNS* ARE CAUGHT IN THE *MIDDLE*.
WE DON'T KNOW HOW OR WHY...
...BUT ANYONE WEARING A GREEN POWER RING HAS FOUND THEMSELVES CAST BACK THROUGH TIME AND SPACE...
...*STRANDED* IN A UNIVERSE THAT WE ALL KNOW IS FATED TO *DIE*.

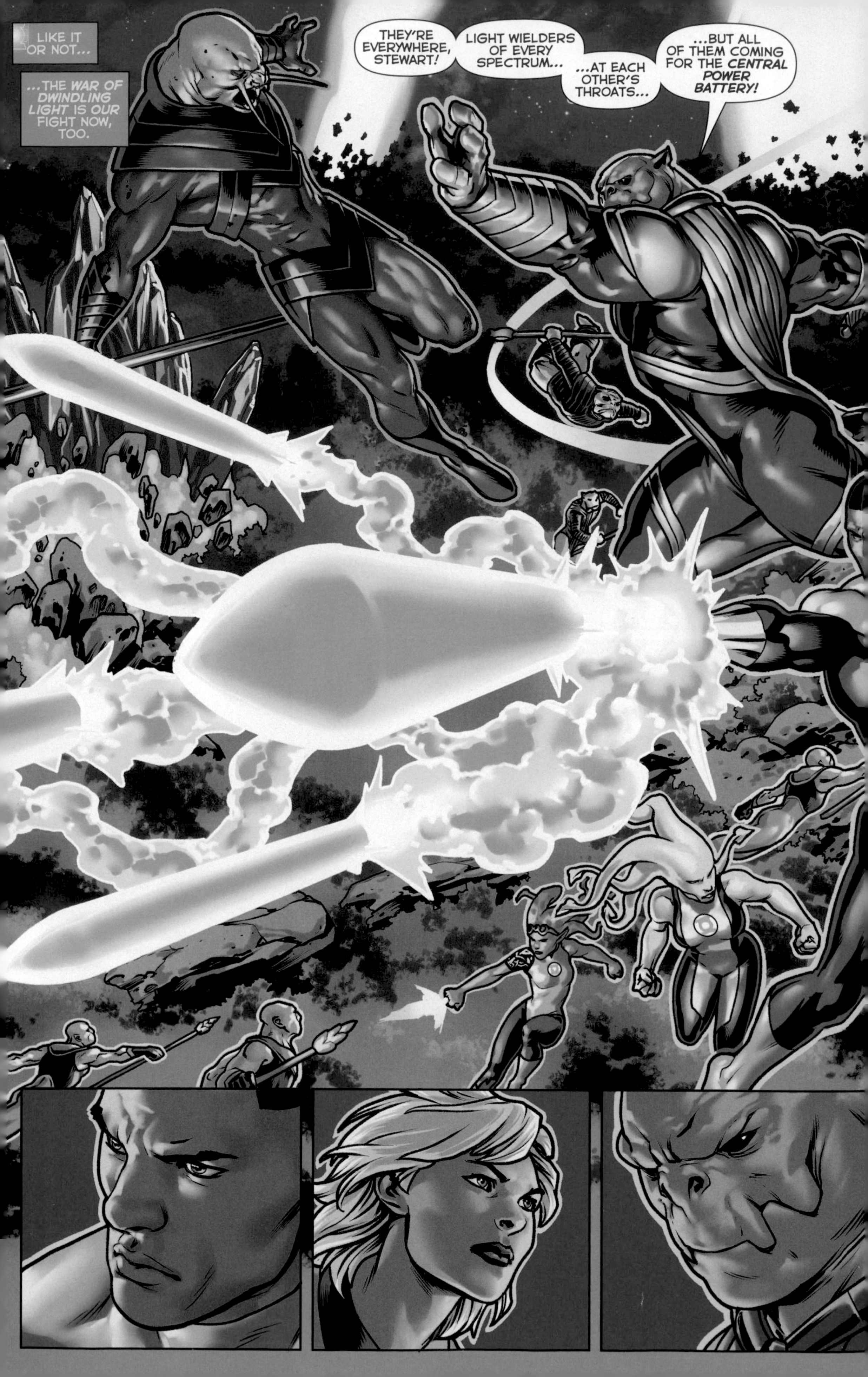
LIKE IT OR NOT...
...THE WAR OF DWINDLING LIGHT IS OUR FIGHT NOW, TOO.
THEY'RE EVERYWHERE, STEWART!
LIGHT WIELDERS OF EVERY SPECTRUM...
...AT EACH OTHER'S THROATS...
...BUT ALL OF THEM COMING FOR THE CENTRAL POWER BATTERY!

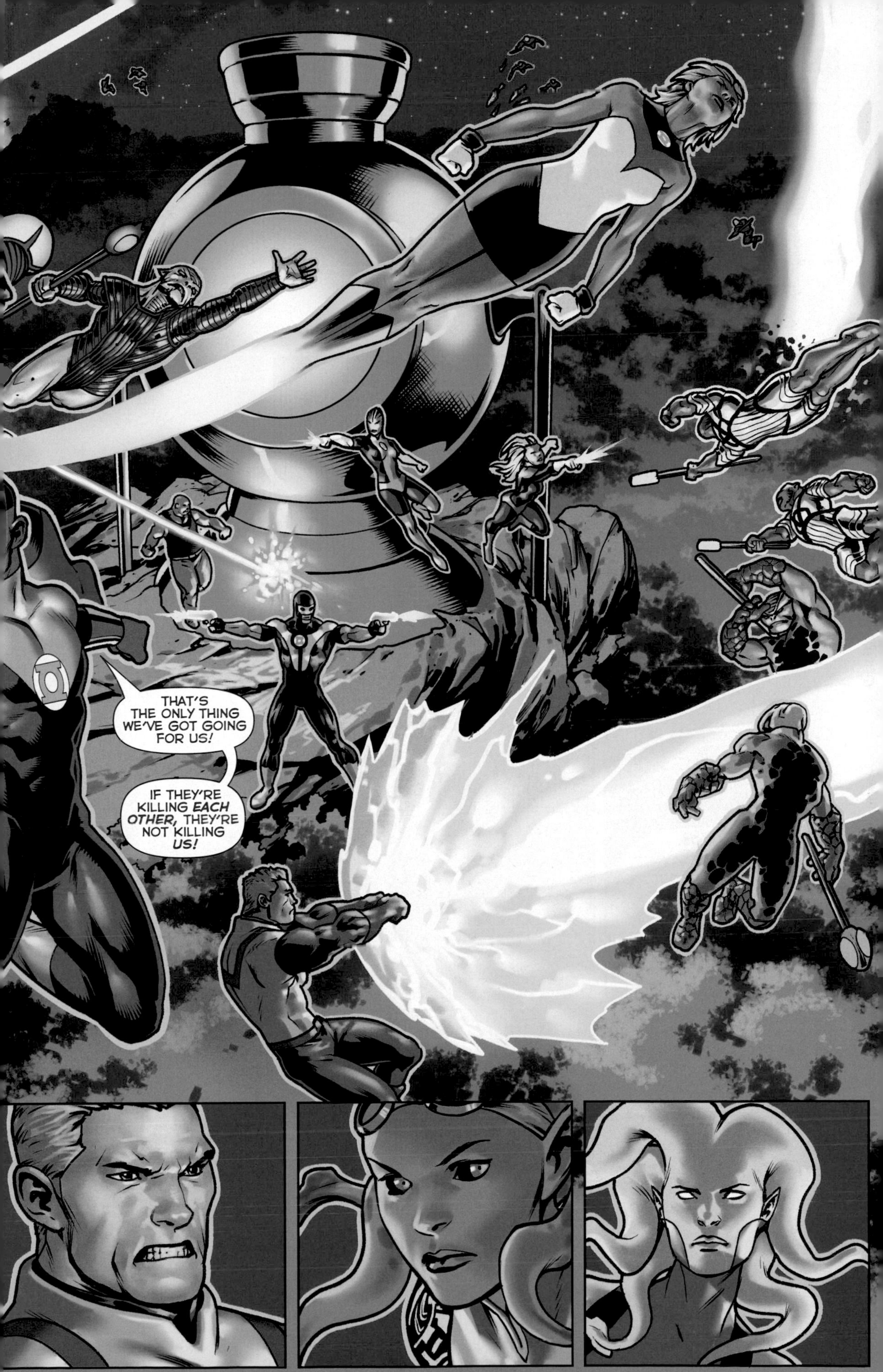
THAT'S THE ONLY THING WE'VE GOT GOING FOR US!
IF THEY'RE KILLING *EACH OTHER*, THEY'RE NOT KILLING *US!*

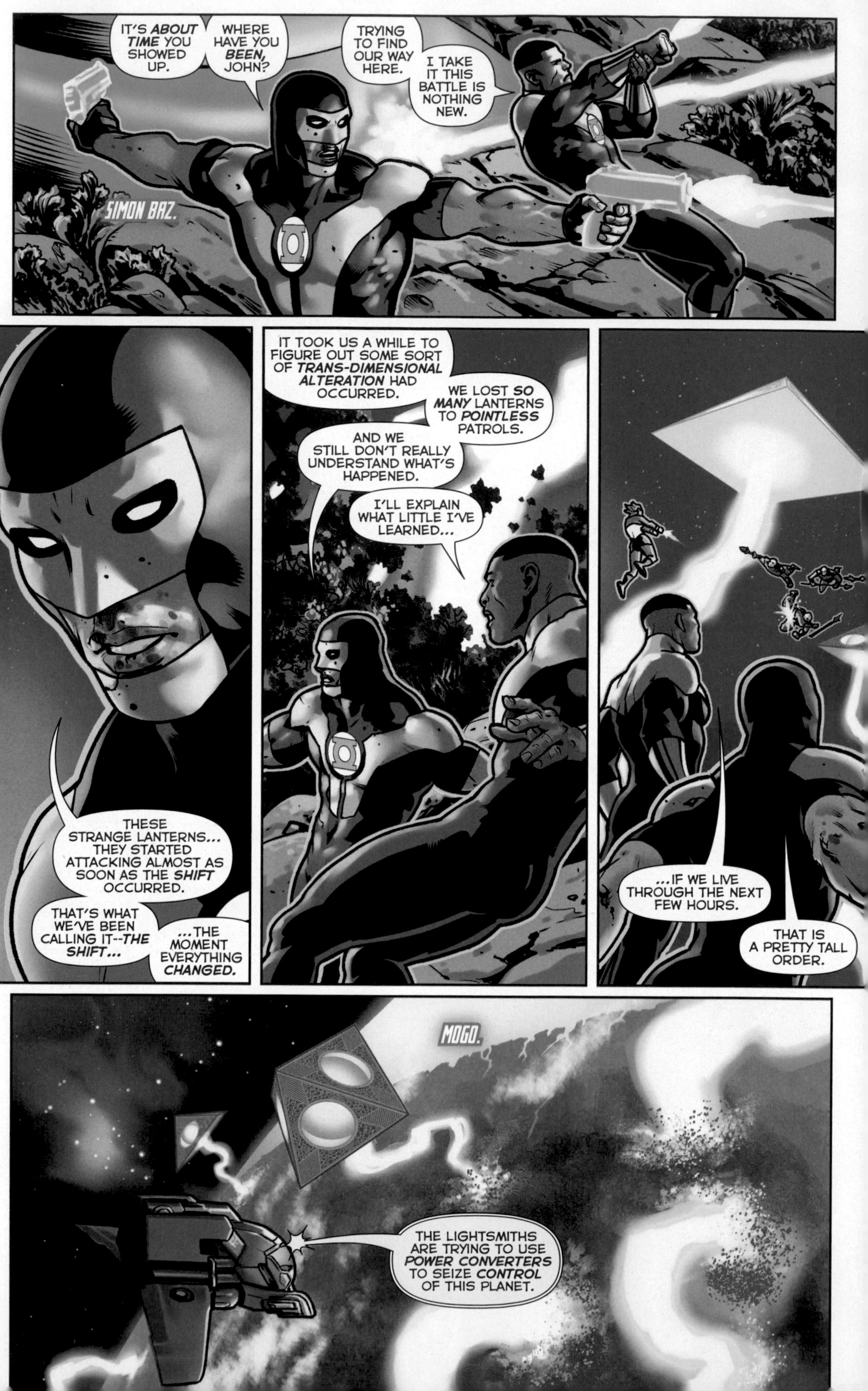
IT'S ABOUT TIME YOU SHOWED UP.
WHERE HAVE YOU BEEN, JOHN?
TRYING TO FIND OUR WAY HERE.
I TAKE IT THIS BATTLE IS NOTHING NEW.
SIMON BAZ.
THESE STRANGE LANTERNS... THEY STARTED ATTACKING ALMOST AS SOON AS THE SHIFT OCCURRED.
THAT'S WHAT WE'VE BEEN CALLING IT--THE SHIFT...
...THE MOMENT EVERYTHING CHANGED.
IT TOOK US A WHILE TO FIGURE OUT SOME SORT OF TRANS-DIMENSIONAL ALTERATION HAD OCCURRED.
WE LOST SO MANY LANTERNS TO POINTLESS PATROLS.
AND WE STILL DON'T REALLY UNDERSTAND WHAT'S HAPPENED.
I'LL EXPLAIN WHAT LITTLE I'VE LEARNED...
...IF WE LIVE THROUGH THE NEXT FEW HOURS.
THAT IS A PRETTY TALL ORDER.
MOGO.
THE LIGHTSMITHS ARE TRYING TO USE POWER CONVERTERS TO SEIZE CONTROL OF THIS PLANET.

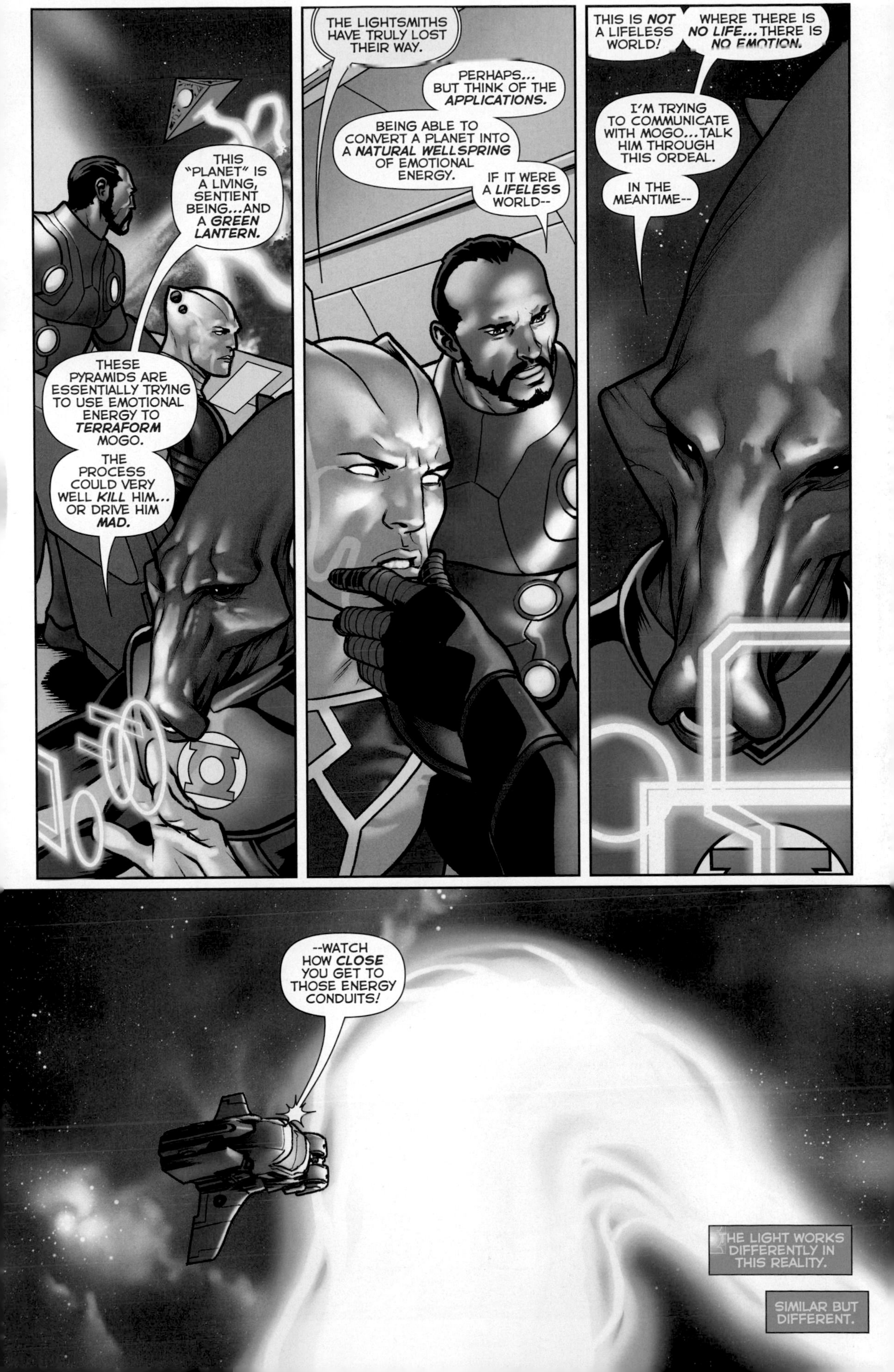
THIS "PLANET" IS A LIVING, SENTIENT BEING...AND A GREEN LANTERN.
THESE PYRAMIDS ARE ESSENTIALLY TRYING TO USE EMOTIONAL ENERGY TO TERRAFORM MOGO.
THE PROCESS COULD VERY WELL KILL HIM... OR DRIVE HIM MAD.
THE LIGHTSMITHS HAVE TRULY LOST THEIR WAY.
PERHAPS... BUT THINK OF THE APPLICATIONS.
BEING ABLE TO CONVERT A PLANET INTO A NATURAL WELLSPRING OF EMOTIONAL ENERGY.
IF IT WERE A LIFELESS WORLD--
THIS IS NOT A LIFELESS WORLD!
WHERE THERE IS NO LIFE... THERE IS NO EMOTION.
I'M TRYING TO COMMUNICATE WITH MOGO...TALK HIM THROUGH THIS ORDEAL.
IN THE MEANTIME--
--WATCH HOW CLOSE YOU GET TO THOSE ENERGY CONDUITS!
THE LIGHT WORKS DIFFERENTLY IN THIS REALITY.
SIMILAR BUT DIFFERENT.

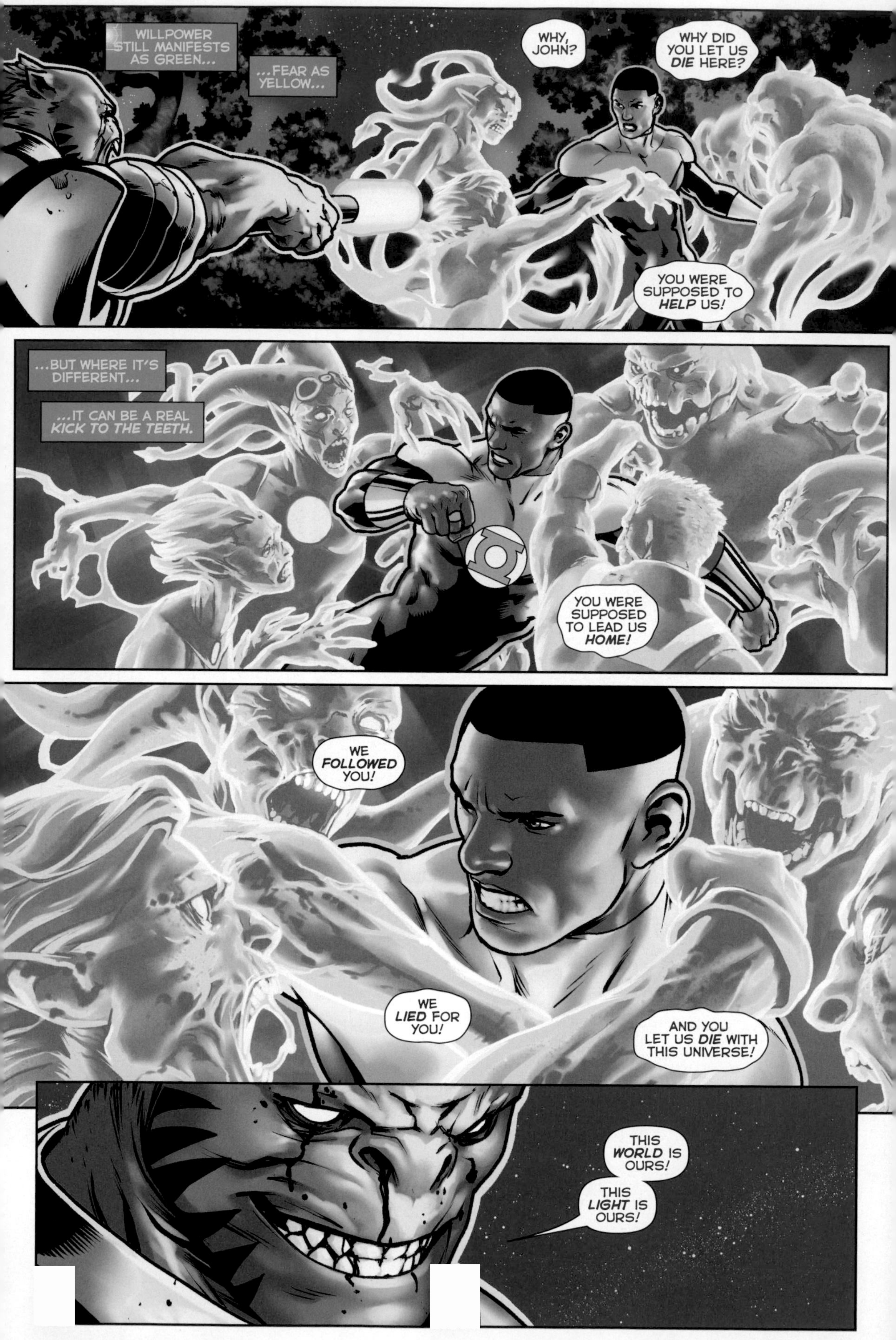
WILLPOWER STILL MANIFESTS AS GREEN...
...FEAR AS YELLOW...
WHY, JOHN?
WHY DID YOU LET US DIE HERE?
YOU WERE SUPPOSED TO HELP US!
...BUT WHERE IT'S DIFFERENT...
...IT CAN BE A REAL KICK TO THE TEETH.
YOU WERE SUPPOSED TO LEAD US HOME!
WE FOLLOWED YOU!
WE LIED FOR YOU!
AND YOU LET US DIE WITH THIS UNIVERSE!
THIS WORLD IS OURS!
THIS LIGHT IS OURS!

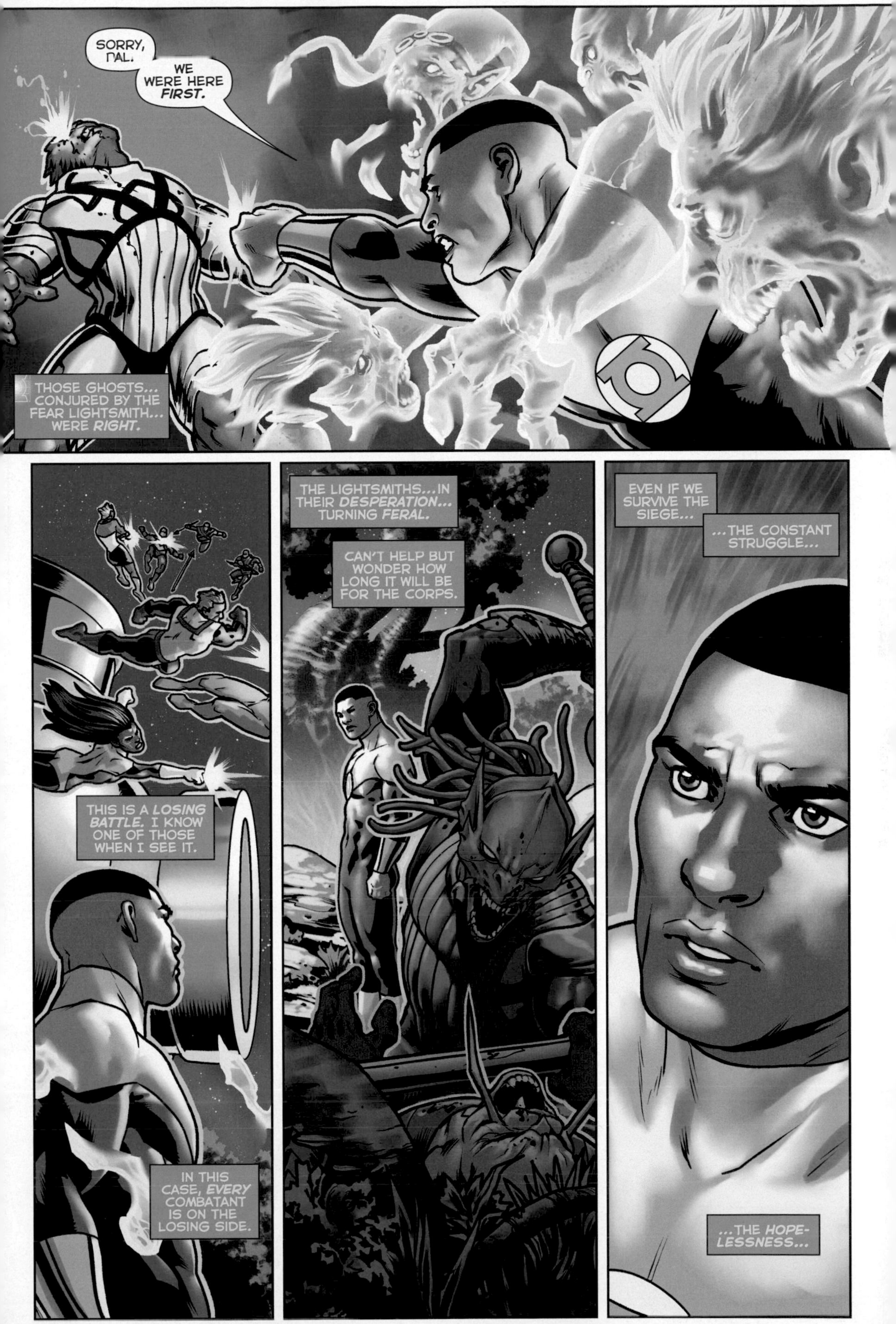

SORRY, HAL.
WE WERE HERE *FIRST.*
THOSE GHOSTS... CONJURED BY THE FEAR LIGHTSMITH... WERE *RIGHT.*
THIS IS A *LOSING BATTLE.* I KNOW ONE OF THOSE WHEN I SEE IT.
IN THIS CASE, *EVERY* COMBATANT IS ON THE LOSING SIDE.
THE LIGHTSMITHS...IN THEIR *DESPERATION*... TURNING *FERAL.*
CAN'T HELP BUT WONDER HOW LONG IT WILL BE FOR THE CORPS.
EVEN IF WE SURVIVE THE SIEGE...
...THE CONSTANT STRUGGLE...
...THE *HOPE-LESSNESS...*

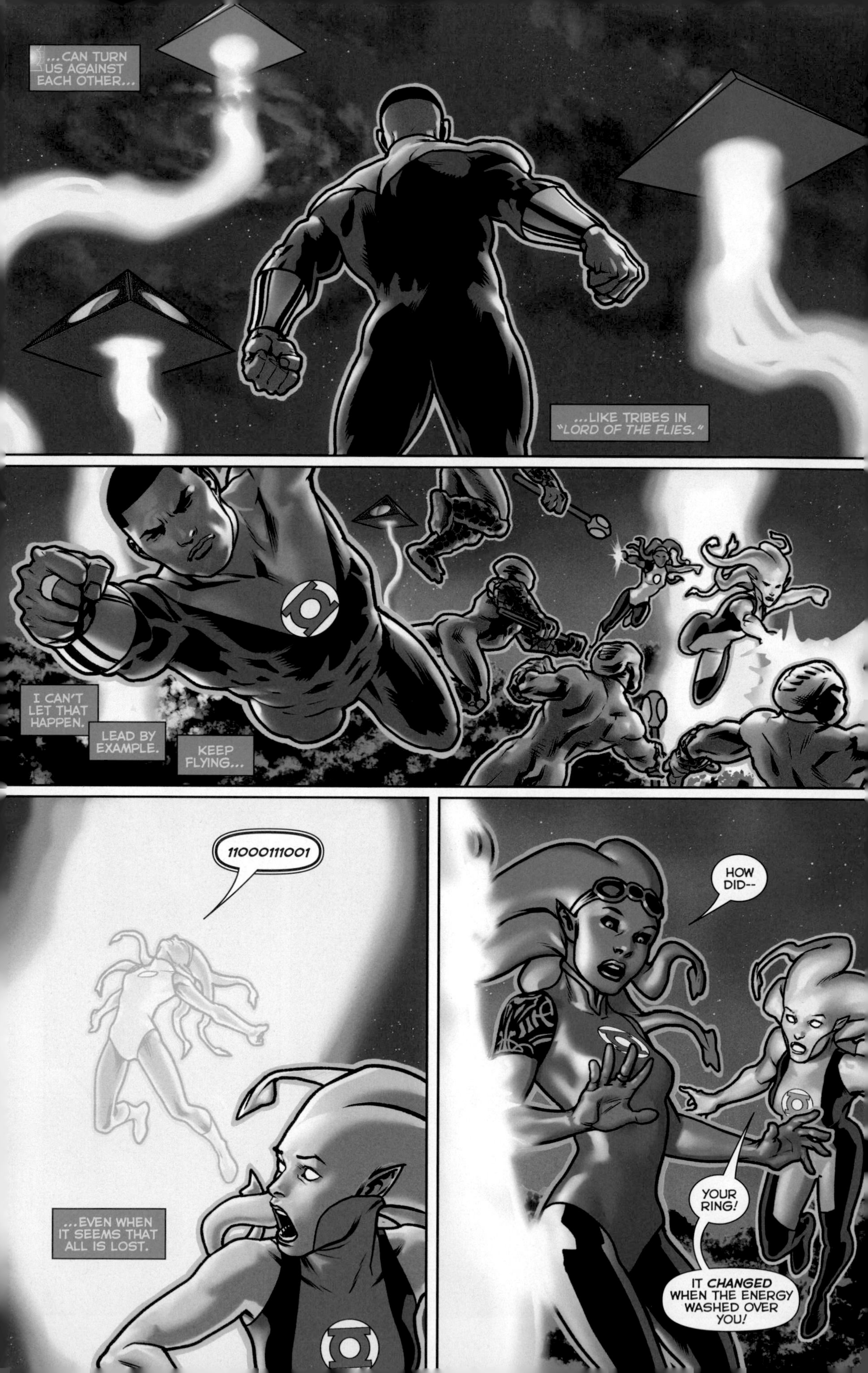
...CAN TURN US AGAINST EACH OTHER...
...LIKE TRIBES IN "LORD OF THE FLIES."
I CAN'T LET THAT HAPPEN.
LEAD BY EXAMPLE.
KEEP FLYING...
11000111001
...EVEN WHEN IT SEEMS THAT ALL IS LOST.
HOW DID--
YOUR RING!
IT CHANGED WHEN THE ENERGY WASHED OVER YOU!

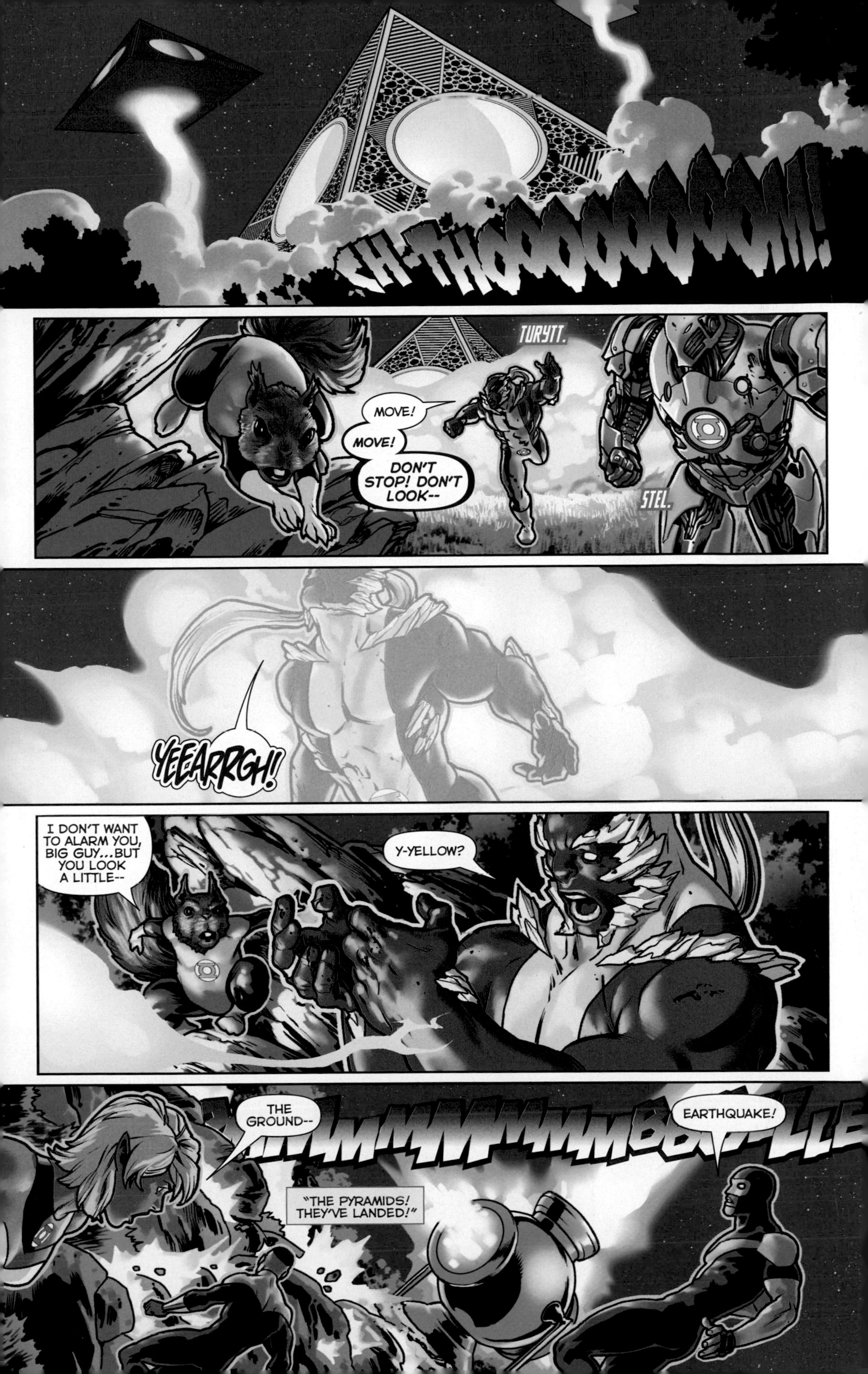
CH-THOOOOOOOM!
TURYTT.
MOVE!
MOVE!
DON'T STOP! DON'T LOOK--
STEL.
YEEARRGH!
I DON'T WANT TO ALARM YOU, BIG GUY...BUT YOU LOOK A LITTLE--
Y-YELLOW?
THE GROUND--
EARTHQUAKE!
"THE PYRAMIDS! THEY'VE LANDED!"

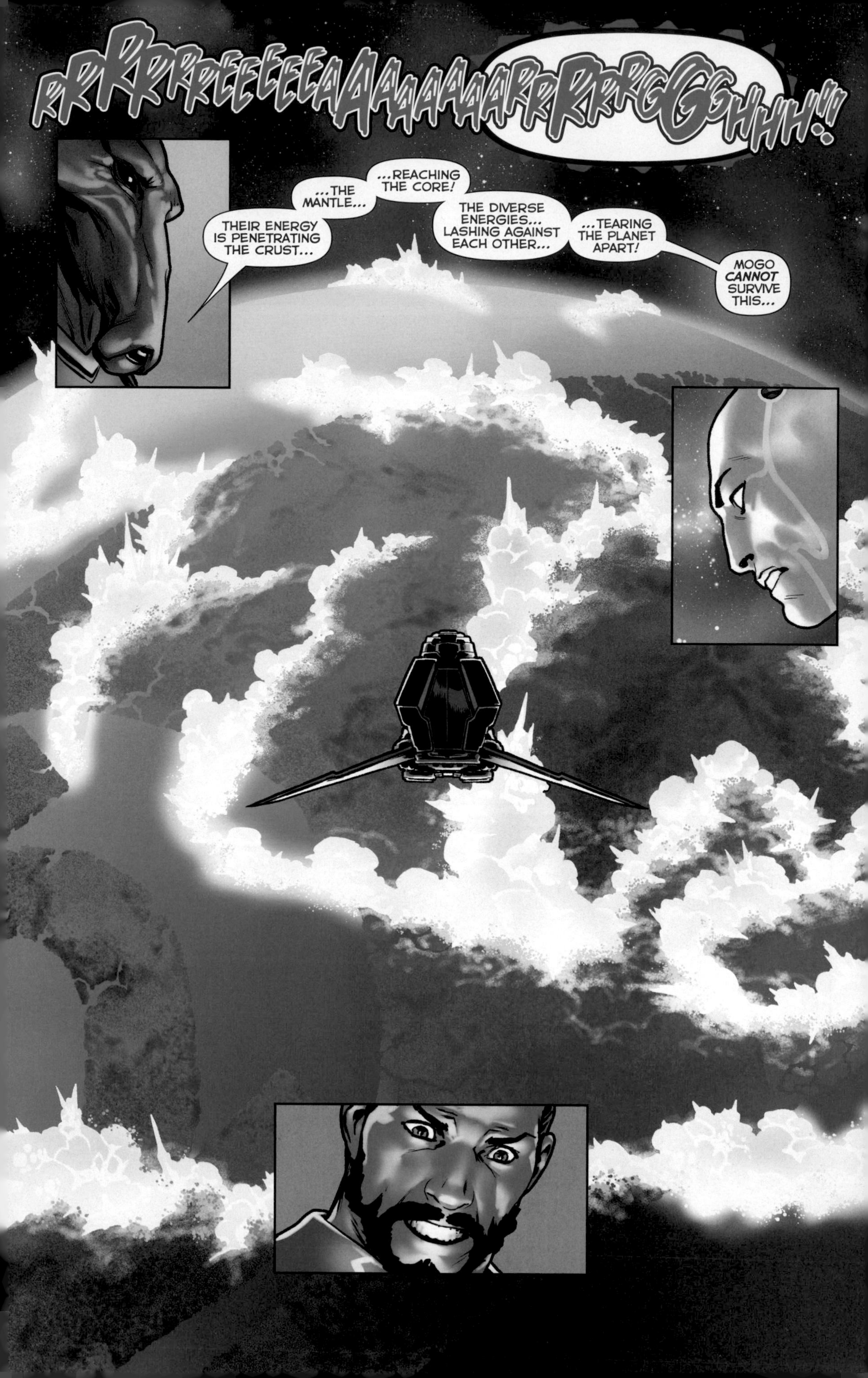

RRRRRRREEEEEEAAAAAAAAARRRRRRGGGHHHH!!!
THEIR ENERGY IS PENETRATING THE CRUST...
...THE MANTLE...
...REACHING THE CORE!
THE DIVERSE ENERGIES... LASHING AGAINST EACH OTHER...
...TEARING THE PLANET APART!
MOGO *CANNOT* SURVIVE THIS...

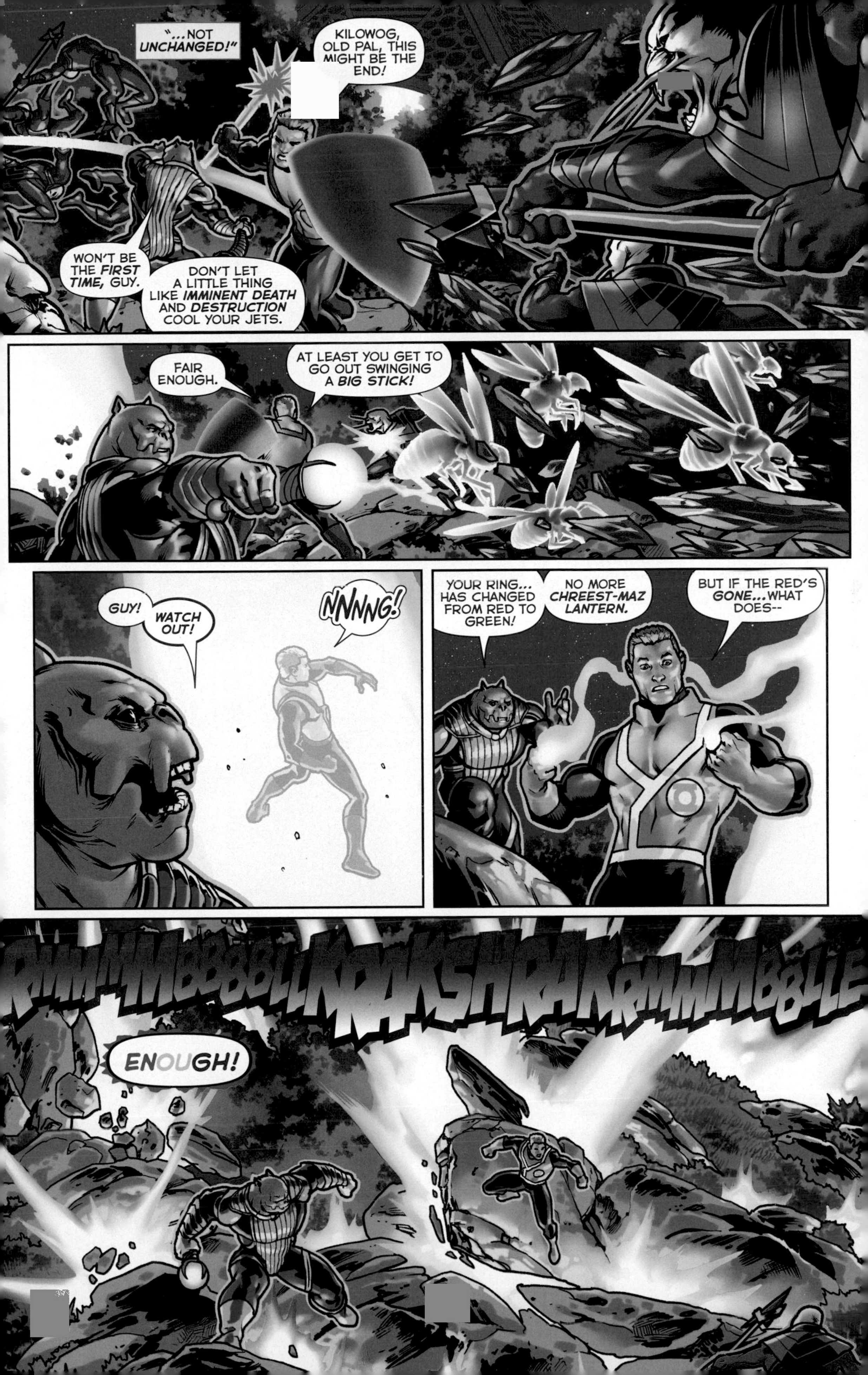

"...NOT UNCHANGED!"
KILOWOG, OLD PAL, THIS MIGHT BE THE END!
WON'T BE THE FIRST TIME, GUY.
DON'T LET A LITTLE THING LIKE IMMINENT DEATH AND DESTRUCTION COOL YOUR JETS.
FAIR ENOUGH.
AT LEAST YOU GET TO GO OUT SWINGING A BIG STICK!
GUY!
WATCH OUT!
NNNNG!
YOUR RING... HAS CHANGED FROM RED TO GREEN!
NO MORE CHREEST-MAZ LANTERN.
BUT IF THE RED'S GONE...WHAT DOES--
RMMMMBBBLLKRAKSHRAKRMMMMBBLLE
ENOUGH!

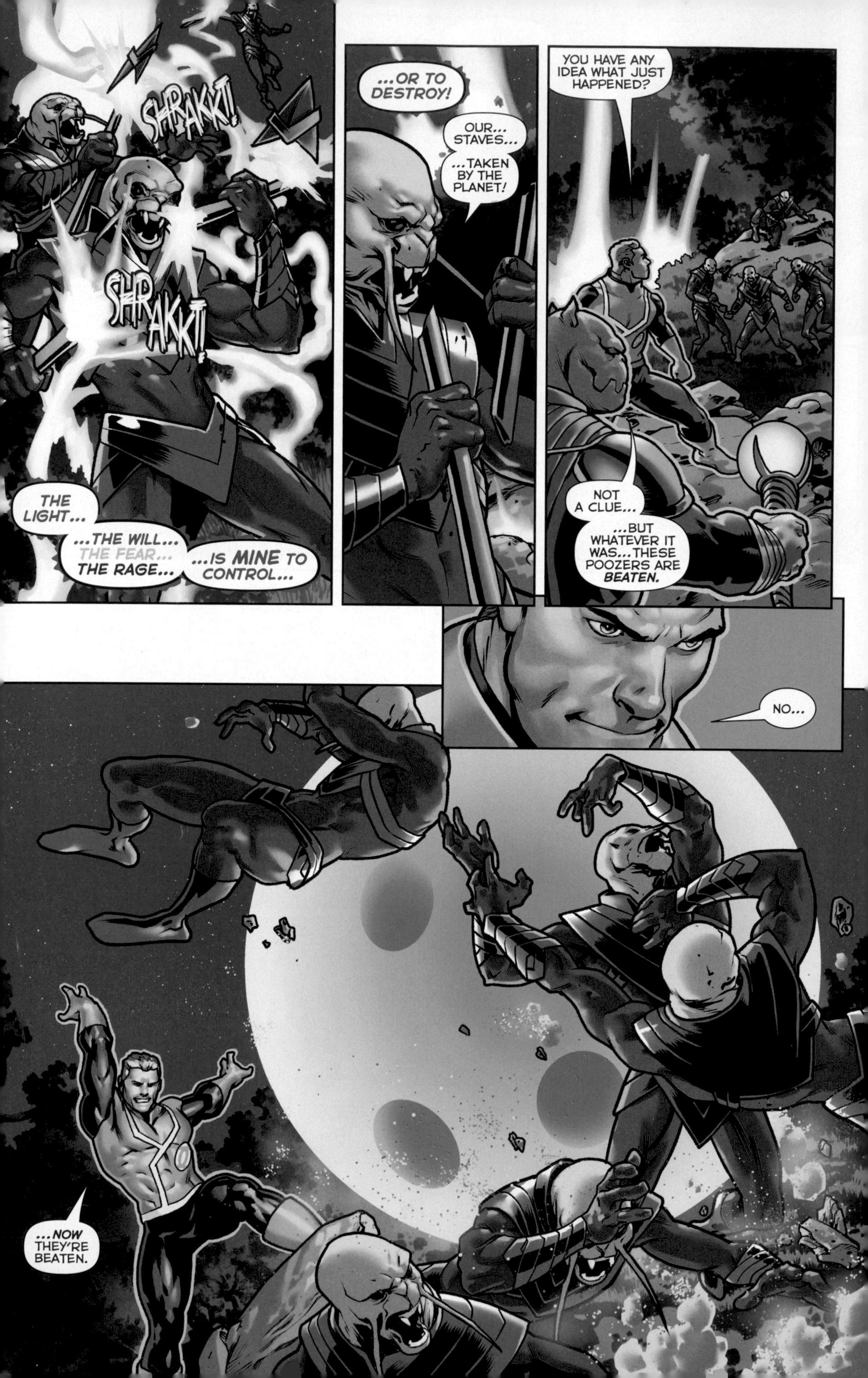
SHRAKK!!
SHRAKK!!
THE LIGHT...
...THE WILL...
THE FEAR...
THE RAGE...
...IS MINE TO CONTROL...
...OR TO DESTROY!
OUR... STAVES...
...TAKEN BY THE PLANET!
YOU HAVE ANY IDEA WHAT JUST HAPPENED?
NOT A CLUE...
...BUT WHATEVER IT WAS...THESE POOZERS ARE BEATEN.
NO...
...NOW THEY'RE BEATEN.

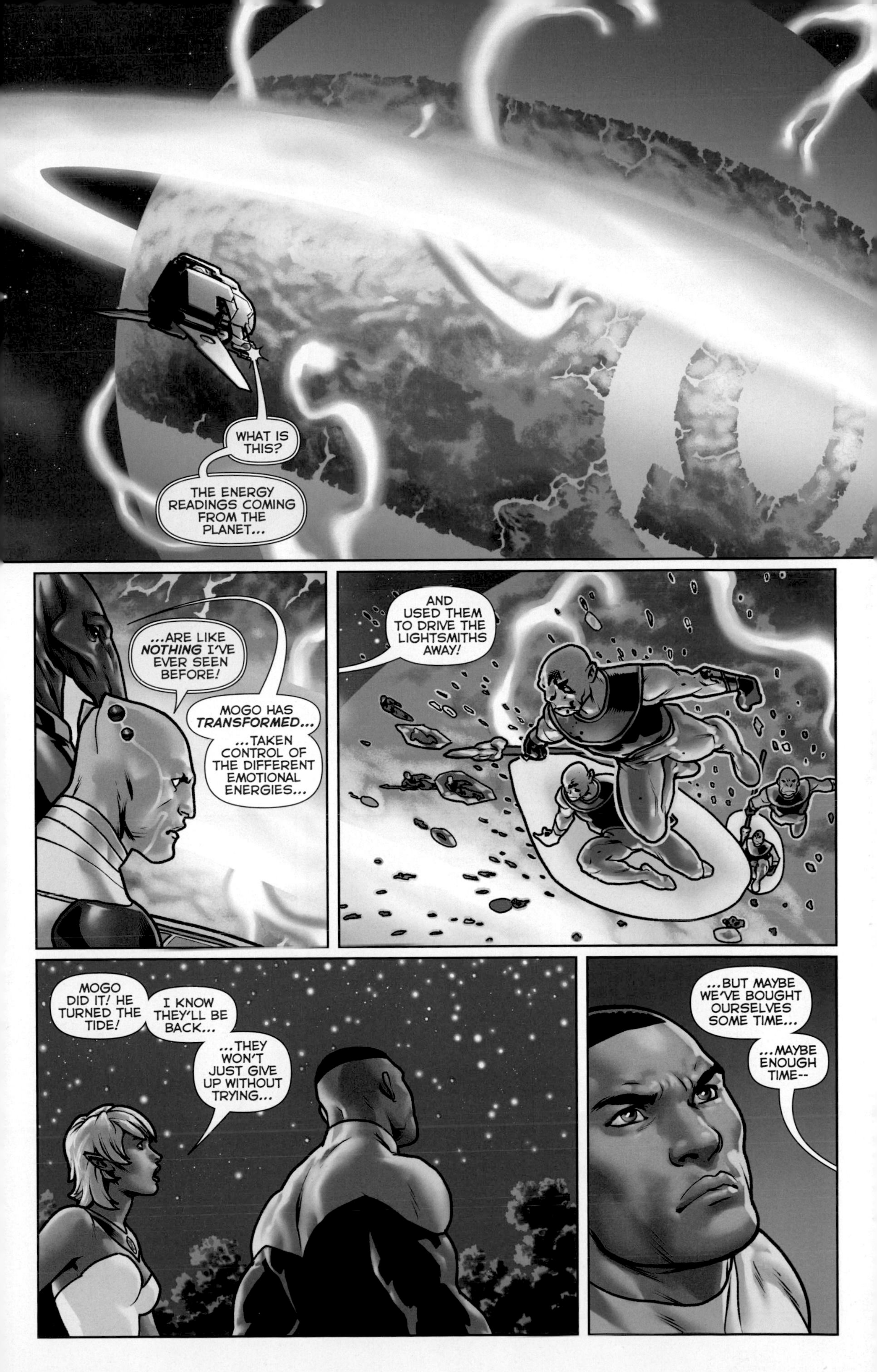
WHAT IS THIS?
THE ENERGY READINGS COMING FROM THE PLANET...
...ARE LIKE NOTHING I'VE EVER SEEN BEFORE!
MOGO HAS TRANSFORMED...
...TAKEN CONTROL OF THE DIFFERENT EMOTIONAL ENERGIES...
AND USED THEM TO DRIVE THE LIGHTSMITHS AWAY!
MOGO DID IT! HE TURNED THE TIDE!
I KNOW THEY'LL BE BACK...
...THEY WON'T JUST GIVE UP WITHOUT TRYING...
...BUT MAYBE WE'VE BOUGHT OURSELVES SOME TIME...
...MAYBE ENOUGH TIME--

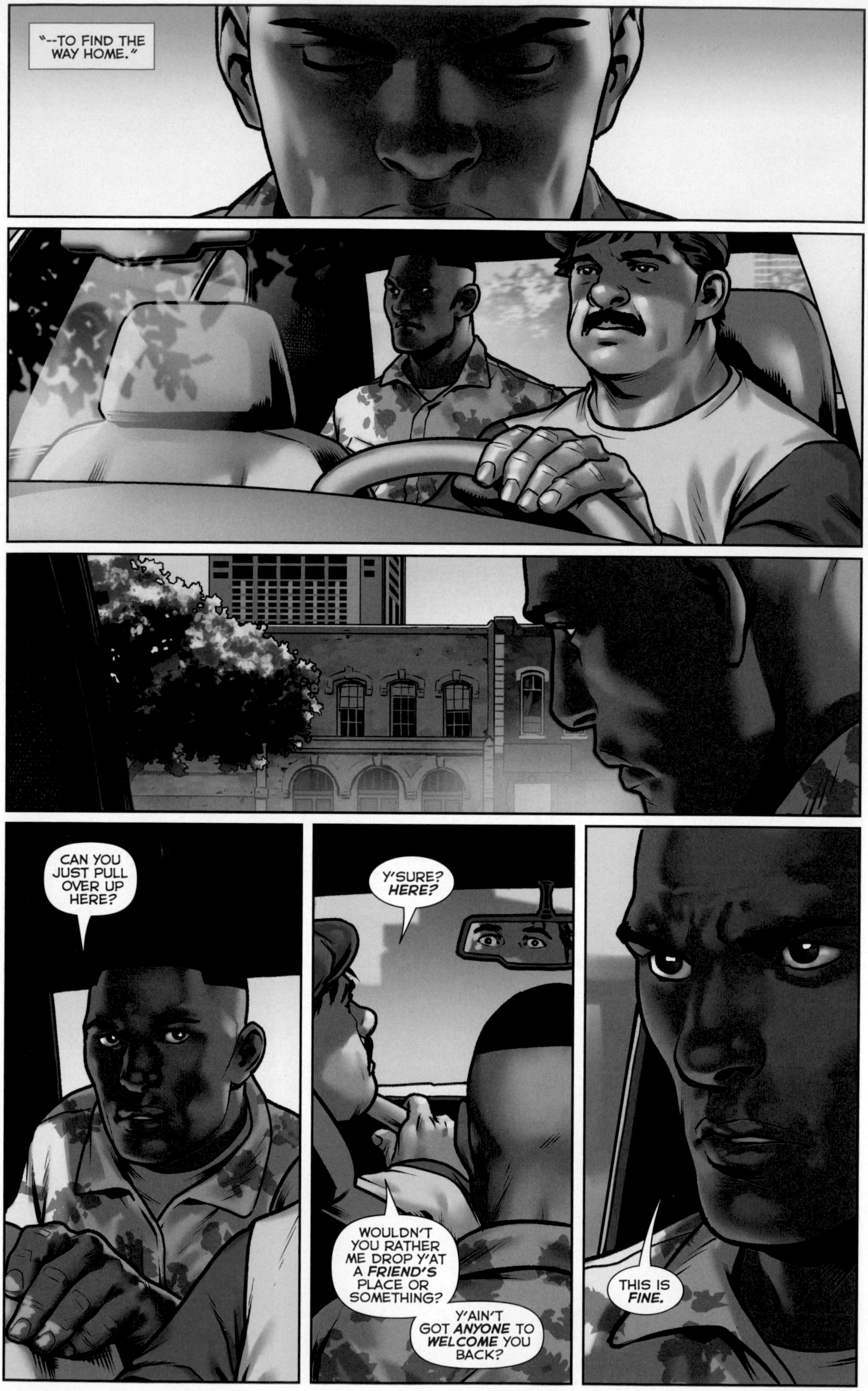
"--TO FIND THE WAY HOME."
CAN YOU JUST PULL OVER UP HERE?
Y'SURE? *HERE?*
WOULDN'T YOU RATHER ME DROP Y'AT A *FRIEND'S* PLACE OR SOMETHING?
Y'AIN'T GOT *ANYONE* TO *WELCOME* YOU BACK?
THIS IS *FINE.*

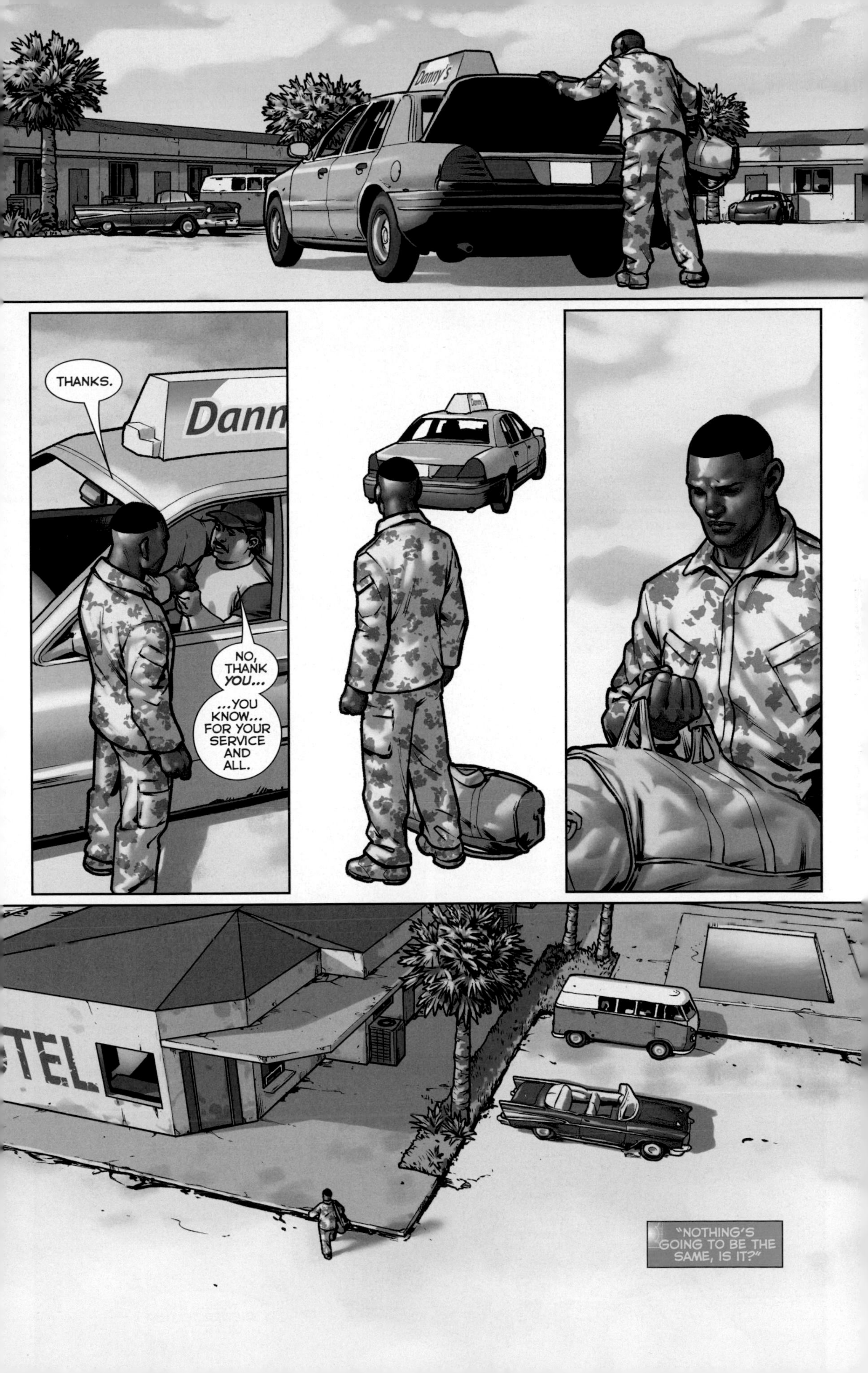
Danny's
THANKS.
Dann
NO, THANK YOU...
...YOU KNOW... FOR YOUR SERVICE AND ALL.
Danny's
TEL
"NOTHING'S GOING TO BE THE SAME, IS IT?"

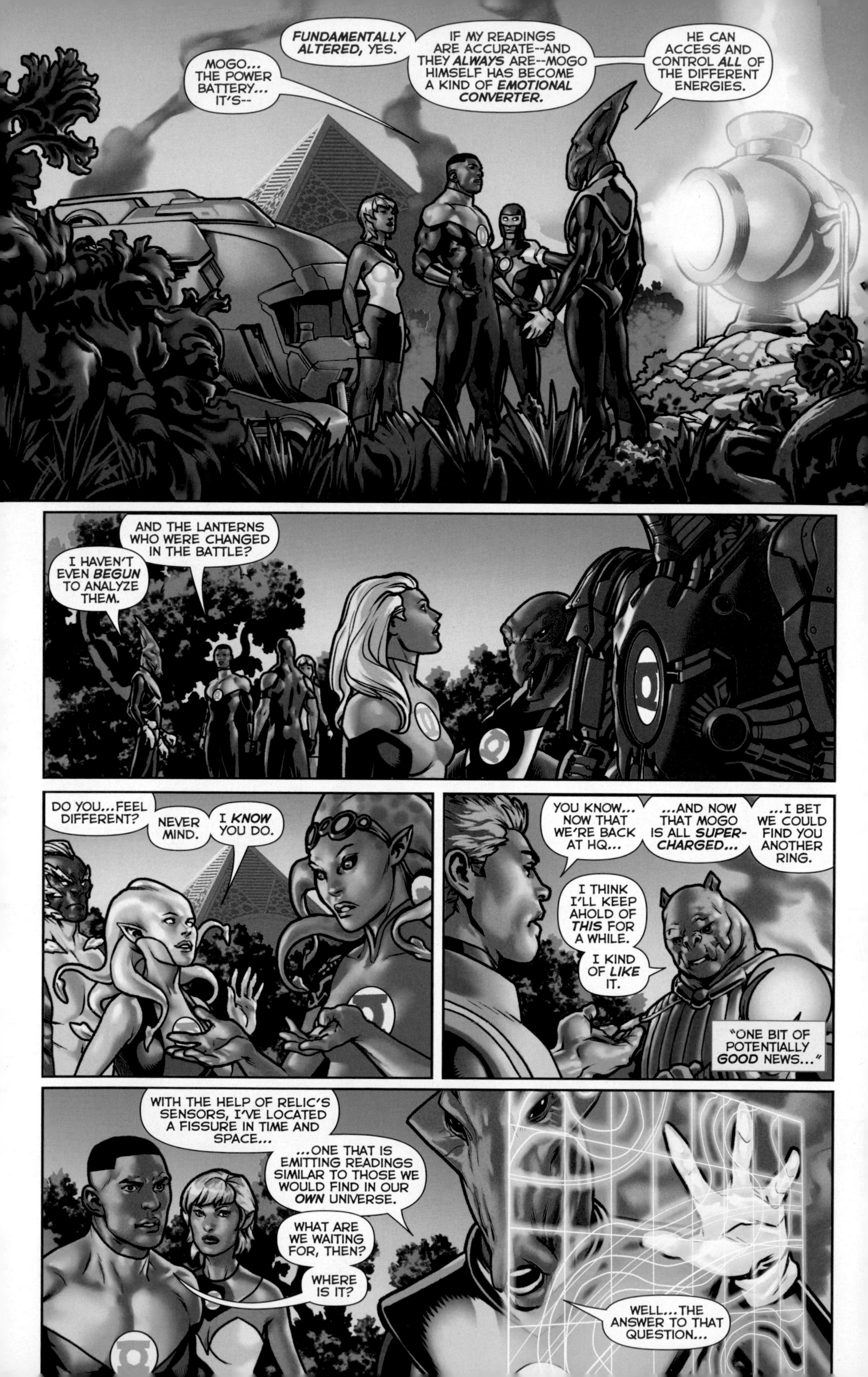
MOGO... THE POWER BATTERY... IT'S--
FUNDAMENTALLY ALTERED, YES.
IF MY READINGS ARE ACCURATE--AND THEY ALWAYS ARE--MOGO HIMSELF HAS BECOME A KIND OF EMOTIONAL CONVERTER.
HE CAN ACCESS AND CONTROL ALL OF THE DIFFERENT ENERGIES.
AND THE LANTERNS WHO WERE CHANGED IN THE BATTLE?
I HAVEN'T EVEN BEGUN TO ANALYZE THEM.
DO YOU...FEEL DIFFERENT?
NEVER MIND.
I KNOW YOU DO.
YOU KNOW... NOW THAT WE'RE BACK AT HQ...
...AND NOW THAT MOGO IS ALL SUPER-CHARGED...
...I BET WE COULD FIND YOU ANOTHER RING.
I THINK I'LL KEEP AHOLD OF THIS FOR A WHILE.
I KIND OF LIKE IT.
"ONE BIT OF POTENTIALLY GOOD NEWS..."
WITH THE HELP OF RELIC'S SENSORS, I'VE LOCATED A FISSURE IN TIME AND SPACE...
...ONE THAT IS EMITTING READINGS SIMILAR TO THOSE WE WOULD FIND IN OUR OWN UNIVERSE.
WHAT ARE WE WAITING FOR, THEN?
WHERE IS IT?
WELL...THE ANSWER TO THAT QUESTION...

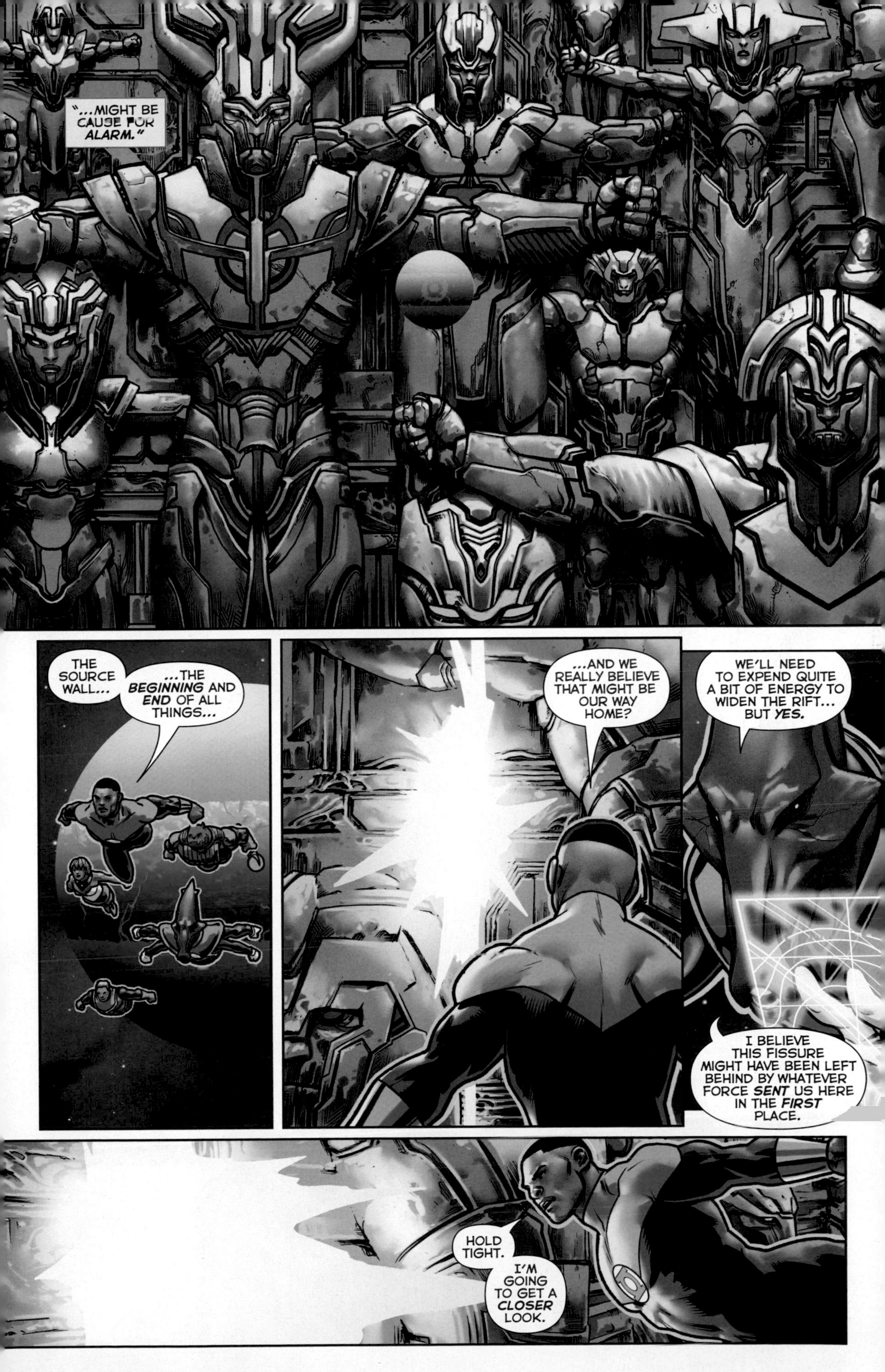
"...MIGHT BE CAUSE FOR ALARM."
THE SOURCE WALL...
...THE BEGINNING AND END OF ALL THINGS...
...AND WE REALLY BELIEVE THAT MIGHT BE OUR WAY HOME?
WE'LL NEED TO EXPEND QUITE A BIT OF ENERGY TO WIDEN THE RIFT... BUT YES.
I BELIEVE THIS FISSURE MIGHT HAVE BEEN LEFT BEHIND BY WHATEVER FORCE SENT US HERE IN THE FIRST PLACE.
HOLD TIGHT.
I'M GOING TO GET A CLOSER LOOK.

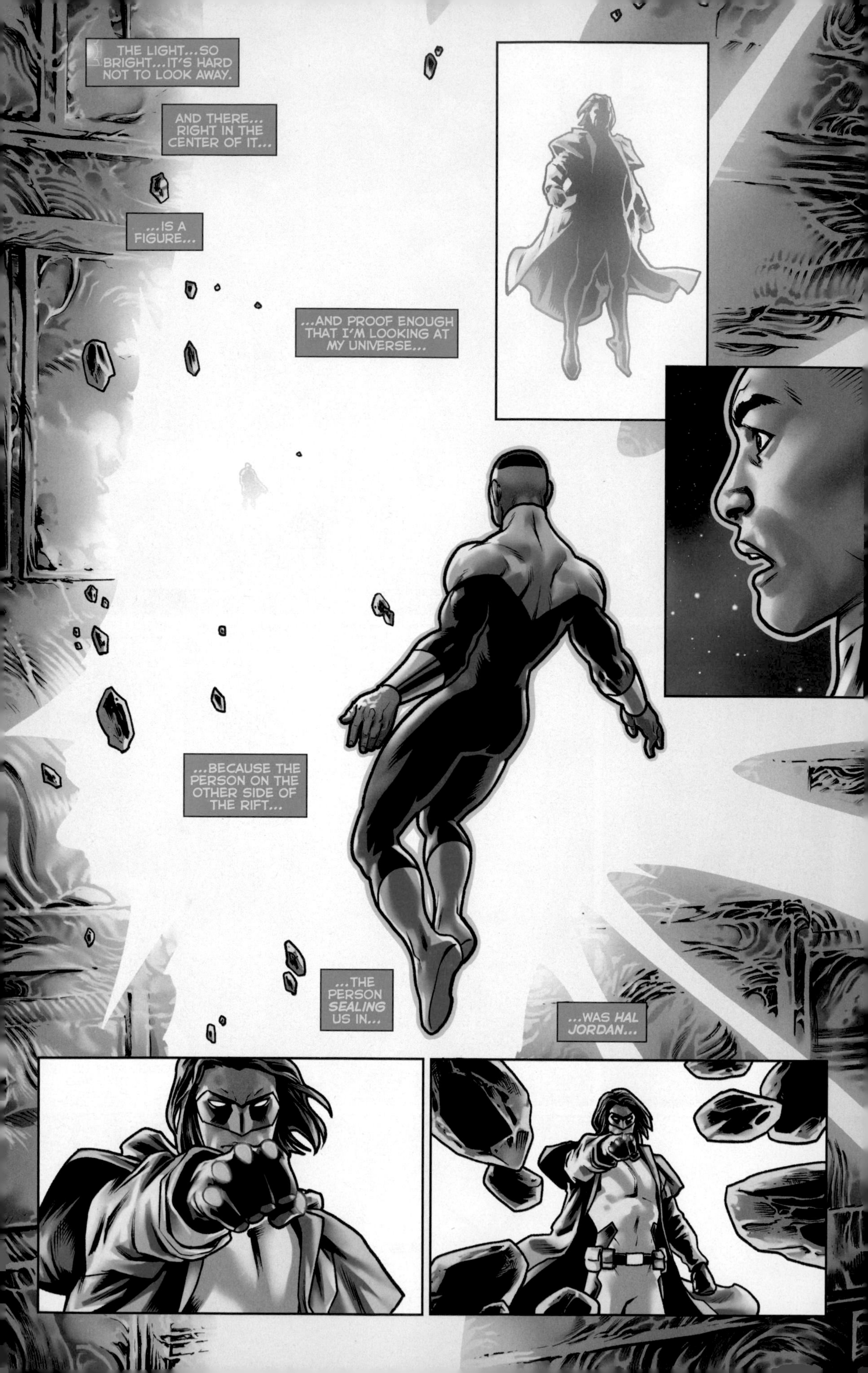
THE LIGHT...SO BRIGHT...IT'S HARD NOT TO LOOK AWAY.
AND THERE... RIGHT IN THE CENTER OF IT...
...IS A FIGURE...
...AND PROOF ENOUGH THAT I'M LOOKING AT MY UNIVERSE...
...BECAUSE THE PERSON ON THE OTHER SIDE OF THE RIFT...
...THE PERSON *SEALING* US IN...
...WAS *HAL JORDAN*...

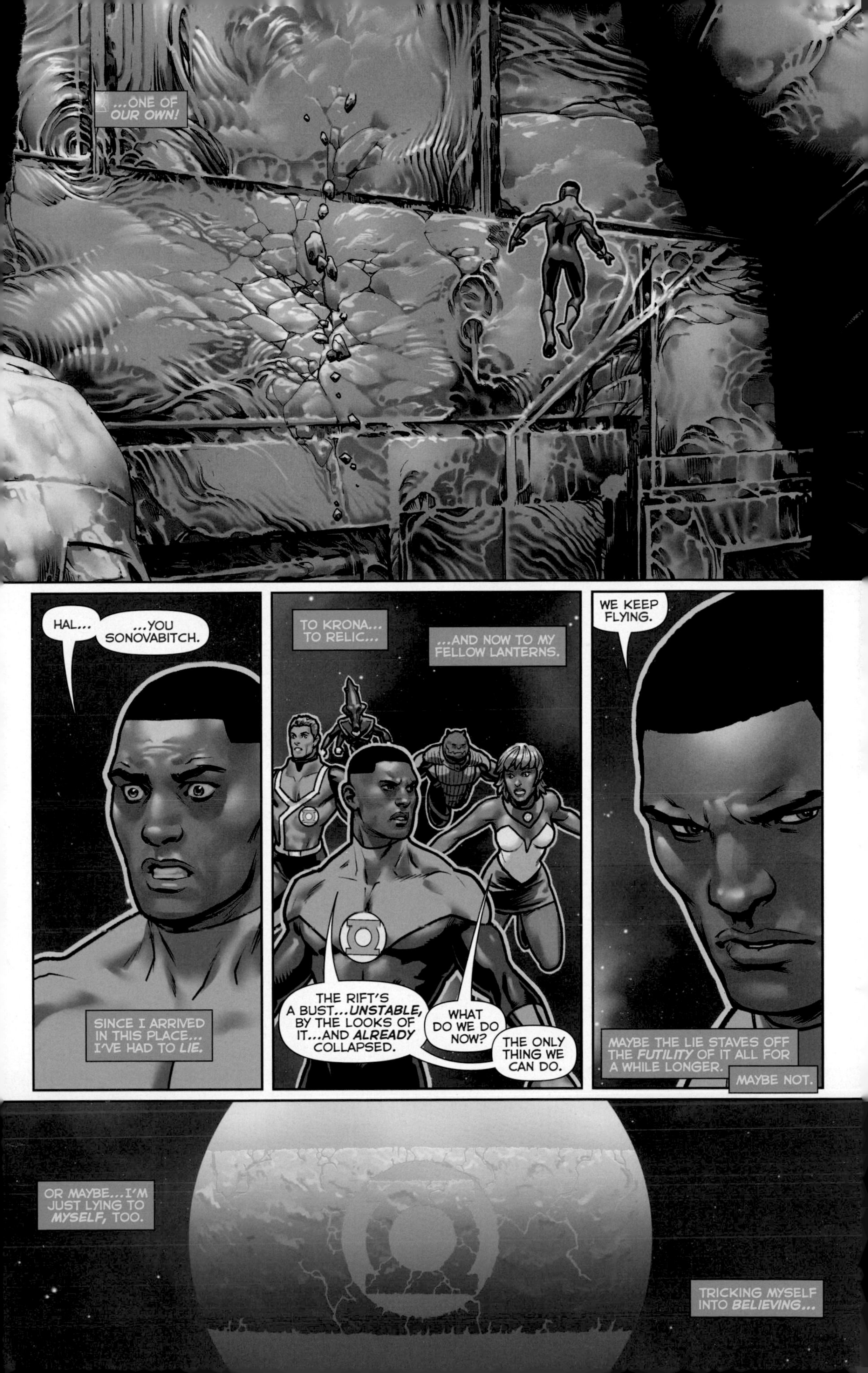
...ONE OF OUR OWN!
HAL...
...YOU SONOVABITCH.
SINCE I ARRIVED IN THIS PLACE... I'VE HAD TO LIE.
TO KRONA... TO RELIC...
...AND NOW TO MY FELLOW LANTERNS.
THE RIFT'S A BUST...UNSTABLE, BY THE LOOKS OF IT...AND ALREADY COLLAPSED.
WHAT DO WE DO NOW?
THE ONLY THING WE CAN DO.
WE KEEP FLYING.
MAYBE THE LIE STAVES OFF THE FUTILITY OF IT ALL FOR A WHILE LONGER.
MAYBE NOT.
OR MAYBE...I'M JUST LYING TO MYSELF, TOO.
TRICKING MYSELF INTO BELIEVING...

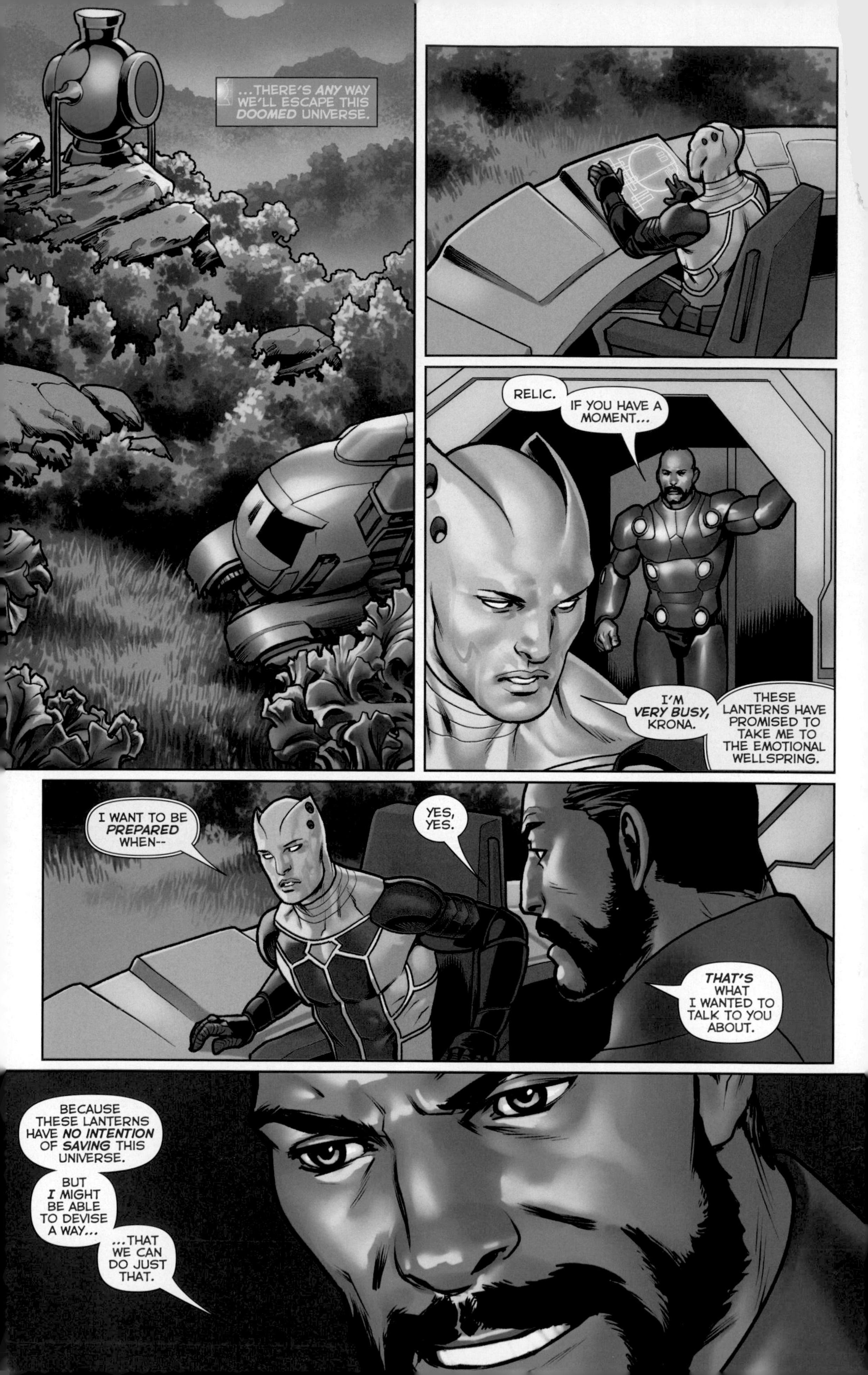

...THERE'S *ANY* WAY WE'LL ESCAPE THIS *DOOMED* UNIVERSE.
RELIC.
IF YOU HAVE A MOMENT...
I'M *VERY BUSY,* KRONA.
THESE LANTERNS HAVE PROMISED TO TAKE ME TO THE EMOTIONAL WELLSPRING.
I WANT TO BE *PREPARED* WHEN--
YES, YES.
THAT'S WHAT I WANTED TO TALK TO YOU ABOUT.
BECAUSE THESE LANTERNS HAVE *NO INTENTION* OF *SAVING* THIS UNIVERSE.
BUT *I* MIGHT BE ABLE TO DEVISE A WAY...
...THAT WE CAN DO JUST THAT.

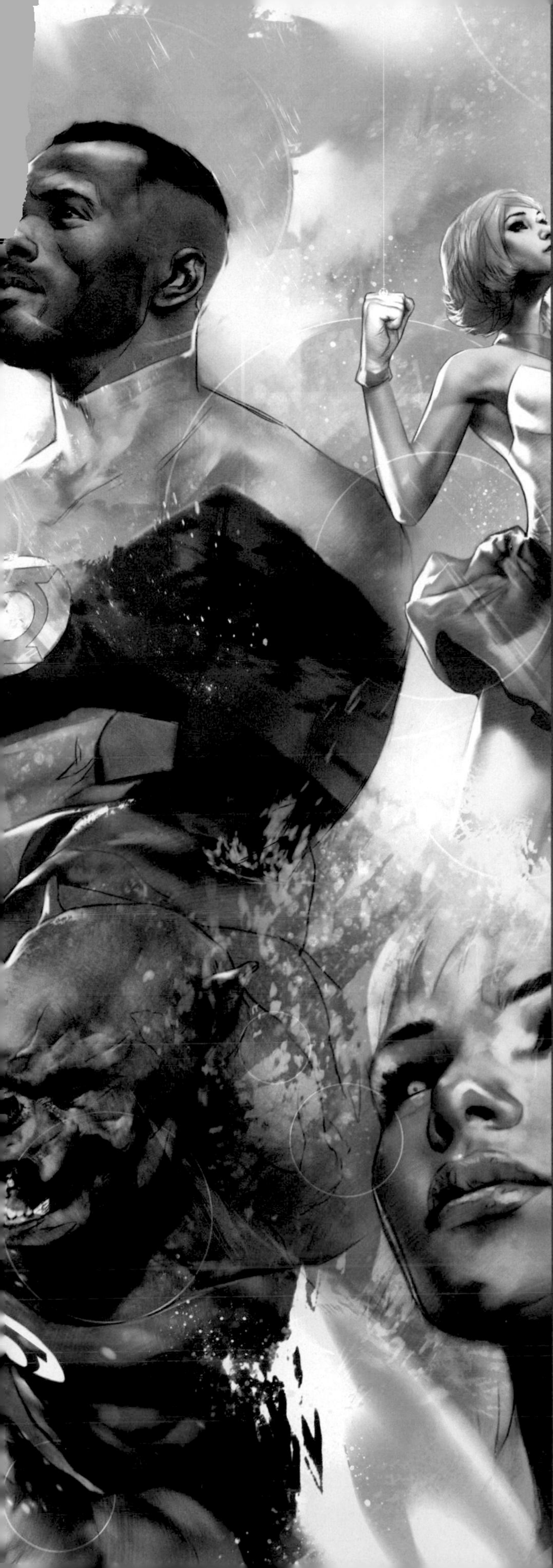

VARIANT COVER GALLERY

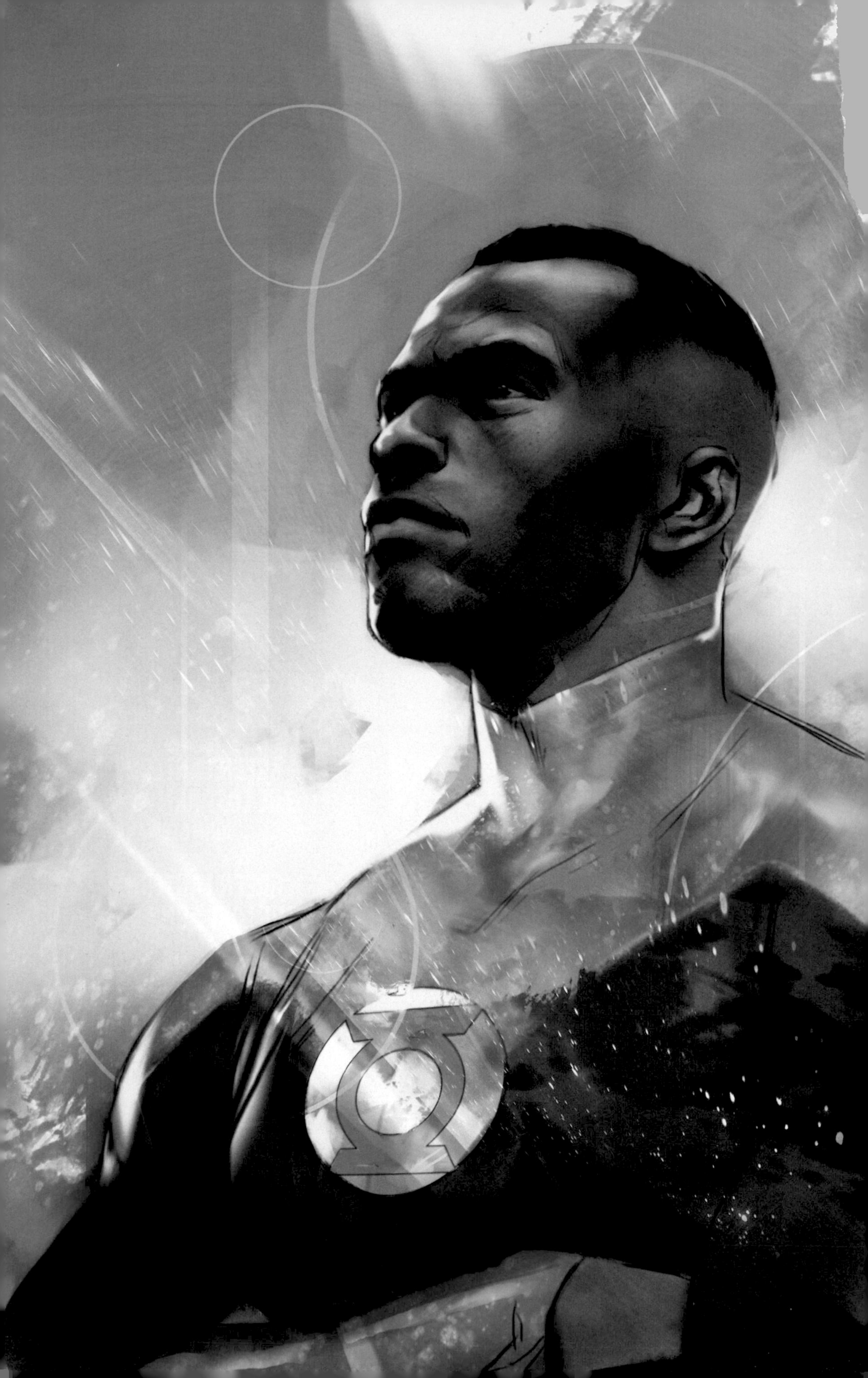

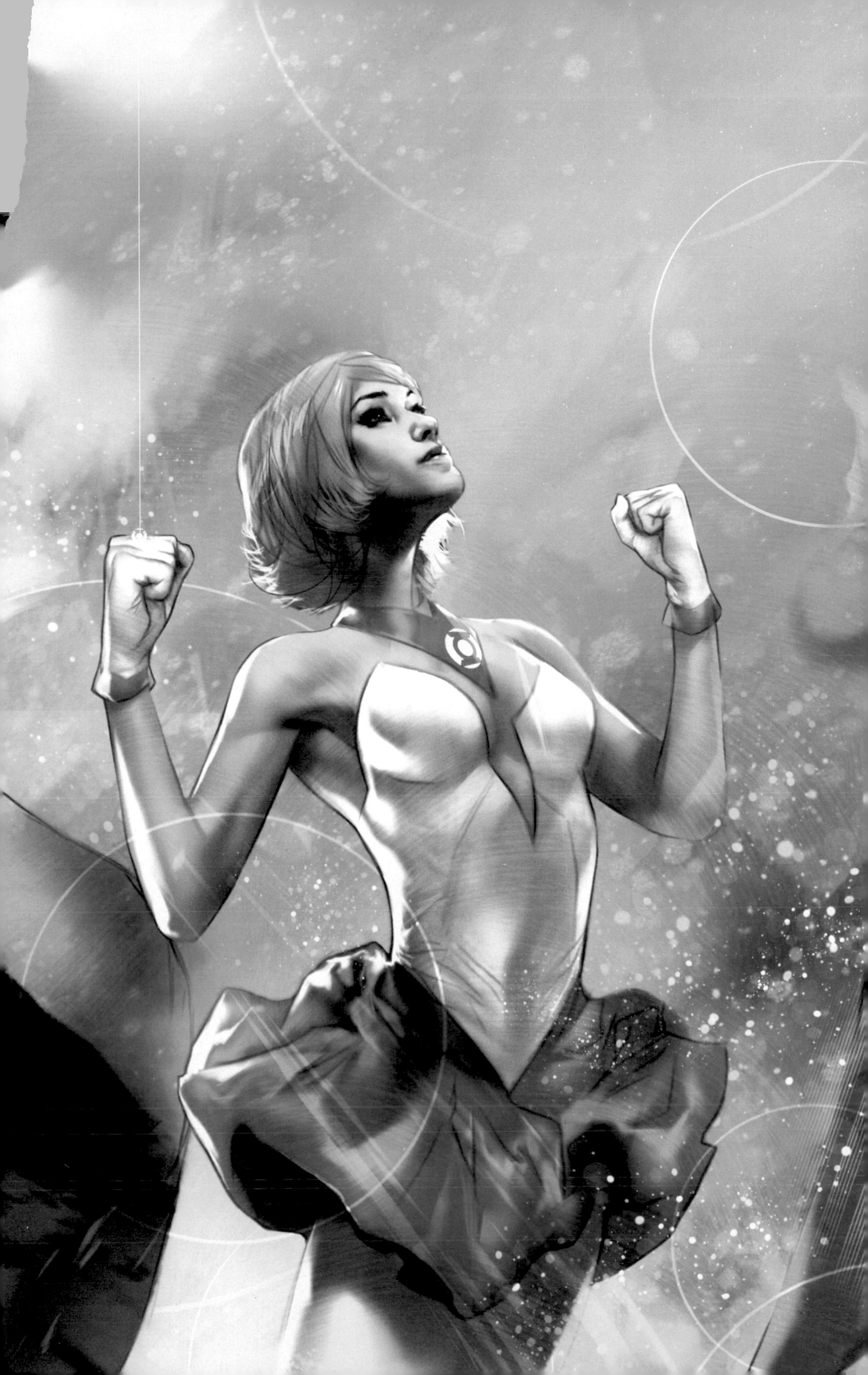

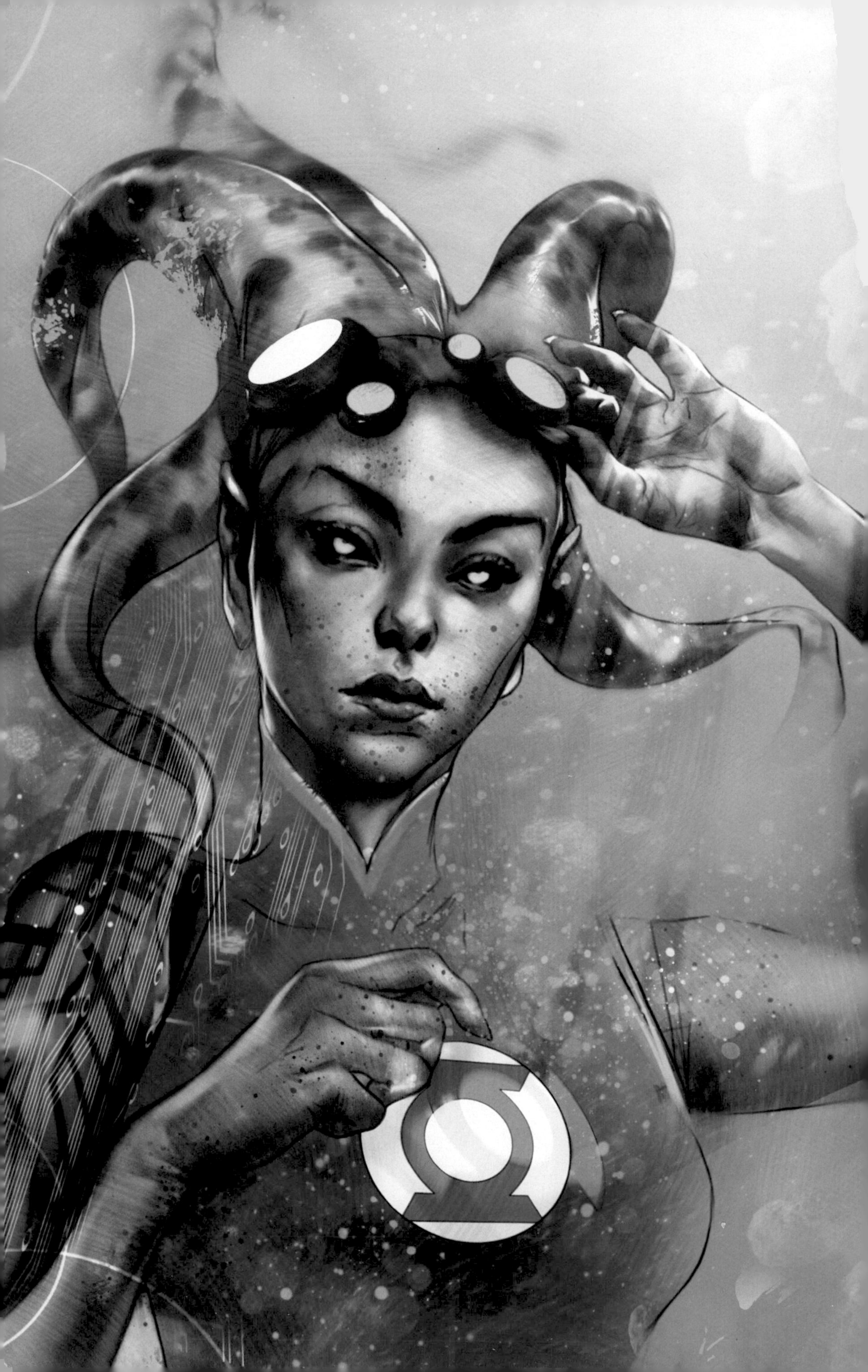

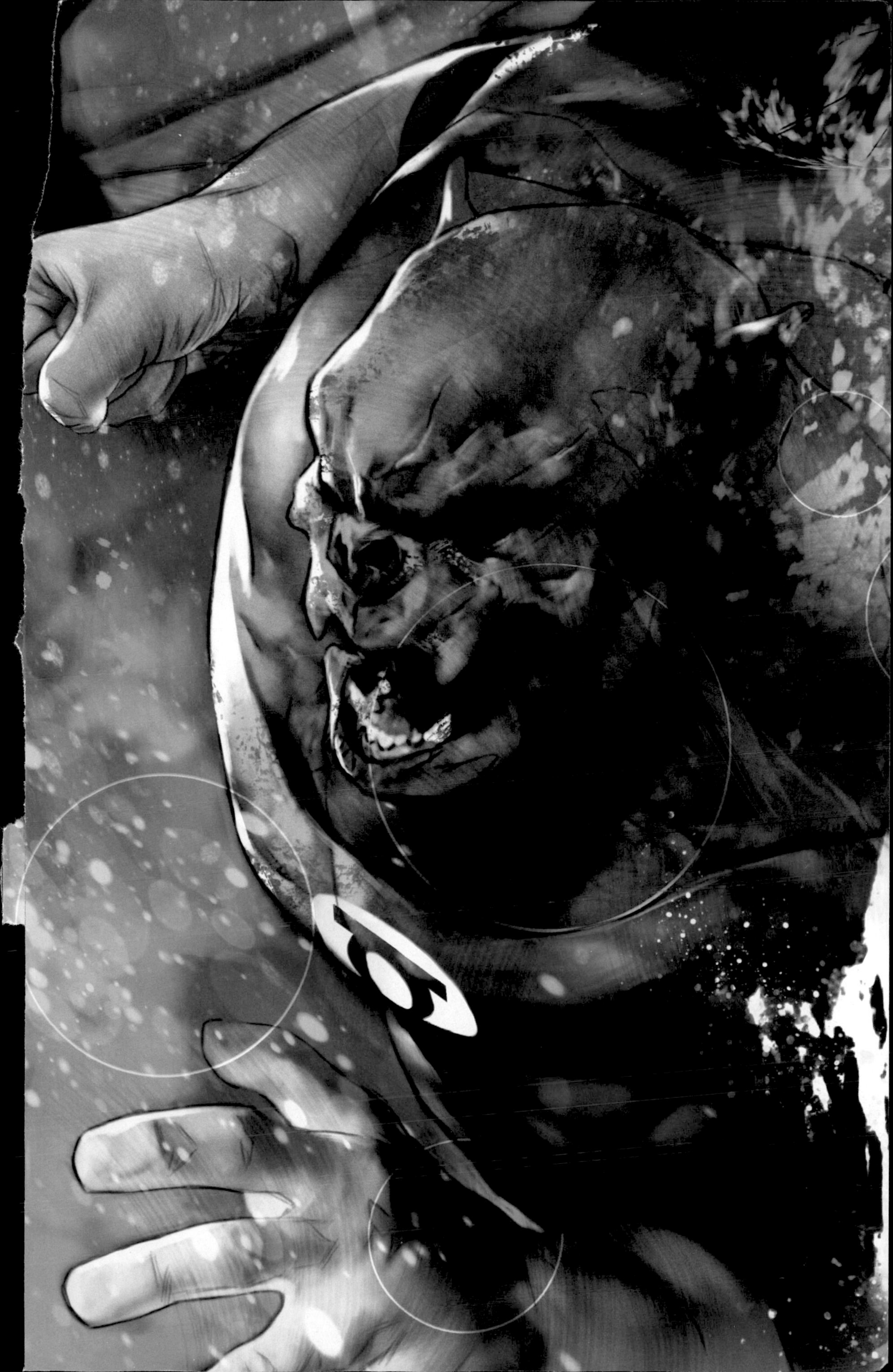

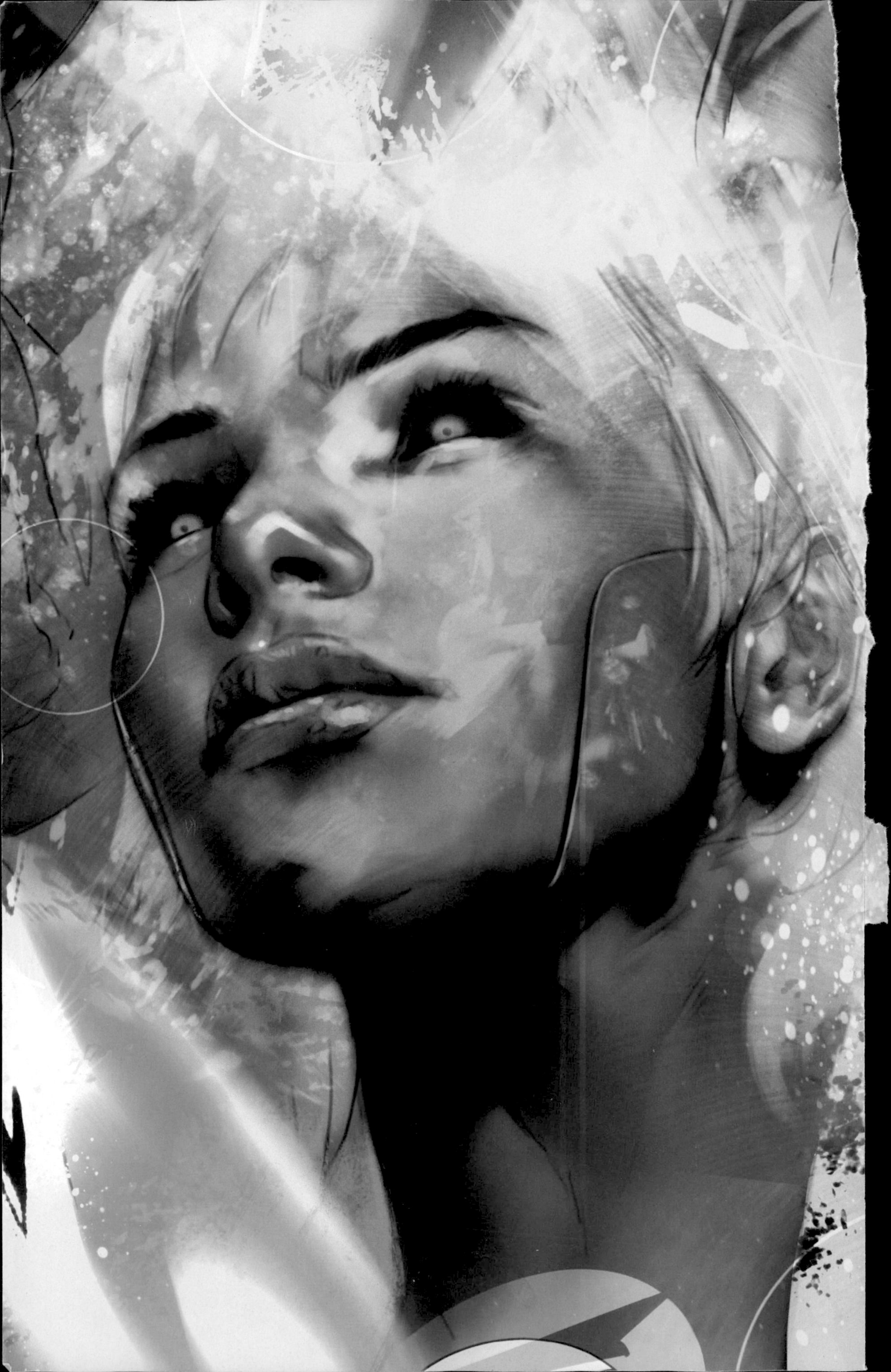

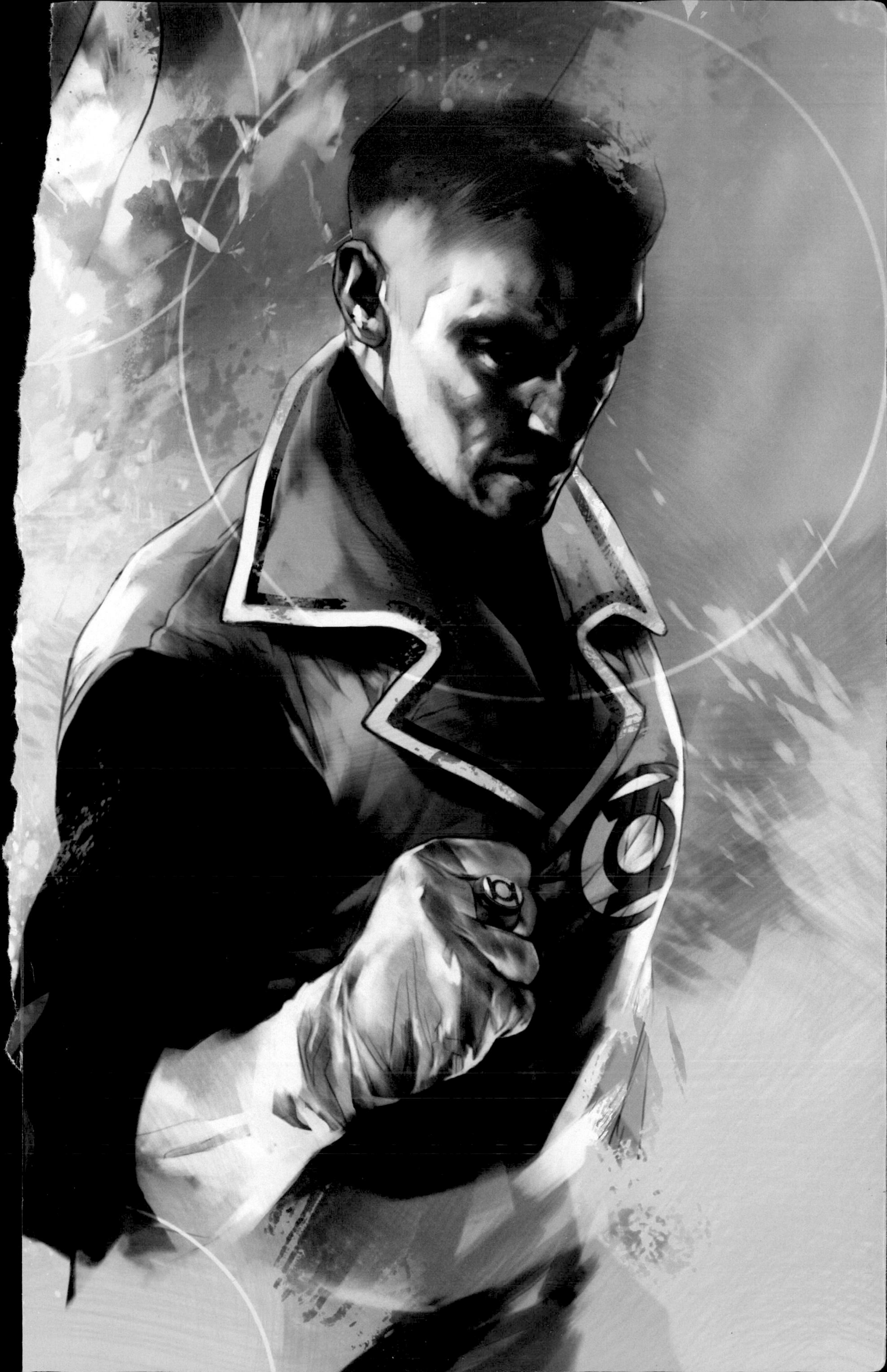

CHARACTER SKETCHES BY JESUS SAIZ

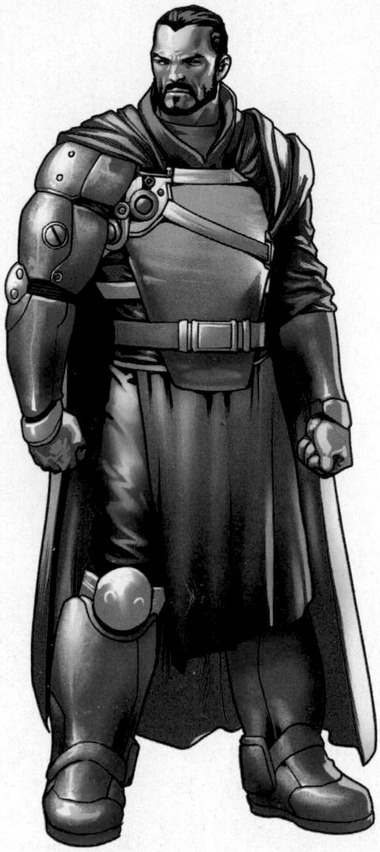

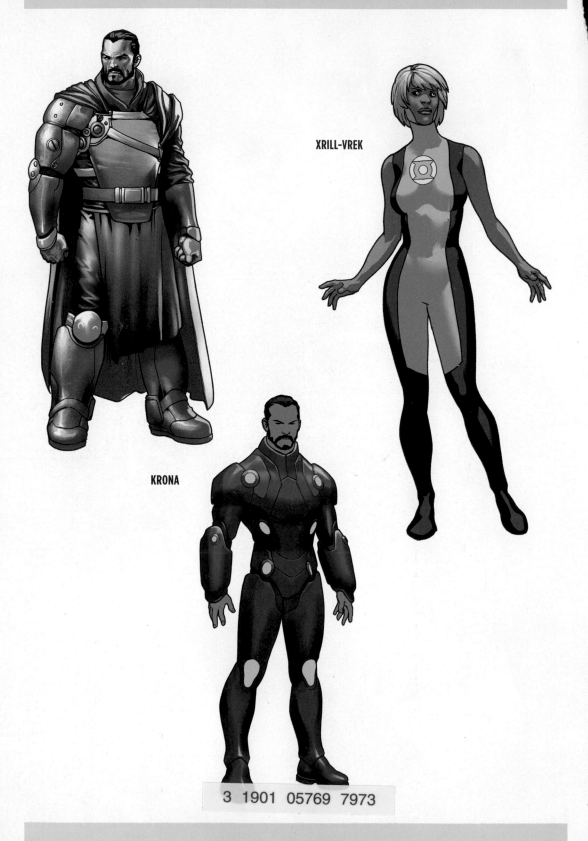

XRILL-VREK

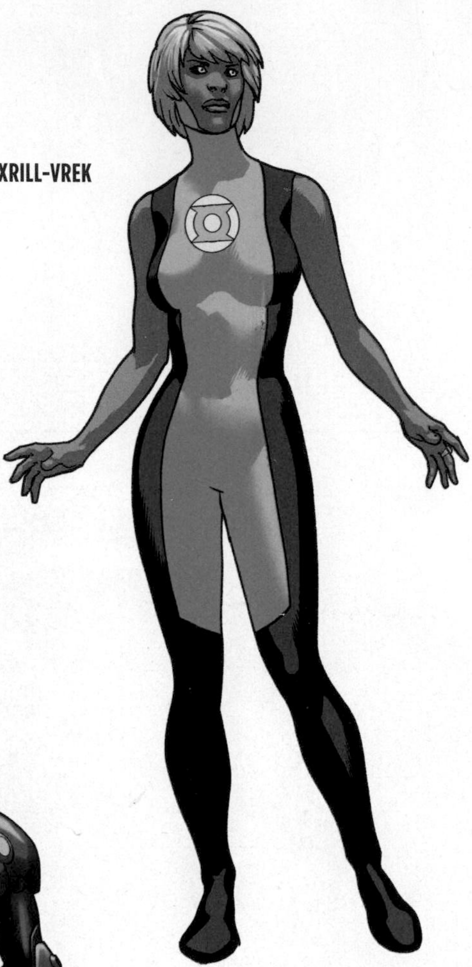

KRONA

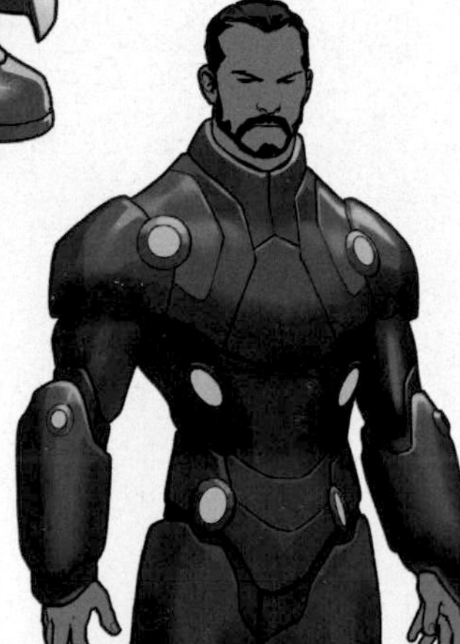